Contents

Tables

Glossary

agricultor	farmer
aguatero	water carrier
aguinaldo	payment for thirteenth month
almacén	local shop
alpargatas	cloth shoes and bags
arrabal	urban slum
barrio	neighbourhood/district
camiseta	Peronist vest
campesino	rural peasant
caño	primitive explosive device
carretillero	stevedor
caudillo	leader
chacarero	sharecropper
chacra	small farm
changador	carrier
clasismo	class struggle tendency
colono	small-holder
comisión de lucha	strike committee
comisión interna	factory committee
comisión paritaria	union wage negotiating committee
comité barrial	district committee
concertación social	social contract
conventillo	tenement block
coordinadora	coordinating body of factory activists and workers
criollo	local-born Spanish
cuerpo de delegados	shop stewards' plenary
delegado de empresa	union representative
descamisado	Peronist
empanada	pasty
entreguista	pro-imperialist
escalafón	job classification
estancia	large estate
estanciero	owner of large landed estate
frigorífico	meat chilling plant
gaucho	Argentine cowboy
golondrina	seasonal migrant worker from Spain or Italy (lit. swallow)
golpista	military coup-maker
gringo	foreigner
guerrillera	female guerrilla
huelga	strike
huelga dominguera	Sunday strike

ingenio	sugar mill
inquilino	tenant
interlocutor	representative
interventor	state overseer
jornalero	day-worker
justicialismo	Peronist doctrine
latifundio	huge estate
matón/ismo	union thug/thuggery
(yerba) maté	green tea
mestizo	of mixed race (part Amerindian)
miguelito	bent nail placed in road to puncture tyres
montonera	guerrilla army
mutual	mutual-aid society
olla popular	soup kitchen
peón	labourer
personería gremial	legal recognition of union
peso	unit of Argentine currency
plan de lucha	struggle plan
plenario	mass meeting
puchero	soup
pueblada	town seizure
pueblo	the people
pulpería	company store
quita zondle	deduction of national wage claimed by employer
quite de colaboración	work-to-rule
rancho	mud hut
retorno	return of Perón
sábado inglés	44-hour week paid as 48
saladero	meat-salting plant
tasajo	dried salted meat
trabajo a desgano	go-slow
vales de pulpería	chits redeemable only at company store
vecinazo	neighbourhood protest
vandorismo	current named after Augusto Vandor
verticalismo	unquestioning obedience to Isabel Perón
zafra	sugar harvest
zurdo	leftist

Preface

Though the three authors share a broadly similar theoretical and political perspective, this is not a fully collective work. For reasons of geography and language the work was based on a division of labour which also reflected each writer's area of historical expertise. Thus Ricardo Falcón was responsible for Chapters 1 to 5, Bernardo Galitelli for Chapters 6 to 9, and Ronaldo Munck for the Introduction and Chapters 10 to 17, as well as the translation of the others and general editing.

The comments by Robert Molteno of Zed Books and Professor Hobart Spalding helped us considerably in producing this final version. We would like to thank CEDLA (*Centro de Estudios y Documentación Latinoamericanos*) in Amsterdam for its support of Bernardo Galitelli during the course of his research for this book. We also extend a vote of thanks to the Publications Committee of the University of Ulster for its financial support of this book.

'Sois obreros, sois trabajadores, a seguir con la huelga, a triunfar definitivamente para conformar una nueva sociedad donde no haya armas, donde no haya uniformes ni uniformados, donde haya alegría, respeto por el ser humano, donde nadie tenga que arrodillarse ante ninguna sotana ni ante ningun mandón'.

'You are workers, carry on with the strike, to triumph definitively, to shape a new society where there are neither poor nor rich, where there are no weapons, where there are no uniforms or uniformed, where there is happiness, respect for the human being, where no one needs to bend the knee to a priest's cassock or before any boss'.

Juan Soto addressing the strikers in Patagonia in 1921, shortly before the massacre of 1,500 of them by the army.

Introduction

The labour movement in Argentina is somehow 'foreign' to workers abroad, in more than the obvious sense. This is mainly because the movement is identified with Peronism, an ideology and type of social movement quite alien to social-democratic or Communist workers. It is therefore important to explain why Socialism and Communism, as Anarchism earlier, failed to provide a successful strategy for the labour movement in Argentina. The rise of Peronism constituted a radical watershed in Argentina's political history, and is therefore a convenient division between the first and second parts of our historical account. The history of the labour movement did not begin in 1945 with the rise of Peronism, and can only be understood in terms of its whole history, from the mid-19th Century onwards. Our historical account ends in 1985 after the collapse of the military dictatorship, which was a result of the unremitting struggles of the labour movement, as much as of the actions of Britain's South Atlantic 'task force'.

Politics

This work represents part of a long-term commitment to the future of the labour movement in Argentina. It is not a propagandist work, being based on serious original research, particularly into the pre-1930 period, which has been generally neglected by labour historians. It is written in an accessible style (we hope) and largely as a narrative, to facilitate its use outside the academic milieu. It is a story with lessons we believe are relevant beyond our national frontiers.

Labour history has traditionally been seen as a means to bolster the labour movement by recovering its past. This can lead to a highly selective, even apologetic, view of the movement, if the main objective is to create a heroic myth. As McLennan writes: 'Labour history can take on unnecessary teleological connotations: the history of the rise of labour, its progressive social prominence.[1] The past can become highly ritualised and contradictions simply evaded; we end up with a history where today's battles are projected into the past, thus distorting it.

1

In Argentina, labour history has always been a highly political affair, being used unashamedly to strengthen particular political currents. Peronist writers, for example, simply begin their accounts of labour history in 1945, with all that went before reduced to a quick sketch of labour's 'pre-history'. With those who recognise that the labour movement did indeed have a history before Perón, the problems are equally serious. Syndicalist and socialist authors reclaim their past militancy but in doing so skim over their weak points and convert Perón into the devil incarnate. Communist writers, for their part, write the most teleological version of labour history, as though an unbroken line runs from the *Communist Manifesto* to the present. Even the supporters of the new class-struggle tendencies of the 1970s delved into the past somewhat selectively to stress the direct-action tactics of the anarchists in another era.

What is to be done, then, to carry out serious historical research while maintaining the role of labour historian as ally of the labour movement? Georges Haupt once noted gloomily that

> Such a conception of a working-class history, which is both engaged and critical because it seeks to be militant, and not a pious exercise in hagiography intended to perpetuate accepted conventions, has not made much headway.[2]

The point is that by reducing labour history to ideology we are not helping the movement we purport to serve.[3] Myths and legends may be beneficial when they are based on fact, but they may also prevent the emergence of a strong principled movement. To be self-critical is not to be less militant, rather it is indispensable for anything other than mindless militancy. This should be a basic starting point for any subsequent work on Argentina's labour history, and one we have by no means resolved satisfactorily.

Method

The traditional approach to Latin American labour history has focused almost exclusively on its political aspects. The history of a class is reduced to a chronology of various labour organisations. Those outside the formal organisations, such as non-union members or women, receive short shrift, and emphasis is laid on leadership struggles rather than the activity of the rank and file. Much of Argentine labour history follows this pattern, being reduced to an endless succession of congresses and resolutions. Even memoirs of labour activists focus almost exclusively on labour politics rather than the day-to-day lives of workers. This 'politicism' has even given rise to a model of capital-relations in Latin America, where 'political bargaining' is the rule, according to James Payne's influential analysis.[4] Payne found that in Peru the government often interfered in labour-management disputes and that violence was often an effective tactic for workers' organisations. He concludes that 'the labour movement in Peru, therefore, is politically oriented'.[5] Certainly trade unions in Argentina have employed varying degrees of class violence in their struggle for survival. Yet even the most stable collective bargaining situations are also characterised by coercion, which may be economic, but can equally be manifested politically. The British labour movement is 'politically oriented', but that does not set it into a Third World model, as somehow different from union practice everywhere else.

Another variant of the traditional approach focuses on the industrial relations machinery which regulates the conflict between labour and capital. A recent example is Efren Córdova's *Industrial Relations in Latin America* which laments the fact that 'the North American model of collective bargaining with its emphasis on bargaining in good faith and prohibition of unfair labor practices, has had no real influence on Latin American law and practice'.[6] The problem in Latin America is diagnosed as 'the aggressive attitude of the trade union movement and its tradition of class struggle' which prevents it from reaching 'the stage of mutual understanding and trust' with capital and the state.[7] Argentina is recognised as one country where industrial relations have reached an advanced stage, with an embarrassed acknowledgement that the 1976 military coup ended some of these practices. The problem with this approach at a theoretical level, is that it elevates a quite distorted model of US collective bargaining into a trans-historical ideal type, against which Latin American practice is measured. Its diagnosis of Latin American reality is quite unrealistic in so far as it ignores the great socio-economic inequalities and the naked exercise of class power by the military state. It is not the 'aggressive attitude' of trade unions that causes the class struggle to be introduced into an otherwise tranquil sea characterised by 'mutual trust and understanding'.

Among the critical approaches to Latin American labour history, the so-called 'dependency' approach has been the most popular. Hobart Spalding, in his broad historical synthesis, argues for a three-dimensional analysis in terms of: (1) the international economic dimension; (2) the relation between the local and the international ruling class; and (3) the composition, structure, and historical formation of the working class.[8] In a general sense one cannot fault this formulation, but Spalding then goes on to prioritise unduly the international dimension, tending to neglect national particularities. Whatever the general merits of the dependency theory, it is an inadequate framework for labour history, which must emphasise Spalding's third point if its objective is to be achieved.

One of the problems involved with the dependency approach arises with Spalding's statement that 'common patterns emerge at roughly the same time throughout the continent. Formative, expansive and explosive, and co-optive–repressive periods emerge everywhere'.[9] Even a cursory acquaintance with Latin American labour history suggests the contrary, that national specificity had a greater role in shaping each country's labour movement. As to the periodisation proposed by Spalding, it is not really a useful guide. Certainly, all working-class movements have a formative phase, and later they tend to expand as they embrace wider layers of the working population. But then to argue that there is a 'co-optive–repressive' phase is really to say very little, because there is no labour movement in the world which has not been subject to both at some stage. The state and the bourgeoisie exercise a judicious blend of repression and coercion to deal with their 'dangerous classes' according to circumstances. Nor can this dichotomy, like others once used, such as reform–revolution, serve as an adequate guide to our research.

The dependency approach essentially prioritises the external dimension. Harding and Spalding, for example, argue that

> The building of pro-capitalist bread and butter unionism in Latin America as elsewhere, aids imperialist penetration in a variety of ways. It dampens class consciousness by concentrating workers' attention solely upon economic issues and preaches that unions should be 'a-political'.[10]

In a sense this verdict is undeniable and concurs with our critique of Córdova above. Yet it is also unrealistic. Firstly 'trade union imperialism', by which we denote the practice of 'metropolitan' states and unions in the Third World, for all the *exposés*, is of quite minor importance in a country such as Argentina. As we will see in our account, a national trade union bureaucracy was thrown up without any substantial aid from the US Embassy and its various departments. Secondly this approach seems to hold as unhistorical a view of US business unionism as do its proponents such as Córdova. Are bread-and-butter issues not important in Latin America, or is the revolution so imminent that such mundane considerations can be dispensed with? The idealism of Harding and Spalding's approach is shown when they argue that: 'In Argentina, the peronista labor bureaucracy shows its false consciousness by combating militant tendencies among the rank-and-file'.[11] Clearly a union bureaucracy which combats internal insurgency is conscious of its interests as a specific class fraction, and not simply misguided. More to the point, it is profoundly unhistorical to label Peronism as 'false consciousness' simply because it does not accord with an abstract model of revolution. The essentially paternalistic implications of the dependency approach are most evident in Kenneth Erickson's history of Brazilian labour, where a corporativist state simply moulds and controls labour to suit its requirements.[12] In this account workers and the labour movement are reduced to passive pawns with no independent volition of their own.

In recent years the dependency approach to labour history has itself been partially replaced by a new critical orthodoxy. But the advances of the 'new' international labour studies are much more sure of what they are against than what they are for. Robin Cohen directs our attention to 'the process of proletarianization and class formation', 'the character of worker struggles in the capitalist periphery' and 'how elements of struggle are contained in counter-ideologies, cultures and institutional practices'.[13] These three elements are indeed crucial and ones we will direct our attention to in our Argentine labour history. What is less clear is how these concerns differ from what the best labour historians have been doing all along: Hobsbawm and Thompson in Britain, Perrot and Trempé in France, Guttman and Montgomery in the US.[14]

The general tendency for critics of traditional labour history is to advocate a 'history from below', and attention to those sectors hitherto ignored. For Eugene Sofer, Latin American labour studies

> focus attention on a minority of workers and give short shrift to the unorganised. They emphasize the role of political parties and thus define politics as synonymous with voting. They overestimate the strike as opposed to other forms of popular protest.[15]

There has thus been a general turn towards social history with its concern for workers' everyday lives and above all culture and consciousness, previously so badly neglected. Certainly our own work is not a genuine 'history from below', and our attention to the social history of labour is insufficient. This work still needs to be pursued but we believe that a general framework, a periodisation of the labour movement's history, is a prerequisite. As regards the Latin American labour movement, Thomas Skidmore is quite right to point out that 'research has been so scant that they have yet to produce an "orthodox" literature large enough to justify a full-scale revisionist reaction'.[16] What this means is that research with more emphasis on social history and oral history does not preclude work such as our own which concentrates on the general relationships between workers, trade unions and politics.

We would not deny that our own work has concentrated more on the labour movement than on the working class as such. It also concentrates largely on Buenos Aires; this is not due to *porteño* (Buenos Aires dweller) chauvinism on our part, but to the preponderant social and political weight of the proletariat in the capital. Having set out the basic periodisation, we can now move on to studies of particular groups of workers and particular periods, as indeed is now being done in Argentina. Our criticism of labour history orthodoxy should not lead us, however, to fall into studying what Haupt described as 'the past of the working-class movement miniaturised in this way into pedantic detailed studies lacking any general perspective and isolated from their context, [which] is capable of arousing only a very limited interest'.[17] A curious antiquarianism is no antidote for the self-serving myths of some labour historians. Recently there has been a growing interest in social history amongst Argentine labour historians. They have broken with the previously dominant institutional approach, but in emphasising working-class culture and daily life, they have tended to abstract from the socio-economic and political context in which these take place. The privilege accorded to 'the popular' as against class divisions and struggles, furthermore, takes these studies away from the global approach necessary. As to oral history, there is also a growing interest in this method, and as yet it has not fallen into facile populism, which is an obvious danger with a depoliticised and naïve collection of popular memories.

Having surveyed various traditional and radical approaches to Latin American labour history, we need to outline our own general perspective. The guiding thread in our historical account is the notion of 'workers' autonomy'. The working class must be seen as an autonomous social and political power which can take initiatives against capital. And capital must be seen as a social relation whereby one class imposes its mode of social organisation on another. The class struggle takes the form of cycles of offensive/defensive strategies employed by capital in response to the resistance of the working class.[18] Jeff Crisp has shown recently that we can avoid 'proletarian messianism' and 'radical pessimism', if we focus simultaneously on the strategies of labour control and the modes of labour-resistance.[19] With this dialectical approach we can see 'how workers respond to the strategies of control imposed upon them, but also how workers constantly take the initiative against capital and state . . . forcing [them] to respond with new strategies of control'.[20]

Our stress should also be on discontinuity, against the epic version of labour history in which teleology guides the analysis to its predestined end. The 'long waves' of capitalist development do not simply produce new machines, but profoundly alter social relations. As James Cronin points out

> Long waves serve not only to re-educate the labor movement in its economic understanding and social and strategic orientation, but in addition to transform the composition of the working class, and to redraw the lines of the class cleavage throughout society and the parameters of collective action.[21]

Economic fluctuations should thus be seen not only as factors favouring or discouraging proletarian insurgency, but as re-drawing the map of class confrontation in key transitional periods.

In a critique of Spalding's approach, Ian Roxborough suggests an alternative set of issues, which Latin American labour history should be concerned with, 'factors such as type of internal union government, the degree of integration of the labour market, the degree of homogeneity of the working class, rates of labour turnover, differing forms of corporatism, etc.'.[22] These are indeed some of the issues which we will concentrate on, and they also provide a basis for a more nuanced understanding of the labour movement. If we were asked to specify one key area of concern, however, it would be the labour process. As John Humphrey has argued on the basis of the Brazilian experience,

> the analysis of the working class must be grounded in an examination of the relation between labor and capital at the point of production. Without such a grounding, analyses of strikes, labour-movement organisations, and the political development of the class will continue to oscillate between reductionism and mere description.[23]

Reductionism has been present in much of the literature on Peronism where recent rural migrants are assumed to have a certain political orientation (authoritarian), or workers in the advanced capitalist sector, such as automobiles, are characterised as a 'labour aristocracy' on the basis of high wages alone. On the other hand, many labour histories display a voluntarism in which strikes take place purely on the basis of free will, thus ignoring the vital social and economic context in which they take place. The struggle of the working class takes place on a terrain formed by the capital accumulation process. Above all, a historical perspective is necessary if we are to grasp the complexity of the present labour movement.

Finally, our critique of the dependency approach in labour studies should not blind us to the condition of dependency as a framework within which labour's activity takes place. After all, Argentina was Lenin's model at the turn of the century for 'the diverse forms of dependent countries which, politically, are formally independent, but in fact, are enmeshed in the net of financial and diplomatic dependence'.[24] This version of dependency theory is not a simple model of metropolis and satellite, but allows a country such as Argentinta 'relative autonomy' and does not necessarily deny a central role for the internal class struggle. By the same token, we can accept a 'weak' version of the dependency approach, as presented by Charles Bergquist, as a framework for early 20th Century Latin American labour history. Bergquist argues in relation to the Chilean case that economic specialisation within the world system 'influences social structure and political developments and shapes the cultural perception of members of all classes'.[25] This in turn determines the considerable influence of workers in export production on the evolution of the entire labour movement. Whether nitrate workers in Chile, or the port and rail workers in Argentina linked to grain and meat export, this is undoubtedly true, and a dimension we should not ignore.

History

We have said that any critical approach to Latin American labour history needs to be historical. Following that advice, we have summarised the basic historical background to our account which commences in 1855.

The territory now known as Argentina was first colonised in the 16th Century by Spanish *conquistadores* who met little resistance from the indigenous peoples. The provinces of the River Plate were not a priority for the Spanish invaders, because mineral resources were lacking. The fertile *pampa* region was simply used to hunt wild cattle and there was only a minor trade in tallow and salted beef. This pattern persisted into the mid-18th Century, when a slightly more rational use of resources began. Even so, the scarcity of labour and remoteness from the Spanish centre of Upper Peru, led, as James Scobie describes, to the creation of 'an economy in which commercial and grazing interests reigned supreme over artisan industries or cultivation of the soil'.[26] A vigorous contraband trade helped counteract Spanish fiscal restrictions designed to limit the role of Buenos Aires. This, and the commercial reforms of the 18th Century, led to the emergence of the city as an important transit point for the whole southern region. The *criollo* (local-born Spanish) merchants and landowners were to lead a struggle for independence from Spain in the early 19th Century, after having first repulsed British invasions in 1806 and 1807.

Who were the labourers in this vast under-developed territory? The rural economy drew its labourers from the ranks of the *gauchos*, semi-nomad horsemen, skilled in the management of cattle. The once-wild cattle were gathered together during the 18th Century to form the basis of the *estancia* (large estate), the mainstay of the rural economy to this day. The *saladero*, or meat-salting plant, introduced a new element into this pastoral economy at the beginning of the 19th Century. In these establishments labour-power was provided by the *gauchos* who became the real predecessors of the modern proletariat. The *estancia peón* (labourer) and the *saladero* workers were gradually joined by a host of artisans in Buenos Aires, the capital city, and several provincial centres. The slave trade was abolished in 1813, but the 1822 census in Buenos Aires indicated that one-quarter of the population was Black. Around the time of the independence movement, the dominant tradesmen were the carpenters, tailors, shoemakers, blacksmiths and brick-layers. The growing *criollo* élite began demanding better services, and after independence in 1810, more artisans were brought in from Europe to join the slaves and ex-slaves. Apart from this service economy, including a great number of Black women in domestic service, there was a group of trades related to the import and export of goods. These included the carriers (*changadores*) and ship unloaders (*carretilleros*) of Buenos Aires and La Boca, who concentrated on the internal trade. Black, immigrant and indigenous *jornaleros* (day-workers) were matched by a group of mobile sellers of water, milk, fish and *empanadas* (pasties). The skilled trades could command relatively high wages, especially in the decades following the independence struggle when forced conscription decimated the ranks of the workers. However, as William McCann noticed in 1847, rents were high, and apart from meat, the cost of living was also high.[27]

The social life of the artisans and day-workers took diverse forms. The ex-slaves congregated by nation – the Angola, Cabundi and Conga among others – and organised the Sunday dances known as *candombé*. The *gauchos* and *criollos* met in the bars where they played cards, drank rum and played the guitar. In the ports, sailors of all nations, according to William McCann 'danced in the bordellos to the tune of a violin or flute to the amazement of the *criolla* girls'.[28]

As we turn to the periodisation of the labour movement in Argentina we must confront one further theoretical question: the making of the working class. There is one tradition within Marxism, represented by Jurgen Kuczynski, for whom 'the modern working class is the product of the machine. It is the creation of the machine—to be exact, of the mechanical tool. No machines would mean no working class'.[29] In this, which we might call an 'objective' view, the proletariat becomes a class passively under the inexorable advance of capital, or more crudely, the machine. Against this, E.P. Thompson stresses that 'the making of the working class is a fact of political and cultural, as much as economic history. It was not the spontaneous generation of the factory system'.[30] The point for Thompson and others, is not how capital made the working class, but rather how the working class made itself. We would argue that neither Kuczynski nor Thompson is correct on his own, and that they are both partly right. The two concepts of 'class against capital' and 'class for itself' are not two separate processes, but are in constant interplay. If labour is understood as an integral component of the capital relation, then any false counter-position disappears. The capital accumulation process is at once the accumulation of wealth, and of a working class with its struggles, which are sometimes muted and subterranean, at moments stridently political.

Whereas our sympathies lie with the 'new' labour history represented by E.P. Thompson, we cannot ignore its weaknesses. As Perry Anderson notes, in Thompson's classic *The Making of the English Working Class* there is 'a disconcerting lack of objective co-ordinates as the narrative of class formation unfolds'.[31] We cannot reject occupational categories as simply a stupid sociological concern with quantitative measurement. Rather, we have constantly accompanied our narrative of labour's development with an account of its 'objective co-ordinates'.

Proletarianisation in Argentina did not follow Marx's path mechanically, i.e. through the dispossession of the peasantry from its means of production. Yet, at the same time, the process of mass immigration was accomplishing a classical proletarianisation at one remove – the European peasant who was driven from the land became the immigrant worker in the 'New World'. The process was more complex because there were also an indigenous work force and the descendants of Black slaves, who in Argentina fused into the modern working class. Our first chapters describe, albeit schematically given the lack of data, what Perry Anderson has called

the whole historical process whereby heterogeneous groups of artisans, small-holders, agricultural labourers, domestic workers and casual poor were gradually assembled, distributed and reduced to the condition of labour subsumed to capital . . . [32]

This complex process is only imperfectly described by the term 'proletarianisation', which does not adequately embrace the uneven spatial and temporal displacements involved.

Notes

1. G. McLennan, (1981) *Marxism and the Methodologies of History*, London, New Left Books, p. 115.
2. G. Haupt, (1978) "Why the History of the Working-class Movement?" *Review* 11, 1, p. 13.
3. cf. E. Hobsbawm, (1974) "Labour History and Ideology", *Journal of Social History*, vol. 7, no. 4.
4. G. Payne, (1965) *Labor and Politics in Peru. The System of Political Bargaining,* New Haven, Yale University Press.
5. Ibid., p.11.
6. A. Córdova, (ed.) (1984) *Industrial Relations in Latin America,* New York, Praeger, p. 97.
7. Ibid., p.172.
8. H. Spalding, (1971) *Organized Labor in Latin America. Historical Case Studies of Urban Workers in Dependent Societies*, New York, Harper and Row, p. 282.
9. Ibid.
10. T. Harding and H. Spalding, (1976) "The Struggle Sharpens: Workers, Imperialism and the State in Latin America, Common Themes and New Directions", *Latin American Perspectives,* vol. III, no. 1, p. 5.
11. Ibid., p. 9.
12. K. Erickson, (1977) *The Brazilian Corporative State and Working Class Politics,* Berkeley, University of California Press.
13. R. Cohen, (1980) The *"New" International Labour Studies: A definition,* Centre for Developing-Area Studies, McGill University, Working Paper Series, no. 27, pp. 14, 15, 16.
14. See respectively E. Hobsbawm, (1971) *Labouring Men.* London, Weidenfeld and Nicolson; E.P. Thompson, (1971) *The Making of the English Working Class*, Harmondsworth, Penguin; M. Perrot, (1974) *Les ouvriers en grève, France 1871–1890,* Paris, Mouton; R. Trempé, (1971) *Les mineurs de Carmaux 1848–1914,* Paris, Ed. Ouvrières; H. Guttman, (1976) *Work, Culture and Society in Industrializing America,* New York, Knopf; D. Montgomery, (1980) *Workers' Control in America*, Cambridge, Cambridge University Press.
15. E. Sofer, (1980) "Recent trends in Latin American Labor Historiography", *Latin American Research Review,* vol. 15, no. 1, p. 175.
16. T. Skidmore, (1979) "Workers and Soldiers: Urban Labor Movements and Elite Responses in Twentieth Century Latin America", in V. Bernhard (ed.) *Elites, Masses and Modernization in Latin America*, Austin, University of Texas Press, p. 80.
17. G. Haupt, (1978) "Why the History of the Working-Class Movement?" p. 7.
18. see P. Bell, (1978) "Cycles of Class Struggle in Thailand", *Journal of Contemporary Asia,* vol. 8, no. 1.
19. J. Crisp, (1984) *The Story of an African Working Class. Ghanaian Miners' Struggles 1870–1980,* London, Zed Books.
20. Ibid., p. 12.
21. J. Cronin, (1980) "Stages, Cycles and Insurgencies: The Economics of Unrest" in T. Hopkins and I. Wallerstein (eds.) *Processes of the World-System*, London, Sage, p. 112.

22. I. Roxborough, (1981) "The analysis of Labour Movements in Latin America", Typologies and Theories, *Bulletin of Latin American Research,* vol. 1, no. 1, p. 93.

23. J. Humphrey, (1981) *Capitalist Control and Workers' Struggle in the Brazilian Auto Industry*, Princeton, Princeton University Press, p. 244.

24. V.I. Lenin, (1970) "Imperialism: the Highest Stage of Capitalism", in *Selected Works Vol. 1*, Moscow, Progress Publishers, p. 734.

25. C. Bergquist, (1981) *Exports, Labor and the Left: An Essay on Twentieth Century Chilean History,* The Wilson Centre, Latin American Program, Working Papers no. 97, p. i.

26. J. Scobie, (1971) *Argentina. A City and a Nation,* New York, Oxford University Press, p. 66.

27. Cited in L.A. Romero, (1983) "La convivencia acriollada", in J.L. Romero and L.A. Romero (eds.) *Buenos Aires. Historia de cuatro siglos*, Buenos Aires, Editorial Abril, p. 228.

28. Ibid., p. 237.

29. J. Kuczynski, (1967) *The rise of the working class,* London, Weidenfeld and Nicolson, p. 51.

30. E.P. Thompson, (1971) *The Making of the English Working Class*, p. 213.

31. P. Anderson, (1980) *Arguments Within English Marxism*. London, New Left Books, p. 33.

32. Ibid.

1. Artisans, Mutual-Aid Societies and Socialism (1855–1870)

The earliest origins of the modern labour movement in Argentina can be traced back to the first attempts at autonomous organisation of workers, and socialist propaganda, inside a layer of artisans and wage-earners which emerged in Buenos Aires during the 1850s. In spite of the profound transformations which have occurred over the years, there is an unbroken thread running through from that period to the present day.

The emergence of this layer of manual workers, of largely immigrant origin, was a consequence of the productive diversification of the pre-capitalist mercantilist structure of the country, through the development of wool production and export. With this wool, Argentine producers broke into the European market, which had previously banned the import of *tasajo* (dried and salted meat) which was destined instead for the slave markets of Cuba and Brazil.

The production of wool rose from barely 350 tons per annum in 1829 to 7,680 in 1850, reaching 65,760 in 1870. In 1862 wool represented half the total value of all Argentina's exports. Though its scope was limited, the wool cycle led to changes which were of greater importance than those produced by the earlier *saladero* (meat-packing plant) cycle.[1] The new product acted as a spur for the conversion of the *gaucho* (a semi-nomad horse-mounted shepherd) into an agricultural labourer. It also led to the emergence of an agricultural sector to complement the raising of sheep; the appearance of initially weak subsidiary industries such as the processing of animal fat; and finally, the need for massive immigration of European workers to provide the labour force for agriculture and the artisan trades.

Though the workers and artisans of European origin were the main sector which gave rise to the first experience of a labour movement, they were not the only type of workers in Argentina in that period. There was also in Buenos Aires a layer of Black manual workers, and in the provinces of the interior mainly indigenous or *mestizo* (mixed-race) workers in agriculture and the pre-capitalist artisan industries. Nevertheless, neither of these two sectors fulfilled the necessary conditions to produce autonomous forms of organisation, if for different reasons.

The Black workers who had played an important role in the artisan industry of Buenos Aires during the colonial and post-colonial periods, were relegated to domestic or bureaucratic employment with the arrival of the immigrants. Already in the last years of this period the demographic weight of the Black population had declined appreciably. The type of capitalist development which was forseeable in Buenos Aires and the littoral region made the introduction of a new wave of slave labour both costly and unnecessary. Paradoxically, at the very moment when they began to decline as a productive sector the Black workers began to produce a significant political literature.[2] The most radicalised sectors of the Black community, though continuing to express their grievances in ethnic terms, posed the need for the organisation of Black workers in clearly socialist terms. However, their social isolation prevented them from fulfilling an important role in the organisation of the labour movement.

The rural workers of the interior provinces did not produce their own organisational expression either. Their incorporation into the labour movement began towards the end of the 19th Century as an extension of the propaganda and activities of the political organisations generated by the urban immigrant workers. The persistence of pre-capitalist forms of exploitation in the interior – sometimes in spite of the nominal existence of wages – prevented the emergence of collective labour demands and activities.

Immigrant workers

The low population density inherited from the agro-livestock economic structure of the colonial and post-colonial periods forced the state to turn to immigration to fulfil the labour requirements of the developing agricultural and artisan sectors. The encouragement of overseas immigration was a constant concern of all governments after 1852. Different laws were adopted to encourage immigration and agrarian colonisation, by setting up freeholds and land concessions. The lack of an adequate infrastructure to absorb immigration, however, led to these legislative measures having little effect. From the end of the 1850s steps were taken to set up an office to place the newly arrived immigrants in jobs and to house them for their first days in the country. Finally, in 1876, an Immigration Law, inspired by the US's Homestead Act, was adopted.

The first relatively reliable statistics on the flow of immigrants date from 1855. Between that date and 1879, 626,003 immigrants arrived in the country.

As we see in Table 1.1, the flow of immigrants maintained a generally upward tendency throughout this period, although momentary declines due to epidemics, political disturbances or economic crises, such as that of the mid-1870s, can be noted.

This wave of immigration led to important changes in the social profile of the country. The first national census in 1869 registered a total population of 1,737,026 inhabitants, of which 210,292, that is 12.1%, were

Table 1.1   Migration to and from Argentina, 1855–1879

Years	Entries			Exits	Balance
	Overseas	Via Montevideo	Total		
1855–1859	24,928	–	24,928	–	24,928
1860–1864	40,663	–	40,663	–	40,663
1865–1869	93,565	16,112	109,677	–	109,677
1870–1874	160,788	81,758	242,546	59,415	183,131
1875–1879	104,800	103,389	208,189	95,971	112,218
Totals	424,744	201,259	626,003	155,386	470,617

Source: *Second National Census, 1895* and *Extracto Estadístico de la República Argentina*, Buenos Aires, 1915.

foreigners. The percentage of foreigners in the capital city Buenos Aires was much higher, however, reaching 49.6%. Of the total number of foreigners, Italians represented 34%, Spaniards 16.5%, French 15%, British 5%, Swiss 3% and Germans 2%.[3]

During these first years of immigration a certain proportion of migrants came from north-eastern Europe (and in general the more developed areas of the continent) where the process of industrialisation led to a surplus labour force. Even in the first years of the 1880s, 19% of immigrants came from north-eastern Europe. In the 1890s, on the other hand, the proportion of migrants from the south-east of Europe rose to 86%, a tendency which was to deepen in the years which followed.[4] This changing trend in migration patterns is significant because, in general, the two areas were associated with different types of migration. The migrants from north-eastern Europe, and the more developed areas, were generally workers with a certain level of education and skill, even in some cases with small capital savings. During the 20th Century, on the other hand, migrants were generally peasants from the poorest regions of southern and central Europe. The first wave of skilled urban immigrants formed the basis of a new layer of artisans in Buenos Aires and the littoral provinces.

Immigrants were attracted to Argentina mainly by the prospects in agriculture. During the 1860s and 1870s the government made great efforts to encourage the development of agricultural colonisation. The persistence of the *latifundio* structure of huge estates, however, made it increasingly difficult for the immigrants to gain access to land ownership. Only in the province of Santa Fé did agrarian colonisation achieve a certain importance. In 1872, the agrarian colonies of that province represented 83% of the total number throughout the country.[5] Some of the newly arrived foreigners, who did not achieve their ambition of land ownership, remained as tenants. Many, however, turned back to the cities, where they swelled the ranks of the nascent proletariat.

In 1885, when immigration became a systematic enterprise and the first mutual-aid societies were formed in certain trades, Buenos Aires boasted 1,265 'industrial' establishments. The majority were in fact small artisan workshops producing for local consumption or for subsidiary activities of the agro-livestock export trade. Nevertheless, that figure nearly doubles the 674 establishments accounted for in the 1822 census.[6] These 1,265 establishments brought together few personnel and had a low level of mechanisation. Some 223 of them were classified as being in the Alimentary sector; they were mainly bakeries and cake shops. Under the Clothing heading there were 278 workshops, and under Construction there were 179 carpentry shops, 34 brick kilns and various other workshops. There were 57 furniture workshops, 145 metal-working shops, and the rest were engaged in small-scale productive activities linked to agro-livestock export and local consumption. There were 114 printing establishments, this being one of the trades of particular importance in the development of an organised labour movement.[7]

It was from this layer of artisans that the first initiatives for autonomous workers' organisations sprang. These were the mutual-aid societies (*mutuales*) structured on a trade basis and having generally as their objective reciprocal help amongst members and defence of their profession. The first organisation of this type, of which we have definite proof, was the *Sociedad Tipográfica Bonaërense* (Buenos Aires Print-workers Society) formed on 25 May 1857. Apart from its mutual-aid and corporative objectives, this society had as one its aims that 'workers should always be remunerated in accordance with their skills and knowledge so that these may be safeguarded'.[8] Nevertheless, all indications are that the society was based predominantly on mutual-aid.

Shortly afterwards the shoe-makers were organised in a society named after their patron St Crispin, followed by other urban artisan sectors and the rural day-workers (*jornaleros*). During the 1860s and 1870s new associations were formed, among them those organising the brick-layers, bakers, construction workers, carpenters and tailors.[9] In all likelihood many of these initiatives were ephemeral, and in many trades there were several abortive attempts at setting up an organisation. Also, there were probably many organisations in other trades which were simply not recorded.

Notwithstanding their predominantly mutual-aid character, these organisations represented a step forward in the formation of workers' organisations. To the extent that they were organised on a corporative professional basis, they can be distinguished from the mutual-aid societies formed on the basis of national origin. In these latter organisations, workers were swamped by the mass of immigrants, and their political objectives were generally linked to the bourgeois and petty bourgeois layers who formed the élite of the immigrant communities.

In many cases these mutual-aid trade-based organisations changed in shape and purpose as their social base of urban workers was transformed.

Frequently the *mutuales* became 'resistance societies', in other cases they maintained their ambiguous character midway between mutual-aid society and trade union. In the case of the printers, the early mutual-aid society provided the foundation for an association based on more specifically trade union principles.

Early political developments

Along with the formation of the *mutuales* there emerged a socialist political literature, which found its most important expression in the journal *El Artesano* (The Artisan) which appeared in 1863 under Bartolomé Victory y Suárez, one of the main pioneers of the Argentine labour movement.[10] *El Artesano* directed its message to the three classes which in its view made up the world of work: the workers, the artisans and the industrialists. This ambiguous stance, frequently repeated in its pages, reflected the low level of internal social differentiation at that time amongst the mass of urban workers. The journal's correspondents defined themselves as workers, and in its last issues they lamented the fact that only a third of their subscribers were workers.[11]

El Artesano was, overall, a faithful reflection of the ambiguous social position of the artisans, who were caught between the expectations of social progress in the 'New World', and their exclusion from national politics. As Julio Godio has pointed out, in a certain way the lack of a true industrial bourgeoisie led these artisans to become the main proponents of an industrialist ideology.[12]

The most important trade union of this whole period was that of the printers. Not only were they in the forefront in 1857 with the formation of the first trade-based mutual-aid society, but towards the end of the 1870s they established the first links with the International Working Men's Association (or First International) and in 1878 founded the first specifically trade unionist organisation in Argentina. Several factors favoured this vanguard role. On the one hand, they were helped by the fact that 60 per cent of them were native-born Argentinians. On the other hand, their trade was one which required a certain level of skill, at a time when literacy was rare among workers. Finally, their very trade familiarised them with the art of running a workers' press, which resulted in their producing numerous journals in those years.

Two documents produced by the printers give us more insight into the political thinking of militant workers in the 1870s. In them we find an advance from the stance of *El Artesano*, though they are still characterised by a reformist socialism, not too deeply influenced by either Marxism or anarchism.

The first of these documents, written by Bartolomé Victory y Suárez, was published in the first issue of *Anales* produced in 1870 by the Buenos Aires Print-workers Society. This journal was, incidentally, reprinted by the

Barcelona journal *La Federación* (an organ of the First International) which served as the first point of contact between the Argentine printers and the International Working Men's Association.[13] In this article, 'association', or the coming together of workers, was seen as the motor or the axis of social action. The first step, according to Victory y Suárez, had to be the organisation of affiliates by trade, profession, industry or other corporative forms. The second step would be the constitution of co-operative forms of production which would allow 'work-capital [to gain] sufficient strength to resist money-capital and ensure for the worker his rights to work and the full fruit of his labours'.[14] Workers had to fight to achieve 'freedom', but this in itself was seen as insufficient to achieve the full liberation of the workers, who had to be 'free, politically and socially speaking'. Workers should only participate in political life to demand from their representatives a guarantee for their freedom to exercise their rights. Political freedom would allow the association of workers, who would thus some day become as powerful as capital.

Another document from this period is the written version of a speech delivered by the president of the Buenos Aires Print-workers Society, José María P. Méndez, at its annual conference on 25 May 1871.[15] This document allows us to glimpse the thinking of the printers just *before* they established firm contacts with the First International, which led to new influences on their thought. The printers' leader called for a peaceful revolution led by the working people, which necessarily had to be preceded by changes in the law and workers' rights. The objective of this revolution was seen as the formation, through association, of a federation of all the working classes which would put an end to the exploitation of man by man. It would do so by 'establishing a judicious and stable legislation which guaranteed, for rich and poor alike, the legitimate exercise of their trade . . . '[16]

In the two documents referred to above, we find a common set of themes: the idea of a peaceful revolution, a society which would guarantee the dignified existence of the worker, at the same time limiting the need for a prior reformist step to achieve protective legislation for workers. In the Méndez speech, however, we also find references which imply a knowledge of certain First International texts. He stated explicitly that he was inspired by some of its documents on subjects related to the labour process and workers' organisations. He also said it was necessary to learn from European workers' associations what might be useful and adaptable for Argentina's workers. Finally, there is explicit mention of the sentence 'the emancipation of the working classes must be conquered by the working classes themselves' from the Provisional Rules of the International.[17]

In spite of the appearance of a new class vocabulary, however, there is no evidence that Victory y Suárez or Méndez supported at that time any of the strategies emerging from Marx's or Bakunin's camp of the International. In this respect, it is interesting to refer to the contemporary comments by Francisco Mora, secretary of the Spanish Federal Council of the

International, who wrote in relation to the Victory y Suárez article in *Anales*, cited above, that 'judging by their writing they are internationalists, even though they ignore the mechanisms and development of this, the First International'.[18]

In all likelihood the militants of the first phases of the labour movement in Argentina referred to diverse ideological sources, including Proudhon, but adapted these to correspond more closely to the social and political aspirations of the majority of manual workers of the period.

Notes

1. R. Ortiz, (1971) *Historia Económica de la Argentina*, Buenos Aires, Plus Ultra, p. 52. For an overview of early economic development in Argentina see J. Scobie, *Argentina: A City and a Nation,* New York, Oxford University Press.

2. G.R. Andrews, (1981) *The Afro-Argentines of Buenos Aires.* Wisconsin, Wisconsin University Press, refers to several journals such as *La Raza Africana* (The African Race) and *El Látigo* (The Whip) which appeared between 1858 and 1870.

3. First National Census, 1869.

4. J. Alsina, (1910) *La inmigración en el primer siglo de la Independencia,* Buenos Aires, F.S. Alsina, p. 22.

5. Second National Census, 1895.

6. Ibid.

7. Ibid.

8. Quoted in S. Marotta, (1976) *El movimiento sindical argentino t.l.,* Buenos Aires, Ed. Libera.

9. For more detils see R. Falcón (1980) *La Primera Internacional y los orígenes del movimiento obrero en Argentina (1857–1879)*, Paris, CEHSAL, and R. Munck, (1984) Formation and Development of the Working Class in Argentina (1857–1919) in B. Munslow and H. Finch (eds.) *Proletarianization in the Third World.* London, Croom Helm.

10. Bartolomé Victory y Suárez was born in the Spanish-ruled Balearic Islands in 1833, coming to Argentina in 1860 where he worked as a printer and journalist. Active in the organisations of his trade, he was also a freemason. He published various books and collaborated with several journals. He died in 1897. For more biographical details see R. Falcón (1980) *La Primera Internacional.*

11. For more details on *El Artesano* see D. Cuneo, (1945) *El primer periodismo obrero y socialista,* Buenos Aires, La Vanguardia.

12. J. Godio (1973) *Historia del movimiento obrero argentino*, Buenos Aires, Tiempo Contemporáneo.

13. *La Federación* (Barcelona) no. 71 (25 December, 1870).

14. Ibid.

15. *La Federación* (Barcelona) no. 130 (11 February 1872).

16. Ibid.

17. K. Marx, (1974) *The First International and After.* Harmondsworth, Penguin, p. 82.

18. Letter from Mora to the International's General Council in London (14 December 1870). Original in Instituut Voor Sociale Geschiedems (1156) in Amsterdam, Fonds Jung 836.

2. The First International in Argentina (1871–1876)

An important step was taken in the development of a labour movement in Argentina when sections of the First International were set up in the country from 1872 onwards. In spite of contacts between the International and the printers of Argentina since at least 1870, the first organised activity of the movement did not take place until the arrival of numerous exiles from the repression which followed the fall of the Paris Commune in 1871. The changes set in motion did, however, have certain objective limits set by the level of economic development of the country and the conditions of its working masses.

The conditions of the working class had changed significantly since 1855, although the transformations were not yet complete. The national census of 1869 shows the existence of 115,794 farmers (*agricultores*), 13,532 shepherds and cowhands, and 46,542 *estancieros* (owners of large landed estates or *estancias*) which covered extra workers as well as owners. There were also 163,989 day-workers (*jornaleros*) of whom a proportion presumably worked on the land, if only seasonally, while others were employed in the cities.[1] In the provinces of the interior the census pointed to 94,032 spinners and weavers, along with 1,236 miners. Of the nearly 100,000 involved in the artisan textile industry, the vast majority were women. This pre- or non-capitalist sector suffered severely from the competition of British manufactured goods, a decline expressed in the reduction of workers in this sector to 39,380 by the 1895 census.[2] Of the main non-agricultural manual trades, the construction workers were the most numerous, with the 1869 census accounting for 9,647 brick-layers, 14,028 carpenters and 1,175 painters. At least one-third of the construction workers lived in the capital city, Buenos Aires.[3] The bulk of the artisans were concentrated in Buenos Aires, where in 1869 34,522 people were classified under the 'manual trades' rubric. Of these, nearly 10,000 belonged to construction-linked occupations, and what were at the time classified as metallurgical trades. There were a further 15,000 involved in artisanal activities for local consumption, 10,000 day-workers (*jornaleros*) and another 32,000 engaged in the transport and services sector.[4]

When we refer to industrial production, we must not forget that the majority of the establishments were artisanal or pre-capitalist in nature. In

Table 2.1   Occupational categories, 1869

Category	Number	Percentage
Industrial production	280,543	35.60
Raw materials production	187,869	23.84
No fixed employment	170,060	21.58
Service personnel	120,177	15.25
Transportation	29,394	3.73
Manual occupations sub-total	788,043	100
Those exercising a profession	857,167	84.5
Those not exercising a profession	156,908	15.5
Total population over 14	1,014,075	100

Source: National Census, 1869.

many cases, particularly in the provinces of the interior, wages were nominal, with payment by chits redeemable only at the company store being a common practice.

Another common pre-capitalist practice of the time was the requirement that workers in certain skilled trades have their own tools. For the artisans and wage-workers without stable employment during the 1860s and 1870s, owning one's tools was a means of upward social mobility. The absence of an industrial structure or bourgeoisie facilitated the transition of many of these workers into the ranks of the small property owners. Even when that was not achieved, as happened in the majority of cases, the ownership of tools, along with the constant demand for labour, favoured the workers in their struggle to obtain concessions from their employers. This type of manual worker was mid-way between artisan and wage worker, on the one hand marginalised by his condition as an immigrant, but on the other hand spurred on by the expectation of social mobility.

It was this type of worker which confronted the internationalists when, in 1872, the first organisations of the International Working Men's Association were set up in Buenos Aires. As we have mentioned, the contacts between the General Council of the International in London and the Argentine printers dated back to mid-1870. These links had been brought to the attention of Marx and Engels by Francisco Mora, secretary of the Spanish Region. The leaders of the International immediately thought that the print-workers of Argentina, through their links with Brazil, Uruguay and Chile, could serve as a vanguard for spreading the International's influence in South America. But difficulties of communication prevented them from advancing the organisational drive in any concrete way. Early in 1872, however, with the arrival of numerous French militants who had participated in the Paris Commune, the *Section Française de l'Association Internationale de Travailleurs* (French Section of the International Working Men's Association) was formed in Buenos Aires.[5] Shortly after, in July 1872, two further sections had been formed by Italian and Spanish immigrants respectively. The latter grouping united with the French section to form a Federal Council comprising 273 members, run by a two-member Central Committee.[6] A fourth section was formed in Córdoba city, in the interior, in 1874.

Little is known of the founders of the First International in Argentina. Both E. Flaesch, who signed the correspondence with London with the title 'founder of the International in Buenos Aires', and A. Aubert, who was secretary of the Federal Council, appear to be pseudonyms for French émigré militants. The two best-known figures were Désiré Job, one of the leaders of the Marseilles Commune in 1871 and a follower of Louis Blanc, and Raymond Wilmart, a Belgian friend of Paul Lafargue, who corresponded with Marx from Buenos Aires.

In spite of its rapid numerical growth–probably due in great measure to the regrouping of militants with previous political experience–the International in Argentina faced grave difficulties. Its sections introduced a new type of organisation, based on a political programme, quite different from the corporative mutual-aid societies, which corresponded better to the social characteristics of the workers of that period. The internationalists, many of whom had passed through the crucible of the Paris Commune and other social and political struggles in Europe, found the conditions in Buenos Aires quite different from those they had known previously. After the first flush of enthusiasm it dawned on them that their work would be difficult in a social milieu where many workers still had hopes of upward social mobility.

One of the main activities of the International's supporters in Argentina was the publishing of a journal, which only appeared sporadically and, due to financial difficulties, only survived for eight issues.[7] They also attempted to link up with the existing workers' organisations and even proposed the formation of a trade union federation.[8] There is no record of what resulted from that proposal, but the signs are that if it did materialise it could only have had an ephemeral existence. In a letter to Karl Marx, Raymond Wilmart referred to these difficulties, not without bitterness, disillusionment and maybe some exaggeration: 'There are too many prospects of becoming a small owner and exploiting the newly arrived workers for people to chose to act in any way'.[9]

In 1875 the backlash of the international capitalist crisis created an unprecedented opportunity for the International's supporters in Argentina to engage in action. In 1872 and 1873 there had been a sharp increase in the number of immigrants arriving. With the start of the economic crisis, there was a large mass of immigrants in the city of Buenos Aires without work and showing clear signs of discontent. At the same time the internal political struggles within the ruling classes sharpened the climate of social unrest. In 1874 General Bartolomé Mitre led an abortive uprising against the elected president, Nicolás Avellaneda. In this case, as with other confrontations and conspiracies which occurred in 1875, some liberal and masonic elements within the immigrant communities appeared to be linked with Mitre's attempted coup.

In February 1875, there was an anti-clerical demonstration in Buenos Aires in which many workers participated. The press helped to create a climate of xenophobia and the police raided the headquarters of the French section of the International. Eleven militants were imprisoned. They were released a month later, having been absolved by the judge of any involvement in the burning of the Jesuit college of El Salvador, which had occurred during the demonstration. Though we do not know the extent of their participation in the 1875 events, the internationalists certainly took advantage of the circumstances to deepen their links with the working class.

The Argentine sections of the International Working Men's Association maintained contact with the tendency led by Marx and Engels. However, this does not allow us to characterise them as 'Marxist'.[10] Some militants maintained close links with Marx, as in the case of Raymond Wilmart, but others supported Blanquist ideas or were non-aligned socialists. There were also some sympathisers of Bakunin, but they do not seem to have maintained an open tendency until after the International's sections in Argentina were dissolved. This happened in 1876 following the lead of the Council in New York. Some of the local members returned to their countries of origin, as in the case of the French, following an amnesty for the exiles of the Paris Commune. Others continued their activity in Argentina, participating in the 'resistance societies' which were being formed at the time, and setting up socialist or anarchist propaganda groups.

Notes

1. First National Census 1869.
2. Ibid.
3. Ibid.
4. Ibid.
5. For more information on the First International in Argentina see R. Falcón, (1980) *La Primera Internacional y los origenes del movimiento obrero en Argentina (1857–1879)*, Paris CEHSAL, and more generally M. Segall, (1972) En Amérique Latine, Developpement du mouvement ouvrier et proscription, *International Review of Social History*, 17.
6. Letter from E. Flaesch to the General Council in London (14 April 1872). Original in Instituut voor Sociale Geschiedenis (IISG) in Amsterdam, Fonds Jung 627/2.
7. There are different versions on the name of this journal but most authors

agree on *El Trabajador* (The Worker).

8. Letter from Raymond Wilmart to Marx (27 May 1873). Original in Instituut voor Sociale Geschiedenis (IISG) in Amsterdam, Karl Marx Correspondence D. 4604.

9. Ibid.

10. It is wrong anyway to call the First International "Marxist". See G. Haupt, (1982) 'Marx' and 'Marxism' in E. Hobsbawm (ed.) *The History of Marxism*, vol. 1, Brighton, Harvester.

3. The Formation of the Proletariat

Towards the end of the 1870s and throughout the 1880s there was a series of transformations in the productive structure of the country, which led to an important change in the composition of the working class. Just as the production and export of wool had led to the formation of a layer of urban artisans, so now meat and grains would lead to a transformation of these early workers into a proletariat subject to modern capitalist exploitation. The concentrated and accelerated rhythm of Argentina's capitalist transformation was due to the fact that it sprang from the requirements of the world market and the development of European and international capitalism. This factor left its mark on the development of capitalism in Argentina, determining its agro-export nature, which resulted in a weak and subsidiary development of industry, constantly thwarted by competition from British manufactured goods.[1]

Argentina's export trade increased dramatically during this period, doubling between 1880 and 1889. A major role was played first by grains and then meat.[2] The area of the country devoted to wheat production increased eight-fold between 1875 and 1888. At the same time cattle herds expanded along with the *frigoríficos* (meat-chilling plants) which allowed the export of meat to rise to prominence from the 1890s onwards. This general increase in agrarian exports led to fundamental changes in the country's economic structure. A key sector in this expansion was that of transport and communications. In 1879 the extent of railways in Argentina was only 2,516 kilometres, but by 1892 there were 13,682 kilometres of track. Alongside this there was a development of maritime transport; the ports were modernised, and the whole infrastructure of foreign trade was organised. In a few years, an important banking and financial network was created. Finally, foreign capital, particularly British, flowed into the country to take advantage of generous concessions.

This set of economic transformations led, albeit indirectly, to an expansion of industry. The growth of the railways favoured the development of some provincial industries processing agrarian produce. In the littoral provinces of the River Plate, industries which depended on the agro-export economy were strengthened, and workshops producing for local consumption multiplied. Industrial growth, however, was subordinated to the agro-export nature of capitalism in Argentina. Industrialisation usually occurred in periods of international economic crisis when local industry could substitute products which were previously imported from abroad.

A determining factor leading to these social and economic transformations was the successful centralisation of the national state and the accompanying political reforms. Under the commercial and agrarian hegemony of Buenos Aires an alliance was forged with the major provincial oligarchies, which allowed the formation of a centralised (and centralising) state power. Some of the main political tasks of the bourgeoisie during this period were the consolidation of the national army as against the provincial militias; the so-called 'desert campaigns' against the indigenous peoples, which led to the incorporation of large tracts of land into the dominant economic system; and the separation of state (and education) from the Church. The governing élite, however, maintained only the formalities of democracy and the parliamentary system, based on political exclusion and the effective absence of universal suffrage.

Mass immigration

One of the most important tasks of the new nation-state was to attract increasing numbers of immigrant workers to service the new needs of agriculture and industry.

Between 1880 and the end of the century 1,949,593 immigrants entered Argentina and 727,210 people emigrated, leaving a balance of 1,222,383.[3] During the first half of the 1880s the rate of immigration was only slightly higher than that of the 1870s, but in the second half of the decade it rose spectacularly, with an average of 120,000 immigrants per annum. The 260,909 immigrants who arrived in 1889 set a record which was not surpassed for many years. This rise in migration to Argentina can be accounted for in terms of the constant demand for labour, the expansion of agriculture, government propaganda abroad, state subsidies of travel costs, and the economic conditions in Europe itself. The economic crisis of 1890 and its political consequences led to a temporary halt in the flow of immigrants, with 1891 being the first year in which emigration was higher than immigration in Argentina. However, this negative trend was not repeated until 1914 and the outbreak of the First World War. Between 1892 and 1895 net immigration stabilised at an annual average of 37,000 people, with a new rise in 1896 due to economic recovery in Europe, which led to a net intake of 89,284 immigrants. In the three years which followed there was an annual average of 46,000 immigrants entering Argentina.

The percentage of immigrants who returned to their country of origin rose from 17% in the 1880s to 57% in the 1890s. This was due not only to the economic crisis mentioned above but also to the spreading of the practice of seasonal migration by which largely Spanish and Italian workers (known as *golondrinas* or swallows) travelled to Argentina for the harvest season and then returned home.

Immigration played an important role in the demographic expansion of Argentina during the second half of the 19th Century. The population grew from 1,830,000 at the time of the 1869 census to 4,044,911 by the second national census of 1895.[4] In 1895 the 1,014,500 foreigners represented 25.4% of the total population compared with 12% in 1869. Of these immigrants, 87.8% were concentrated in the littoral provinces. In the city of Buenos Aires immigrants represented 52.2% of the population. The social and economic importance of the immigrants was even greater than their sheer numbers. In 1895 they accounted for 90% of property owners; 75% of enterprise owners; 64% of industrial employees; and 42.6% of commercial employees.[5] As to the national composition of the immigrants, Italians continued in the majority, representing 49% of the total; immigrants from Spain increased their relative weight to 19.8% of the total; and those from France, while still occupying third place, now only represented 9.4% of all immigrants.[6]

The working class

Wage labour was concentrated in four main sectors from the 1880s to the beginning of the 20th Century: firstly in agrarian activities and the processing of primary goods in the interior provinces; secondly in semi-artisan industries producing for the local market; thirdly in construction of infrastructure associated with the urbanisation of Buenos Aires; fourthly in transportation and the commercial and services sector generally. The 1895 census noted that out of an economically active population of 2,451,761, there were 1,645,824 who exercised a profession or trade and 805,937 who did not. The latter sector (composed largely of women) had increased noticeably since the 1869 census, from 15.5% of the total to 32.9%.[7] Table 3.1 provides a breakdown of occupations in 1895:

Table 3.1   Employment by sector, 1895

Sector	Number	Percentage of economically active population
Primary goods, processing	393,948	16.2%
Industrial production	366,087	14.9%
Transportation	63,000	2.6%
Services	222,774	9.1%
No fixed employment	342,493	14.0%
Sub-total manual trades	1,388,302	56.8%
Non-manual professions	257,522	10.3%
Total trades or professions	1,645,824	67.1%

Source: Second National Census, 1895.

The primary goods processing sector was linked to agriculture and livestock raising. The number of those working in this sector had doubled since 1869, with 261,453 farmers, 28,724 shepherds and cow-hands, and 81,074 *estancieros* (which covered both owners and ranch hands). Some 58% of overseas immigrants who had arrived in Argentina between 1876 and 1897 declared their occupation as that of tenant farmer (*agricultor*). Some of these were active in the 709 agrarian colonies, covering 6,188,013 hectares, which existed in 1895, half of which were concentrated in the province of Santa Fé.[8]

As to industrial production, in 1895 there were 22,204 industrial establishments employing 145,650 people, with capital of 284,101,367 pesos, and an installed capacity of 27,227 internal combustion engines, 2,348 steam engines and 31,700 engines of various other kinds. The majority and the most important of these establishments were concentrated in the littoral provinces, where 84% of the total labour force was employed. The capital, Buenos Aires, accounted for 34% of the total number of establishments, and 57% of employees.[9] In Table 3.2 we can see the breakdown of industrial employment at the turn of the century.

Table 3.2   Industrial employment, 1895

Sector	Number of Firms	Number of Workers
Food and beverages	4,082	27,071
Textiles	5,713	32,599
Construction	3,955	30,519
Furniture	2,259	12,721
Decorative Trades	949	2,560
Metallurgical	3,163	14,631
Chemicals	317	4,712
Printing and Publishing	427	5,080
Other	1,339	15,757
Total	22,204	145,650

Source: Second National Census, 1895.

In spite of the economic transformations which had taken place, the vast majority of industrial establishments in 1895 were semi-artisanal in character. This is confirmed by the fact that there was a low level of labour concentration, the overall figure being six workers per establishment.

In the construction industry there were 28,067 brick-layers in 1895, which represented an increase of 290% since 1869. The strong demand for labour in this sector led to the highest growth rate of all the trades or professions. As Adolfo Dorfman points out, a brick-layer earned more than double a printer's wage and three times that of a *saladero* (meat packing plant) *peón*.[10] Not only brick-laying but all skilled trades linked to the construction industry were in strong demand. In 1884 the newspaper *La Prensa* declared that 'the demand for carpenters, ironmongers and brick-layers continues to grow, constantly pushing up wages, including those for *peones*'.[11] We can safely assume that an important proportion of day-workers (*jornaleros*) and those 'without fixed employment' were involved sporadically in the unskilled building trades.

In the transport sector, the most important group of workers at the turn of the century were the railworkers. In 1896 there were 34,056 railway workers and employees, along with 4,266 tram-workers distributed across 19 towns. In this sector there were also 20,851 cart drivers, 4,619 carriers and 16,989 seamen.[12]

Apart from the breakdown by industrial sector mentioned above, the Special Bulletins of the 1895 census allow us to examine the composition of the labour force in the primary goods processing sector, where in general there was a higher level of capital invested. Table 3.3 shows the main employers in this sector.

Table 3.3   Primary goods processing, 1895

Sector	Number of Firms	Number of Workers
Meat salting plants (*saladeros*)	39	5,574 (including 160 administrative personnel)
Flour mills	659	3,910 (at the 586 mills who provided this data)
Sugar mills	51	293 technicians
		998 artisans
		9,577 unskilled workers (*peones*)
		7,509 permanent agricultural workers
		17,440 seasonal workers
Wine plants	949	4,568 permanent workers
		18,630 seasonal workers
Beer plants	61	957 (many women and children)
Alcohol distilleries	–	2,530
Total	1,759	71,986 (includes 36,070 seasonal workers)

Source: Industry Special Bulletin, Second National Census, 1895.

The degree of labour concentration in the primary goods processing industries was greater than in the artisan workshops. There was also a higher proportion of seasonal workers, including women and children. These industries were less open to trade union organising and were only drawn into the labour movement at the beginning of the 20th Century through the efforts of the urban trade unions.

In the formation of a working class in Argentina the presence of immigrants is overwhelming, especially in the provinces most affected by the process of modernisation. In 1895 those who were born abroad represented 36% of the economically active population, 38% of those with a trade or profession, and 64% of all those employed in industry. The presence of immigrants was particularly strong in certain sectors, such as the food industry, bakeries and the construction industry.

Women represented only 15% of the total number of workers employed in industry. The proportion of female workers was higher in the chemical industry, sugar factories and leather works. The higher proportion of women workers usually occurred in those sectors where there was a higher proportion of native-born workers. Also, as already mentioned, women represented the majority of the 39,380 workers employed in the artisanal textile industry of the interior provinces. The 1895 census also points to the existence of 119,180 seamstresses, 75,539 washerwomen, 8,536 tailoresses and 25,492 ironing women. Of the immigrant women 34.3% declared a trade or profession, as against 48% of those who were native-born. In general terms, the presence of a female labour-force was linked to the sectors least affected by capitalist modernisation and those where the proportion of native-born workers was highest.[13]

The workers of Buenos Aires

Buenos Aires was the axis of capitalist modernisation in Argentina, and had the major concentrations of the work-force. It was virtually in that one city that the labour movement of Argentina was born.[14]

During the second half of the 19th Century Buenos Aires experienced one of the most important growth processes in international terms. The city had 90,076 inhabitants in 1855, growing to 177,787 in 1869, 433,375 in 1887, reaching 663,854 in 1895.[15] Immigration played an important role in the capital's demographic expansion: in 1869 immigrants represented 49.3% of the city's inhabitants, in 1887 52.7%, and in 1895 47.9%.[16]

One of the major sources of labour recruitment was the very process of urban expansion needed to cope with the city's population increase. The urban area grew threefold between 1867 and 1887, and the number of houses grew from 20,858 in 1869 to 50,000 in 1895, of which more than 5,000 were over one storey high.[17] Apart from the building programme, the last decades of the 19th Century and the early years of the 20th saw a number of major urban development schemes which absorbed an important amount of labour power. One of these was the port of Buenos Aires which expanded in various phases. Running water, waste disposal and gas systems were built, and after 1899 an electric lighting system spread throughout the city. Towards the end of the century, eight large thoroughfares were constructed and the first asphalt roads were laid.

In 1887 there were 10,414 brick-layers in Buenos Aires, along with 10,074 carpenters, 540 stonemasons, 3,123 painters and 442 plasterers.[18] Apart from these specialised trades the urbanisation works recruited, for a time, a large number of unskilled workers, especially day-workers (*jornaleros*). In the transport sector there was also an important concentration of workers: between 1887 and 1897 tram-workers increased threefold and there was a strong nucleus of coach drivers. The 1895 census also shows the existence of 8,439 manufacturing workshops in Buenos Aires, producing largely for local consumption, and employing 70,469 people. The average concentration of labour – eight workers per workshop – was still low, but there were some factories employing up to 800 workers.

Conditions of the working class

The socio-economic transformations of the 1880s not only led to a change in the objective conditions of the working class but also in its subjective manifestations.[19] Until approximately 1887 working-class life, particularly for the immigrants, was marked by a relatively justified expectation of social mobility. The steady demand for labour led to the rapid placement of the newly-arrived workers and, in many cases, led to their obtaining favourable wage rates. The absence of a real industrial sector, the ownership of their own tools, and sometimes the ownership of a small sum of capital, allowed some of the early immigrants to become property owners. However, the transformations of the 1880s accelerated the proletarianisation of the vast bulk of the work-force. The arrival of a large number of immigrants towards the end of the 1880s led to a new situation, which was aggravated by the ensuing economic depression. The increase in the supply of labour favoured the employers' ability to impose stringent working conditions.

The development of the first large factories also led to a general change in working conditions and the labour process. The characteristic closeness of the small workshop gave way to the modern forms of capitalist exploitation. The Rufino Varela workshops for instance, established work norms which were common practice at the time: the working day in winter and summer alike was to be ten hours; obligatory night work was established; strict labour discipline codes prohibited smoking and absence without leave from the premises; and those who were dismissed were furnished with a certificate detailing the cause of dismissal.[20] These draconian conditions of labour discipline were one of the earliest concerns of the labour movement. Thus in the 1891 petition from the *Federación Obrera* (Workers' Federation) to President Carlos Pellegrini there was a protest against the severe fines inflicted on workers by the bosses for various reasons. The employers were able to make handsome additional profits in this way, the *Federación* alleged.[21]

Referring to the early factories and workshops Adolfo Dorfman writes that 'the sheds where the first industrial machines began operating were, in general, primitive, inadequate and dangerous'.[22] Not surprisingly, accidents were frequent, particularly in the building industry, as even the conservative *La Nación* newspaper noted with alarm in 1887.[23]

For the majority of workers the working day was 10 hours or more. According to Adrian Patroni's calculations, of 134,772 workers surveyed, 65% were working 10-hour days, 22.5% worked between 11 and 14 hours daily, 8.5% did a 9-hour day and only 4% had achieved an 8-hour working day.[24] It was during the 1890s that the labour movement began to agitate in earnest on the length of the working day. In 1896 nearly half of all strikes included a demand for the reduction in working hours, which began to achieve some results in the first decade of the 20th Century.

All writers and contemporary accounts agree that real wages in Argentina increased until at least 1886. Following a 19th Century study carried out by the US Consul in Buenos Aires, William Buchanan, it is usually maintained that after that date wages declined steadily.[25] However, recent research by Roberto Cortés Conde, based on rural wages and those in the Bagley biscuit factory, throws some doubt on the earlier view. Cortés Conde sets out a periodisation of wage patterns which includes periods of wage declines and also steady real wages.[26] The periods in which wages rose seem to coincide with peaks in the rate of unemployment, and those in which wages declined, with the periods in which strike activity reached its highest peaks.

One factor which led to sharp oscillations in the supply of labour was the nature of the immigration process. One of the earliest concerns of the labour movement was the uncontrollable migratory flow, which was seen as an obstacle to workers' struggles.

The exploitation of female and child labour in far worse conditions than those of men, was characteristic in Buenos Aires as much as in the interior provinces. According to Germán Ave Lallemant's contemporary testimony, 'child labour is exploited at between 0.06 and 0.15 *pesos* [per day]',[27] at a time when the lowest daily wage of an unskilled worker was one *peso*. According to Lallemant, in some establishments seamstresses were paid 0.23 for a 15-hour day.[28]

The characteristic working-class housing in the cities was the *conventillo* (little convent) which was a large building divided into rooms, with a whole family living together in one room. In 1890 there were 2,249 of these tenement blocks in Buenos Aires, housing 94,743 people (of which 67,770 were immigrants) in 37,063 rooms.[29] The average was 2.5 people per room, but in many *conventillos* a figure of 5 people per room was not uncommon. In 1887 infant mortality in the *conventillos* was 67 per thousand live births, compared to 24.4 per thousand for the population at large.[30] The rent for this accommodation accounted for nearly one-quarter of the average working class family's expenditure. From the beginning of the 1890s there was agitation against the bad housing conditions and high rent of the *conventillos*. These moves culminated in a number of important rent strikes by the *conventillo* tenants. While the housing situation in the cities was bad, it was still common in the provinces of the interior to see straw and wood (or even mud) *ranchos.*

The situation of the recently-arrived immigrant workers was not easy either. On arrival they were placed in the Immigrants' Hotel, where living conditions and food were not of the best, as letters to families back home in Europe testified.[31] On various occasions inquiries were launched into irregularities and abuses committed by the Immigrants' Hotel management. Some immigrants were placed in jobs in the provinces by a specially created government department, but the majority had to make their own way in the New World. In this context, the national immigrant societies fulfilled an important role in certain cases. The immigrant was a worker, but above all a foreigner. Solidarity within national groups was of great importance in the first days after landing in Argentina.

Working conditions were worse for the majority of native-born workers, and the minority of immigrants, who were employed in the vineyards, *maté* tea plantations, timber mills and *saladeros.* In these areas pre-capitalist exploitation practices persisted for a long time in spite of the existence of nominal wages in some cases. In the northern provinces in particular, indigenous labour was exploited under serf-like conditions.[32]

Notes

1. For an overview see F. Ferns, (1960) *Britain and Argentina in the Nineteenth Century*, Oxford, Clarendon Press, and A. Ferrer, *The Argentine Economy*, Berkeley, University of California Press.

2. For the major economic sectors of the period see J. Scobie, (1964) *Revolution on the Pampas: A Social History of Argentine Wheat, 1860–1910,* Austin, University of Texas Press, and P. Smith, (1969) *Politics and Beef in Argentina: Patterns of Conflict and Change,* New York, Columbia University Press.

3. Second National Census, 1895.

4. Ibid.

5. Ibid.

6. Ibid.

7. Ibid.

8. Ibid.

9. Ibid.

10. A. Dorfman, (1970) *Historia de la Industria Argentina.* Buenos Aires, Solar/Hachette, p. 103.

11. *La Prensa* (7 October 1884).

12. Second National Census, 1895.

13. Ibid. On the position of women workers in the provinces see D. Guy, (1981) "Women, Peonage and Industrialization: Argentina, 1810–1914", *Latin American Research Review*, XVI (3).

14. For an excellent study of urbanisation and workers in Buenos Aires see G. Bourdé, (1974) *Urbanisation et Immigration en Amérique Latine. Buenos Aires (XIX et XX Siècles),* Paris, Aubier.

15. First National Census, 1869, Buenos Aires Municipal Census, 1887 and Second National Census, 1895.

16. Ibid.

17. Buenos Aires Municipal Census, 1887 and Second National Census, 1895.

18. Buenos Aires Municipal Census, 1887.

19. For an overview of the conditions of the working class during this period see J. Panettieri, (1967) *Los Trabajadores*, Buenos Aires, Jorge Alvarez.

20. *La Unión Gremial* (31 October 1895).

21. *El Obrero* (24 January 1891).

22. A. Dorfman, (1970) *Historia de la Industria Argentina*, p. 105.

23. *La Nación* (28 August 1887).

24. Cited in J. Oddone (1934), *Historia del Socialismo Argentino*, Vol. II, Buenos Aires, La Vanguardia, p. 188.

25. W.I. Buchanan, (1898), "La moneda y la vida en la República Argentina", *Revista de Derecho, Historia y Letras* (Buenos Aires), I (2).

26. R. Cortés Conde, (1979) *El Progreso Argentino 1880–1914*. Buenos Aires, Editorial Sudamericana, Part IV: "El Mercado de Trabajo".

27. G.A. Lallemant, (1985) *Die Nieu Zeit*, 1, cited in Paso, I (1974) *La Clase Obrera y el Nacimiento del Marxismo en la Argentina. Selección de articulos de Germán Ave Lallemant*, Buenos Aires, Anteo, p. 164.

28. Ibid.

29. S. Gache, (1900) *Les logements ouvriers à Buenos Aires*, Paris, C. Steinheil, p. 62–3.

30. G.A. Lallemant, (1895) *Die Nieu Zeit*, 1.

31. G. Gauderlier, (1889) *La verité sur l'émigration des travailleurs et des capitaux belges dans la République Argentine*, Brussels, p. 33.

32. J. Bialét Masse, (1904) *Informe sobre el estado de la clases obreras en el interior de la República*, Buenos Aires, A. Grau. An abbreviated version was reprinted as J. Bialét Masse, (1971) *Los obreros a principios de siglo*, Buenos Aires, Centro Editorial América Latina.

4 The Emergence of a Labour Movement (1877–1899)

Between 1877 and the end of the century, the formative stage of labour's history drew to a close and a modern labour movement began to take shape.[1] The first strikes in 1877 and 1878 were followed by the formation of the first trade union organisations. The development of anarchist and socialist groupings also belong to this period. The social and economic transformations of the 1880s had a profound effect on the working class, and from the end of the decade, the state of class struggle became virtually permanent. By 1897 an important step in the formation of a labour movement had been taken with the consolidation of the Socialist Party and the launching of *La Protesta Humana* (The Human Protest) by the anarchist currents favourable to involvement in the labour movement. These changes created the conditions for a fundamental step forward in 1901, when the first united labour confederation was formed, and another in 1902 when the first general strike took place. With these events (see Chapter 5) the labour movement assumed a major role in the social and political life of the country. The 'labour question', as it was known at the time, was to be the major problem for the state and the bourgeoisie from then on.

First strikes and trade unions

It is quite certain that there were isolated and sporadic strikes before 1877 which were not recorded, but the first known strike was carried out by the *aguateros* (water-carriers) of Rosario that year.[2] It left the city without water for several days and had major repercussions. Of much greater importance was the 1878 strike by the Buenos Aires printers, which was the first carried out by a workers' organisation for specifically trade union demands.

From the early *Sociedad Tipográfica Bonaerense* (Buenos Aires Print-workers' Society) a new grouping had emerged, the *Unión Tipográfica* (Print-workers' Union), formed by militants who saw that the first body's mutual-aid society nature prevented more direct demands and struggles. Its inaugural meeting in 1878, in which over 1,000 workers took part, was presided over by M. Gauthier, probably an exile of the Paris Commune. Shortly afterwards, following the mandate given by this meeting, the print-workers declared a strike in pursuit of higher wages, regulated working hours, and the abolition of child labour.[3] The strike was successful, but the victory was short-lived, as the introduction of piece rates led to competition between the printers, and again the length of the working day was pushed up. The *Unión Tipográfica* was then dissolved by order of the *Sociedad Tipográfica Bonaerense*, as one organisation for the trade was considered quite sufficient. Behind this simple argument lay the mutual-aid ideology still shared by many of the workers.

Between 1877 and 1887 there were only 15 strikes recorded. Though the disputes occurred in various trades they predominated in the skilled construction and service sectors and the artisanal sector producing for the local market. The most frequent demands in these disputes concerned wage increases, back pay, the length of the working day and general working conditions. In approximately 60% of these strikes the workers gained all or some of their demands, and in nearly all cases the state abstained from any intervention.

During this same period there was a development of 'resistance societies', particularly among the skilled fractions of the proletariat: three were formed in the commercial sector, another three in the transport industry, two in the skilled construction sector, and several others in the food and clothing industries. In many cases the lifespan of these associations was quite short. The first association to achieve a certain continuity was that organised by the bakers; the second was probably the footplatemen's *La Fraternidad* (The Fraternity) formed in 1887, which was also the first to achieve a level of organisation which went beyond the local level.[4]

The socialist and anarchist groups which emerged during the 1880s played an important role in these early organisations of the working class. After the dissolution of the local sections of the First International (see Chapter 2), several socialist journals appeared, but these were reformist and republican in outlook and both pre-Marxist and pre-Bakuninist. In 1875 *Le Révolutionnaire* (The Revolutionary) was launched by Stanislas Pourille, who had participated in the Paris Commune under the pseudonym 'Blanchet'. This journal had a republican orientation and was fiercely anti-clerical. Another example was *El Descamisado* (The Shirtless One), subtitled 'Red Journal', which was only short-lived. It proclaimed a revolution which would be achieved without spilling a drop of blood. There were numerous other journals which began publishing in these years.[5]

The first known anarchist group was the *Círculo de Propaganda Obrera* (Workers' Propaganda Circle) formed by the pro-Bakunin minority in the Buenos Aires section of the First International, who began to organise independently once that body was dissolved. In 1879 they published a pamphlet entitled *Una Idea* (An Idea) in which they expounded the principles of the dissident fraction of the International as agreed by the

Saint Imier Pact.[6] An attempt to reform the International in 1879 was also probably an anarchist initiative. In connection with this a journal, *La Vanguardia* (The Vanguard), was launched by Eduardo Camaño.[7] Several other anarchist journals then appeared: *La Anarquía* (Anarchy) in 1880, *La Lucha Obrera* (The Workers' Struggle) in 1884, and *La Questione Sociale* (The Social Question), edited by Italian anarchist Errico Malatesta, which appeared in 1887. The anarchist movement in Argentina began to establish a stable presence in 1884 with the formation of the *Círculo Comunista Anárquico* (Anarcho-Communist Circle) which still proclaimed itself a section of the First International.[8] Other groups were formed subsequently in which the role of Errico Malatesta, who resided in Argentina for several years, was of great importance.[9] Another pioneer of anarchism was Ettore Mattei, who launched the Italian-language journal *La Questione Socialista* (The Socialist Question) in 1887. By the end of the decade four different Anarcho-Communist Manifestos had been published in Buenos Aires.

The socialist groups also began to organise in the 1880s, with the ephemeral *Le Proletaire* (The Proletarian) appearing in French in 1882. The socialists received encouragement from the formation of *Verein Vorwärts* (Forwards Club) that same year, which brought together German exiles on the basis of the German Social Democratic Party programme. In 1886 this group launched the journal *Vorwärts* (Forward) and its members went on to play a major role in the local labour movement.[10]

Permanent class struggle

The situation of the working class was to change dramatically in 1888: a sharp drop in real wages led to a rash of strikes which continued until mid-1890. In those two years there were over 30 strikes, double the number that had occurred in the whole previous decade. Around one-third of these strikes involved the railway workers, who thus became established as a vanguard within the labour movement.

An important event in this period was the emergence of an employers' federation, the *Unión Industrial Argentina* (Argentine Industrial Union) in 1887, which refused to recognise trade unions or engage in collective bargaining.[11] This attitude had not yet hardened in 1888 however, when they proposed to striking foot-wear workers the formation of worker-employer committees to resolve disputes. This was rejected by the anarchist and socialist activists,[12] and the employers subsequently pressurised the government into maintaining an intransigent attitude towards labour. When the industrialists organised a large demonstration in 1899 to demand protectionist measures for local industry, the workers' journal *La Vanguardia* (The Vanguard) declared that another contradiction had been established between workers and industrialists, given the free-trade orientation of the labour movement.[13]

In July 1890 two fractions of the ruling class clashed in what is known as

La Revolución del Noventa (The 1890 Revolution).[14] These events led to a momentary suspension of strikes, and when they were resumed towards the end of the year, the situation had changed considerably. The onset of an economic depression halted the upturn of the struggle of the working class which had begun in 1888: from 1890 to 1893 there were only 20 strikes. Wage demands were still central, though for the first time there were a number of strikes calling for a reduction in working hours. Unemployment became probably the most important concern for the labour movement during this period. A petition from the *Federación Obrera* (Workers' Federation) to the President in 1891 referred to the existence of 10,000 unemployed in Buenos Aires alone.[15] Paradoxically, while strikes decreased, trade union organisation advanced, with the formation of the first labour confederations.

The labour movement began to take its first steps in the political arena during this period. The socialists in particular promoted the formation of a trade union confederation which could put a united expression to labour. An early attempt at forming a confederation was that by *Vorwärts* (Forwards) militants who formed the *Comité Internacional Obrero* (International Workers' Committee) following the resolutions of the 1889 international socialist congress in Paris. Formed early in 1890, before the decline of the strike wave, this committee had several objectives: to celebrate 1 May as the international workers' day; to create a trade union confederation; to publish a journal to defend the interests of the working class and to send a petition to congress.[16]

On 1 May 1890, between 2,000 and 3,000 workers participated in an assembly at which speakers used Spanish, Italian, French and German in their speeches, such was the cosmopolitanism of the early labour movement. A group of anarchists from the *Círculo Socialista Internacional* (International Socialist Circle) agreed to participate in this socialist-organised event, but they did not support the other proposals concerning a trade union confederation. That May Day celebration was nevertheless the first mass political expression of the nascent labour movement. The *Comité Obrero Internacional* (International Workers' Committee) programme, which served as the basis for subsequent confederations, was centred around wages, hours, working conditions and the situation of women and minors at work.

Following the May Day celebration steps were taken to form the *Federación Obrera* (Workers' Federation), which was established in mid-1891 by five Buenos Aires based unions and some federations from the interior provinces. The Federation's political programme called for the seizure of political power by the working class, the socialisation of the means of production, the organisation of society along the lines of an economic federation, the international harmonisation of production, and social and political equality for all.[17] However, its life was too short to achieve such lofty aims, as the economic depression which began towards the end of 1890 gripped the country. The Workers' Federation did, however, launch a journal in 1890: *El Obrero* (The Worker), which was the first in Argentina, and probably in Latin America, to stand clearly for Marxism. This journal, edited by the German socialist Germán Ave Lallemant, also expressed the first serious attempt by émigré militants to understand the social and political reality of Argentina.[18]

Following the collapse of the first Workers' Federation in 1890 the socialists tried again in 1894 to form a similar body along the same lines. The new federation did stress much more the importance of economic demands, and one of its statutes stated that it 'would abstain from all political and religious matters'.[19] After a short life this organisation also died through sheer inertia.

The general strike debate

With the decline of strike activity the anarchists, who had opposed intervention in the class struggle through labour organisations, received a certain boost. The socialists found themselves in competition with these 'anti-organisers' who were hegemonic within the anarchist ranks through to 1895. Amongst their prolific press we should mention *El Perseguido* (The Persecuted), which had a substantial circulation. By the mid-1890s however, the 'organisers' current amongst the anarchists began to grow in strength. They pursued a vigorous unionisation campaign and helped organise strikes.[20] One of the first anarchist journals to support this trend was *El Oprimido* (The Oppressed), edited by an Irish doctor, John Creaghe, who had been active in the Sheffield labour movement before becoming one of the main figures of anarchism in Latin America. In 1897 the famous journal *La Protesta Humana* (The Human Protest) also threw its weight behind the pro-organisation anarchists.

With the economic recovery following 1895 the rhythm of strikes accelerated, as did the formation of new trade unions. Between 1895 and 1896 there were more than 40 strikes, largely centred around wage demands but also for the reduction of working hours. In 1895 around three-quarters of the disputes were successful for the workers, but the following year more disputes were lost than won. The industrialists, alarmed by the extent of strikes, hardened their positions and called for police support in some cases.

From 1880 to 1930 uncontrolled foreign immigration was perceived by the labour movement as a source of weakness in its struggle. In 1892 an article in *El Obrero* argued that 'the high level of immigration is a misfortune for the working class of Argentina, because it increases the supply of labour when there is no work for those already here'.[21] The increase in the reserve army of labour in 1896 because of high immigration rates may be seen as a factor in the larger number of working-class defeats in strikes. By 1898 the Socialist Party had included an article in its programme which condemned any artificial encouragement of overseas immigration. Similar positions were adopted in the anarchist and revolutionary syndicalist press throughout the first decades of the 20th Century.

In 1895 a new journal was launched, *La Unión Gremial* (The Trade Union) by various resistance societies. It expressed a somewhat inorganic trade union current, which was neither socialist nor anarchist, although its differences with the first were greater.[22] In its pages there was an important early debate on the possibility of launching a general strike. In 1896 a number of trade union organisations signed a pact which led to the formation of the *Convención Obrera* (Workers' Convention). Its first declaration posed the need for workers to prepare for a general strike.[23] The Convention was not, however, a full-blown trade union federation; rather it was a flexible agreement between various unions. The independent and anarchist-led unions, who supported this body did not go along with a socialist attempt to re-launch the *Federación Obrera* (Workers' Federation) in 1897.

The upsurge in strike activity did not last beyond 1897 anyway: unemployment was on the rise, reaching 40,000 in Buenos Aires by 1899. In this context the debate on the general strike became academic. The axis of the labour movement became unemployment again, a struggle which united socialists and anarchists on occasion.

Formation of the Socialist Party

Apart from the rise of the 'organiser' tendency of the anarchists, the other major event towards the end of the 19th Century was the formation of the Socialist Party. Its origins went back to the German *Vorwärts* (Forwards) group and, after 1890, the supporters of the journal *El Obrero* (The Worker). In those early years the socialists tended to merge political and trade union action. *El Obrero*, while it claimed to be Marxist, also acted as the organ of the union body *Federación Obrera* (Workers' Federation). Their political programme combined republican reforms with the 'socialisation of the means of production'. At the same time their internationalist orientation was much stronger than it would be subsequently.

The fusion of political and trade union work was in fact the source of a split in the socialist ranks in 1893. While one tendency continued publishing *El Obrero,* a second group recognised the weakness of the *Federación Obrera* and the difficulties of building a socialist party on the basis of the trade unions. They thus launched a new journal *El Socialista* (The Socialist) which proclaimed itself the organ of the *Partido Socialista Obrero* (Socialist Workers' Party).

During this period the socialists still tended to organise along national lines in the immigrant community. In 1891 the group *Les Egaux* (The

Equals) was formed by French immigrants, and Italian workers formed the *Fascio dei Lavoratori* (Workers' League) the following year. These two groups, along with the German *Vorwärts* group, the supporters of *El Socialista* and a dissident sector of *El Obrero*, came together in 1894 to lay the basis for the formation of a socialist party.

In 1894 there was another important change in the make-up of the socialist movement. For the first time a group of locally-born or naturalised intellectuals joined the movement, along with doctors, lawyers, journalists, artists and students. Prior to this, the socialist movement had been led almost exclusively by foreigners. This nucleus of middle-class socialists (and also anarchists) who moved towards the labour movement was the first expression of an 'intellectual left' in Argentina. Their turn towards labour often followed disillusionment with the radical democratic movements of 1890 and 1893. The new militants rapidly moved into leadership positions, among them Juan B. Justo, Leopoldo Lugones and Nicolás Repetto. The well-known poet Alberto Ghiraldo joined the anarchists. Also in 1894 the *Centro Socialista Universitario* (University Socialist Centre) was formed by a medical student, José Ingenieros.

The socialist programmes of the mid-1890s marked certain changes from those adopted earlier. While internationalism still formed part of their declarations, the 1894 programme of the *Centro Socialista Obrero* (Socialist Workers' Centre) stood on the platform of the international socialist movement, but 'with the modifications demanded by local circumstances'.[24] The relationship between the party and the unions also changed. At the 1896 founding conference of the Socialist Party, the socialist trade unions were represented, but they could only vote on trade union matters. The programme furthermore stressed the element of republican reform rather than the full Marxist platform. This meant that the 'minimum programme' of labour claims assumed a larger role in socialist agitation.

The socialist organ *La Vanguardia* (The Vanguard) was launched in April 1894; it was to continue as the movement's main newspaper into the 20th Century. Its editor was Juan B. Justo, who soon became the leading figure in the socialist movement. In 1895 the movement selected candidates for the 1896 elections, in which it obtained 1 per cent of the vote. This showing was due to a limited electoral register, electoral fraud, and also to the fact that most foreign workers, who were deprived of political rights, were not highly motivated by this type of political activity. This was to be a major concern for the socialists after 1896. They encouraged the naturalisation of immigrants and made Argentine citizenship a condition for holding party office. This last move was considered discriminatory by various socialist branches and led to the party's first split in 1898. A large number of socialist organisations, led by the electrician Francisco Cuneo, broke away to form the *Federación Obrera Colectivista* (Workers' Collectivist Federation). The dissidents also developed a critique of what they considered to be electoralism in the party's orientation, arguing instead that the economic struggle of the working class should be their main concern.

The 1898 split–which was healed in 1900 after the party statutes were reformed–posed the broader issue of the difficulties to be faced organising a socialist party in Argentina.[25] How could a strategy of reforms to be gained through parliamentary activity prosper when a democratic regime did not really exist, and when a large proportion of the working class was marginalised from politics? A further important issue was raised in the 1896 congress concerning the means of the socialist struggle. A group of delegates, led by José Ingenieros, won the vote on an amendment to the party's founding principles, which stated that socialist strategy did not rule out the possibility of using violent means to achieve its political ends. Party leader Juan B. Justo managed to have this amendment removed at the second party congress in 1898, thus setting the party firmly into the peaceful electoral mould. In 1897 José Ingenieros and the writer Leopoldo Lugones published a journal, *La Montaña* (The Mountain), which called itself 'revolutionary socialist' and expressed the views of a socialist left opposition. However, this tendency was not able to consolidate itself and was dissolved in 1898.

By 1899 the 'preparatory' stage of the labour movement had been completed: trade unions had spread widely, workers had taken their first broad-scale strike actions, and the anarchist and socialist currents had been consolidated. All these elements were to play a major role in the new phase which began in 1900.

Notes

1. For an overview of this period see J. Godio, (1972) *El Movimiento Obrero y la Cuestión Nacional. Argentina: immigrantes, asalariados y lucha de clases, 1880–1910.* Buenos Aires, Editorial Erasmo; see also the useful collection of contemporary documents in H. Spalding, (1970) *La Clase Trabajadora Argentina. (Documents para su historia—1890/1912),* Buenos Aires, Editorial Galerna.

2. F. Gonzalo (1924), "La Prehistoria del Anarquismo en América", *La Revista Internacional Anarquista, t, 2,* Paris, p. 31.

3. S. Marotta, (1970) *El Movimiento Sindical Argentino. t. 1.* Buenos Aires, Ediciones Libera, p. 31.

4. For a history of *La Fraternidad* see F. Agnelli, and J. Chitti, (1938) *La Fraternidad, fundación, desarollo, obra, 1887–1937,* Buenos Aires.

5. see R. Falcón, (1981) *Bibliografía para el Estudio de Movimiento Obrero Argentino en el Siglo XIX,* Paris, Documento de Trabajo CEHSAL.

6. M. Nettlau, (1927), "Contribución a la Bibliografía Anarquista de América Latina hasta 1914", *Certámen Internacional La Protesta,* Buenos Aires, p. 9.

7. F. Gonzalo, (1924) La Prehistoria del Anarquismo, pp. 31–2.

8. *La Protesta* (10 September 1909).

9. On Malatesta's role see G. Zaragoza Ruvira, (1978), "Anarchisme et mouvement ouvrier en Argentina à la fin du XIXe siècle", *Le Mouvement Sociale*

no. 103 (April–June). For a major history of anarchism and the labour movement in Argentina consult Oved, I. (1978) *El Anarquismo y el Movimiento Obrero en Argentina*, Mexico, Siglo XXI.

10. On the *Vorwärts* group see J. Ratzer, (1969) *Los Marxistas Argentinos del 90*. Córdoba, Pasado y Presente.

11. *La Unión Industrial, Reseña Histórica (1910)*, Buenos Aires, Compañía Sudamericana de Billetes de Banco.

12. S. Marotta, (1970) *El Movimiento Sindical Argentino*, pp. 68–71.

13. *La Vanguardia* (15 July 1899) and *La Protesta Humana* (6 August 1899).

14. On the 1890 Revolution see N. Jitrik, (1968) *La Revolución del 90*, Buenos Aires, Centro Editor de America Latina.

15. *El Obrero* (24 January 1891).

16. *El Obrero* (9 January 1891).

17. *El Obrero* (12 February 1893).

18. On Germán Ave Lallemant see J. Ratzer, (1969) *Los Marxistas Argentinos del 90;* for his own writings see G.A. Lallemant, (1974) *La clase obrera y el nacimiento del marxismo en la Argentina*, Buenos Aires, Editorial Anteo.

19. *La Vanguardia* (23 July 1894).

20. On the organiser/anti-organiser debate see I. Oved, (1978) *El Anarquismo y el Movimiento Obrero Argentino*.

21. *El Obrero* (13 February 1892).

22. *La Unión Gremial* (4 April 1895).

23. The original document is lodged in the "Dosier Max Nettlau" in the Instituut voor Sociale Geschiedenis of Amsterdam.

24. *La Vanguardia* (11 August 1894).

25. For further details of the 1898 split see R. Falcon, (1979), "Lucha de tendencias en los primeros congresos del Partido Socialista Obrero Argentina (1896–1900", *Apuntes,* no.1 (October–December).

5. Immigrants, Anarchists and General Strikes (1900–1910)

The first decade of the 20th Century was of crucial importance in the formation of the Argentine working class. The proletariat expanded numerically as industrialisation advanced, the transport network spread and the agro-export sector continued to thrive. There were also major qualitative changes in the structure of the working class which had an impact on the formation of a working-class consciousness. Around 1901–2 the 'labour question' made its definitive entry on to the national social and political scene in Argentina.

During this period the rural labour movement and the urban labour movement of the interior provinces began to take their first steps, but the city of Buenos Aires (and to some extent Rosario) remained the centre of labour's social and political activities. The limited but steady development of industrialisation was largely concentrated in the capital city and in the littoral provinces. Buenos Aires also attracted the majority of the immigrants who flowed into the country during this period.

Immigrants and class unity

After the economic recession of the early 1890s the pattern of mass immigration was re-established, and indeed it accelerated in the 1900s. Between 1900 and 1904, 601,682 immigrants entered Argentina, while 356,468 left the country, leaving a balance of 245,214 or 40% of those who had arrived. After 1905 the rate of immigration increased owing to a succession of good harvests, the favourable balance of trade and the upward tendency in wages. Between 1905 and 1908 there were 1,363,055 immigrants entering the country of whom 57% (589,227) remained. While the proportion of immigrants who returned to their country of origin remained high, the reasons for this were apparently different from those which applied in periods of crisis. A large proportion of those who returned were the seasonal migrants known as *golondrinas* (swallows), who were mainly Spanish and Italian agricultural labourers who travelled to Argentina for the harvest period. The relatively high wages and the low cost of the sea passage made this tremendous voyage worthwhile, and was for many European workers a means of escaping temporary unemployment in their own countries. Between 1909 and 1914 the flow of immigrants remained at a high level, though it diminished sharply as the First World War began to loom on the horizon. Overall, between 1900 and 1914. 3,517,681 immigrants arrived in Argentina, of whom 48% (or 1,677,893) remained permanently.[1]

Census data on industrial employment in Buenos Aires, which excludes home workers, points to 36 main trades and an increase in the work-force from 50,000 in 1895 to 57,000 in 1904, reaching 63,000 in 1908.[2] To these figures we must add important concentrations of non-industrial workers in the capital city: railway, tram-way, coach and port workers for example. On a smaller scale, the littoral city of Rosario presented similar characteristics. During this period Rosario was, along with Buenos Aires, the epicentre of the major working-class mobilisations. Bahía Blanca, an important port in Buenos Aires province, and some other lesser port towns, also witnessed a significant working-class presence.

If one were to consider only the degree of industrialisation attained in the first decade of the 20th Century, the strength and verve of the labour movement in Argentina would be surprisingly high compared with Europe. The agro-export nature of capitalist development in Argentina led to the working class assuming a different composition from the countries of Europe and the rest of Latin America. The large industrial concentrations already present in many countries of Western Europe were lacking or were at least rare. The working class taking shape in Argentina took on particular characteristics due to the geographical concentration of small industry, the development of a major transportation network linked to the export trade, the existence of an important rural and semi-rural proletariat concentrated in the cereal-growing zones close to the cities, and the presence of a strong nucleus of port and maritime workers. Furthermore, the accelerated process of urbanisation, particularly in Buenos Aires,[3] led to the development of activities linked to internal transport, construction and services which employed considerable numbers of workers, also in a highly concentrated area.

During the first decade of the 20th Century the workers of Argentina demonstrated a high degree of activity and a relatively well-defined class outlook, particularly through the formation of a labour movement. This process, through which the proletariat became a working class, entailed a constant struggle for unity and homogeneity against the centrifugal tendencies caused by the heterogeneity of the proletariat. One of the main problems in this respect was to transform the mass of immigrants into a working class. Many of the immigrants arrived in Argentina with social aspirations and expectations, which were in conflict with the moral and even material interests of the already established workers and their class practice. Whereas the prospects for upward social mobility were not even remotely comparable to those of the artisans of the 1870s and 1880s, there was, for some reduced sectors, the possibility of rising in the social scale through individual endeavour. In any case the myth of social mobility persisted in some sections of the proletariat, and in particular among the recently disembarked immigrants. The vast majority of immigrants came to '*fare l'America*' (make America), and their adaptation to the social practices of class was a process which required time, and the disillusionment of the previously held hopes for industrial advancement.[4]

Very early in its development the labour movement began to sense that uncontrolled immigration was prejudicial to the interests of the working class (see Chapter 4). This stance was common to all the political currents within the labour movement during the 1900–10 period. Agreements were in fact reached with the Spanish and Italian trade union movements to fight jointly against artificial immigration. The erratic rhythm of immigration was seen by trade unionists as a cause of unemployment and the subsequent decline in wage levels. Furthermore, the expectations of individual advancement held by the immigrants was seen as an obstacle to united action by the different fractions of the working class.

The social integration of the wage-earning immigrants into the working class depended on their breaking with the feeling that they belonged to the national community of their origin. The Socialists waged a particularly strong battle against national particularism, but the Anarchists had a far more flexible attitude. In fact, the Anarchist periodical *La Protesta* (Protest) sometimes included an Italian- and a Yiddish-language section.

The aspiration for unity within the labour movement during this period was also threatened by the existence of different professional categories ('grades and trades') as well as gender and age divisions.

Women Workers

During the early 1900s female labour became generalised across the industrial sectors of Buenos Aires. Women constituted an important proportion of the labour force in the textile and clothing industries. Women and minors formed the bulk of the labour-force in the tobacco and glass factories, in the manufacture of cloth bags and shoes, and in the laundry and ironing workshops.[5] If a certain proportion of women workers were employed in factories and workshops, the women engaged in home-based work were more numerous. In 1913 there were an estimated 60,000 women engaged in outwork, the majority in dress-making.[6] The workshops of the seamstresses were usually in the same 9ft by 12ft rooms of the *conventillos* (tenements) in which they lived with their families, where health conditions were deplorable. Young women workers generally preferred to go out to work in the factories, where wages were higher and they did not need to buy their own tools and materials.

Within the labour movement there was a debate on whether women and children should work in the factories. The socialists were whole-heartedly in favour of women working, as an instrument of women's emancipation and as training for the class struggle, according to them the main task was to obtain for women better working conditions and equal pay. To this end they pursued the objective of winning labour legislation which would limit super-exploitation. It was Alfredo Palacios, the socialist deputy elected in 1904, who put forward the first legislative proposals to regulate the work of women and minors.

The anarchists and revolutionary syndicalists had a more ambiguous attitude towards working women. Trade unions on several occasions condemned female employment on the grounds that it devalued the family and led to serious problems in the health and education of children. The general argument was that women working in factories was an evil caused by capitalism. Behind these so-called moral arguments was the cold economic fact that in so far as women and minors were paid less than adult male workers, their presence in factories and workshops was a factor in depressing wages. Even the socialists, who were generally in favour of women working, did on occasion raise this objection. For example, during a debate on the work of women in the printing industry the socialists claimed that its legalisation by the government was aimed at reducing wages and employment levels.

Labour activists did on the other hand always strive to incorporate women and young workers into the strike movements. Frequently the authoritarianism of the foreman acted as a brake on struggles, particularly in the workshops where young women workers predominated. So the search for unity across gender and age divisions within the proletariat was a constant preoccupation, even though internal contradictions inevitably persisted.

The division of the working class according to trades and professions also conspired against the unity of the working class. For some time the trade unions organised the skilled workers of each trade, leaving the unskilled *peones* outside their orbit. However, during the early 1900s the level of participation in the trade unions increased greatly, embracing the *peones* and the unskilled trades generally. The persistence of trade-based divisions did create secondary contradictions on certain occasions. Towards the end of the first decade of this century, the anarchist activists of the printers' union, the *Federación Gráfica*, somewhat naïvely launched a campaign to abolish grades within their trade. The socialists and syndicalists adopted a rather more prudent attitude to this question.

As we have already mentioned, the uncommon level of importance attached to the national community of origin by wide sectors of the proletariat created a tendency towards divisions on certain occasions. In many cases workers from one particular nationality would occupy a whole trade or a large part of it. For example, Italians predominated among bricklayers, local-born workers predominated among saddlers and harness-makers. In certain circumstances the employers and the state would seize on these national distinctions to create divisions within the working population. On some occasions local workers were brought from the rural areas to act as strike-breakers. In other cases, recently disembarked Russian Jewish workers were used as scabs to break strikes of the Buenos Aires port workers. Nevertheless, the extent of geographical and professional mobility did not permit these national tendencies to crystallise into an element which would prevent the structuring of the proletariat into a working class.

Labour and the state

The diverse political and ideological tendencies within the labour movement were also a major factor conspiring against a unified working class. The whole decade following 1900 was in fact dominated by this theme. These were the years in which the debate on working-class unity achieved national dimensions, while trade union involvement spread its influence across the country.

During this decade there were important changes in the patterns of consumption and the standards of living of the workers. As a result of the expansion of foreign trade on the one hand, and the consolidation of the trade union movement and labour struggles on the other, the proletariat, particularly in Buenos Aires and the littoral zone, made considerable gains.

The general strike of 1902, preceded by the foundation of the *Federación Obrera Argentina* (Argentine Workers' Federation), marked an important shift in the attitude of the state and the ruling class towards the working class. In 1902, for the first time in their history, the workers of Argentina led a unified class struggle on a national scale and demonstrated their growing social and political weight in the life of the nation. This tendency was amply confirmed by the partial and general strikes in the years which followed, as well as by the rapid development of the trade union movement.

Faced with this rise of the labour movement the state was forced to abandon its previous non-interventionist stance towards capital-labour conflicts, only dropped previously for short, sharp repressive interventions. Now repression became more systematic, with strikes and demonstrations usually leading to bloody episodes as the intervention of the police and the army took its toll of dead and injured. Immediately after the 1902 strike the government sanctioned the first major legislative repressive measure, the so-called Law of Residence. This law led to the expulsion from the country of hundreds of anarchist militants and foreign-born workers, with some Argentinian workers thrown in for good measure.

At the same time as the systematic policy of repression was launched, the ruling class sought a long term solution to the 'labour question'. The presence of a socialist deputy in parliament favoured the sanctioning of some early labour laws. The first of these established Sunday as a day of rest; the second, approved shortly thereafter, regulated the work of women and minors, though with some limitations. In 1907 the *Departamento Nacional de Trabajo* (National Labour Department) was established, being charged with the enforcement of the new labour legislation, the collection of statistics on workers' conditions, and the arbitration of industrial disputes when both sides agreed to it.

The most daring legislative initiative was the attempt in 1904 to adopt a comprehensive Labour Code (*Código de Trabajo*) drawn up by the Minister of the Interior, Joaquín V. González, advised by intellectuals close to the Socialist Party or sympathisers of the labour cause. This proposed legislation marked a real shift in the policy of the hegemonic sectors within the state towards the workers. It established a series of important demands, amongst which was the eight-hour day, while at the same time it rigidly regulated the activity of the trade unions, maintaining some of the repressive principles of the 1902 Residence Law. The unspoken objective of this law was to favour an agreement with the socialists, while marginalising the anarchists.

The project failed because it came up against two obstacles: first, the employers' association, *Unión Industrial Argentina* (Argentine Industrial Union), was fiercely opposed to it on the grounds that it accorded excessive advantages to the workers; second, the labour movement rejected it fearing its repressive and coercive aspects. However, the fact that the project was even considered demonstrated that at least a section of the ruling élite understood that a policy had to be adopted towards the labour movement, which had now become an important factor in the life of the nation.

The new labour laws, though limited in scope and even more in their application by the industrialists, represented a significant advance in the living and working conditions of the proletariat. Furthermore, outside the scope of this legislation, many unions imposed on their employers agreements on the eight-hour day or at least substantial reductions in working hours.

Since the end of the 19th Century there had been considerable improvements in living conditions. Health measures launched in Buenos Aires in the 1870s and 1880s had by now been largely completed. For example, the installation of a new underground sewage system had a very positive effect on workers' health. There was a general decline in the epidemics which had previously hit the popular quarters with weary regularity.

Housing conditions remained an important problem for working-class families. The overcrowded tenements known as *conventillos* persisted into the first decade of the 20th Century. The Buenos Aires Municipal Census of 1904 revealed 2,462 workers' lodgings, in which 138,188 people lived in 43,873 rooms.[7] These figures indicate a net increase in the *conventillo* population since the 1887 census, and a higher density of inhabitants per room (over three).

From 1906 onwards the number of *conventillos* began to decline due to cheaper tramway fares which made access to the suburban areas easier. The city centre *conventillos* were thus abandoned by many workers' families who sought small plots of land in the suburbs on which to build their homes. If this represented a gain in terms of comfort and fresh air, there was in many cases a loss of the sanitation facilities which were beginning to be installed in the city-centre *conventillos*.

First trade union federation

The process of trade union formation, attempts at forming trade union federations and the debates on the general strike, all of which took place in the 1890s, formed the basis for a leap forward in organisation after 1901. As we mentioned above, the definitive constitution of the Socialist Party and the united front of the pro-organisation anarchists around the journal *La Protesta* (Protest) were also decisive factors in this advance of the labour movement.

In 1900 there was yet another attempt by the socialists to form a labour federation, but it was not supported by the anarchists and therefore failed. Although there were some trade union struggles that year, the effects of high unemployment towards the end of the 1890s tended to dampen the strike movement. Despite the virtual absence of strikes there were important mass actions against unemployment which united socialists and anarchists. This unity created a precedent for the agreements which led to the formation of the *Federación Obrera Argentina* (Argentine Labour Federation) in 1901. A group of socialist-led trade unions (or resistance societies as they were then known) called for a labour federation and this time the anarchists heeded the call. The labour struggles of the previous decades and in 1900–01 created a climate of opinion in the labour ranks which pressurised the anarchists into accepting this unifying move.

Within the anarchist current itself there had also been a number of significant changes. Now, a majority of the anarchist tendencies favoured an intervention in the class struggle; they had taken over the leadership of various unions and influenced others still politically independent. Two foreign anarchist leaders, Pietro Gori and Antonio Pellicer Paraire ('Pellico'), then living in Buenos Aires, favoured the development of that current and the moves towards creating a mass union federation. Gori was an Italian anarchist of international renown who had a great influence on some anarchist sectors in Argentina between 1898 and 1902. Not only did he encourage anarchist participation in the incipient labour federation but he actually played a prominent role in its founding congress. 'Pellico' was a Spanish printer active in the First International who arrived in Argentina in 1891. In 1900 he published a series of articles in *La Protesta Humana* (The Human Protest) on 'Labour Organisation', in which he advanced the basic principles for a labour federation. He posed the need for a dual though interrelated organisational structure, one economic and trade-based represented by the labour federation, the other revolutionary, and specifically anarchist. These principles were later advanced in the founding documents and in the practice of the anarcho-syndicalist FORA

(*Federación Obrera Regional Argentina*): Argentine Regional Labour Federation).

In 1900 and the first half of 1901 there were several strikes in Buenos Aires and the interior provinces, where the process of organisation and consolidation of trade unions proceeded apace. The unions organising workers engaged in production for consumption, who were usually of an artisan background, continued to be in the vanguard of strike movements and of trade union organisation. However, other sectors such as factory workers and those engaged in transport were beginning to form part of the growing labour movement.

On 25 May 1901 the journal *La Organización* (Organisation), backed by a group of trade unions, launched the *Federación Obrera Argentina* (Argentine Labour Federation) in a congress attended by 27 resistance societies—15 from Buenos Aires and 12 from the provinces. The significant representation from the interior revealed the growing weight of the labour movement across the country. This participation should be placed in perspective by the fact that many of the provincial trade unions were represented by Buenos Aires militants, in some cases not even labour activists but intellectuals.

Many of the themes which were to concern the labour movement during the early 1900s were raised at that first congress of the *Federación*, amongst which were the type of union organisation needed, the question of strikes, arbitration of industrial disputes, the attitude to be taken towards labour legislation, and so on. As Julio Godio notes, the joint participation of anarchists and socialists in this venture required a certain degree of compromise on all these topics.[8] The spirit of unity meant that in many debates the dividing line was not along party lines, and socialists and anarchists often found themselves arguing for similar positions. But this unity within the ranks of labour was not to last long. As early as the second congress in 1902, the inevitable split materialised. The anarchists were by then less disposed to compromise given their growing popularity in many trades and the launching of other trade union federations in which they maintained a strong position, such as the *Federación Nacional de Portuarios* (National Port-workers' Federation).

General strikes

In November 1902 the first general strike in Argentina took place, preceded by a series of partial strikes and a general climate of class struggle. The general strike was actually precipitated by state repression, as were most of the general strikes which took place between 1902 and 1910. The majority of these were political confrontations between the state and the labour movement. Major episodes of the class struggle took place in 1902, 1904, 1905, 1909 and 1910.[9]

Institute of Latin American Studies

31 Tavistock Square

London WC1H 9HA

In 1902, strikes in the ports of Buenos Aires, Rosario and Bahía Blanca and by the workers in the Central Fruit Market created a radical and combative spirit which led to a general strike against the Law of Residence. The workers' quarters of Buenos Aires effectively became armed camps leading to the occupation of the city centre by infantry and cavalry for fear of a workers' 'invasion'. In 1904 there was a general strike in the littoral city of Rosario which led to it being referred to as 'the Barcelona of Latin America'. That year also saw the first strike by workers on the sugar plantations of Tucumán. The general strike of 1905 marked the high point of anarchist influence in the labour movement and by 1907 factory stoppages seemed to have replaced the massive confrontations of the general strikes. An important event was the 1907 national strike organised by the railway engineers' union *La Fraternidad*. Then on May Day 1909 repression against the workers' commemoration marches led to a dozen deaths and over one hundred injured. The following day anarchist, socialist and independent unions called a general strike to free the imprisoned workers and ensure the reopening of union offices.

Though successful, this strike led to a renewed repression which by 1910 left Buenos Aires under a state of siege and the gaols full of workers. A symbol of these times was the execution of Coronel Falcón, who had led the cavalry charge on May Day 1909, in a bomb attack by a young anarchist militant, Simon Radowitsky. Our account of the revolutionary general strikes of this period should not lead us to a romantic vision of masses of workers consciously following the anarchists in their struggle against state and capital. As Ruth Thompson has recently reminded us, in previous studies of this period 'the importance of anarchism has been exaggerated' and 'strikes in the period owed little to ideological consciousness'.[10] This negative view may itself be 'exaggerated' but it is an antidote to the exalted account of contemporary anarchist labour historians.

The scope and content of the general strike was one of the central debates within the labour movement throughout this period, being raised at most union conferences and in the frequent polemics between the various labour federations. For the anarchists, or at least their hegemonic sectors, the general strike was given an insurrectional character and was seen as an instrument in the struggle to abolish the state and install a new society.[11] For the revolutionary syndicalists, who appeared as an independent current around 1906 after a split in the Socialist Party, the general strike was seen above all as a school for the working class and an instrument of unity. The socialists saw the general strike as being limited in scope and useful only in specific circumstances.

It was the failed anarchist attempt to drown out the centenary celebrations of national independence through a general strike, and the ensuing repression, which in 1910 marked the end of this phase of Argentina's labour history. This was the last great anarchist attempt at insurrection through a general strike, and it also marked a shift in working class consciousness. In 1910, as in 1902, the working class paid a high price for the general strike in terms of workplace expulsions and arrests, and recovered only after a considerable period of recomposition.

Apart from the general strikes there was a tremendous increase in partial strikes in the 1900s compared with the previous decade. Prior to 1907 there were no official strike statistics but contemporary press reports allow us to estimate that there were on average around 100 strikes per year between 1901 and 1906. The *Departmento Nacional de Trabajo* (National Labour Department) provides statistics for Buenos Aires from 1907 onwards, which, though incomplete, do indicate the general pattern across the country. It is interesting to note that whereas in 1903 and 1904 around half of all strikes occurred outside the capital, this trend was reversed between 1907 and 1909 when strikes in Buenos Aires accounted for nearly three-quarters of the total. Spalding puts forward the idea that 'this trend probably reflects a second wave of organisational activity that began in the capital and then spread to other areas'.[12]

In Table 5.1 we can follow the evolution of strikes from 1907 to the end of the decade.

Table 5.1   Strikes in Buenos Aires city, 1907–1910

Year	No. of Strikes	No. of Strikers
1907	231	169,107
1908	118	11,561
1909	138	4,762
1910	298	18,806

Source: Annual bulletins, *Departamento Nacional de Trabajo.*

We note a peak in 1907, then a sharp decline, with a relative upturn in the number of strikes and strikers (though less in the latter) in 1910. The overall figures mask the fact that in 1907, 161 of all the strikes were lost by the workers whereas in 1910, 185 were won. As to the causes of strikes, 40% of all strikes between 1907 and 1910 were centred around wage demands. A further 30% of strikes were to defend trade union organisation or were against employers' reprisals, a further 15% were concerned with the length of the working day and 10% were focused on working conditions. The most active fractions of the working class in this strike movement were those in the food industry, textiles and clothing, the wood industry and transport.

Labour politics

The other big debate of this period centred around the question of trade union unity. After the split in the *Federación Obrera Argentina* (Argentine Workers' Federation) the socialists formed the *Unión General de Trabajadores* (General Workers' Union) in 1903. There was then a split in the UGT between the socialists and the revolutionary syndicalist current. The latter began as a workers' opposition within the socialist movement, but later acquired a more defined character when it adopted the ideas of George Sorel, Arturo Labriola and the contemporary French syndicalists.

The tendency which created the revolutionary syndicalist current already existed prior to its definitive ideological formation. It had become consolidated in internal opposition to the socialist leadership over some of the major issues in the labour movement around 1904–6. These included the struggle against acceptance of the González project (see above) and the party's attitude to the 1905 failed Radical rising which was followed by widespread repression, including that of the labour movement. Furthermore, anarchist influence was growing within an expanding and constantly active labour movement, thus placing the socialist trade unionists under pressure. Paradoxically, the election of the first Socialist Party deputy, Alfredo Palacios, in 1904 increased the contradictions within the socialist ranks. On the one hand it strengthened the strategy of participation in parliamentary politics as dictated by the early party congresses, but on the other hand it increased anarchist pressure on the trade-union wing of the party.[13]

Though the opposition was a minority within the Socialist Party – at the Seventh Congress in 1906 it was 'invited to withdraw' by the majority – it achieved a majority in the leadership of the UGT (*Unión General de Trabajadores*) in December 1906. The rise of the revolutionary syndicalists was to have a considerable effect on the labour movement. The new labour current became the champion of unity and constantly exerted pressure on the anarchists to move in that direction. Several fusion congresses held by the revolutionary syndicalist UGT and the anarcho-communist FORA failed owing to the intransigence of the latter. The anarchists were all agreed on rejection of this unity offensive, though opinions were divided on the nuances. They argued that unity in itself was worthless, and that content was essential. In 1909 the revolutionary syndicalists formed the *Confederación Obrera Regional Argentina* (Argentine Regional Workers' Confederation), but the bulk of the anarchists stayed out of the new body and thus postponed the longed-for labour unity.

The revolutionary syndicalists edited a journal *La Acción Socialista* (Socialist Action) and attracted to their ranks some intellectuals and leaders of the Socialist Party such as Aquiles Lorenzo, Gabriela de Coni, J.A. Arraga, E. Troise and B. Bosio, as well as many of the party's most distinguished trade union militants. The syndicalists evolved in their ideology from a conditional acceptance of parliamentary politics to an adoption of the ideas of Sorel and the guiding principles of French and Italian syndicalism. At first, following Sorel's *Reflections on Violence*, they stressed the importance of the revolutionary general strike and displayed a catastrophic vision of the future of capitalist society. Then, gradually, a parallel discourse began to predominate which placed its emphasis on the constructive nature of the trade unions and the importance of educating the working class through the class struggle. By adopting these positions they became differentiated from the anarcho-syndicalists as well as from the socialists. Particularly after 1910 the revolutionary syndicalists began to gain influence.

During the decade following 1900 the trade union movement was definitively consolidated. In 1908 a *Departamento Nacional de Trabajo* (National Labour Department) survey accounted for 45 labour organisations in Buenos Aires, with 23,438 members, that is, slightly less than 10% of the total number of workers in the 45 trades involved. However, as the survey itself notes, 'It is well to bear in mind that these figures for the number of affiliates vary from month to month, increasing in periods of conflict with the employers and diminishing in peaceful times'.[14] The year 1908, when the survey was conducted, for example, was not a period of high trade union activity. The number of affiliates also varied because of the repression to which the labour organisations were periodically subjected, their highly politicised character and the often violent nature of their economic struggles. For these reasons the labour organisations themselves even disappeared on occasion, to be reconstituted later. In any case, the organising potential of the trade unions was much greater than the number of affiliates alone would indicate. For example, during the general strikes and political confrontations with the state, hundreds of thousands of workers heeded the call of the trade union organisations.

Strikes, and to a lesser extent boycotts, were the principal weapons of the labour organisations. In a few cases, however, as for example in the 1907 *conventillo* strikes in Buenos Aires and Rosario, social struggles developed relatively independently from the trade unions. Negotiations with employers were usually short-lived and without any continuity. The first collective contract, and for some time the only one, was that of the printers who had formed a federation embracing the anarchist union and that of the syndicalists and socialists. As to state recognition, the footplatemen's union *La Fraternidad* was the only one for a long time to achieve legal status.[15]

The politics of the labour movement during the first decade of the 20th Century were characterised by the rise of anarchism, particularly the FORA (*Federación Obrera Regional Argentina*) defined as anarcho-communist at its Fifth Congress in 1905. The so-called 'individualist' current of the anarchists, represented by the periodical *El Rebelde* (The Rebel) among others, was gradually displaced by the 'organising' tendency, which by now had fully embraced anarcho-syndicalism. This vigorous tendency published numerous political and trade union bulletins, among which featured the journal *La Protesta* (Protest), which became a daily in 1904.

After 1910 anarchism progressively lost its hegemonic position. Thereafter the revolutionary syndicalists were to move into a leading position within the labour movement. The socialists had more difficulty than either of these two in obtaining a base within the working class. Their explicit reformism and their parliamentary orientation were confronted by a political system which simply did not allow for this type of strategy. Nevertheless, the socialists did experience a relative growth in electoral support during these years. The first socialist deputy, Alfredo Palacios, though blocked by the conservative majority in parliament and by supporters of the employers' association, the *Unión Industrial Argentina*, carried out an intervention which enabled the socialists to achieve support among certain sectors of the working class. The socialist vote in the city of Buenos Aires increased from 204 in 1902 to 1,245 in 1904 (when Palacios was elected), 1,700 in 1906 and 7,556 in 1908.[16] The number of branches did not increase accordingly: there were 24 in 1900 and the same number in 1910 across the whole country, which reflected the electoral nature of the party's support.

To sum up, the first decade of the 20th Century was of singular importance in the formative process of the Argentine working class. During these years the experiences of the last years of the 19th Century were built upon, and traditions were created which would guide the development of the labour movement in the years to come.

There were important regional variations in the pattern outlined above. As recent research by Ofelia Pianetto on Córdoba shows, it was the socialists there who organised the first trade unions in the 1890s and from 1904 onwards organised the first strikes.[17] The labour movement in Córdoba was led by the workers of the footwear industry, who made it independent of the rhythm of agrarian activities, and linked it to the fortunes of the general democratic movement, in particular the 1919 University Reform movement. This point only confirms the general dearth of studies on the provincial variations in the history of the labour movement.

Notes

1. Third National Census, 1914.
2. Departmento Nacional de Trabajo, 1908.
3. For an overview of the city's development see J. Scobie, (1974) *Buenos Aires. Plaza to Suburb, 1870–1910.* New York, Oxford University Press.
4. For one immigrant's account see J.F. Marsal, (1969) *Hacer la América: autobiografía de un inmigrante español en la Argentina.* Buenos Aires, Di Tella.
5. Third National Census, 1914.
6. Departamento Nacional de Trabajo, 1913.
7. Censo Municipal, Ciudad de Buenos Aires, 1904.
8. J. Godio, (1972) *El movimiento nacional y la cuestión nacional. Argentina: inmigrantes asalariados y lucha de clases–1880–1910.* La Plata, Erasmo, p. 152.
9. These are described in detail in I. Oved, (1978) *El anarquismo y el movimiento obrero en Argentina.* Mexico, Siglo XXI.
10. R. Thompson (1984) "The Limitations of Ideology in the Early Argentine

Labour Movement: Anarchism in the Trade Unions, 1890–1920", *Journal of Latin American Studies*, no. 16, pp. 82–83.

11. For the views of an anarchist in this period see A. Gilimón (1971) *Un Anarquista en Buenos Aires (1890–1910)*. Buenos Aires, Centro Editor de América Latina.

12. H. Spalding (1977) *Organized Labor in Latin America*. New York, Harper and Row, p. 25.

13. For a discussion of socialists and the trade unions see M. Mullaney (1983). *The Argentine Socialist Party 1890–1930: early development and internal schisms*. PhD thesis, University of Essex.

14. Departamento Nacional de Trabajo, Boletín 1908.

15. For a discussion of the rail unions see P. Thompson (1978) *Organised labour in Argentina: the railway unions to 1922*. M.Phil thesis, Oxford University.

16. *La Vanguardia*, cited in H. Spalding (1970). *La Clase Trabajadora Argentina (Documentos para su historia – 1890/1912)* Buenos Aires, Editorial Galerna, p. 72.

17. Pianetto, O. (1984) Mercado de trabajo y acción sindical en la Argentina, 1890–1922, *Desarrollo Económico* vol. 24, no. 94, p. 304.

6 Political Reform and Labour Struggles (1911–1915)

The political crisis caused in part by the general strike of 1910 accelerated the reform of the political system; a reformist tendency had been developing within the ruling class during the previous decade. The oligarchic state which had taken shape in the 1880s had achieved its legitimacy by leading the process of agro-export growth and by being able to integrate all the different fractions of the dominant classes within a system of restricted democracy. It now entered into crisis as a result of the social consequences of the economic growth strategy it had itself promoted – urbanisation, growth of the middle classes and development of the working classes. From another angle the high proportion of foreigners within the population (30% in 1914) posed the need for their national integration by the state. In political terms the old regime was being challenged both by the bourgeois-democratic opposition (the Radical Party) and the labour movement.

Political reforms

With the election of Roque Sáenz Peña as president in 1911, the oligarchy took its first step to setting a new level of political equilibrium. Once in office Sáenz Peña submitted a new electoral law to Congress which established secret and obligatory voting, the representation of minorities and the updating of the electoral register. Compared with the old system these mild reforms were truly 'revolutionary', if only because they established norms to guarantee 'clean' elections. The electoral reforms were designed to co-opt the political opposition of the Radical Party by offering it the prospect of integration into the process of political bargaining and a certain political legitimacy. This upset the Radical Party's alliance with the labour movement, which would have presented a more powerful threat and aggravated the crisis. The political reforms were also directed, to a more limited extent, at the labour movement which could now obtain a parliamentary voice through the Socialist Party. Already in 1909 the Chief of Police in Buenos Aires had declared that

Nothing is more urgent at the moment than the opening of that valve to allow the entry of two or three socialist deputies into the parliament, particularly in this period of labour agitation when laws on strikes and working practices will be discussed.[1]

The Sáenz Peña Law of 1911 led to a major change in the country's political system, promoting the entry into politics of the bulk of the native working classes. The increase in electoral participation is eloquent testimony of this: in 1910 there were 191,000 voters under the old system, in 1912 there were 640,852 voters (69% of the electorate) under the new laws.[2] In terms of political representation the new democratic regime led to a restructuring of political organisations, and the stable national development of the Radical and Socialist Parties. It was the Radical Party which, leaving behind its earlier practice of political conspiracies, was able to draw the most diverse social sectors behind the banner of political participation and effective implementation of the democratic reforms. In the presidential elections of 1916 the Radical Party led by Hipólito Yrigoyen won handsomely over the conservatives, thus closing the first period of political proscription in Argentina.

The rise to power of Radicalism in 1916 led to three major changes at state level: its social base was broadened through universal male suffrage; the recruitment of its political personnel was extended to the intermediate social layers; the welfare functions of the state were expanded through social security, labour legislation etc. These changes in the political system and the state also implied a certain shift in the relationship between the working class, the state and the political parties. The political reforms set in motion a far-reaching process of integration within Argentine society. In this regard the role of the labour movement during this period was of crucial importance. The process of simultaneous democratisation and integration set in motion by Yrigoyen had to resolve a problem: how to integrate a working class which was largely foreign, owing to mass immigration, within a system of political bargaining. The question of integration of the working class thus formed part of a broader problem – the crisis of nationality (customs, cultural models, language, etc) – which embraced the whole society. The reforms of 1912 made only limited inroads into the crisis of political participation – foreigners were still excluded from the political process and the Radical Party in power never attempted to go beyond the compromise agreed in 1912. In the economic field the new Radical government continued to operate, with only slight variants, within the agro-export model controlled by the oligarchy and British capital. Thus the movement of social integration was to operate within fairly precise limits, particularly with regard to the working class. It was unable to channel the modernisation process of Argentina without paying the price of the great social upheavals of 1919–21. Radicalism fell, unlamented, in 1930, at the hands of a military coup d'état, after having won handsomely in three successive elections: Yrigoyen in 1916, Alvear in 1922 and Yrigoyen again in 1928.

Labour and the political reforms

The effect within the labour movement of the new electoral law was to reopen the debate on the relation between political and economic action, between parliamentary and direct action. The anarchists and revolutionary syndicalists seized this opportunity to reaffirm their 'anti-politics' position and attacked the Socialist Party in harsh terms. The revolutionary syndicalist current, since its break from the Socialist Party in 1906, had evolved rapidly to a position which, by 1907, rejected parliamentary participation and any electoral activity.[3] In February 1918, during parliamentary elections, they denounced the electoral attitude of the Socialist Party as 'effectively collaborating with the conservative work of the capitalist class'.[4] For the Syndicalists there was no doubt as to the correct tactics to follow in the new situation: 'We may go to gaol but not to the polls'.[5] Within the anarchist ranks there was a general refusal to participate in parliamentary politics, though a group of anarchist intellectuals did vacillate on this question in view of the electroal euphoria which had gripped wide sectors of the masses. During a meeting held at the cart drivers' union headquarters, Santiago Locascio, Alberto Ghiraldo and others proposed that the anarchists should participate in elections. They argued that workers should not throw their votes away. The meeting decided by a big majority not to present anarchist candidates, not to vote, and not to pay the fine which would result from not voting.[6]

It was the anarchist and revolutionary syndicalist position of refusal to engage in any 'political action' which held sway overall within the labour movement. This was manifested in the trade unions' lack of interest in elections. Furthermore, the trade union federation FORA ruled that the holding of union office was incompatible with the holding of any elected political post, be it at national, provincial or municipal level. The FORA congresses thus refused to accept the credentials of delegates who were Socialist members of congress or local councillors.

For the Socialist Party the new situation entailed a fundamental change, because it created the conditions to develop their strategy, set in 1899, which stated that the only possible means of action was 'to awaken the consciousness of the workers, inciting them to political action as the *only means* to begin expropriating the capitalist class'.[7] The new electoral law represented for the Socialist Party not only the opportunity to win a few parliamentary posts, but the chance to pose as the most democratic and reformist alternative in the process of national and social integration of the immigrant masses. When Jean Jaurès visited Argentina in 1911, he had as one of the central themes in his meetings the need for political participation in forging a new nationality.

With the broadening of the limits of political participation, the Socialist Party was led to readjust its tactics. The whole party was turned towards the electoral arena and to the campaign for the naturalisation of foreigners. At the end of 1911 the party created an Elections Central Committee which, according to the party press, would 'be in charge of the political agitation of the Socialist Party'.[8] The objectives of this committee, aided by sub-committees in each electoral district, were to direct Socialist electoral propaganda and the organisation of the Socialist candidates' campaigns. From then on the growing importance of Socialist electoral activity can be gauged by the increasing space devoted to it in the party press.

The results of the first elections under the Sáenz Peña Law in 1912 seemed to confirm the Socialist Party's orientation: in the city of Buenos Aires it made a historic breakthrough with the election of Alfredo Palacios and Juan B. Justo to the national parliament with 35,000 and 13,000 votes respectively. In the 1913 elections the party won two further congressional seats and saw the election of the first Socialist senator in America: Enrique del Valle Iberlucea. On this occasion the Socialist Party overtook the Radical Party in Buenos Aires by 48,000 to 30,000 votes, becoming the main opposition party in the capital city. This level of Socialist votes was not achieved again until 1918, giving rise to speculation that some Conservatives had switched to the Socialists to defeat the Radicals.

The overall evolution of Socialist votes in Buenos Aires gives a clearer idea of the magnitude of the party's advance:

Table 6.1   Socialist Party results in Buenos Aires, 1910–1918

Year	Votes	Senate seats	Congress seats
1910	7,010	–	–
1912	35,000	–	1
	23,000	–	1
1913	48,000	–	2
	42,000	1	–
1914	42,000	–	6
1916	42,000	–	3
1918	49,000	–	3

Source: *Historia del Socialismo Marxista en la República Argentina*, Buenos Aires, 1919, p. 3.

Furthermore, the Socialist Party obtained 47,000 votes in the 1918 Buenos Aires municipal elections, gaining ten councillors' seats. In the provincial elections for Buenos Aires the party gained two seats in 1914, and four in 1915, but lost them in the elections of 1917–18.

In spite of this growth the weight of socialism at the national political level was quite limited. Though the party was, to a certain degree, implanted nationally, its effective political force was restricted to Buenos Aires city. Here, there was not only a high concentration of workers, but also the control and clientelism apparatus of the traditional parties was much weaker. Whereas in Buenos Aires city the Socialist Party overtook the Radicals and Conservatives on various occasions, thus becoming the main opposition party, at a national level it never posed a serious threat to them. In the presidential elections of 1916 the Radicals, headed by Hipólito Yrigoyen, won 340,802 votes, against 96,103 for the Conservatives and 66,397 for the Socialists.

The expansion of Socialist influence was not restricted to the electoral arena. From 1911 onwards it encouraged the development of 'socialist centres' which, according to one young militant, grew from 15 in 1912 to over 100 in 1915.[9] In 1912 the Socialist Federation of the Province of Buenos Aires was formed, and the inflow of new militants and the organisation of new centres spread to the interior provinces, particularly Corrientes, Entre Ríos, Tucumán, Mendoza and Salta. During this period the socialist youth circles began to organise. They were structured at a national level by the Federation of Socialist Youth, which was formed in 1916. The party daily *La Vanguardia* (The Vanguard) had a circulation of around 75,000 by this stage.[10]

The good election results and the expansion of party structures encouraged the party leadership's parliamentary strategy. Tactics in this area had changed since the days in which Alfredo Palacios was first elected to congress in 1904, when the socialist attitude was 'negative', critical and denunciatory. From 1912 onwards the Socialist senators and congressmen developed a more 'positive' parliamentary intervention. They sought to develop reforms and pass laws which would favour the working class, and they also participated actively in the general administration of the state, the problems of military budgets, penal codes, etc.

In spite of all these advances, the development of a parliamentary strategy caused a certain tension between the Socialist Party and the trade union movement. In the first place, there were problems within the party because the priority given to electoral activity led to the withdrawal of worker militants from trade union activity. Party leader Juan B. Justo actually wrote in 1912 that 'the party has nothing to do with trade union organisations'.[11] This led to a situation in 1916 where only 5% of Socialist workers were affiliated to their trade unions. By 1918 this choice between political and trade union activity was such that the Executive Committee of the Socialist Party was forced to make it obligatory for Socialist activists to be affiliated to their respective trade unions. In second place, outside the party, the Socialist parliamentary strategy clashed with the 'anti-politics' tradition of the labour movement, and the fact that the foreign workers were still largely marginalised. This meant that the prestige and influence of the party was restricted to the sectors of the working class who were in a relatively privileged economic and social situation, such as the railway workers and the 'white collar' trades: public employees, teachers, shop-workers, etc. A survey carried out in 1920 gives some idea of the Socialist Party's social composition in its most important bastion, the city of Buenos Aires:

Table 6.2   Socialist Party composition in Buenos Aires city, 1920

Occupational Category	Number of Members	Percentage
Worker	732	20.0
Artisan and small merchant	1,382	37.8
Employee	1,155	31.6
Owner	24	0.7
Professional	293	8.0
Various	73	2.0
Total:	3,659	100.0

Source: R. Walter, (1977) *The Socialist Party of Argentina 1890–1930*, University of Texas at Austin, Institute of Latin American Studies, p. 175.

We note the preponderance of artisans and small merchants (38%) within the party membership. This would appear to confirm the hypothesis that the Socialist Party acted as a channel for the political expression of the newly-emerging intermediate layers. For them, as for the older, more established sections of the working class whose situation had improved with the great social mobility of this period, socialism appeared as a means to enter politics and with that to achieve a rise in social status.

The priority given to electoral work and the deteriorating relations with the trade union movement led to unrest within the Socialist Party. At the tenth Party Congress in 1911 a group of trade union militants, many from the printers' union, confronted the party leadership and denounced the one-sided nature of the parliamentary strategy. They argued for the party's full participation in the organisation of workers' economic struggles. As a result of this debate, the opposition current gained the concession of a Trade Union Propaganda Committee, which began operating in early 1912. During that year the Socialist dissidents extended their critique of the leadership to broader issues, forming a Karl Marx Study Committee and issuing a bi-monthly journal, *Palabra Socialista* (Socialist Word). In this journal the opposition current denounced the party's electoralism, stressing the equal importance of political and economic struggles. It also attacked the 'revisionist' tendency of Edward Bernstein, the German social democrat, with whom they identified the positions of the party leadership.

The Trade Union Propaganda Committee maintained a low profile until 1914 when it began to participate actively in the unionisation of the metal, municipal and foot-wear workers. An internal report of 1917 claimed that the committee had 16,671 affiliates.[12] The opposition current which promoted this trade union work also began to encourage the organisation of a socialist youth movement, and supported the growing anti-militarist campaign. In 1917, when the Socialist Party entered a crisis over the leadership's position towards the war (see Chapter 7) it was this current which led to the breakaway faction which would eventually form the Communist Party.[13] Apart from this left-wing opposition, the Socialist Party also had a nationalist-type opposition led by the party's first elected representative, Alfredo Palacios. He was expelled from the party in 1915 for participating in a duel, which was against party regulations, but he was reincorporated into the party in 1931 after leading the ephemeral *Partido Socialista Argentino* (Argentine Socialist Party).

The increased level of political participation and public rights not only led to the expansion of political and trade union organisation (of which more shortly) but to a significant growth of working-class cultural activities. There was a popular workers' theatre which performed at trade-union-organised parties and picnics. Worker education centres expanded greatly, as did publishing activities. Following an already established tradition, the number of trade union, political and cultural reviews and journals practically doubled between 1910 and 1930 to reach a total of around 350 titles. Working-class culture was certainly thriving in this period.

Having examined the implications of the 1912 political reforms we should also stress their very definite limitations with regard to the working class. For one thing the new electoral law did not concede the right to vote to foreign-born workers, nor to women, nor to working minors. At a stroke over half the industrial working class was excluded from the political process. The percentage excluded is even greater if we take into account foreign-born workers employed in the service and rural sectors. This situation set the context for subsequent attempts by the Radicals to integrate the labour movement, and severely limited the electoral prospects of the Socialists. The continued political marginality of the foreign-born workers, which could not be overcome by the educational system or military service, was a constant source of conflict within Argentine society as a whole. On the other hand, this national marginality had as its counterpart a strong level of integration within the trade union movement. The immigrants were integrated first of all as workers; this *class* integration was followed only much later by their integration as citizens. This meant that the trade unions not only expressed the economic-corporative demands of their members, but also an underlying national conflict.

Urban and rural strikes

The repression following the 1910 general strike, accompanied by the Law of Residence which allowed the deportation of foreign born 'agitators', and the new Law of Social Defence, was a serious blow to the trade union and political organisations of the working class. The second half of 1910 saw a sharp decline in strike activity. During 1911 and 1912 there was a slow recovery of labour militancy, though most conflicts were limited in scope and their results usually unfavourable to the workers. There were some important exceptions such as the successful strikes by the Buenos Aires brick-layers and cart drivers in the early months of 1911. When Roque Sáenz Peña became president in 1912 there was no immediate improvement in the relations between the state and the labour movement. This was seen clearly in the attitude taken by the authorities to the strikes of the Tandil quarry workers, of the Mar del Plata building workers in 1911, and above all to the rail drivers' strike led by *La Fraternidad* (The Fraternity) in 1912.

In Tandil, the quarry workers, whose union was affiliated to the syndicalist-oriented CORA confederation, took strike action in pursuit of a wage claim. When the strike leaders were detained by the authorities, some 3,000 workers marched on the city where they were violently suppressed. After a gun battle between workers and police, three workers and two policemen lay dead in the streets, and there were several wounded on both sides. The strike was lifted without any concessions being granted. In Mar del Plata the building workers launched a strike in September 1911, also in pursuit of a wage claim. The police repressed the workers from the start, arresting various activists. The strike spread throughout the city, with the support of the anarchists, socialists and revolutionary syndicalists. In the course of a demonstration one worker was killed and 15 injured. After ten days on strike the workers were forced to concede defeat, leaving 58 workers to be tried by the courts.

In 1912, strikes were still localised and the result of most was defeat for the workers. The most important case was that of the train drivers and firemen organised by *La Fraternidad*, a union which was independent of the syndicalist CORA and anarchist FORA confederations. The union launched a strike demanding new working regulations and a new scale of wage categories and promotion. The Minister of the Interior attempted to mediate in the dispute as the government was concerned by its effect over the transport of export goods. When the union rejected a compromise deal, the government placed the union membership under martial law. They also lifted certain legal regulations thus allowing the rail companies rapidly to replace the personnel on strike. After 52 days out on strike, the workers returned having received a promise of no victimisation and prompt government arbitration of their demands. These promises were not kept.

The defeat of the *La Fraternidad* strike showed, among other things, the general downturn in labour militancy (there were no sympathy strikes) and the difficulty of sustaining the strike without the support of the rest of the railworkers, who were very poorly organised. The station, workshop, maintenance and railway-crossing personnel were almost totally non-unionised. It was precisely during the *La Fraternidad* strike that the *Federación Obrera Ferrocarrilera* (Railway Workers' Federation) was formed to embrace these categories. Too recently formed to mobilise its members effectively, the new federation was able to lend only moral support to the *La Fraternidad* strike. This new rail union was organised on the initiative of syndicalist activists linked to the CORA confederation. It soon called on the revolutionary syndicalist periodical *La Acción Obrera* (Workers' Action) to appoint an activist to assist the union's organising drive. Francisco Rosanara, who was appointed for this purpose, was elected the general secretary of the new federation, a post he held through various congresses until 1922. With the help of *La Acción Obrera* and the more organic support of CORA, the new rail union began to expand rapidly. In September 1912 it launched the first issue of its periodical *El Obrero Ferroviario* (The Railway Worker) and by 1915, when its first congress was held, it boasted 4,000 full members and 1,500 associates. It was not until 1916–7 that the union organised the vast bulk of the railworkers, which coincided with a number of big strikes.[14]

While the urban working class was relatively quiescent in 1912, an important rural strike occurred in July of that year led by the sharecroppers and small peasants of the central cereal zone.[15] Known as the *Grito de Alcorta* (shout or rising of Alcorta) after the town in the province of Santa Fé where it began, this strike had three main demands: a lowering of rent levels, the freedom for sharecroppers and peasants to buy and sell to whom they pleased; and abolition of unfair tenancy agreements. The strike, which lasted a whole year, led to the social awakening of the small-scale peasant farmers who faced up to the once omnipotent large landowners and the commercial agents who handled agrarian products. When the strike ended in August 1913, the sharecroppers had obtained a general lowering of rents, but the other demands were only acceded to in some areas. Perhaps the most important long-term result of this strike was the formation of the *Federación Agraria Argentina* (Argentine Agrarian Federation) in August 1912, which organised the small proprietors, the sharecroppers and the colonists.

The attitude of the labour movement towards the *Grito de Alcorta* was an ambiguous one. On the one hand, various workers' organisations welcomed the strike because it destabilised the government and helped to unblock the political situation, quite apart from their recognition of the gross exploitation imposed by the large landowners. On the other hand, because the strikers were not wage workers, the workers' organisations' attitude was one of distrust towards those who wished to become bosses and might do so. An example of this ambiguous stance was that the CORA confederation supported the strike and sent a representative to one of the rallies in Santa Fé, but also declared definite limits to its support in so far as the strikers were not genuine proletarians. Sebastian Marotta, who was the delegate sent by the revolutionary syndicalists to Santa Fé made his position clear:

> We thought, in vain, that we might convince the colonists through propaganda that once they 'became workers, their struggle, from the perspective of their new social condition, could lead to effective improvements, such as a reduction in the working day', thus preparing them through the education of the struggle for their 'emancipation'.[16]

With such an unrealistic perspective there was little hope of building a 'worker-peasant alliance' during this period.

Trade union unity

Two attempts by the syndicalists to forge a united trade union movement
were frustrated in 1911 and 1912 by the refusal of the FORA anarchist
unions to participate. Most contemporaries and subsequent writers agree
on the general weakness of the trade unions at this time. In 1913 the
syndicalist confederation CORA claimed 10,000 members though only
5,844 of these paid their dues.[17] For the anarchist FORA there are no
reliable figures, though we can assume that they were considerably higher,
bearing in mind that it had several powerful unions affiliated, such as the
Federación Obrera Marítima (Maritime Workers' Federation) which had
9,000 members. The syndicalists in fact recognised at the time the
numerical superiority of the anarchists. As to the third, independent,
grouping of unions, it grew steadily during these years as a result of the
dispute between the two major confederations, and because of the support
given to it by the socialists. The independents, for example, claimed that the
Federación Gráfica Bonaerense (Buenos Aires Graphical Workers'
Federation) which they led, had more members in 1914 than the two rival
confederations put together.[18]

In the course of 1913 and 1914 three factors increased the pressure
towards anarchist and syndicalist unity: the economic depression; the
arrival of a great number of immigrants which increased the reserve army
of labour; and a certain recomposition of the trade union movement. In
September 1914 a unity congress called by the syndicalist CORA drew 27
trade unions, and it was agreed to dissolve the confederation recom-
mending that its affiliates, along with the independent unions, should enter
the anarchist-led FORA. This decision of the revolutionary syndicalists to
join forces with FORA was taken without a demand for the withdrawal of
the communist-anarchist objectives set by the fifth FORA Congress in
1905, which had historically been one of the obstacles to trade union unity.
The unity was based on a promise by the anarchists to convene a congress
to discuss this issue, but also on a process of political convergence whereby
a sector of the anarchists moved towards syndicalist positions. This sector,
led by Francisco García (secretary of the Maritime Workers' Federation),
Bautista Mansilla (rail union) and others, was to change the balance of
political forces within the trade union movement.

After the syndicalist and independent unions joined forces with FORA
the confederation called its Ninth Congress early in 1915. The conference
brought together the delegates of 57 unions, of which 29 were from Buenos
Aires, 8 from Rosario and Santa Fé, 5 from La Plata and 15 from the rest of
the country. It was a marked success in spite of the withdrawal of some
unions such as the socialist-led Buenos Aires Graphical Workers'
Federation, who argued that it represented a sell-out to the anarchists. The
conference resolutions demonstrated the hegemony of the revolutionary
syndicalists in alliance with a sector of the anarchists, within the labour
movement. The 1905 commitment to communist-anarchist goals was

dropped in favour of a position of neutrality towards the different political currents within the labour movement. The resolution with regard to the general strike adopted at the Congress was also in marked contrast to positions held since 1910. At that time both the socialist UGT and the syndicalist CORA saw the general strike as a major resource of the proletariat in its revolutionary education, and an efficient means, to be used 'without limitations', of destroying the capitalist system. By 1915 the general strike was considered suitable 'only when it is exercised with intelligence and energy to repulse the aggression of capitalism and the state'.[19]

From 1915 onwards, the 'destructive' aspect of working class actions was discouraged and the primacy of its 'positive' aspects became clearly established. These would be represented by actions which tended to 'gain space' in the factory through the organisation of workers. At a broader level it would lead to a challenge to capitalist power in society through the founding of a new producers' law and morality, through independent class action and refusal to engage in the political process. By reducing the sphere of working-class politics to the economic struggle, and rejecting the system of political parties, parliament and so on, this new strategy favoured and developed a corporativist practice focused on wages, working conditions, social security, etc. This in turn led to the establishment for the first time in Argentina of limited negotiating mechanisms between the trade union movement and the state. These measures, representing to a certain extent the 'legitimisation' of the working class, operated as a stabilising factor in society as a whole, a stability which led to the gradual fading away of revolutionary class action.[20]

On the anarchist front, the defeat of the 1910 general strike threw into question the idea of a sudden seizure of power, the proximity of capitalist collapse and the prospect of an immediate insurrection. It was from this starting point that a group of anarchists argued for fusion with the syndicalists after 1911, thus changing their own conceptions of working-class action and strategy. On the terrain of trade union organisation they adopted a position of political neutrality, leaving anarchist propaganda and agitation to 'individuals and groups who are only interpreters of the theoretical, philosophical and scientific foundations of the anarchist ideal'.[21] From this separation of economic struggle, to be waged by the trade unions, and political action, which was left to intellectual groups, the anarchists opened the door to a reformist policy for the trade union movement. In this way the syndicalists, by reducing politics to the economic struggle, and the anarchists, in seeing a sharp divide between the two, had both arrived at a common strategy for the labour movement.

The background to this political convergence between anarchists and syndicalists in 1915 was set by fundamental changes in the structure of the working class. During the decade after 1900, the service sector proletariat had become the leading sector of the working class. The leading unions within the labour movement were the railworkers, the port-workers, the maritime workers and the public employees. The formation of large trade unions in all these sectors placed the trade union leadership at the head of important concentrations of workers. Many of these workers played a key role in the agro-export economy and thus had considerable bargaining weight. Furthermore, the relation between labour and capital was mediated directly or indirectly by the state in most of these service areas.

On the political front, the political reforms of 1912 had, despite their limits, prefigured a growing tendency for the state to intervene in industrial relations. In 1912 the role of the *Departamento Nacional del Trabajo* (National Labour Department) was broadened to give it considerable functions of mediation and control over the labour situation. A fundamental change occurred when Hipólito Yrigoyen became president in 1916, when a continuous and direct policy of negotiations with the unions began, which we will examine shortly. To sum up, the reform of the political system and the more conciliatory attitude of the state made a revolutionary and insurrectionary labour strategy less viable. This led to the restructuring of the labour movement to face the new situation.

After the ninth FORA congress the unity of the trade union movement did not last long. The 'hard' wing of the anarchists, supported by the journal *La Protesta* (Protest), called an assembly of trade unions in May 1915 at the cart drivers' union headquarters. Ten Buenos Aires unions participated, with another seven as observers. The meeting decided not to recognise the decisions of the ninth congress and to re-establish the original communist-anarchist objectives of the old FORA. For the next six years there were therefore two FORA's – FORA IX (ninth congress – syndicalist) and FORA V (fifth congress – anarchist).

While there was an overall picture of labour-movement weakness prior to the ninth FORA congress in 1915, it was the syndicalists who emerged strengthened from the subsequent regroupments. The new relation of forces reflected not only the predominance of the service-sector workers – nearly all were affiliated to FORA IX – but also the growing weight of the more skilled working-class fractions. It also reflected the process of 'nationalisation' of the working class as the native-born workers came to predominate over the foreign-born. The anarchist FORA V organised, on the whole, the less-skilled sectors of the working class and those trades where foreign-born workers still predominated. There were exceptions – such as the syndicalist railworkers who were mainly foreign-born and the anarchist women textile workers who were mainly native-born – but as a general rule the syndicalists were hegemonic in the skilled native-born sectors.

Notes

1. *La Acción Obrera*, no. 218 10 February 1912).
2. D. Canton, (1973) *Elecciones y Partidos Políticos en la Argentina*, Buenos Aires, Siglo XXI, p. 45. For an overview of the political reforms see A. Borón, *The Formation and Crisis of the Liberal State in Argentina 1880–1930*, Harvard University, PhD thesis.
3. *La Acción Socialista*, no. 41 (16 April 1907).
4. *La Acción Obrera*, no. 218 (10 February 1918).
5. Ibid.
6. *La Vanguardia* (25 and 26 March 1912).
7. *La Vanguardia* (23 December 1899).
8. *La Vanguardia* (8 May 1912).
9. E.J. Corbière, (1974) "Conversando con Carlos Pascali", *Todo Es Historia*, no. 81.
10. J. Longuet, *Le Mouvement Socialiste Internationale*, in J. Compère-Morel (ed.) *Encyclopédie Socialiste*, Paris (1912–13) p. 622.
11. *La Vanguardia* (19 January 1912).
12. *Informe del Comité de Propaganda Gremial*, Buenos Aires, 1917.
13. See B. Galitelli, (1981) *Aux Origines du Parti Communiste Argentin*, Paris, Mémoire de Diplôme EHESS.
14. For further details S. Marotta, (1975) *El Movimiento Sindical Argentino. Su Génesis y Desarrollo: 1857–1914*, Buenos Aires, Ediciones Librera. pp. 539–542.
15. On the *Grito de Alcorta* see S. Solberg, (1976) "Agrarian unrest and agrarian policy in Argentina, 1912–1930", *Journal of Interamerican Studies and World Affairs* no. 13.
16. S. Marotta, (1975) *El Movimiento Sindical Argentino*, p. 466.
17. Ibid., p. 514.
18. Ibid., p. 156.
19. Ibid., p. 550.
20. On the Revolutionary Syndicalist current see E. Bilsky, (1982) *La Semaine Tragique en 1919 en Argentine*, Paris, Mémoire de Diplôme EHESS, pp. 300–310.
21. *Orientación* no. 1 (10 November 1915).

7. From the First World War to the *Semana Trágica* (1916–1921)

In this chapter we examine the composition of the working class in 1914 on the basis of census data, which allows us to assess the changes which took place after the 1895 census discussed in Chapter 3. The process of economic growth which occurred between the two census years followed the general orientation established in the 'golden era' of the agro-export economy. The working class which was formed was based predominantly on the service sector, with the development of subsidiary light industry linked to the transformation of primary goods, along with a strong nucleus of rural workers. The second section of this chapter turns to examine the political currents within the labour movement during the First World War period. Under the Yrigoyen presidency there was a certain degree of integration of the labour movement by the state. However, the bloody events of the *Semana Trágica* (Tragic Week) in 1919 showed that there were limits to the reformist tendencies operating within the state.

Composition of the working class

The third national census of 1914 allows us to gain an impression of the composition of the working class around the time of the First World War. We shall examine three main fractions of the working class: the industrial, service and rural proletariat. The overall pattern of industrial employment can be seen in Table 7.1.

The two sectors which had expanded most since 1895 were food and beverages, and the metallurgical sector, which was seen as proof that the basic industries were now set for expansion. The process of growth led inevitably to the adoption of more capital intensive techniques: whereas in 1895 there was an installed capacity of 60,000 horsepower throughout industry, this figure had risen to 678,700 by 1914. The level of concentration of the labour force did not increase by the same proportion however: in 1895 there was an average of 7 workers per industrial establishment, which rose only to 8.4 workers in 1914.

This apparent contradiction is explained by the fact that by 1914 there was an important nucleus of large firms, but alongside these there remained

Table 7.1   Industrial employment, 1914

Sector	Number of Firms	Number of Workers
Food and Beverages	18,983	134,842
Textiles	2,458	15,560
Clothing	7,081	57,764
Construction	8,582	87,317
Furniture	4,441	29,007
Metallurgical	3,275	29,327
Chemicals	567	9,986
Printing and Publishing	1,439	13,286
Decorative Trades	996	4,297
Other	957	28,815
Total	48,779	410,201

Source: Third National Census, 1914.

a multitude of small workshops which brought down the average. We can note the existence of firms employing more than 100 workers in a number of key sectors: the *frigoríficos* (meat-packing plants) had an average of 1,300 workers per plant, the 'Alpargatas' textile plant employed 1,600 workers, the 'Sociedad Italo-Americana' had 800 workers, the 'Establecimientos Americanos Gratry', also a textile firm, employed 650 workers and so on. In the metallurgical industry there were 100 establishments in Buenos Aires employing 1,500 workers, an average of 150 workers per plant.[1] The level of mechanisation of these big firms was also higher than the average: the sugar mills (*ingenios*) of the north-west, which employed around 1,000 workers each, had an installed capacity of 1,000 hp in each plant. The capacity of firms with over 100 workers varied between 180 hp and 500 hp.

An intermediate group of businesses employed between 20 and 100 workers. This category included most firms in the clothing sector, the flour mills, and much of the construction sector. The degree of mechanisation was also considerably lower in this sector varying from an average of 5.9 hp per plant in the construction industry to a maximum of 103 hp in the foot-wear industry. Finally, a third group of small plants, employing less than 20 workers, was to be found in the textile industry (particularly in the provinces), much of the food industry, in printing, in furniture, etc. Here the degree of mechanisation ran from 0.4 hp, 6 hp in some of the small metallurgical plants.

The growing concentration of industry and its labour force also had uneven geographical distribution as we can see in Table 7.2. Whereas industry grew in all areas, acting as a factor towards national integration, it is quite clear that the littoral provinces maintained their historic advantage over the rest of the country. Furthermore, whereas the littoral area as a whole employed 76.4% of the total number of industrial

Table 7.2   National distribution of industry, 1895–1914

Area (provinces)	Number of Firms		Number of Workers	
	1895	1914	1895	1914
Littoral (Buenos Aires, Santa Fé, Entre Ríos and Corrientes)	19,044	34,102	135,971	313,629
Central (San Luis, Córdoba and Santiago del Estero)	1,659	4,011	9,920	31,020
Andean (Mendoza, San Juán, La Rioja and Catamarca)	1,898	5,914	8,435	27,970
Northern (Tucumán, Salta and Jujuy)	1,185	3,282	14,025	25,561
National Territories (all other provinces)	328	1,470	3,431	11,012
Total	24,114	48,779	171,782	410,192

Source: Third National Census 1914.

workers, the city of Buenos Aires on its own accounted for over 50% of the nation's proletariat.

As to the proportion of native-born to foreign-born workers, the 1914 census indicated that for the first time, locally-born workers were in a slight majority. The immigrant workers were concentrated in Buenos Aires and the littoral provinces where they still accounted for over half the industrial work-force. The proportion of immigrants within the work-force varied considerably across industries. Locally-born workers predominated in the textile sector, owing chiefly to the preponderance of female labour (immigrants were largely male). In the printing trade, the Spanish language was indispensable so in that industry locally-born workers were also in a majority, though about one-third of printers were immigrants. This last point can be accounted for partly by the large number of printers from Spain but also by the existence of a number of foreign-language publications in Argentina: *The Review of the River Plate, Le Courier de la Plata, Die Presse, Culmine, Golos Truda* and others. Locally-born workers were also in a slight majority in the construction, alimentary and furniture sectors. Immigrants had the edge in the clothing, chemical and metallurgical industries. These differences would seem to indicate a greater degree of immigrants in skilled occupations requiring a certain level of technical preparation, although the differences are not clear-cut enough to draw definitive conclusions.

Having examined the structure of the industrial working class, we must now turn to the service sector and the rural working class. We have already mentioned how the service sector grew out of the agro-export economy, and as a result of the rapid urbanisation of the littoral zone with its attendant administrative apparatus. The transport sector played a fundamental role within this economic system, employing some 170,000 workers in 1914. The largest concentration of transport workers was on the railways, which employed 113,095 workers. The tram networks in the cities employed a further 11,581 workers and there were 26,000 engaged in cargo transport (of whom three-quarters were immigrants). Between 9,000 and 12,000 worked in the docks in the 1900–20 period, of which some 80% were immigrants. Shipping employed a further 13,000 workers.

According to the 1908 Agrarian National Census there were 578,000 workers permanently engaged in agriculture, with a further 725,000 seasonal workers. This temporary work-force was engaged not only in grain harvesting, but also in sheep shearing in the south of the country (Patagonia) and in sugar-cane cutting in the northern provinces (Tucumán, Salta and Jujuy). The 1914 census thus referred to 14,700 'industrial' workers in the sugar mills (*ingenios*), but there were a further 30,000 workers taken on during the sugar harvest (*zafra*) along with an unspecified number of labourers *(peones)* drawn from the indigenous population of Santiago del Estero and the Chaco provinces. With regard to the nationality of rural workers, an overwhelming majority (70% to 90%) of sugar, forestry and *yerba maté* tea plantation workers of the northern provinces were native-born. In the central provinces there were considerably more immigrant workers engaged in the cereal economy, including the seasonal immigrants, the *golondrinas* (swallows). In the southern sheep-rearing provinces, foreign workers—mainly from Chile— also came into the country occasionally.

Taking an overall view of the composition of the working class at the time of the First World War we can draw several general conclusions:

- The numerical predominance of rural workers in the productive structure was not translated into a hegemonic political role within the labour movement. This was due largely to the dispersion of these workers throughout the vast national territory—with the exceptions noted above—usually without direct communciation with the urbanised and dynamic littoral area.
- There was a growing service sector proletariat, owing to the modernisation of the littoral area and the dynamic agro-export economy. These workers were relatively concentrated and were in direct contact with the state, which led them to play a vanguard role within the trade union movement.
- The industrial workers were, in general, only just approaching the condition of a modern industrial working class. Apart from a few islands of relatively concentrated firms with a certain level of technical development, these workers were dispersed in a myriad of small workshops with strong artisanal features. This did not prevent their emergence on to the political scene, though their role in this period was still subordinate to that of the service sector workers.

- Immigrants still predominated over native-born workers in the great urban centre of Buenos Aires and its environs. The labour market was swollen by the arrival of the sons and daughters of the first generation of immigrants, who had been absorbed by a productive structure in the throes of modernisation. Furthermore, immigration led to divisions with the working class at a time when the state was trying to socialise and 'nationalise' the immigrant worker.

Effects of the war in Argentina

The inter-imperialist war launched in 1914 had as one of its foreseeable effects the retrenchment of world trade. This was bound to have serious consequences in a country which exported primary goods and imported manufactured goods.[2] The war led to a significant drop in Argentina's exports and a much sharper decline in imports. The effect of this decline affected each economic sector in different ways. The slight decline in the physical volume of Argentina's exports was more than compensated for by the high prices for these goods on the international market. The more drastic reduction in imports resulted in a favourable balance of trade for Argentina and allowed the state to pay off most of the foreign debt. This new 'golden era' for the agrarian oligarchy and the exporters was made possible by the political neutrality of the governments of Victorino de la Plaza (1914) and Yrigoyen (1916), which kept Europe's ports open to Argentine produce.

But the decline in imports had a detrimental effect on the population as a whole, with consumer goods not produced locally becoming scarce. Industry was deprived of essential inputs and fuel. At the same time, this drop in imports led some industrialists to produce goods locally which had previously been imported. This 'import substitution industrialisation' was limited because the depression was relatively short-lived—1915–1918 approximately. Nor was the scarcity of consumer items so great or so prolonged as to lead to a substantial expansion of national industry, though the longer the depression continued the more acute the scarcity of machines, tools, and fuels became. Within these limits, import substitution advanced furthest in the metallurgical, textile and alimentary branches of industry.

It was only really in metallurgy that import substitution took place, because the others expanded due to the warring nations' increased demand for food and clothing. Lloyd George was later to say that the Allied powers had won the war thanks to the tons of grain and meat received from Argentina.

The lack of manufactured goods and machinery also led to a slump in the construction industry, both in the public and private sectors. Port renewal works were suspended and the expansion of the urban transport network stopped. On the railways the freeze on further extensions of the network was total, as was the suspension of repair work.

The second major effect of the imperialist war in Europe was to halt the flow of immigrants to Argentina. Table 7.3 gives a clear idea of the war's impact on immigration to Argentina.

Table 7.3   Migration to and from Argentina, 1903–1929

Period	Entries	Exits	Balance
1903–1913	3,007,089	1,403,685	1,603,404
1914–1919	513,278	726,068	–212,790
1920–1929	1,358,441	510,898	847,543

Source: G. Bourdé, (1974) *Urbanisme et Immigration en Amérique Latine.* Paris, Aubier Montagne, p. 162.

During the First World War the arrival of new immigrants not only slowed down, but emigration increased to such an extent that the net balance was a loss of around 200,000 people. This was due to the desire of many immigrant workers to return to their countries of origin to enlist, and a decline in living standards in Argentina itself.

For the workers who remained in Argentina the war led to rising unemployment, a fall in real wages and an increase in working hours as we see in Table 7.4.

Table 7.4   Conditions of the working class, 1914–1921

Year	Working day (hours/minutes)	Unemployment (percentage)	Cost of Living (1929=100)	Real Wages (1929=100)
1914	8.42	13.7	108	68
1915	8.58	14.5	117	61
1916	8.56	17.7	125	57
1917	8.46	19.4	146	49
1918	8.28	12.0	173	42
1919	8.12	7.9	186	57
1920	8.11	7.2	171	59
1921	8.02	–	153	73

Source: G. Bourdé, (1974) *Urbanisme et Immigration en Amérique Latine,* Paris, Aubier Montagne, p. 237; G. Di Tella and M. Zymelman, (1973) *Los Ciclos Económicos Argentinos.* Buenos Aires, Paidos, p. 150 and p. 175.

We note a slight annual increase in the working day until 1916 (although this data masks considerable disparities), a considerable rise in unemployment until 1917 and a steady decline in wages until 1918. Unemployment was particularly severe for workers in the construction industry and the transport sector, for public employees and some of the rural workers. On the other hand there was an increase in employment in the alimentary, tobacco, textile and leather industries. Regarding the composition of the labour force the proportion of males declined (they constituted the majority of emigrants) while the employment of women and minors increased. Minors in particular were taken on after 1918 as the economic recovery began and employers sought to reduce their wage bills.

According to contemporary accounts the rising cost of living was the worst burden which the working class had to carry. In 1919 the austere *La Nación* (The Nation) daily newspaper declared:

> There is a large group, which we could call an intellectual proletariat, composed of teachers, public employees with special technical skills . . . many of whom have seen no improvements [in living standards] over a long period.[3]

This would seem to indicate how widespread the effect of the rising cost of living was. The same newspaper article recognised that the situation was even more precarious in the interior provinces, where goods were more expensive owing to extra transport costs and provincial and municipal taxes.

The labour movement and the war

The dominant feeling within the Argentine labour movement when war broke out in 1914 was that a global catastrophe was approaching. The crisis was seen to have two main elements: first, it was thought to be the inevitable destiny of a tired monarchist and anti-democratic Europe, where the revolutionary spirit had given way to colonialism and to the war between different capitalist interests; second, it was regarded as the result of the betrayal of the leaders of the social democratic parties which led the proletariat to forsake the socialist alternative and instead support its own bourgeoisie. This dual crisis was seen in similar terms by the various political currents within the Argentine labour movement.

Nicolás Repetto, delegate from Argentina at the congress of the neutral countries held at The Hague in 1915 declared:

> I cannot hide the fact that in the first instance your civil war had disconcerted us almost totally. We did not expect, nor would ever have suspected, that so many survivals from past periods would lay hidden within your civilisation and culture.[4]

Repetto himself had earlier that year denounced the weaknesses of the Second International in the struggle against the war, especially the nationalist deviations maintained by the Swiss social democrat, Branting.[5] He further accused the German Social Democratic Party of favouring the outbreak of the war as a means of achieving political reforms in Germany.

The revolutionary syndicalists blamed German social democracy and also the German trade unions for the *débâcle*. Probably most representative of this current were the views of José Ingenieros who in 1914 wrote:

> The feudal civilisation, which dominates the barbarian nations of Europe, has decided to commit suicide, hurling itself into the abyss of war . . . A past full of violence and superstition entered its death throes. It has had its merits, which we admire. It had its heroes; they are part of the historical record. It had its ideals; they were fulfilled.[6]

This article, entitled *The Suicide of the Barbarians*, was reproduced and commented on in most of the workers' press of the period. In it Ingenieros not only expressed a vision of *débâcle*, but also argued quite originally that it represented the end of a historical model. It marked the limits of the idea that harmonious social development could take place on the basis of a complacent organised labour movement which would soften the worst aspects of capitalism. The cycle of 19th Century Europe was closed and, according to Ingenieros, the crisis opened up a new era:

> The present disaster is a bridge to the future. It is best that it be truly catastrophic so that the suicide does not rest at a failed attempt . . . With the barbarian armies wiping each other out, two forces will emerge as the nucleus of a future civilisation which will forge the nations of tomorrow: labour and culture.[7]

Later, after the triumph of the Russian Revolution, Ingenerios would take up again this idea of the suicide which regenerates. He became one of the main supporters of the new Bolshevik regime as the incarnation of the new era.

The second question to consider is the attitude of the various currents within the labour movement towards the belligerent powers as the war progressed. As in Europe, the outbreak of the war led to a split in the labour movement. Nearly all political tendencies within it agreed on an anti-militarist and neutralist strategy. The Socialist Party of Argentina, at its tenth congress in 1912, adopted the position of the Kier Hardie amendment – general strike in the case of war breaking out – which had earlier been approved by the Basle congress of the Second International. The various anarchist and revolutionary syndicalist currents also accepted this position implicitly. In the trade union movement itself, condemnation of the war and the call for a general strike were adopted by the ninth FORA congress in 1914. This position was ratified by the Pro-Peace Congress of Revolutionary Workers' Organisations held in São Paulo, Brazil, in 1915 to which FORA sent delegates. However, formal support for an anti-militarist and neutralist line could not conceal the different attitudes within the socialist and syndicalist currents, as we shall see.

The Socialist Party condemned the war and called for immediate peace negotiations. In 1917 it sent a telegram to US President Wilson supporting his peace proposals. Later, when the US entered the war, the Socialist Party called a mass meeting in support of the US congressmen who had opposed the decision. Behind its pacifism, however, the Socialist Party concealed a sympathy for the Allied powers against German militarism and Russian absolutism. In an article in 1916, Socialist senator Enrique del Valle Iberlucea praised the position adopted by Karl Liebknecht in so far as it undermined the position of German militarism.[8] In February 1917 the party actually demanded that Argentina break off diplomatic relations with Germany. This move was caused by the sinking of an Argentine ship by the German navy and the publication (by the US secret service) of letters by the German ambassador in Buenos Aires to Count Von Luxburg, in which he recommended the sinking of Argentine cargo ships bound for Allied ports.

As the submarine war became more acute, Argentina's export drive was placed in jeopardy, which drove a section of the ruling class to adopt a pro-war policy. That the Socialists also adopted this position was due largely to national politics, because Argentina's role in the war could only remain at the propaganda level given the country's geographical position. This orientation expressed the growing integration of the socialists into the country's political structures since the 1912 electoral reform. The Socialist parliamentary bloc had to express its support for Argentina's export drive as it was an essential element in their own economic strategy. Furthermore, a pro-war stance served as a useful means to attack the Yrigoyen regime, which remained firmly neutral and was therefore accused of being pro-German. The Socialists hoped to win votes away from the Radicals, by showing how Yrigoyen's neutrality led to artificial protectionism, which in turn led to a decline in wages, a rising cost of living, and unemployment. This patriotic stance could also be seen as an act of good faith towards the ruling class as whole. As Ricardo Sáenz Hayes, a Socialist councillor in Buenos Aires, declared in relation to the Socialist parliamentary bloc's presentation: 'It is a clear and intelligent document through which our party proves it is a party of government.'[9]

The parliamentary declaration in favour of war caused grave concern in the party ranks where there was a deeply rooted pacifist and neutralist tradition. As internal protests mounted, the Executive Committee called an extraordinary congress in April 1917 to debate the question. Three reports were presented: the first, from the Executive Committee majority and the parliamentary bloc, supported Argentina's entry into the war; the second, presented by an Executive Committee minority, opposed any participation in the war; the third, presented by Deputy Augusto Bunje, opposed participation in the war but called for military defence, if necessary, of Argentina's foreign trade. The debate centred on the first two positions. The minority took its stand on 'proletarian internationalism', denounced the capitalist nature of the war and supported the Zimmerwald (1915) and Kienthal (1916) anti-war resolutions of the European socialists. The submarine war was seen simply as a natural consequence of the war and an even greater argument to bring it to an end, not as a reason for supporting one side or the other. When the vote was taken, 4,204 votes went to the internationalist position against 3,564 for the pro-war position of the leadership majority. The parliamentary bloc was mandated to abstain in any further debates on the war, and the party press was directed to develop a pacifist line. The internationalists were not able to impose either of these two decisions in practice, however, as they did not control the party apparatus.

The internationalists then took the step of forming a 'Committee in defence of the Third Extraordinary Party Congress resolutions' and published its own journal *La Internacional* (The International) to compete with the official party organ, *La Vanguardia* (The Vanguard). The first issue of the new journal appeared in August 1917 and its critical stance seemed confirmed in September when the Socialist parliamentary bloc ignored the Congress resolutions and voted for the breaking of diplomatic relations with Germany. The internationalist tendency demanded a re-call conference to discuss the situation and the parliamentary representatives presented their resignations from the party. A referendum was organised, not to judge the parliamentary bloc's breaking of party discipline, but rather to decide on whether to accept the resignations. Presented in this way, the party voted 5,345 against acceptance (which would have deprived the party of any parliamentary representation), with 909 in favour and 2,000 abstentions. Following the referendum, the Executive Committee condemned the 'Committee in defence of the Third Extraordinary Party Congress resolutions.' The editor of *La Internacional*, José Fernando Penelón, and another member resigned from the Executive Committee, leaving the internationalists outside the party.

In January 1918 49 delegates representing 22 socialist centres and 750 party members gathered to found the International Socialist Party, which in 1920 became the Communist Party. At first sight it was disagreements over the First World War which caused the split in the socialist movement. However, the war only brought out into the open a dissident fraction which had been maturing for several years previously. This can be seen in the founding principles of the new International Socialist Party which added three points to the parent party's platform:

- trade union work was seen as equal to political activity as a means of struggle, and parliament was seen as a platform to denounce capitalism;
- a clear internationalist position was taken vis-à-vis the war;
- the socialist youth movement was organised around an anti-militarist platform.

The new party addressed a report to the Socialist International which accused the Socialist Party of 'reformist degeneration' and of upholding a social patriotic and electoralist policy.[10] It outlined its history as a 'Marxist opposition' within the party and called for the exclusion of the Socialist Party and for the recognition of the new party as the official section of the International in Argentina.

The themes indicated above, and the names of the party members who led the split, point to continuity with the socialist opposition of 1912, with the Trade Union Propaganda Committee which they created, and with the formation of the socialist youth movement in 1915–16. Before the First World War a certain communality of language allowed for the coexistence of various political positions and interpretations of socialism within the same movement, but this was no longer the case after the war broke out. Now the incompatibility of the two tendencies became clear and the decision to split appeared both necessary and revolutionary to the left opposition. After its inaugural congress the International Socialist Party participated in the 1918 elections, obtaining 2,750 votes in the parliamentary elections and 3,258 votes in the municipal contest.

In the trade union field the new party supported the syndicalist confederation, FORA IX, where it obtained five seats out of fifteen on the executive committee. Its trade union strength was greatest amongst the printers, foot-wear workers, municipal employees, and in the newly-formed metallurgical workers' union. As we shall see in Chapter 8, a major axis of party propaganda was around the 1917 Russian Revolution. At the Second Party Congress in 1920 it declared its support for the Communist Third International. At an extraordinary party congress that same year it accepted the so-called '21 Conditions' of the Comintern and changed its name to 'Communist Party – Argentine Section of the Third International'. It was accepted as a section of the world communist movement at the Third Congress of the Comintern in 1921, when Rodolfo Ghioldi attended as delegate from Argentina. During these early years the party extended its implantation to the interior provinces, doubling its membership to 1,400 between 1918 and 1919. In the 1920 Buenos Aires municipal elections party leader Penelón became a councillor with 5,061 votes. That same year the party participated in a series of teachers' strikes in Mendoza province and organised a local trade union movement in Córdoba. In spite of these advances the new Communist Party was still a marginal force within the labour movement, caught between the prestige of the Socialist Party in the electoral arena, and the revolutionary intransigence and prestige of the anarchists and the revolutionary syndicalists in the trade unions.

The syndicalists were also divided over what attitude to adopt towards the war, in spite of their early recognition that it was the product of capitalism's contradictions. Some sectors began to defend the position advanced by L. Johaux and most of the French trade union movement: to condemn the German unions. Though this position was debated in the main revolutionary syndicalist journal. *La Acción Obrera* (Workers' Action) it did not prevent unified support of the Radical Government's policy of neutrality. This stance was maintained throughout the World War, particularly when the submarine war sharpened in 1917.

The neutral and pacifist stance of the labour movement vis-à-vis the war (except for the Socialist Party's position at its close) has usually been explained in terms of Argentina's geographical distance from the conflict and the neutral position adopted by the local bourgeoisie. Though these factors were important, we should also stress the weak level of the labour movement's integration into the state and the political system. While in Europe the World War marked a high point in labour's integration ('social patriotism' etc), in Argentina this type of social integration had only just begun between 1912 and 1916. This fact strengthened the anarchist position, for example, which distanced itself from the war in the same way as it had from the political system in Argentina itself. On the other hand, when a sector of the bourgeoisie adopted a pro-war stance in 1917, this had immediate repercussions in the most integrated element of the labour movement, namely the Socialist Party.

Strikes under the Yrigoyen government (1916–1921)

When Hipólito Yrigoyen came to power in October 1916 the whole political scene in Argentina began to change.[11] That Yrigoyen became president through the support of the newly enfranchised masses, with all their aspirations and demands, meant there was a new social protagonist on the scene to challenge the dominant conservative élite and foreign capital. Yrigoyen's labour policy was critical for a number of reasons: the Radicals did not have an absolute majority in Congress, nor did they control the province of Buenos Aires (which was in the hands of the conservatives); the Socialist Party had a strong presence in the Buenos Aires administration; anarchists and syndicalists dominated the trade union movement; and finally, the World War had led to a critical economic situation.

On the labour front, the new Radical government's main innovation was to intensify state intervention in industrial relations. Apart from this, Yrigoyen personally developed relations with leaders of some of the bigger trade unions and of the syndicalist FORA IX. State intervention was carried out through the National Department of Labour which had been created in 1907. In 1912 this body decreed that the President could call and preside over works' councils composed of workers and employers. In 1916 this conciliatory machinery was actually put into practice, and the National Department of Labour began to oversee the implementation of labour legislation through its labour inspectors. It also began to regulate the labour market, setting up a labour register and controlling other private employment agencies. One of its tasks was to recruit labour for the seasonal rural tasks, thus cutting across the speculation of private labour agencies.

Yrigoyen's first presidential intervention in a labour conflict occurred in the maritime workers' strike of November 1916. The strike began over a wage claim and when the National Department of Labour called the parties to a conciliation meeting, the shipping companies refused to participate. The Minister of the Interior condemned the employers' refusal and they in turn called for arbitration by the President. Yrigoyen delegated his powers to the Buenos Aires Chief of Police who ruled in favour of the workers. A second maritime strike in 1917 was settled in a similar fashion. Also in

81

1917, the railway repair-shop workers of Rosario came out on strike to protest two arbitrary dismissals, and again the government forced the employers to concede to the workers' demand that they be reinstated.

The government's attitude in these strikes involving key unions, and its general policy of negotiations, meant a *de facto* legalisation of the trade union organisations. This naturally encouraged the numerical expansion of the unions, which began during the First World War. Another factor encouraging trade union growth was the decline of immigration during the war, which stabilised the labour market and reduced the number of seasonal workers who would have been less amenable to unionisation. The syndicalist FORA IX grew from 20,000 members in 1915 to nearly 70,000 in 1920. The anarchist FORA V, for which figures are less readily available, was at this time clearly a minority current.

Faced with socialist electoral pressure in the capital, and the conservative opposition, Yrigoyen took direct control of government relations with the syndicalist FORA IX. A 'special relationship' was established with Francisco García, general secretary of the *Federación Obrera Marítima* (Maritime Workers' Federation). Even during the bloody *Semana Trágica* (Tragic Week) of 1919 Yrigoyen was to call a meeting of labour intellectuals to seek a solution to the conflict. There were several reasons for the Radicals' conciliatory attitude towards the syndicalist FORA IX. They were trying to consolidate a 'moderate' unionism as a counterweight to the anarchists, and to use the 'anti-party' syndicalists to block socialist penetration in the unions. Then by establishing good relations with the maritime and port unions, they were simultaneously removing sources of conflict which might impede agro-export activities and threatening the socialist electoral implantation in the workers' quarters of La Boca and Riachuelo. Good relations were established with rail unions for similar reasons, and the new role of the state as arbiter gave it increased leverage with regard to foreign capital, in particular the British owners of the railway system.

The Radical government's new attitude towards the trade unions was not universal, however. A hard line was taken in labour conficts where no electoral advantage could be gained, where the state itself was directly involved, or where the government's relations with the ruling élite or foreign capital was threatened. These factors were at play in a number of strikes between 1916 and 1918. The mainly US-owned *frigoríficos* (meat-packing plants) of Berisso in Buenos Aires province were out on strike several times towards the end of 1917 and the beginning of 1918. The government responded by sending in troops to protect the scab labour and to break the strikes. In this case, foreign capital had threatened to withdraw its operations to neighbouring Uruguay if the government did not ensure 'labour peace'. Furthermore, most workers in these plants were foreign (chiefly from Russia and the Balkans) and therefore electoral criteria did not apply. Finally, the trade union movement in Berisso was weak and linked to the anarchist FORA V. The refuse collectors of Buenos Aires also launched a strike in 1917 over a wage claim and the government responded by sacking all the workers and sending in the police to break the strike. In this case, the Socialist Party had supported the organisation of these workers into the *Unión Obrera Municipal* (Municipal Workers' Union) which provided a useful scapegoat. It was only pressure from the syndicalist FORA IX which led the government finally to compromise, offering limited re-hiring of the unionised workers and compensation for the rest. As Rock points out, this strike shows how 'the government was much less favourable to the strikers during disputes which affected public services and to which it was itself a party'.[12]

Finally, the government's attitude was seen to change in the course of a second rail strike in 1917. In September of that year *La Fraternidad*, together with the new *Federación Obrera Ferrocarrilera* (Rail Workers' Federation) and the signalmen's union, launched a general strike for better wages and consistent working regulations. The strike paralysed most of the country's economy, particularly all activities linked to the export trade. This time, unlike the earlier rail strike of 1916, the government did not support the workers. Repression was used instead, and the press (including that of the socialists) openly condemned the strike. After a month the strike was lifted on the insistence of the rail engineers' union *La Fraternidad*, while the Rail Workers' Federation began to collapse as the rivalry between the various sectors sharpened with the skilled categories focusing on fringe benefits, while the unskilled concentrated on the wage claim. The Federation, which had grown rapidly up to that point, was later replaced by unions more amenable to negotiation. In 1918 the government banned any interruption of the rail service by the unions (or employers) in a bid to guarantee the profitable export contracts signed with the Allied powers. As Rock concludes, 'The main effect of the general strike on the railways in 1917 was thus that it crystallised the real nature of the relationship between foreign capital and the élite'.[13] The few strike movements which followed were rapidly crushed and the rail unions as a whole entered into a decline which was to last until the mid-1920s.

Taking a more general view of strikes during this period, we can note that 1917 marks the beginning of an upsurge in labour activity. The data for strikes in Buenos Aires alone as shown in Table 7.5 are eloquent testimony of this. These statistics, which do not include general strikes, show a dramatic rise in the number of strikes and workers on strike after 1917, which peaked in 1919. From then on there was a gradual decline until 1922 when the number of workers on strike was the lowest since 1909. Throughout the period from 1912 to 1922 wage demands lay behind one-third to a half of all strikes – more, if hours and conditions are added. Strikes over unionisation and more generally related to organisation at work, accounted for a third or more of the remaining strikes including a remarkable 62% in 1921 as the Radical government's attitude towards the unions hardened. In the interior provinces there were important strike movements in Rosario, Córdoba and Mendoza. During this period there was also a strong unionisa-

Table 7.5   Strikes in Buenos Aires city, 1912–1922

| Year | No of Strikes | No of Strikers | Wages | Hours | Causes (in percentage) | | |
					Condi-tions	Unioni-sation	Other
1912	99	8,992	37	16	6	27	13
1913	95	23,698	36	12	5	42	7
1914	64	14,137	50	8	8	33	1
1915	65	12,077	49	6	15	29	–
1916	80	24,321	40	3	19	31	8
1917	138	136,062	41	7	2	34	17
1918	196	133,042	40	12	2	35	15
1919	397	308,967	66	6	2	25	3
1920	206	134,015	45	4	9	40	2
1921	86	139,751	32	3	2	62	2
1922	116	4,737	31	5	9	47	16

Source: Annual bulletins, *Departamento Nacional de Trabajo*, Buenos Aires.

tion drive among the rural workers of the north-east (Chaco and Misiones provinces) led by the anarchists and in particular the syndicalists through the *Federación Obrera Marítima* (Maritime Workers' Federation).

There were various underlying reasons for this strike wave. First of all, the increased political freedom following the Radical victory of 1916 encouraged workers to pose demands they might previously have shelved and to attempt to reconquer rights they had lost: hence the increase in struggles in defence of, or to rebuild, the trade unions. Secondly, the improvement in the general economic situation after 1917 stabilised employment, allowing wage claims to be pursued more easily. Thirdly, the government's failure to control the rail workers through 'moderate' unions and the repression of the *frigorífico* and municipal workers led to an impasse in the Radicals' labour policy, hence sharpening labour discontent. Finally, from mid-1918 onwards, the repercussions of European revolutionary politics after the armistice, and in particular the Russian Revolution, reintroduced the idea of imminent revolution into the discourse and practice of the local labour movement.

These factors, which encouraged the upsurge in labour militancy, were set in the wider context of broad social crisis which affected the whole society. The continuous process of modernisation and urbanisation centred around Buenos Aires had included a shift of the working-class population from the inner-city tenements, the *conventillos*, to the new suburban quarters, a process which was completed in the 1920s. The emergence of new intermediate layers in the cities, including the children of the early immigrants, led to a questioning of the educational system, as access to knowledge became a recognised means of upward social mobility. Yrigoyen had no problem in broadening the catchment of the primary and secondary level education, which was favoured by the bourgeoisie as a whole. At university level, however, demands for increased participation clashed with the archaic administrative structure and led to the massive mobilisation of students which began in Córdoba in 1918. This movement for university reform succeeded in winning a tripartite system of university government (staff, students and graduates) and freedom of teaching, which spread throughout the country and ultimately to the rest of Latin America.[14] The student strike gained the support of the labour movement in Córdoba and when the university was closed down the students held their meetings at one of the local union headquarters. This was an early example of the 'worker-student alliance' which was to have considerable importance in a later period.

The *Semana Trágica* of 1919

It was in this general climate of working-class militancy and wider social crisis that a strike movement broke out in January 1919 which became known as the *Semana Trágica* (Tragic Week). This bloody episode is one of the events in the history of the labour movement which has been most written about.[15] It began in the city of Buenos Aires on 7 January 1919 when the police launched a fierce attack on the Vasena metallurgical plant workers, who had been on strike for some days. The following day, a peaceful procession followed the cortège of one of the workers who had been killed. Throughout the day, the anarchist FORA V denounced repression and called for a revolutionary response. That afternoon it called for a general strike the next day, to which several unions sympathetic to the anarchists agreed. On 9 January a large march began from the Socialist Party Headquarters in Nueva Pompeya suburb for the funeral of another worker. It was led by 150 armed workers and the FORA V leadership. When the 200,000 strong procession reached the Vasena works a fierce gun battle with police broke out, and this continued to the cemetery gates. That afternoon, as the police were overwhelmed by the workers, the government decreed the mobilisation of the army, which promptly marched on the city.

The much larger syndicalist FORA IX confederation had till that point been concerned with a separate maritime strike. So as not to be outflanked by the anarchists it called a general strike for 10 January against the repression. With the syndicalists backing this call, the general strike on 10 and 11 January was total. After that it began to decline as the level of repression was stepped up and as individual unions began to break ranks. As the strike wave subsided the repression got worse. The police, the army and groups of right-wing civilians launched themselves on the workers' quarters, raiding union buildings and murdering workers. According to the socialist press the final toll was 700 dead and 4,000 injured. Repression had centred on the Jewish community, partly as a result of a police-concocted 'Bolshevik plot' which was supposed to be planning to seize power under the leadership of a Russian Jewish journalist, Pedro Wald, who was a member of the Socialist Party.

The background to the *Semana Trágica* is complex. At one level it appears to have been an immediate inorganic response to the police assault on the Vasena metal workers. It was not organic in the sense that it developed outside the framework of the political and trade union organisations of the labour movement. This does not mean that it was spontaneous in the sense that there were no organisers of the strike or of the street-fighting. It was also inorganic in that the strike had no clear political or economic objectives, and that the anarchists and syndicalists failed to provide these. Furthermore, the violent response of the workers to police repression was part of a long tradition in the labour movement, from the Red Week of 1909 onwards. At another more analytical level the 1919 events appear as the outcome of an accumulated social crisis. This had been caused by the continued political marginality of the working class, the conflictive national integration of the immigrants, and the ambiguous position of the sons and daughters of the early immigrants, who were politically Argentine while sharing 'foreign' cultural models and family background. To this social crisis of the working class we must add the broader social crisis discussed above.

It is also worth noting that the *Semana Trágica* showed the role of the armed forces in a new light.[16] Though the strike was lifted following negotiations between the government and the syndicalist FORA IX, it was the army's intervention which in fact re-established order, enabling negotiations to take place. The army intervened on its own initiative, and this was only later ratified by the government. This demonstrated the weakness of the political system and the growing influence of the now professional army. It also revealed a tendency, later to be confirmed, for the army to intervene, rather than the crisis-ridden conservative parties, when the Radical government met an impasse. This was precisely what happened in September 1930 when a military coup overthrew the Radical government.

As to the labour movement itself, the electoral reforms of 1912 had not automatically broken the anti-political and anti-parliamentary traditions of the working class. This could be seen in the political hegemony of the syndicalists, the continued relevance of the anarchists and the great difficulty the socialists had in becoming a mass political alternative at a national level. The clear dominance of the syndicalist FORA IX after 1915 was a product of the restructuring of the labour movement's relations with the state. The changes in the productive structure also led to a growing 'professional' orientation of the trade unions, but this could only partially overcome the deep social crisis of the country. This crisis of participation, or condition of marginality, was reflected in the events of 1919: in the participation of a great number of young people not directly involved in the strike and the support of the non-working-class population generally; the limited geographical scope of the movement which was largely restricted to Buenos Aires; and its inorganic nature already mentioned, the lack of a clear programme or objectives. That there was a latent crisis of integration is also indicated by the fact that after the *Semana Trágica* there was a resurgence of anarchism within the trade unions and of the strategy of smashing the state.

This leads to another point because, as we shall see in the following chapter, a section of the anarchists identified with the revolutionary breakthrough in Russia in 1917. With regard to the Russian Revolution it would be futile to seek a 'Bolshevik plot' in Argentina in 1919: the presumed 'president of the Soviet', Pedro Wald, was in fact freed by the judge in his subsequent trial. What the Russian Revolution did lead to in Argentina was a general political radicalisation and the renewal of the previous belief that the end of capitalism was near.

The *Semana Trágica* led to a process of political agitation and radicalisation which affected both the working class and the dominant classes. The general strike and the crisis of Yrigoyen's labour policy led to the creation of a reactionary self-defence movement organised by the conservative opposition and the right wing of Yrigoyen's own Radical Party. Already in 1918 the *Asociación del Trabajo* (Labour Association) had brought together the *frigorífico*, railway and export-house bosses along with the traditional *Sociedad Rural* (Rural Society) to form a primitive employers' federation. Its objective was to intervene in strikes to 'defend' the members' factories and to organise scab labour. Immediately after the 1919 general strike, the *Liga Patriótica Argentina* (Argentine Patriotic League), known also as the White Guards, were formed with the blessing of the employers, the military, sections of the church, the conservatives and a good part of the Radical Party. The League, recruited from among the sons of the oligarchy, became an assault group directed against the unions, the anarchists and above all the immigrants, in particular Russian Jews who were systematically accused of Bolshevism. This direct action against the labour movement had its intellectual counterpart in the resurgence of a nationalist current pledged to assert Hispanic values against the flood of foreign culture. Its politics were to support a 'strong' state against parliamentary democracy. In the course of the 1920s most of this current became identified with Mussolini's corporativist project in Italy.

The bloody end to the 1919 general strike did not lead immediately to a decline in labour struggles. As we saw in Table 7.5 above, 1919 was in fact a peak year for strikes, with 259 strikes involving over 100,000 workers in the first three months of the year alone. The trade unions also continued to expand, as we mentioned above. The most remarkable point was the resurgence of the anarchist FORA V. Its affiliate, the *Federación Obrera Local Bonaërense* (Buenos Aires Local Workers' Federation) received a monthly average of 148 pesos in dues in 1918, which rose to 1,041 pesos in 1920 representing an average monthly figure of 20,448 dues-paying workers.[17] According to its own estimates, the anarchist FORA V as a whole had 128 affiliated unions, representing 25,000 workers.[18] At an extraordinary FORA V congress in 1920 there were between 248 and 273 trade unions represented of which approximately 220 were FORA V affiliates (representing 180,000 workers) the rest being observers.[19] Finally, we note that the report sent from Argentina to the 1920 Berlin Congress of Anarcho-Syndicalists claimed the following membership for FORA V: 47,000 port workers, 43,000 transport workers, 28,000 agricultural workers and 35,000 workers in the Santa Fé local workers' federation.[20] Though the political crisis and the international climate favoured the growth of the anarchists, these figures seem to be exaggerated. However, there was a real increase of anarchist influence within the labour movement. After 1920 the anarchist FORA added the adjective 'Communist' to its name, becoming FORA C.

The second great crisis of the Radical government's labour policy occurred in the cold arid plains of Patagonia between 1920 and 1921. The Patagonia strikes were in a way the rural counterpart of the urban insurrectionary strike of 1919.[21] The strikes developed to the province of Santa Cruz, which had an archetypal *latifundio* (large estate) structure: 20 million hectares of land were held by a mere 600 landowners. Immigrants represented 43% of the total population and 70% of the working population. The workers included 4,432 rural *peones* (labourers), 3,297 day-workers, 1,178 in manual trades, 1,050 self-employed workers, 706 commerical employees and 671 ranch workers. The major aspect of the economy was sheep-rearing, wool being exported mainly to Britain. The only industries in the area were the British and American *frigoríficos* (meat-packing plants) situated mainly in port towns such as Río Gallegos and Puerto Deseado. Since the end of the First World War the fall of international wool prices had thrown the Patagonian regional economy into crisis. The big companies were being forced to liquidate their stocks at rock-bottom prices. For the working class the crisis also had the usual consequences of increased unemployment, a drop in wages and deteriorating working conditions.

Since the beginning of 1920 there had been several strikes in Río Gallegos and Puerto Deseado led by the local workers' federation. In July the workers of Río Gallegos called a general strike in the port and in the town's hotels. At the same time the workers' federation began to organise the rural *peones* who suffered barbaric levels of exploitation. In November 1920 the workers' organisations of the area called a general strike centred on the *peones*' demands. These included the payment of wages in money and not in kind, provision of hygienic living quarters, free lighting, one free afternoon per week to wash clothes, the right not to work outdoors in the rain and, above all, recognition of the *peones*' trade unions and workplace delegates. Organised into horse-mounted squads, the *peones* left work and rode around the *estancias* collecting provisions, horses and arms. When the government sent in the army to crush the strike, negotiations were held which led to the strike being lifted and the workers' demands being forwarded to the governor for arbitration.

The governor ruled in favour of the workers, and though this verdict was at first accepted by the *estancieros* (landowners) they then refused to recognise what they saw as yet another display of Radical weakness towards labour. A new general strike was called in October 1921 to enforce the agreement. The government again sent its troops to the southern provinces, with the broad mandate of 're-establishing order'. Under Colonel Varela the army engaged in vicious pursuit of the ill-armed and isolated *peones*. By December Varela's army had 'pacified' the area by sending over 1,500 strike leaders and ordinary workers to the firing squad. In most cases this occurred after they had surrendered and had been forced to dig their own graves. The British landowners of the area organised a reception in Varela's honour where they sang 'For he's a jolly good fellow'. With the workers' federation destroyed, the *estancieros* were able to reduce *peones'* wages. As for Varela, he was killed in 1923 by a bomb hurled by Kurt Wilckens, a German anarchist of the Tolstoyan tendency who did not believe in violence but thought that in extreme cases violence from above could only be answered in kind.

Notes

1. A. Dorfman (1970) *Historia de la Industria Argentina.* Buenos Aires, Solar Hachette, p. 304.
2. On the economic situation during the First World War see G. Di Tella and M. Zymelman (1973) *Los Ciclos Económicos Argentinos.* Buenos Aires, Paidos, Chapter 6.
3. *La Nación* (16 January 1919).
4. N. Repetto (1917) *Problemas de la Guerra*, Buenos Aires, Ideal Socialista.
5. *La Vanguardia* (1 May 1915).
6. J. Ingenieros (1914) "El suicidio de los bárbaros", *Caras y Caretas* (September).
7. Ibid.
8. *La Vanguardia* (7 March 1916).
9. *La Vanguardia* (19 April 1917).
10. *Historia del Socialismo Marxista en la República Argentina*, Buenos Aires, 1919.
11. For an overview of labour during the Yrigoyen period see D. Rock (1975) *Politics in Argentina 1890–1930. The Rise and Fall of Radicalism*, Cambridge, Cambridge University Press.
12. Ibid., p. 134.
13. Ibid., p. 145.
14. On the Córdoba University Reform movement see R.J. Walter, (1968) *Student Politics in Argentina. The University Reform and its Effects, 1918–1964.* New York, Basic Books.

15. For an overview see J. Godio (1972) *Le Semana Trágica de enero de 1919.* Buenos Aires, Granica, and the critique by D. Rock (1972) "La Semana Trágica y los usos de la historia". *Desarrollo Económico,* vol. 12, no. 45.

16. For a survey of the army's rise to prominence see R. Potash (1969). *The Army and Politics in Argentina, 1928–1945. Yrigoyen to Perón.* California, Stanford University Press.

17. *La Protesta* (19 September 1918).

18. *La Organización Obrera* (1 May 1921).

19. *Tribuna Obrera,* (1920) vo. 1, no. 10, also *El Libertario* (1920) vol. 1, no. 14.

20. *Bericht Die Internationale Syndikalistische Konferens. Gehöltin Zu Berlin.* December 1920.

21. On the Patagonia events see O. Bayer (1980) *La Patagonia Rebelde.* Mexico, Nueva Imágen.

8. The Russian Revolution in Argentina

Towards the end of 1918 several thousand workers marched through the main cities of Argentina to celebrate the first anniversary of the Russian Revolution. This marked the beginning of a period of political restructuring within the labour movement under the impact of the revolutionary wave then sweeping through Europe. This restructuring was not a simple reflection of events in Europe; it was modified by the particular reality of the labour movement and the country itself. The global significance of 1917 could only spread through particular mechanisms of diffusion, being interpreted and applied according to the concrete situation of each country.

Diffusion

The first news of the Russian Revolution arrived in Argentina through the international news agency network. As in Europe the press as a whole celebrated the fall of the Tsar as bringing hope of peace, thinking that the Tsar's vacillations in waging the war would now be overcome. The praise for the revolution from European socialists engaged in the imperialist war led to a confused perception of these events by the various currents of the Argentine labour movement. Though the revolution was seen as the result of the rising of the oppressed masses, its full significance as a historical movement was not at first clearly grasped. This confusion, introduced by the bourgeois press agencies, led one anarchist militant, M. Portiero, to write as late as 1919 that:

> The Russian Revolution is nothing more than a result of the excited temperament of the peasants, who, under pressure from a despotic and feudal regime and a war which was annihilating them, rose bloodthirstily against their most immediate tyrants, without understanding the cause of their problems.[1]

For the anarchists and socialists, though the revolution had overthrown Tsarism, to a 'peasant uprising' (as it was presented in the press) they could not be wholeheartedly sympathetic. For both currents, the peasants represented a survival of barbarism, as against the redemptive class: the industrial proletarians.

The second source of news on Russia was the foreign revolutionary press which began arriving in Argentina after 1917: *L'Avanti* from Italy, *L'Humanité* from France, *The Revolutionary Age* from the US, *Rote Fahne* from Germany, etc. This press began to recognise, particularly after April 1917, that the Russian Revolution represented the beginning of a new era of social transformation. This international workers' press helped to rectify the catastrophic and savage image presented by the bourgeois press, particularly with regard to the actions of the workers, the formation of the soviets and the role of the Bolsheviks.

After the October revolution when the Bolsheviks seized power, the diffusion of the new revolutionary ideas was to take new channels. Though the bourgeois press continued to disseminate its version of events there was now direct access to news from Russia itself, and to the writings of the revolutionary leadership. In the course of 1918 the International Socialist Party in Argentina published the new Soviet Constitution, and *On the Russian Revolution* by Lenin and Zinoviev. In 1919 their journal *Documentos del Progreso* (Documents of Progress) carried articles and speeches by Lenin, Trotsky, Zinoviev, Bukharin and others. In 1920 this same journal published Lenin's 'The reconstruction work of the Soviets' and Trotsky's 'The coming of Bolshevism', and in 1921 Lenin's 'Left-wing Communism – An infantile disorder'. After October a number of accounts by the early 'tourists of the revolution' also began to arrive in Argentina. The local press took up the accounts of life in revolutionary Russia by Arthur Ransome, W.T. Goode and the 'Bullit Report on Conditions in Russia'.[2] Local travellers also published their accounts: the anarchist Vidal Mata published his 'Impressions of a Trip to Russia' in 1921, and a local Russian resident, Komin Alexandrovsky, had his account 'Six Months in Revolutionary Russia' published in 1923 by *La Internacional* (The International), the press of the new Argentine Communist party.

This flood of publications radically changed the local perception of events in the Soviet Union. It was no longer seen as a disastrous movement which would continue to pursue the imperialist war. It was now seen as the beginning of a social revolution and an end to the war by the rising of the masses who were tired of being used as cannon-fodder. The revolution also required its local representatives who could carry out its national 'legitimisation'. It was a famous lecture by José Ingenieros in November 1918 on 'The historical significance of the Maximalist movement' which began this process.[3] Ingenieros was an intellectual who was recognised by anarchists, socialists and syndicalists alike, so he could speak with authority above party politics. He declared that Maximalism (Bolshevism) was the expression of a 'new order' which other nations would join as a result of the catastrophe of the war. For Ingenieros, the importance for America of the social revolution initiated in Europe lay in America's relation to European civilisation; as in Europe, its coming was inevitable, be it through the peaceful strength of the 'new ideals', or through the violence of the peoples.

The Ingenieros speech resounded throughout Latin America – it was commented on in Mexico, Brazil and Cuba.[4] In Argentina it was taken up by the anarchist, socialist and syndicalist press, and presented as a booklet. Even Portiero, the anarchist whose hostile view of the Russian Revolution was cited above, later recognised the Ingenieros speech as one of the fundamental influences in his understanding of these events.[5] Among intellectuals, views similar to those of Ingenieros were by no means uncommon. Leopoldo Lugones, Constancio Vigil and Anibal Ponce were among the intellectual figures who turned to Russia from diverse backgrounds to seek a new model, a new ideal. The writer Jorge Luis Borges published poems in the pro-Bolshevik magazine *Cuasimodo* under the pseudonym Alba Roja (Red Dawn).

The diffusion of the new ideal within the labour movement was carried out fundamentally by the militants, through publications of the International Socialist Party (later the Communist Party) and by a section of the anarchist movement which had shifted to a pro-Bolshevik position. The publications of the Communist International and of all the main Bolshevik leaders became available between 1918 and 1922. The anarcho-Bolsheviks published a newspaper called *Bandera Roja* (Red Flag) carrying this type of material, and they also produced 20,000 free copies of the *Boletín de la Liga de Educación Racionalista* (Bulletin of the Rationalist Education League), which carried articles by Lunacharsky, Gorky and Kollontai.

The Russian community

The repercussions of the Russian Revolution in Argentina were increased by the presence of a strong Russian community which had a long tradition of involvement in labour politics. Among those who came to Argentina were: a number of exiles from the defeated revolution in 1905; in 1907 and 1908 several sailors from the battleship Potemkin; and in 1909 the social democrat Boris Vladimirovich, who had participated in the Russian party's conference in Geneva in 1904.[6] Apart from this political immigration there had been a broader flow of immigrants from Russia, who by 1914 totalled 93,634 people, of whom 28,846 lived in Buenos Aires. Two points must be made concerning these figures: they include inhabitants from the whole Russian Empire, including Poles and other nationalities; and they were largely Russian Jews fleeing from the pogroms. A healthy workers' press emerged from this milieu, for example *Der Avangard* in 1908 and *Novi Mir* in 1914, and in 1905 a Russian library was established which became a cultural centre for the labour movement. The Russian emigrés were able to make the 'Russian question' an important issue in the local labour movement after 1905. In 1907 the South American

Printers' Congress held in Buenos Aires had solidarity with the Russian workers and the condemnation of the Tsarist regime as the only points of discussion in relation to the international labour movement.

In 1917 the Russian community in Argentina received the news of the revolution with great enthusiasm. It led to a certain reunification of the various political tendencies within the local Russian socialist movement. In 1917 they established a Federal Organisation of Russian Workers in South America, which published a weekly, *Golos Truda* (The Voice of Labour). In 1918 another Russian language journal *Bread and Work* appeared, and the local Jewish workers' organisation, the Bund, published *Avantgard*, edited by Pedro Wald. Within the Federation the anarcho-Bolsheviks were the dominant tendency. The predominance of the anarchists within the Russian community and the importance which the anarcho-Bolsheviks were to achieve later, was due to the early 'anarchistic' perception of events in Russia. In 1919 the Federation held its third congress where it resolved to send a delegate to the Second Congress of the Comintern and seek recognition as the sole representative of the Russian workers in South America.

The Russian emigrés also contributed a great number of articles on the history of the Russian revolutionary movement to the local workers' press. *Documentos del Progreso* (Documents of Progress) published a lengthy article 'Studies on the Russian Revolution' by M. Jarochewsky in its October 1919 issue. *Bandera Roja* (Red Flag) published a series of biographies of Russian anarchists by Stepniak in the course of 1919.

Assessment

The various political currents within the labour movement were to make different assessments of the Russian Revolution's significance and its relevance to Argentina. Contrary to the canons of Leninist orthodoxy the revolution was not seen as a proletarian class revolution, but rather as a popular revolution with a certain peasant content. It was seen as a profound movement of the whole society; for this reason it was called a 'social revolution'. This somewhat ambiguous assessment allowed each tendency to find what it wanted in the Russian Revolution. The socialists saw it as a democratic revolution and fervently supported the government which emerged from the February revolution, and in particular Kerensky. The anarchists saw it as a revolutionary convulsion, a continuing process in which the masses controlled the streets in spite of the constitutional government.

The revolution was not seen as two distinct episodes – February and October – but rather as a single process which began with the fall of the Tsar and in which the Bolshevik seizure of power represented merely an internal change. Ingenieros, for example, referred to October as 'the crisis of the Bolsheviks'. This perception allowed the Socialist Party to support the

Bolshevik regime (though they had previously backed Kerensky against Lenin) in so far as the Bolsheviks were: 'the most daring socialist fraction, which best understood at the precise moment what the needs of the country were, and moved resolutely to serve them'.[7]

The October revolution was thus seen as setting the stable socialist course for the revolution, though fierce controversy raged at this point. One anarchist tendency began to reassess its critique of 'socialism', which had apparently been redeemed by the Russian revolutionaries, whereas another current simply deemed that the Bolsheviks were not socialists at all.[8] For a time agreement was reached around the term 'maximalism' which was interpreted as the expression of the maximum aspirations of the exploited.

Different tendencies within the labour movement were to seek their own 'legitimisation' by appropriating the Russian Revolution for themselves. For the anarchists, their hopes and aspirations were confirmed: the revolution was a rising of all the exploited; its methods were direct action and insurrection rather than adherence to the parliamentary system; it was also institutionalised through new means of political representation (the Soviets) as against bourgeois forms of democracy. Until 1919 no anarchist fraction dared criticise the Russian Revolution. It was only when the confrontation with the anarchists in Russia began, as the Bolshevik regime sought stabilisation, that the old and prestigious journal *La Protesta* (The Protest) linked to the anarcho-individualists, clearly condemned the Soviet regime as a new dictatorship, and drew its distance from Bolshevism. However, for another sector of the anarchists, expressed through the journals *Bandera Roja* (Red Flag), *El Trabajo* (Work) and others, the Russian Revolution continued to be a source of legitimacy.

These debates formed the subject of a pamphlet *Anarchism and Maximalism* written in 1919 by Santiago Locascio, editor of the journal *Via Libre* (Free Road or Path to Freedom). He not only sought to demonstrate the 'anarchist' character of the Russian Revolution but also to draw out points of disagreement. He argued that article 2 of the Soviet constitution – 'The USSR is based on the principle of a free union of free nations forming a federation of national Soviet republics'[9] was equivalent to the anarchist social ideal – a federation of citizens who will form a free association of nations. Locascio went on to define his terms: 'Maximalism is the revolution. Anarchism is the full realisation of man's real rights'.[10] He thus effectively denied any contradiction between the two doctrines, and opened the way for justifying the 'dictatorship of the proletariat' as simply an original aspect of this revolution.

The importance of the anarcho-Bolsheviks during the years between 1918 and 1921 was considerable. In 1919 *Bandera Roja* (Red Flag) sold 20,000 copies daily until it was closed down by the government. In 1920 this current gained control of FORA V and in 1921 took it into the *Unión Sindical Argentina* (Argentine Syndicates' Union) along with the syndicalist- and communist-led unions. Such was the weight and prestige of this current that it prevented the International Socialist Party (Communist Party after 1920) from becoming the sole representative of Bolshevism in Argentina, in spite of the latter party's labour of diffusion and propaganda. The anarcho-Bolsheviks could further point to the parliamentary emphasis of the Communist Party and to the Amsterdam 'yellow' International, already anathematised by Zinoviev. This balance of forces was to change as the Comintern theses on parliamentary work became known, along with the '21 Conditions', and so on.

The South American Russian Workers' Federation mandated Alexandrovsky, its delegate to the Second Congress of the Comintern in Moscow in 1920, to 'warn the Russian revolutionaries about the manoeuvres of the false delegate of the working class; Penelón' (the CP delegate). Alexandrovsky was close to *Bandera Roja* (Red Flag) as we can see from the report 'The Labour Movement in Argentina', which was the first ever to be presented to the Communist International.[11]

Labour movement realignment

The Russian Revolution had thoroughly shaken up the labour movement in Argentina. It was a real revolution which not only had survived, but was spreading through Europe. It was seen as the start of a world movement which would soon reach the American continent. Thus the labour movement had to define its position towards this revolution and the new international movement which it had spawned: the Third, or Communist, International. A process of realignment within the labour movement was inevitable.

Within the Socialist Party, the group *Claridad* (Clarity) was formed in 1920, led by Socialist senator Del Valle Iberlucea. *Claridad* pressed for the party's affiliation to the Communist International. At an extraordinary congress held in Bahía Blanca in 1921, this tendency managed to win the vote on dis-affiliation from the Second International, but lost the vote to affiliate to the Third International. Following this congress most of the left opposition, though not its leader Iberlucea, left the Socialist Party to join the Communist Party.

In the revolutionary syndicalist movement a pro-Bolshevik trend emerged in 1919 to form an autonomous federation. It sent A. Pellegrini as delegate to the Fourth Congress of the Comintern and the Red International of Labour Unions (RILU) Congress in 1923, where he joined the CP delegates, F. Penelón and J. Greco.[12]

With the formation of the Communist International in 1919 the evolution of the International Socialist Party to a 'marxist-leninist' position was completed. In December 1920 it accepted the '21 Conditions' set by the Comintern for potential affiliates and became its official section in Argentina. In 1921 Rodolfo Ghioldi attended the Comintern's Third Congress, where this affiliation was ratified.

In the trade union movement the process of realignment began in earnest in 1921 when the Red International of Labour Unions was formed. In the syndicalist FORA IX, the debate centred around the withdrawal of the communist-led unions, who had gone because the confederation had remained affiliated to the Amsterdam International. For its part, the anarchist FORA V held an extraordinary congress in October 1920, where the pro-Bolshevik tendency gained a majority. They could not get agreement on affiliation to any international body, the congress calling instead for a new movement along the lines of the First International. The congress also added the adjective 'communist' to FORA, as mentioned above. The supremacy of the pro-Bolshevik tendency only lasted until 1921, when a new congress resulted in the victory of the 'hard' anarcho-syndicalists who promptly removed the 'Communist' from FORA. Left in a minority position, the anarcho-Bolsheviks joined forces with the syndicalists and some independent unions to form the *Unión Sindical Argentina* (Argentine Syndicates' Union) in 1922. This new confederation was quite sympathetic to the Russian Revolution but did not join any international body.

This process of realignment within the labour movement represented a certain turn to the left, apparently contradicting the tendency towards reformist communism of 1918-19. It was based on generalised revolutionary expectations after the triumph of the Russian Revolution and the growing upsurge in Europe. The Russian Revolution had a powerful mobilising effect. As Carlos Astrada wrote in the anarchist review *Cuasimodo* in 1921:

> Russia is something more than a national or geographic category; it is the great myth which has taken root in the spirit of the people and the consciousness of each man.[13]

The triumphant revolution created a mobilising myth, and the working class was reconstituted as the historical universal subject which would achieve the transformation of society.

The revolution also created a Utopia, the vision of a New Jerusalem—the Universal Republic of Soviets. This idea, which eventually proved illusory, marked a clean break in the ideological structuring of the labour movement, and in its forms of appropriation of revolutionary theory, particularly of Marxism. With the formulation of the Leninist theory of imperialism, and the Comintern theses on the backward countries, Marxism was renewed. As Paris has pointed out, Marxism became anew 'a universal doctrine, by proposing an anti-imperialism which broke with the exclusively workerist and profoundly European reference points of the original doctrine'.[14] This process not only affected the local Communist Party, but nearly all the anti-imperialist currents within the labour movement, and even Peronism in the 1940s (see Chapter 10).

Notes

1. M.S. Porteiro, (1919), Los partidos reaccionarios frente a la Revolución Rusa, *Bandera Roja* no. 35, 4 May.

2. A. Ransome, (1919–20), Diez Semanas en Rusia, *Documentos del Progreso*; W.T. Goode, (1921) El Bolshevismo en la obra, *Documentos del Progreso*; Informe Bullit sobre las condiciones en Rusia, *La Vanguardia*, January 1920. The first two works were first published in *The Manchester Guardian*, the third in *The New Statesman* (New York).

3. The reception of Ingenieros' speech is discussed in D. Kamia, (1957) *Entre Yrigoyen e Ingenieros*. Buenos Aires, Meridión. See also the article by his disciple A. Ponce, (1980) La revolution d'Octobre et les intellectuels argentins, in M. Löwy (ed.) *Le Marxisme en Amérique Latine*. Paris, Maspèro.

4. For its reception in Brazil and Cuba see M. Bandeira, (1980) *O Ano Vermelho*, São Paulo, Editora Brasiliense; and E. Dumpierre, (1977) *La Revolución de Octubre y su Repercusión en Cuba*, La Habana, Editorial de Ciencias Sociales.

5. M.S. Portiero, (1919) *Los partidos reaccionarios frente a la Revolución Rusa.*

6. For further details see O. Bayer, (1975) *Los Anarquistas Expropiadores*. Buenos Aires, Galerna; and A. Cherenko, and A. Shliajov, (1981) "Participantes de la Primera Revolución Rusa en América Latina", *América Latina*, no. 1–2.

7. N. Repetto, (1918) *Puntos de Vista Sobre la Cuestion Rusa*, Buenos Aires, La Vanguardia, pp. 8–9.

8. see S. Locascio, (1919) *Anarquismo y Maximalismo*. Buenos Aires.

9. Ibid., pp. 2–3.

10. Ibid., p. 40.

11. *Le Mouvement Communiste International (1921).* Rapports addresses au Deuxième Congres de l'Internationale Communiste, 1920, Petrograd, Editions de l'Internationale Communiste, pp. 367–375.

12. *La Internacional* (24 February 1923).

13. C. Astrada, (1921) El renacimiento del mito, *Cuasimodo*, II no. 20.

14. R. Paris, *Diffusion et appropriation du Marxisme en Amérique Latine,* Colloque "Marx Marxismes", Programe UNESCO, Paris, June 1983.

9. Syndicalists, Socialists and Communists (1922–1929)

For the working class the 1920s were marked by the economic transformations of the post-war period. The protectionist moves begun by the imperialist countries spread to Argentina, though there they developed in an 'inorganic' manner, as Dorfman notes.[1] During the First World War, the national industrial sector was given a boost, and although world trade resumed in 1918, this tendency continued under the Alvear government (1922). Alvear announced protectionist measures to encourage national industry, to complement an increased promotion of agrarian exports.

Though there is no official data on the extent of industrial development, the study by Alejandro Bunge in 1926 is worth citing:

Table 9.1   Manufacturing industry, 1926

No. of Establishments	61,000
No. of Workers	600,000
Capital Invested	2,467 million pesos
Installed Capacity	1,000,000 hp
Value of Production	2,886 million pesos

Source: A. Bunge, (1929) *Revista de Economía Argentina*, p. 168, cited in A. Dorfman, (1970) *Historia de la Industria Argentina*. Buenos Aires, Solar-Hachette, p. 358.

If we compare these figures with those of 1914 (see Chapter 7) we find that the number of establishments had risen by 30%, the number of workers by 50%, capital investment by 50%, installed capacity by 45% and the value of production by 40%. This industrial expansion followed previous lines of development, being mainly concentrated in Buenos Aires and the littoral provinces. The process of capital concentration was most clear-cut in the textile industry and to a lesser degree in the metallurgical branches. The level of mechanisation in the textile branch created a genuine textile manufacturing *industry* for the first time.

With regard to labour, the level of immigration picked up after 1919, though the tendency was for a growing predominance of local-born workers in manufacturing, as the children of first-generation immigrants (Argentine through *jus solis*) entered industry. The economic recovery led to some stabilisation of real wages, and unemployment rates returned to their pre-war levels. The 1920s saw a considerable decline in the level of strikes after the peak year of 1919 as we see in Table 9.2, which also shows the evolution of real wages in this period.

Table 9.2   Strikes and wage rates in Buenos Aires city 1919–1930

Year	No. of Strikes	No. of Strikers	Real Wages (1929=100)
1919	397	308,967	57
1920	206	134,015	59
1921	86	139,751	73
1922	116	41,737	84
1923	93	19,190	86
1924	77	277,078	85
1925	89	39,142	89
1926	67	15,880	90
1927	58	38,236	95
1928	135	28,170	101
1929	113	28,271	100
1930	125	29,331	91

Sources: Strike data from annual bulletins, *Departamento Nacional del Trabajo,* Buenos Aires. Wages data from G. Di Tella and M. Zymelman, (1973) *Los Ciclos Económicos Argentinos*, Buenos Aires. Paidos, p. 175, p. 200, p. 229.

The outstanding number of strikers in 1924 was due to trade union resistance to a new pensions law, a struggle we will examine in the next section. The cause of strikes in the 1920s followed the pattern of the previous decade, with approximately 40% centred around trade union and organisational matters, while around 35% were in pursuit of wage claims. It is also worth noting that strikes occurred mainly in small industries (of less than 50 workers) and to a lesser extent in the medium-sized plants (51–500 workers) with only a handful of strikes taking place in the large plants employing more than 500 workers.[2]

In this period there was a continuation of the integrationist policy begun under the first Yrigoyen government. Among the important labour laws approved by Congress we can mention the 1925 wage protection legislation which banned fines and made payment in cash obligatory, and the 1929 law regulating working hours, which established the 8-hour day, and the 6-hour day in unhealthy conditions. The 8-hour day did not extend to agrarian and domestic labour, however. Social security legislation was also extended with a new pension scheme for state-sector workers.

Decline of the trade unions

During the economic upturn of the 1920s there was a decline in the trade union movement as a whole. For example, the syndicalist FORA IX, which claimed to have grown to 700,000 in 1920, claimed only 46,562 members at its eleventh Congress in 1921. The anarchist FORA V, which in 1920 had claimed approximately 180,000 members, could claim only 60,000 members at its ninth Congress in 1923; and at its tenth Congress in 1929 this figure had declined to 40,000. Within this context of a general retreat of the labour movement, there was a certain redistribution of forces among the various trade union confederations.

The *Unión Sindical Argentina* (Argentine Syndicates' Union) had been formed in 1922 by 102 trade unions from FORA IX, 14 from FORA V and 60 independent unions. These 176 trade unions together covered around 262,000 workers. The *Unión Sindical Argentina* had the political support of the socialists, the communists, the syndicalists, and the anarcho-Bolsheviks who had been expelled from FORA V. It was this last sector, along with the more pro-Bolshevik syndicalists (who had eclipsed the old reformist leadership) which held the upper hand within the new trade union confederation, giving it a much more revolutionary image than the old FORA IX. The confederation openly espoused 'class struggle', and described the epoch now opening up as 'revolutionary'. It stressed the struggle for the maximum programme for social revolution – summed up in the slogan 'All power to the trade unions!' – which set it apart from socialists and communists alike. It reaffirmed the practice of trade union independence, the critique of parliamentarianism, and the incompatibility of holding trade union posts and public office. This was to lead to a split by the socialists, who argued for the right of workers to participate in parliamentary affairs and who, together with the old-guard syndicalists, urged a more reformist course of action for the union movement. The communists were also split off, because of their support for working class electoral participation, and because they failed to persuade the confederation to join the Red International of Labour Unions (RILU).

The Socialists withdrew from the *Unión Sindical Argentina* in 1924, after its first Congress. The socialist-led trade unions remained within the Socialist Trade Union Information Committee until 1926, when a new confederation was formed: the *Confederación Obrera Argentina* (Argentine Workers' Confederation). In spite of its reduced number of affiliates – 12 unions and one local federation – this socialist body gained considerable influence. This was because it gained the support of the hitherto independent, powerful Railway Confederation – embracing *La Fraternidad* and *Unión Ferroviaria* – with its 60,000 members. Another 10,000 members were affiliated by the *Unión Obreros Municipales* (Municipal Workers' Union), giving the socialist confederation a total of 79,650 members in 1926.

The communist-led unions withdrew from the *Unión Sindical Argentina* in 1926 after its second Congress, and remained unaffiliated until 1929 when the *Comité Sindical de Unidad Clasista* (Trade Union Committee of Class Struggle Unity) was formed. Judging by the small number of trade unions from Argentina (seven unions and one federation) which attended the 1929 communist regional union conference in Montevideo,[3] communist influence in the labour movement was quite low.

Towards the end of the decade, this picture of divisions within a weakened labour movement was to change with a move towards the creation of a united labour confederation. A movement towards trade union unity was formed in 1929 by the *Unión Sindical Argentina*, the socialist *Confederación Obrera Argentina* and a number of independent unions. This led to the creation in September 1930 of the first *Central General de Trabajadores* (General Labour Confederation).[4] The CGT was at first composed of the 90,000 members of the socialist confederation and 15,000 from the *Unión Sindical Argentina*. After the inaugural meeting several other unions affiliated: the 10,000-strong tram-drivers' union, the 7,500-strong state workers' association and the 2,000-strong telephonists' union. By the end of 1930 the first united labour confederation in Argentina could claim 130,000 members.

The formation of the CGT – a body which has continued to the present day – put an end to the long-term dichotomy between on the one hand, a relatively stable social and political situation with a state open to negotiation, and on the other, a radicalised labour movement which did not even organise the most important trades. The trade union movement now achieved a unity it had previously lacked, and adopted a more 'moderate' attitude which was more attuned to the orientation of the state. The CGT was formed as an apolitical organisation, though it was not 'anti-politics' as earlier confederations had been. The dominant political tendencies within the CGT were a fraction of the syndicalists who had dropped all revolutionary pretensions, and in second place, the now openly reformist socialists. The CGT professed an outlook of 'political abstention', arguing for a 'professional' relationship with the state, which it hoped would be willing to negotiate with the working class. Two groupings remained outside the CGT: FORA V, which was steadily losing strength; and the communist unions, totalling some 5,000 members, which criticised the collaborationism of the new labour confederation.

Political developments

Paradoxically perhaps, the general weakening of the trade unions in the 1920s was matched by a radicalisation of the labour movement's political expression. The anarchist FORA V remained an important factor; the traditionally 'moderate' big rail unions were marginalised within the movement; and the revolutionary syndicalists and anarcho-Bolsheviks set the political tone. This political radicalism was an indirect effect of the

Russian Revolution, but also represented the dying throes of a labour movement which had not changed with the times. This movement had effectively lost its traditional identity in the course of the process of social and political integration begun in 1916; it had yet to forge a new one.

In 1923 this radicalism was manifest in the labour movement's fierce resistance to a new pensions law, which culminated in a general strike. Two other general strikes showed this radical political outlook: in 1923 a general strike was called to protest the murder in prison of Kurt Wilkens, the avenger of the Patagonia massacre; and in 1927 a general strike formed part of the broad international solidarity campaign for the reprieve of Sacco and Vanzetti.

Many of the debates within the labour movement during the 1920s centred around the strategy for 'social revolution' in the light of the Russian Revolution.[5] A further source of dissension was the attitude to be taken towards the international labour organisations. The *Unión Sindical Argentina* remained independent, the socialist-led *Confederación Obrera Argentina* was affiliated to the Amsterdam International, and the anarchist FORA joined the Berlin-based International Workers' Association. The communists called constantly for the Argentine trade unions to affiliate to the Red International of Labour Unions (RILU) and in 1929 were instrumental in setting up the RILU-associated *Confederación Sindical Latinoamericana* (Latin America Trade Union Confederation).

A further deabate in the labour movement was over the best form of trade union organisation. Some favoured industry-wide unions and others trade-based unions. The anarchists flatly rejected industrial unions – at its 1923 congress FORA V actually withdrew its recognition of the *Federación Obrera Portuaria* (Port Workers' Federation) over this issue. While the other confederations had many trade-based unions, they also accepted, and in fact promoted, industry-wide unions. This position recognised more clearly the changing structure of industry in Argentina.

Finally, we shall assess the role of the socialists and the communists, the two currents which could have been expected to impose a new image on the labour movement, either reformist or revolutionary. The expulsion of the left opposition in 1922 did not put an end to the dissension within the Socialist Party which had begun in 1917.[6] On the contrary, the party's relative withdrawal from the trade union movement gave increased importance to its political, that is parliamentary, role. Electoral advances in Buenos Aires city and province were in fact to lead to a split in 1928 which was the most serious in the party's history.

Several years of economic prosperity and political stability had led a sector of the party to adopt pro-liberal positions and to establish links with the anti-Yrigoyen sector of the Radical Party, which was led by Alvear. The dissidents split in 1927, forming the Independent Socialist Party which presented its own candidates in the 1928 elections (won by Yrigoyen). The socialist 'independents' gained 50,000 votes in Buenos Aires city against 45,000 votes for the old party, thus splitting the socialist vote. They went on to triumph over the Radicals in the 1930 congressional elections for the city, gaining 110,000 votes against 83,000 for the Socialists and 82,000 for the Radicals. Only one deputy resulted from these votes, representing the worst electoral defeat for the socialists since 1912. The socialist 'independents' centred their politics around an attack on the Yrigoyen administration which came to power in 1928. They allied with the conservatives and the anti-Yrigoyen Radicals to attack the President's 'populism'. They also criticised the government's lack of interest in the deteriorating economic, political and social situation following the 1929 international capitalist crisis. In 1930 the Independent Socialist Party threw its weight behind a military conspiracy to overthrow Yrigoyen, receiving its reward when party leader Antonio De Pomasso became Minister for Agriculture under the new military regime.

For the Communist Party the 1920s was also a period of internal dissension, which was only stifled in 1928 with the definitive 'Stalinisation' of the party.[7] These were the years in which the party ranks were purged of dissidents and when the integration into the apparatus of the Comintern was achieved. Already in 1920 there were two clear tendencies: those who argued for a united front with the socialists and those who stressed the value of economic struggles in the new revolutionary era opened up since 1917. The latter published a journal called *Chispa* (Spark) and were therefore known as the *chispistas*, while the first tendency was called *frentista* ('frontist'). The *frentista* tendency was expelled from the party in 1923 by an alliance of the *chispistas* and the centrist leadership. The *chispistas* were themselves expelled in 1925 when the leadership was able to obtain a majority at the party congress. Until then the *chispistas* had dictated the political line of the party, but had been unable to replace the leadership, which owed its strength and legitimacy to its links with the Comintern.

With the right and left opposition expelled, the centrist leadership consolidated its position and became faithful executors of the international communist movement in Argentina. In 1925 the 'Bolshevisation' of the party was carried out following Comintern instructions. In 1926 the leadership of the Argentine CP was placed in charge of the International's South American Bureau, and its organ *La Correspondencia Sudamericana* (South American Correspondence) was edited by the party's general secretary, José F. Penelón. The Comintern's turn towards a 'class against class' policy after 1927 led to a new split in Argentina, this time led by Penelón himself. He had opposed the 'ultra-left' turn of 1928, arguing for the need to maintain working-class unity and for a reformist political orientation. Penelón and his supporters were expelled from the party in 1927. They went on to form a dissident CP which became known as *Concentración Obrera* (Workers' Concentration) in 1930. This party carried out strong reformist intervention in Buenos Aires where Penelón remained a deputy until 1954.

It was only at the 1928 party congress that the CP 'historic leadership' took up its position. This was achieved only after the gradual expulsion of all opponents, and through a letter from the Comintern leadership in 1928 which imposed the 'Third Period' line on the rank and file and legitimised the leadership's position. The reconstituted party played a central role in organising the First Latin American Conference of Communist Parties in Buenos Aires in 1929.[8] This conference, with Jules Humbert-Droz as the Comintern's representative, set the 'Third Period' course for Latin American communism as a whole.

Notes

1. A. Dorfman, (1970) *Historia de la Industria Argentina* Buenos Aires, Solar Hachette, p. 358.

2. Ibid., p. 264.

3. For a report see *Internacional Sindical Roja*, June 1929, Paris.

4. On the formation of the CGT see R. Rotondaro, (1971) *Realidad y Cambio en el Sindicalismo*. Buenos Aires, Editorial Pleamar, pp. 130–150.

5. For the syndicalist, socialist, and communist views see respectively S. Marotta, (1961) *El Movimiento Sindical Argentino*, Buenos Aires, Lascio; J. Oddone, (1949). *Gremialismo Proletario Argentino* Buenos Aires, La Vanguardia and R. Iscaro, (1958) *Orígen y Desarrollo del Movimiento Sindical Argentino*. Buenos Aires, Editorial Anteo.

6. On the Socialist Party see R. Walter, (1977) *The Socialist Party of Argentina 1890–1930*. Austin, University of Texas, Institute of Latin America Studies; and also J. Ratzer, (1981) *El Movimiento Socialista en Argentina*. Buenos Aires, Ediciones Agora.

7. On the Communist Party see the official party history: Comité Central (1947) *Esbozo de Historia del Partido Comunista de la Argentina*. Buenos Aires, Editorial Anteo; and also J. Abelardo Ramos, (1969) *Historia del Stalinismo en la Argentina*. Buenos Aires, Ediciones del Mar Dulce.

8. For a report see *El Movimiento revolucionario latino-americano, versiones de la Primera Conferencia comunista latino-americana*, June 1929, Buenos Aires, Correspondencia Sud-Americana.

10. Labour Realignment and the Rise of Perón (1930–1944)

The year 1930 was a watershed in Argentina's economic and political history. It also marks the beginning of a period of transition for the labour movement because between 1945 and 1946 the nationalist Peronist movement began its long dominance over the working class. Though it would be wrong to read Argentina's history before 1945 as the mere pre-history of Peronism, it is undoubtedly true that Peronism represented a fundamental 'remaking' of the Argentine working class. This chapter examines the various interpretations of the rise of Peronism within the labour movement. First we examine the changing composition of the working class due to industrialisation and internal migration in the 1930s. We follow the evolution of labour politics after the formation of the CGT in 1930 and the splits in 1935 and 1943. There was a fundamental realignment of the labour movement, which explains how a movement such as Peronism was able to arise at that time. As in other chapters we survey the pattern of strikes in this period, focusing on some of the major workers' actions. We also examine the policies and actions of the working-class parties, focusing in this case on the Communist Party which played a major role in the rise of industrial unions during this period.

The international economic crisis of 1929 upset Argentina's agro-export economy dominant since the 1860s, as the prices of agrarian produce slumped. A lucid fraction of the agrarian oligarchy decided to embark on a limited policy of industrialisation so that in future the economy would not be so dependent on international fluctuations.[1] This entailed an increase in import duties on consumer goods, creation of multiple exchange rates to favour exporters, and a depreciation of the peso. This did not represent a break with imperialism, as can be seen by the Roca-Runciman pact of 1933. Under this pact Britain agreed not to restrict the entry of Argentine chilled beef and Argentina granted Britain 85% of the import licences it required to consolidate the British meat-packing plants (*frigoríficos*) in Argentina. Through a range of other trade and import duty agreements the Argentine government ratified the traditional arrangements of unequal exchange imposed by British imperialism.

In politics, the overthrow of the Radical government of Hipólito Yrigoyen in 1930 marked the beginning of a long line of military interventions. The first military president, General Uriburu, aimed to instal a full-blown corporativist system in Argentina and to dispense with elections. In 1932, however, the traditional ruling class, committed to maintaining a façade of constitutional rule, imposed the presidency of General Justo. Popular discontent was circumvented by controlled elections and open fraud. These reached such a level that nationalist writers have dubbed the 1930s the 'Infamous Decade'.[2] In 1938 President Ortiz took over from Justo who was succeeded by his vice-president, Ramón Castillo, in 1940. In 1943 a new military coup was carried out to prevent the succession to the presidency of a pro-British candidate. The coup in its turn provided the vehicle for the rise of Colonel Perón.

Transition period (1930–1935)

Industrialisation accelerated in the 1930s in response to the depression and to the need to produce locally manufactured goods which had previously been imported. The 1941 industrial census showed that 40% of all existing industrial establishments had been formed since 1930. Import substitution was particularly marked in the textile industry– in 1930 only 8% of cotton textiles consumed was produced locally; by 1934 this had risen to 31% and by 1939 it had reached 58%. Perhaps of greater long-term importance was the rise of a dynamic metal- and machine-production sector. This not only produced a growth in the size of the working class but a change in its internal composition. Though small-scale industry persisted, the industrial working class was now increasingly employed by large establishments. For example, the ten largest textile firms (only 4% of all establishments) employed 44% of the textile work-force and accounted for a similar proportion of the country's total production. Figures for 1937 show that factories with over 250 workers (barely 0.5% of the total) employed one-third of the total number of industrial workers. Taking the secondary sector as a whole we find that the manufacturing industry employed half of the labour force in 1946 against 30% in 1936; conversely the artisan sector (less than 10 workers) dropped from 52% to 30% of the labour-force over the same period.

Where did workers come from to toil in the new factories? Before 1930, as we have seen, a major factor in the make-up of the working class was international migration. After 1930 this slowed down to a trickle and was largely replaced by internal migration from Argentina's impoverished rural areas. Nearly half the total number of unemployed in the early 1930s were from the rural areas. Not surprisingly, the mid-1930s saw a wave of internal migration to the cities to escape poverty and unemployment. Overseas immigration had averaged an annual 88,000 people prior to 1930; during the 1930s the annual average was 7,300 people and between 1940 and 1946 this fell to 5,500. According to Germani's calculations, in 1945 internal migrants represented three-quarters of the unskilled workers in

Buenos Aires, three-fifths of the semi-skilled and about half of the skilled workers.[3] In 1935 there were less than 500,000 internal migrants to the greater Buenos Aires region but in 1947 there were over 1,500,000, who came to the city in search of work. Recently, there have been doubts cast on the importance of internal migration as an explanation for the rise of Peronsim. We shall return to this debate at the end of the chapter, but there can be little doubt about the objective change in the composition of the working class in the 1930s. There was a massive process of urbanisation and industrialisation along with a reversal of the previous dominance of overseas immigrants within the Argentine working class.

The organised labour movement was slow to respond to these objective changes and for much of the 1930s it followed the rhythms of an earlier period. The response to the military coup of 1930 was minimal in spite of some talk of a general strike. The newly-formed CGT issued a statement declaring its political neutrality in the new situation, in keeping with a certain interpretation of syndicalist principles. This did not prevent the new military regime from carrying out a number of repressive measures. As Baily explains, the government first suppressed the anarchist and communist-led unions and then the more moderate syndicalist elements; more generally Uriburu 'denounced the minimum wage law, interrupted labor meetings, instituted a system of labor spies, broke strikes by police action, and made no effort to fulfill existing labor legislation'.[4] Employers throughout the country took advantage of the new situation to attack the social and economic gains the workers' movement had achieved in previous decades. Average industrial wages in Buenos Aires dropped from an index of 100 in 1929 to 92 in 1930, 85 in 1931 and 81 in 1932. The recently-won 8-hour day was everywhere under attack as was the 'English Saturday' (half-day work on Saturdays). Legislation governing night-work and health regulations was left inoperative. The anarcho-syndicalist historian Diego Abad de Santillan wrote that the working class 'sealed its destiny for years to come . . . by neglecting to defend its rights and liberty in the crucial hour'.[5]

The trade union movement was weakened by its lack of representativity. Little argues that 'the most important characteristic of the working class as a whole (before 1943) was its generally low level of organisation'.[6] Only the transport unions organised a majority of their trade; of the 228,356 metallurgical workers in 1941 only 4,459 were union members; agricultural workers were almost completely unorganised. Of the CGT unions only the railway union *Unión Ferroviaria* had a genuine nationwide organisation with strong local branches. In 1930 the CGT barely organised 200,000 of Argentina's 4,500,000 workers. Unemployment in the early 1930s was also high–running at over 300,000 until 1935–which effectively thwarted the mobilising potential of the organised labour movement, and kept it on the defensive. Yet one cannot absolve the leadership of the trade union movement which, as one labour leader of the time wrote, played 'a bureaucratic type role which did not reflect the anguish through which workers were passing or the unrest provoked in popular quarters by the government's policies'.[7] Lack of basic unity caused by divisions such as the separation of the train-drivers' union *La Fraternidad* from the CGT until 1933 owing to a demarcation dispute, prevented the CGT from becoming a strong organic expression of the working class during the 1930s.

For many writers the objective divisions within the working class also resulted in political divisions. A privileged 'labour aristocracy' emerged in the transport unions, the vanguard of the labour movement prior to 1930. Cheresky argues that the railway workers

> were an integrated social sector, who, benefiting from collective bargaining bodies, worker-employer grievance committees and worker participation on the board of pension funds, were differentiated from the rest of the wage earners and could be susceptible to sectional solutions by means of negotiations.[8]

This is undoubtedly true, but it did not prevent the rail companies from sacking thousands of railworkers during the 1930s depression. The strategically important maritime and port workers were also severely attacked during this period when overseas trade was disrupted. Little explains this in terms of the fact that 'far from being divided the urban working class seems to have been relatively homogeneous in both its lack of privilege and its poor organisation'.[9] He cites the case of the reputedly highly organised printing industry having a lower rate of unionisation than the reputedly ill-organised clothing industry. This seems to be a simple reversal of the dualist theory which diagnoses a traditional and non-traditional sector of the working class. It could be that the divisions were not watertight and that in a period of economic downturn they could be levelled out, but the fact remains that some sectors of the working class were better paid, better integrated into a collective bargaining structure and open to a reformist solution to their problems.

The political divisions within the CGT culminated in 1935 in an 'internal coup' led by the socialist leaders of the rail unions along with those of the commercial employees and state workers. Against the 'apolitical' stance of the syndicalists the new socialist leaders of the CGT stressed the need to confront fascism at an international and local level. The crisis began in the powerful railworkers' *Unión Ferroviaria* where the Tramonti leadership was held responsible for reduced wages and unfavourable contracts.[10] At their 1934 congress the railworkers elected a socialist, José Domenech, to lead their union, thus changing the balance of forces with the syndicalists within the CGT. In the 1931 and 1934 elections the Socialist Party had increased its vote and was now keen to consolidate its labour base. After a series of internal wrangles Domenech led a group of union leaders to seize the CGT offices and set up a new provisional executive. The displaced syndicalist sector eventually dropped the CGT label in 1937, taking up the old name of *Unión Sindical Argentina* from the 1920s. The 'bread and butter' unionism of the syndicalists had not delivered the goods in the 1930s and was dangerously oblivious to the new international political situation created by the rise of fascism. Discredited by their collaboration with the military government, and outflanked by the socialists who had more weight in the state apparatus through their parliamentary work, the syndicalists now became, like the anarchists before them, a spent force.

Though labour resistance to the military coup of 1930 was virtually non-existent, in the years which followed there was a gradual revival of working-class militancy. In 1931 there were fewer strikes and strike participants than in any of the years since strike statistics were first recorded in 1907. Thwarted by economic conditions and political repression, the fledgling CGT turned its energies to committee work. As Tamarin describes, they

> concentrated on aiding and securing the release of social and political prisoners, working for the repeal of the residence law, fighting salary cuts, petitioning the government for a public works program to ease unemployment, and fighting for the maintenance and enforcement of labor legislation.[11]

Throughout this work, stress was laid on the need to collaborate with the state. The communists on the other hand promoted a class-struggle approach, which was put into practice in the 1932 *frigorífico* strike and the 1934 wood-workers strike.

In 1932 there was not only the *frigorífico* strike, called against a change in working practices, but also a 24-hour strike by the tram-workers over a wage claim, a victorious 52-day strike by telephone workers over redundancies and working conditions, and an important strike by small farmers. In September the communist-sponsored *Comité de Unidad Clasista* (Committee of Class Struggle Unity) held its second congress with delegates from 73 unions. In 1933 two foot-wear workers' unions came together to call a strike for a wage demand. By now the employers' offensive, which had been partially detained in 1932, had gathered steam, and the strike was defeated when the dispute went to a second round in 1934. In 1934 the upturn in labour struggles took a more organic form. In June the wood-workers launched a strike in pursuit of a wage increase and a 44-hour working week. In spite of fierce repression which included the gaoling of successive strike committees and of many activists, this strike was successful after 46 days. In 1935 these workers were out on strike again, this time demanding a 40-hour week. Though this was the most memorable strike in the first half of the 1930s, the more 'traditional' railworkers were also active against wage cuts. Their mobilisation in 1934, though it did not reach strike action, successfully resisted wage cuts and work-sharing in spite of the mobilisation of the army against them. This last dispute is particularly interesting because it was settled by presidential arbitration (which called for wage retention by the company, instead of an out-right cut) thus beginning a trend towards state intervention in industrial relations. The labour situation was bad in these years, as one labour leader recalls:

> With unemployment, total in some cases, partial in others, the trade union

movement, split by internal struggles which had intensified in the last decade, had come to naught. Brought low, it was illusory to propose action between 1930 and 1935 in defense of the members . . . The few organisations which risked taking action only obtained limited results.[12]

The Communist Party

In 1935 the labour movement shifted from its earlier 'apolitical' syndicalism, as Socialist Party sectors gained hegemony within the CGT. We shall return shortly to the process which led to the formation of a labourist current which was to be instrumental in the rise of Perón. First we have to examine the rise within Argentine labour politics of the Communist Party, which was to provide a vital new ingredient in these years. We have already mentioned its trade union front – the *Comité de Unidad Clasista* – which was set up in 1929. The period from 1930 to 1934 was dominated by the 'class against class' line advanced by the Third International, but in 1935 the Argentine CP, like other national sections, adopted the Popular Front strategy. The previous class-struggle line was now denounced by the party as sectarian and ultra-left.[13] Rather than setting up rival unions, the CP was now orienting its forces in the labour movement towards work in the socialist-dominated CGT. The party rapidly became a major organisational and political force within the trade union movement. The four largest CP-led industrial unions – construction, *frigorífico*, textile and metallurgical workers – accounted for nearly 95% of the total growth in union membership between 1936 and 1941.[14] The communists were practically unique in stressing the need to extend unionisation to agricultural workers, an area where they had considerable success in spite of major difficulties.

The Communist Party had a history of intervention in the provinces going back to 1918, when, as the International Socialist Party, it had become the leading force in the Córdoba labour movement. Though it attempted to organise rural 'soviets' during strikes in the province, its electoral support was negligible. This would seem to imply that CP militants were elected to union office because of their honesty and efficiency, rather than their politics. During the 1930s the party launched an organisation drive in the sugar plantations of Tucumán, the *yerbales* (mate tea plantations) and *quebracho* (a hard wood) fields of Misiones and the Chaco, and in the vineyards of Mendoza and San Juán.[15] Their achievements, though modest, were significant in so far as the labour movement was achieving a foothold in the rural areas. Whereas efforts by party workers to organise the cotton fields of the Chaco province were repulsed by employer and state resistance, in other areas they were more successful. A notable advance was the organisation by the party in 1931 of an oil workers' union in the remote Comodoro Rivadavia field. In a momentous struggle, union recognition was achieved and dismissed workers were reinstated.[16] In some cases, urban unions such as the construction and food workers' organisations under communist influence, were used to spear-head the organising drive in rural areas.

The communists led several major strikes in this period, and according to one calculation, 'the bulk of strike activity during the late 1930s and early 1940s was initiated by the communist-led industrial unions'.[17] In the course of several strikes by construction workers between 1935 and 1937 the communists organised the powerful *Federación Obrera Nacional de la Construcción* (National Construction Workers' Federation) which was second only to the *Unión Ferroviaria* in its weight within the labour movement (by 1941 it had 40,000 members). During these strikes they were able to draw in hitherto unorganised sectors of the working class, co-ordinate struggles across different categories, and call a 48-hour solidarity strike in 1936 when the CGT refused to back the striking building workers.

Towards the end of 1936 there was a big strike in the textile industry, which gave the impetus for the *Unión Obrera Textil* (Textile Workers' Union) to double its membership to 10,000 by 1941. Though the construction strike may have been 'a model of organisation, combativity and solidarity'[18] as the CP history declares, their record was not always so excellent. The communist-led *Federación Obrera de la Industria de la Carne* (Meat Industry Workers' Federation) held a strike in 1943 for a series of economic demands and for the release of their leader, José Peter. When Peter was released, he promptly called for an end to the strike without any of the other workers' demands being met. All this was in aid of the continued supply of beef to the Allied troops, since the Soviet Union had entered the war in 1941.

The shortcomings of the Communist Party did not lie in its industrial policy, but rather in its uncritical pursuance of Third International shifts. Argentina, a country clearly dominated by imperialism and where the national question was growing daily in importance, was analysed in terms of a simple fascism/democracy dichotomy. The CP declared in 1941 that 'There is no opposition between the foreign and the Argentine: the only opposition is that existing between those serving nazi-peronism and those supporting democracy. . . .'[19] This reached the absurd level of distinguishing between 'Nazi' firms (Siemens, Bayer and others and 'democratic' firms (the *frigoríficos,* the railways, etc.) where British capital prevailed and where the CP advised the workers to make 'sacrifices'.[20] In simple terms the 'democratic' sectors in Argentina were the landowners and the traditional oligarchy. Against this was emerging a pro-German ('fascist') sector which was also more pro-industrialist and favoured state intervention. By choosing to ally with the first, the Communist Party isolated itself from the working class and thus found itself in a weaker position to criticise the more reactionary aspects of Peronism (e.g. state-run trade unions). The CP's serious misinterpretation of Peronism will be returned to. Here we need only stress that the CP had achieved a major role in the labour movement and was well placed to have a decisive effect on the future of the working class in the late 1930s.

Labour upsurge (1935-1942)

There was a marked increase in strikes after 1935 compared to the first half of the decade as we see in Table 10.1.

Table 10.1   Strikes and strikers, 1926–1939 (By index numbers: 1926–30=100)

Years	Strikes	Strikers
1930–1935	62.5	86.4
1936–1939	71.3	146.6

Source: M. Murmis and J.C. Portantiero, (1974) *Estudios sobre los orígenes del peronismo/1*, Buenos Aires, Siglo XXI, p. 87.

In terms of the number of strikers, working-class mobilisation in the second half of the 1930s surpassed that of the 1920s, even though the number of strikes still lagged behind. If we are to examine which sectors of the working class were most prone to strike (Table 10.2) we find that it was largely the new industrial unions and the building trade.

Table 10.2   Strikes, days lost and union membership, 1934–1942 (percentage)

	Strikes	Days lost	Union Members
Manufacturing Industry	72.0	48.7	16.0
Construction	23.3	49.1	16.8
Others	4.7	2.2	67.2
Total	100.0	100.0	100.0

Source: I. Cheresky, (1981) Sindicatos y Fuerzas Políticas en la Argentina Preperonista (1930–1943), *Boletín de Estudios Latinoamericanos y del Caribe,* 31, p. 38.

Workers in industry, who represented barely 16% of union members, accounted for nearly half the days lost through strikes in this period. Even more remarkable, those in manufacturing and construction together accounted for over 90% of strikes and days lost, yet they made up barely one-third of the union membership.

It is interesting to examine the percentage of strikes won or lost by the workers, because it is now widely accepted that an accumulation of unsatisfied labour demands played a certain role in the rise of Perón. The basic figures are provided in Table 10.3. Murmis and Portantiero conclude from this data that 'the percentage of strikers involved in disputes which obtain the satisfaction of their demands is low, which obviously accentuates dissatisfaction and tensions'.[21] Some authors reach this conclusion more easily by simply amalgamating the figures for strikes lost and unresolved.[22] This interpretation is only strictly true for 1934 when over half of the strikes were lost and only a minimal amount won. Leaving aside

113

Table 10.3   Results obtained by strikers over the total number of workers on strike, 1934–1939

	1934	*1935*	*1936*	*1937*	*1938*	*1939*
Won	2.4	55.8	14.7	8.2	11.3	18.4
Lost	55.9	7.8	11.2	3.6	13.8	6.3
Unresolved	41.67	36.2	74.1	88.2	74.7	75.3

Source: M. Murmis and J.C. Portantiero, (1974) *Estudios sobre los orígines del peronismo/1.* Buenos Aires, Siglo XXI, p. 89.

the category of 'unresolved' where we have no clear criteria of definition, the figures actually tell a different story.[23] Except in 1934 and 1938, more workers were involved in strikes which were won than lost. We cannot assume that there will be *less* strikes when demands are met – the logical conclusion if unsatisfied demands are seen to lead to labour activity. Historical experience would seem to indicate that strikes increase when their chances of success are greater.

If we investigate the strike statistics further we find that the degree of success varied directly in proportion to the number of workers involved. We see in Table 10.4 that where more than 200 workers were involved – either in a large factory or because the strike involved several factories – there were considerably more strikes won by the workers and very few lost.

Table 10.4   Results of strikes according to size, 1935 (in percentages)

Results	*Size of Strike*			
	Below 50 workers	*From 51–200 workers*	*More than 200 workers*	*Total*
Won	15.8	–	24	17.1
Unresolved	13.2	28.6	48	28.6
Lost	68.4	57.1	16	48.6
Unknown	2.6	14.3	12	5.7
Total	100	100	100	100

Source: R. Gaudio and J. Pilone, (1976) "Estado y relaciones obrero-patronales el los orígense de la negociación colectiva en Argentina". *Estudios Sociales*, 5, Buenos Aires, CEDEX, p. 13.

In 1936 the percentage of successful large strikes rose to 35%, whereas more of the smaller strikes were lost. This all seems to indicate that the success of labour mobilisation depended on the degree of organisation which had been achieved.

Finally, we can note from Table 10.5 that though the majority of strikes were over wages, the proportion does not appear to be as high as the 90% or more usually indicated.

Table 10.5   Causes of strikes in selected areas, 1937–1943 (absolute figures)

Causes	Chemicals	Construction	Metallurgical	Textile	Graphic	Total
Wage Related	12	37	20	18	15	102
Working Conditions	4	1	4	10	1	20
Union Organising	–	4	1	–	–	5
Solidarity	4	18	14	12	6	54
Others	5	24	12	8	10	59
Total	25	84	51	48	32	240

Source: C. Durruty, (1969) *Clase obrera y peronismo*, Córdoba, Pasado y Presente, p. 121.

It appears that around half the disputes were in demand of higher wages, opposing reductions or claiming back-pay. Except for the textile industry there were few strikes over working conditions, shifts, piece-work, etc. Only in the construction industry was the issue of union recognition still important at this stage. Finally, we note a far from negligible proportion of strikes in solidarity with workers in other firms or sectors, reaching a quarter of the total in some cases.

The trade unions experienced a period of growth after 1935 in contrast to the first half of the decade. We have already mentioned the new industrial unions organised by the communists. The long-standing *Unión Ferroviaria* also increased its membership from 70,000 in 1930 to 96,000 in 1940. The trade unions were also centralised in this period, with the CGT becoming the undisputed pole of attraction for organised labour as we see in Table 10.6.

Table 10.6   Union membership, 1936–1941

Tendency	1936	1937	1939	1940	1941
CGT	262,630	289,320	270,320	311,076	330,681
USA	25,095	32,111	26,980	23,079	26,980
Catholic Employees' Federation	8,012	8,079	18,500	18,675	21,500
Autonomous Unions	72,834	68,105	120,809	120,038	118,838
No tendency	1,398	21,214	–	–	8,709

Source: R. Rotondaro, (1971) *Realidad y Cambio en el Sindicalismo,* Buenos Aires, Pleamar, p. 142.

The 1940 trade union census found that the CGT had 217 affiliated unions (61% of the total), the Unión Sindical Argentina had 31 (9%) and there were 83 (23%) autonomous unions. These latter, who were a significant force, adopted a pragmatic attitude, often co-operating with the CGT. The communists controlled the construction, *frigorífico* and metallurgical unions; the socialists had their main bastions among the commercial, municipal and state workers and the footplatemen, whereas the syndicalists were dominant among the railworkers and tram drivers.[24]

It would be wrong to exaggerate the growth of the trade union movement because it is a simple fact that it did not keep up with the growth of the working class. Trade unions in the wood industry, transport, commerce and state sectors actually lost members between 1936 and 1941. Even the industrial unions which rose from 40,000 to 70,000 members over this same period only covered 14% of wage earners in 1941 (compared to 12% in 1936). The level of representation was undoubtedly higher in Buenos Aires and strikes tended to mobilise non-unionised workers. Another index of rank-and-file participation is attendance at union meetings which we can examine in Table 10.7:

Table 10.7   Trade union meetings, 1935–1942 (By index numbers)

Year	1935	1936	1937	1938	1939	1940	1941	1942
Number of meetings	100	142	126	129	125	109	67	64
Attendance	100	90	45	45	38	30	20	27

Source: D. Tamarin, (1977) *The Argentine Labor Movement in an Age of Transition, 1930–1945*, PhD thesis, Washington University, p. 267.

Repression certainly played a role in restricting the number of meetings and attendance. In 1937 over 1,000 union meetings were banned in Buenos Aires alone. However, the fall-off in union meetings after 1941 matches the consistently declining number of members who attended meetings. It is not only fear of deportation or gaol which accounts for this but a general tendency towards bureaucratisation and consequent decline of rank-and-file activity. In 1935 there were 5,600 trade union meetings attended by one million workers; in 1941 there were only 3,000 meetings with 300,000 participants.

Labour politics

Labour politics after 1935 were dominated by controversies within the socialist camp, and between the Socialists and the Communists. The 1936 CGT Congress placed the trade union movement squarely in the political arena, and from then on its political weight could only grow. The May Day celebrations of that year brought together for the first time the CGT, the independent unions, the democratic political parties and the student associations.[25] From 1936 the trade union movement played a prominent role in the solidarity displayed by broad sections of the population with the Republicans during the Spanish Civil War. In the broader international sphere the trade unions were pledged to peace and the defence of democracy. The relative harmony between the left-wing parties and the trade unions surrounding all these aims ended abruptly in 1939 with the signing of the Nazi-Soviet pact, which led the Communist Party to characterise the war as inter-imperialist and call for the neutrality of Argentine workers. This switch from a popular-front strategy to an anti-imperialist position found a certain degree of support among syndicalist sectors of the trade union movement. It was also reflected in the May Day celebrations of 1940 where the tone of the declaration was decidedly anti-capitalist and anti-imperialist, though the CGT later returned to its pro-Allied position. This debate exacerbated divisions among the Socialist Party trade unionists, reflected in the cancellation of the 1941 May Day celebrations because of disagreements with the party. The *Unión Ferroviaria* had begun to re-adopt essentially syndicalist positions, which led it, and indirectly the CGT, to abstain from national politics (although it still advanced a workers' programme to beat the crisis).

These political divisions within the labour movement came to a head in 1943 with a new split in the CGT. One group, led by Domenech of the railworkers' unions, was aiming for the construction of a labour party to represent directly the interests of the working class. The other, which became known as CGT No. 2, saw the role of the trade unions as remaining loyal to the Socialist or Communist parties. We should not exaggerate the ideological content of this dispute, because to a large extent it was a clash over personalities, specifically over Domenech, who had become a *caudillo* figure in the union movement. One writer refers to 'the heavy handedness of union leaders, irregularities in union finances and administration, and alienation between the leadership and the rank and file' throughout this period.[26] There was a certain crisis of legitimacy within the union movement. More broadly, there was a crisis of perspectives among the political parties claiming to represent labour. The Socialist Party in particular suffered from an inability to come to grips with the national question. Its social democracy was simply unable to cope with the problems of the Argentine working class in a period of dynamic change. The Socialists still lived in the ideological world of the 'golden era' before 1930. The split in the socialist leadership of the CGT in 1943 and the emergence of a labourist current brought out in the open a process of deep transformation which would play a key role in the rise of Perón.

Reorientation (1943–1944)

In June 1943 Generals Rawson and Ramírez seized control of the government, and in 1944 Colonel Juan Domingo Perón emerged as vice-president. This new coup was decidedly nationalist in that the military government refused to enter the Second World War on the Allied side (they finally did some months before it ended) or to enter into the Pan-American system being promoted by the new imperial power in the north. The dominant political voice within the army was the *Grupo de Oficiales Unidos* (Group of United Officers), a lodge of which Colonel Perón was a prominent member. It is his activity within the labour movement to which we now turn.

The de facto military government moved rapidly to disarm the labour movement which in 1942 had organised a record number of strikes. Indicative of this new mood was the strike in the remote oil fields of Comodoro Rivadavia to obtain the right to unionise, and to stop the practice of the imperialist-owned companies from deporting labour activists. The government's first move was to suspend the CGT No. 2 led by Socialists and Communists, accusing it of being an 'extremist organisation'. Many of its members transferred to CGT No. 1, which retained a favourable attitude towards the government, even when it passed a new Law of Professional Associations which increased state intervention in labour affairs. Having dealt with the 'extremists' the government then turned to the 'moderates'. The two powerful rail unions, *Unión Ferroviaria* and *La Fraternidad*, were subjected to government intervention and had to leave the CGT. As the unions began to reject the new labour laws and launched a series of strikes towards the end of 1943, the government responded with widespread arrests of labour leaders. Perón now came on to the scene when he was appointed head of the Department of Labour, which was soon upgraded to ministerial status as the Labour and Social Security Secretariat.

Perón had already made contact with labour leaders through his friend Colonel Mercante (whose brother was a railworker) and had met Borlenghi, head of the commercial employees' union and prominent in the now banned CGT No. 2. Mercante recalled later how a series of trade union leaders began discussions with Perón. They were seeking his support on labour demands; he was seeking their compliance in a broad populist project.[27] The communists had led a militant metal-workers' strike in 1942 and Perón sought to disarm them too: 'When I speak with these communists, they shall cease being that or be replaced'.[28] Perón sought to halt the advance of communism through the implementation of 'social justice', the vague ideology of *justicialismo*, which was to be the corner-stone of Peronism in power. His work in the trade unions also had a more practical dimension, as was seen in his management of the Avellaneda meat-packers' dispute in 1943. He allowed the communist leader of the union, Peter, to return from the southern gaol he had been placed in by the military government. As we saw above, Peter called off the strike but did not give due thanks to Perón as he had agreed. As Peter was not cooperative, Perón encouraged a rank-and-file leader, Cipriano Reyes, to set up a new packing-house union.[29] This was duly recognised in 1944 after Perón had granted a small wage increase and improvements in working conditions in return for a no-strike pledge. Perón was able to walk through the streets of Berisso (a meat-workers' quarter of La Plata) with his arms around the shoulders of Reyes and pose as the genuine 'worker colonel'.

With the metal-workers too, a new leadership emerged after the defeat of the 1942 strike when the CP leadership agreed to Church mediation. During the 17-day strike Communist leaders of the union were publicly calling for settlement with the 'anti-fascist' firms like Siam di Tella. In the aftermath 5,000 union activists were sacked and the CP leadership was widely discredited. In 1943 a new union, the *Unión Obrera Metalúrgica* (Metallurgical Workers' Union) was formed with Trotskyist Angel Perelman at its head. The UOM rapidly grew from its 1,500 members under the CP leadership to some 300,000 who were to become a bastion of the organised workers' movement. Perelman justified his role saying that

so deep was the need for the country to defend its political independence and economic sovereignty and that the working class at last organise its large-scale unions that, faced by the betrayal of the parties of the left, this need was embodied by a military figure coming from the ranks of the army'.[30]

The policy of setting up alternative unions was less successful when Perón tried to undercut the powerful CP-led construction workers' union. Repression effectively broke the FONC, but Perón's alternative could boast only 14,300 members in 1945 compared to the 74,300 members of the old union in 1941. Elsewhere Perón promoted the organisation of workers who had not previously had unions. He aided the organisation of the Tucumán sugar workers in the *Federación Obrera Tucumana de la Industria Azucarera* (Tucumán Sugar Workers' Federation) which was to play a major role in the union movement, the wine workers of Mendoza and the *yerba mate* (tea) workers of Misiones. Perón also approved the first complete rural legislation, the *Estatuto del Peón* (Statute of the Rural Worker) which fixed minimum wages, paid holidays and free medical services for the down-trodden rural proletariat.

Perón not only worked on hitherto unorganised sectors of the working class, or helped establish parallel unions, but also directed his sights at central elements of the existing labour movement. In 1943 he placed his associate, Mercante, as government overseer in the *Unión Ferroviaria*. Mercante promptly reversed the divisive measures of the previous military intervention and allowed the return of the Domenech leadership. The union rejoined the CGT. Perón visited several branches and promised 'social justice' and extended material concessions. He also warned that the 'foreign ideologies' of socialism and communism would no longer be tolerated, explaining that they were 'the worst sickness of the working masses. The politicians have always exploited this factor to divide the working classes and to use them for their benefit'. In their place, Perón argued for Argentine nationalism in the political and economic domains. This also meant, as Perón said: 'We seek to abolish the struggle between classes, replacing it by a just agreement between workers and employers, under the auspices of the justice which emanates from the state'. Peronist railway worker Luis Monzalvo explains in his memoirs how Perón built up massive support in the union on the basis of satisfying long-felt material needs.[31] An interesting point he makes is that 'the initiative to reach out to the army was through our own determination. There were no suggestions from any civilian or military personnel'.[32] It was figures like Monzalvo who would go on to form the Labour Party in 1945, which expressed a genuine labourist tendency in spite of its support for Perón's candidature in the 1946 elections.

Statism

A constant parallel to the rise of Perón was the growing role of the state in the management of industrial relations. Collective-bargaining was not born in 1943, but it certainly spread rapidly after that year. Whereas between 1936 and 1940 there were only 46 agreements signed at the National Department of Labour, in 1944, after the formation of the Labour and Social Security Secretariat, there were 142 signed for the capital alone, and 279 for the rest of the country. Some authors argue that these figures under-estimate the real degree of state intervention before 1943, but nevertheless we must admit to an increased role concomitant with the rise of Perón.[33] He extended the scope of labour law and encouraged workers to look to the state to resolve problems regarding wages, conditions, pensions, holidays, dismissal, etc. In 1944 the first *Tribunales de Trabajo* (Labour Tribunals) were set up and the commercial employees were covered by the *Caja de Jubilaciones* (Pension Fund). Perelman recalls how

> from 1944 onwards we saw incredible things in our trade union work: labour laws which had previously been ignored were now being obeyed; there was no need for court appeals to obtain holidays; recognition of factory delegates and guarantees that they would not be victimised were kept to rigorously.[34]

In this context it is not surprising that a whole generation of labour leaders (and activists) should have looked to the state and rejected the pre-1943 unions as élitist and incapable of forming mass organisations.[35] Nor is it surprising that the displaced trade union leaders should see 1943 as the end of a period of 'free unionism'.[36]

A footnote to the growing tendency of the labour movement to look towards the state to solve its problems, is the tendency throughout the 1930s for unions to adopt protectionist economic policies. Whereas prior to 1930 the labour movement invariably supported the free-trade ideology of the oligarchy, by the end of the decade most sectors were calling for tariffs in their area and more generally supporting a pro-industrialising economic policy.

Interpretations

At this stage we should consider the various explanations put forward to account for Perón's mobilisation of a working-class base. Until recently the orthodox view stressed the support for Perón from the 'new' working class recently arrived in the city. They supposedly held a traditional view of society and were susceptible to the authoritarian paternalism (or 'charisma') of Perón. Stress is laid on the 'irrational' element of Peronism – the mass rallies and slogan chanting – which even led some authors to detect a form of 'left-wing fascism'.[37] The established working class is analysed in terms of its European origins and political allegiance to constitutional socialism. It is contrasted with the new arrivals who supposedly flocked towards Perón without a clear consciousness of their class interests. The radical divide between the established and the 'new' working class is a widespread image, shared even by serious writers like Baily who says, without any foundation, that 'the internal migrants and the organised workers viewed each other with hostility and suspicion'.[38] One of the popular labour histories, that of Alberto Belloni, refers to the growth of industry in the 1930s:

> A whole army of workers is concentrated in these new factories who share an extremely important characteristic; they are of clearly native stock and have no complicity with the inglorious past of our 'left-wing' parties.[39]

Supporters and detractors of Perón alike operate with an image of a new, politically inexperienced working class ripe for a political adventure.

In recent years a series of 'revisionist' interpretations have seriously questioned the validity of this perspective. One debate centres around the precise weight of internal migration, with several authors questioning Germani's assertion that 'by 1945–1946, the major part of the native and urban working class had been replaced by those recently arrived from the provinces'.[40] Other authors have shifted the terrain of the debate away from the demographic arguments to consider the orientation of the working-class leadership prior to 1945. Murmis and Portantiero put forward three basic hypotheses:

1) the organisations and leaders of the 'old' working class participated intensely in the rise of Peronism;

2) the participation of the working class in the national popular movement cannot be characterised as passive, short sighted or divided;

3) the joint participation of old and new sectors of the working class in the rise of Peronism follows a pre-existing labourist programme.[41]

121

The major stress of the 'revisionist' writers is to question the radical divide which the previous authors detected between the established working class and the immigrants. Walter Little goes even further arguing that 'far from being divided the working class was remarkably homogeneous and . . . explanations of popular support for Peronism must be developed on this basis'.[42] As we saw above, this assertion is factually doubtful and plays down the degree of objective and subjective divisions within the labour movement.

It is not a question of trying to achieve a balance between the orthodox and revisionist interpretations, but we should draw some conclusions. The demographic argument appears to be somewhat sterile and there is little denying the fundamental social changes occurring in Argentine society during this period. What is important is the political interpretation placed on this data, and here the revisionist critique cannot be faulted. There was no clear-cut division between an anti-Peronist established working class and a 'new' Peronist working class. At times the case is pushed further as when Little argues that 'the evidence for structural and behavioural differentiation within the working class is in no way significant'.[43] There seems to have been a degree of segmentation within the working class, and political divisions as great (if not greater) than elsewhere. It was Perón's nationalist project which achieved that unification and forged the modern labour movement. Likewise, the argument of Murmis and Portantiero that the main characteristic of this period was the unity of the working class through a process of industrialisation without income redistribution, is at best partial. Wages stagnated, but did not fall, through most of the 1930s, and actually began rising after 1936. It is a form of economism to explain the rise of Perón purely in terms of his ability to satisfy pent-up demands.[45] His rise, and the popular movement he led, is better explained by the social dynamic unleashed by his strategy, in particular the employers' resistance to his reforms and later the fervent anti-Peronism of the oligarchy.

The essential point we need to make is that the workers' movement was not simply duped by a clever politician. There was, it is true, a certain amount of disorientation in the labour movement and a failure to adapt to new realities. In this sense there was little option but to support Perón, though a minority of the craft unions and the communists held out, bitterly defending their political independence. In the circumstances the dominant trend towards a labourist policy, which emerged in the late 1930s, found a natural ally in Perón. The labour movement went into this alliance in 1943 and 1944 to defend its own interests, not those of Perón. Support for Perón came from all sectors of the movement. Perón achieved the support of trade union leaders from the dissident socialists of the CGT No. 1, some of the major unions of the orthodox CGT No. 2, and in particular from the autonomous or independent unions, not forgetting the remnants of the syndicalist USA which had favoured this type of alliance since the 1935 split. Support from the leadership was matched by support from the rank and file. It is difficult to disagree with Baily's simple conclusion that by the end of 1944, the CGT and many of the leading unions of the country supported Perón and the government, because together they had given labor new status within society. Perón had won popular support . . . because of his active sympathy for the working class.[46]

Later events were to show that this sympathy was more than just tinged with self-interest.

At the end of the period from 1930 to 1944, several factors stand out. Industry had overtaken agriculture as the leading contributor to national income. The number of workers in the manufacturing sector had doubled since 1935. The industrial working class had become the backbone of the labour movement in Argentina. The industrialisation of this phase was based largely on import substitution in the textile and food-stuffs industries, with the metallurgical sector growing towards the end of the period. It was largely labour-intensive and based on the extraction of absolute surplus value. The major political expressions of labour–anarchism, syndicalism and socialism–were either in decline or unable to express adequately the current needs of the working class. One new political current–communism –gained a major foot-hold in the working class but its political subordination to an international tendency made its full adaptation to the national reality difficult. Finally, Perón came on to the scene at a fortuitous moment and through agile political manoeuvring positioned himself at the head of a mass nationalist movement. But Peronism had been inscribed in the internal logic of working-class development since 1930 and did not represent simply the imposition of an alien political scheme on the labour movement.

During this period the position of women in the economic and political structures of the country changed fundamentally. As we have seen above, around the time of the First World War, women accounted for one-third of the industrial workforce. By 1939 women represented one-third of workers in the chemical, pharmaceutical and paint industries, 48% of the workforce in the rubber industry and 58% of textile workers.[47] Cheap female labour-power was thus a prime ingredient in the industrialisation of the 1930s. Furthermore the internal migration of that period was predominantly female, as against the mainly male overseas migration of an earlier era. By 1947 women represented only 20% of the total labour force but they still predominated in the textile, tobacco and clothing sectors. With factory production overtaking the craft and cottage industries, the overall economic power of women was declining. As Hollander notes 'many women were left isolated in their houses, relegated to the role of housewife and separated from much of the productive labor for which they had historically been responsible'.[48] The other side of the coin was an increased political role for women, who under Perón gained the vote and a major role in the political system from then on.

Appendix 1

Table 10.8   Strike volume and real wages in Buenos Aires, 1930–1944

	No of strikes	Workers Affected	Days Lost	Real Wages (1925/1929: 100)
1930	125	29,331	699,790	95.80
1931	43	4,622	54,531	103.16
1932	105	34,562	1,299,061	109.47
1933	52	3,481	44,779	101.05
1934	42	25,940	741,256	104.21
1935	69	52,143	2,642,576	106.32
1936	109	85,438	1,344,461	100.00
1937	82	49,993	517,645	101.05
1938	44	8,871	228,703	101.05
1939	49	19,718	241,099	102.11
1940	53	12,721	224,599	103.16
1941	54	6,606	247,598	103.16
1942	113	39,865	634,339	106.32
1943	85	6,754	87,229	112.63
1944	27	9,121	41,384	124.21

Source: Strike statistics: R. Rotondaro, (1971) *Realidad y cambio en el sindicalismo,* Buenos Aires, Pleamar, p. 240.

Wages: R. Gaudio and J. Pilone, (1976) "Estado y relaciones obrero-patronales en los orígenes de la negociación colectiva en Argentina", *Estudios Sociales*, 5, Buenos Aires, CEDES, p. 36.

Note. These figures do not include general strikes or factory occupations.

Notes

1. See M. Murmis and J.C. Portantiero, (1974), "Crecimento industrial y alianza de clases en la Argentina (1930–1940)", In *Estudios sobre los origines del peronismo/1* Buenos Aires, Siglo XXI.

2. For a general political history of this period see A. Ciria, (1974) *Parties and Power in Modern Argentina, 1930–1946*, Albany, State University of New York Press.

3. G. Germani, (1980) "El surgimiento del peronismo: el rol de los obreros y de los migrantes internos", in M. Moray Araujo and I. Llorente, (eds.) *El voto peronista*. Buenos Aires, Editorial Sudamericana, p. 107.

4. S. Baily, (1967) *Labor, Nationalism and Politics in Argentina*. New Brunswick, Rutgers University Press, p. 53.

5. D.A. de Sanitallán, (1958) "El movimiento obrero argentino ante el golpe de estado del 6 de septiembre de 1930", *Revista de Historia*, no. e, p. 130.

6. W. Little, (1975) "The Popular Origins of Peronism", in D. Rock (ed.) *Argentina in the Twentieth Century* London, Duckworth, p. 168.

7. A. Lopez, (1974) *Historia del movimiento social y la clase obrera argentina.* Buenos Aires, Pena Lillo, p. 299.

8. I. Cheresky, (1981) Sindicatos y Fuerzas Políticas en la Argentina Preperonista (1930–1943). Boletín de Estudios Latinoamericanos y del Caribe. 31, p. 28. See J. Horowitz, (1979) *Adaptation and change in the Argentine labor movement (1930–1943) A study of five unions.* PhD thesis, University of California, Berkeley, for useful case studies of rail, textile, commercial, municipal and telephone workers' unions during this period.

9. W. Little, (1975) "The Popular Origins of Peronism", p. 168.

10. On the internal situation of the rail unions see D. Tamarin, (1977) *The Argentine Labor Movement in an Age of Transition, 1930-1945*, PhD thesis, University of Washington, Ch 5.

11. Ibid., p. 155.

12. Sebastián Marotta, cited in M. Murmis and J.C. Portantiero, (1974) *Estudios sobre los orígenes del peronismo/1*, p. 84.

13. See Comité Central del Partido Comunista (1947). *Esboza de Historia del Partido Comunista de la Argentina*, Buenos Aires, Editorial Anteo, p. 76.

14. On the CP work in the unions see D. Tamarin, (1977) *The Argentine Labor Movement*, Ch 6.

15. Ibid., p. 248.

16. For an account see R. Gómez, (1973) *La gran huelga petrolera de Comodoro Rivadivia (1931–1932).* Buenos Aires, Ediciones Centro de Estudios.

17. D. Tamarin, (1977) *The Argentine Labor Movement*, p. 245.

18. Comité Central del Partido Comunista (1947), *Esbozo de Historia del Partido Comunista*, p. 83. For a case study of CP intervention in the construction workers' union see C. Durruty, (1969) *Clase obrera y peronismo*, Córdoba, Ediciones Pasado y Presente.

19. Orientación (16.01.46) cited in E. Nash, (1976) *The Argentinian Communist Party and the Rise of Peronism: 1943-1946.* Mimeo, University of Essex, p. 13.

20. According to CP dissident J.J. Real, (1976) *Treinta Años de Historia Argentina*, Buenos Aires, Ediciones Crisol, p. 74.

21. M. Murmis and J.C. Portantiero, (1974) "El movimiento obrero en los orígenes de peronismo", in *Estudos sobre los orígenes del peronismo/1*, p. 88.

22. See H. Spalding, (1977) "Labor and Populism: Argentina and Brazil", in *Organized Labor in Latin America*, New York, Harper and Row, p. 162. This is nevertheless an excellent essay.

23. This argument follows R. Gaudio and J. Pilone, (1976) "Estado y relaciones obrebo–partonales en los orígines de la negociación colectiva en Argentina". *Estudios Sociales*, 5, Buenos Aires, CEDES, pp. 9–10.

24. This follows CP historian R. Iscaro (1958) *Orígen y Desarrollo del Movimiento Sindical Argentino.* Buenos Aires, Anteo, p. 179, which despite obvious bias is an excellent source.

25. This paragraph draws on the account by I. Cheresky, (1981) Sindicatos y Fuerzas Politicas en la Argentina Preperonista. pp. 21–23.

26. D. Tamarin, (1971) *The Argentine Labor Movement*, p. 264.

27. La Historia del Peronismo. *Primera Plana* (24.8.65).

28. Ibid.

29. On the "Peronisation" of the meat-packers union see W. Little, (1971) "La tendencia peronista en el sindicalismo argentino; El caso de los abreros en la Carne". *Aportes*, 19.

30. A. Perelman, (1961) *Como Hicimos el 17 de Octubre.* Buenos Aires, Coyoacán, p. 45.

31. L. Monzalvo, (1974) *Testigo de la primera hora del peronismo.* Buenos Aires, Pleamar.

32. Ibid.

33. See R. Gaudio and J. Pilone, (1976) "Estado y relaciones obrero-patronales". pp. 16–19.

34. A. Perelman, (1961) *Como Hicimos el 17 de Octubre*, p. 46.

35. e.g. A. Taconne in C. Fayt (ed.) (1967) *La Naturaleza del Peronismo.* Buenos Aires, Viracocha p. 232.

36. e.g. J. Oddone, (1975) *Gremidlismo Proletario Argentino.* Buenos Aires, Libera p. 565.

37. For a critique, see E. Laclau (1973) "Argentina: Peronism and Revolution", *Latin American Review of Books.* 1.

38. S. Baily, (1967) *Labor, Nationalism and Politics*, p. 81.

39. A. Belloni, (1960) *Del Anarquismo al Peronismo – Historia del Movimiento Obrero Argentino.* Buenos Aires, Lilla, p. 59.

40. G. Germani, (1980) "El surgimiento del peronismo", p. 109.

41. M. Murmis, and J.C. Portantiero, (1971) "El movimiento obrero en los orígenes del peronismo'. p. 73.

42. W. Little, (1975) "The Popular Origins of Peronism", p. 175.

43. Ibid., p. 175.

44. M. Murmis and J.C. Portantiero, (1971) "El movimiento obrero en los orígenes del peronismo", p. 76.

45. Di Tella (1981) Working-Class Organization and Politics in Argentina. *Latin American Research Review.* XVI.2. begins to break out of earlier discussions.

46. S. Baily, (1967) *Labor, Nationalism and Politics*, p. 79.

47. N. Hollander, (1974) *Women in the Political Economy of Argentina*, Los Angeles, University of California, PhD Thesis, p. 75.

48. Ibid., p. 88.

11. Perón in Power and the Consolidation of the Trade Unions (1945–1955)

This period begins with an event – on 17 October 1945 – which has passed into the mythology of the Argentine labour movement. On that date the working class entered the political scene in a massive and explosive manner. We assess the significance of 17 October and the process leading up to Perón's election as president in 1946. Then we follow the quantitative expansion of the trade unions and their qualitative advances in terms of workplace organisation. In spite of the gradual bureaucratisation of the trade unions under Perón, the working class displayed a marked capacity to defend its living standards through a number of important strikes. Within this Peronist period there is a phase beginning around 1951, when the industrialists began to pull out of the Peronist coalition and economic conditions worsened. As polarisation increased, the question of forming trade union militias to defend the regime was posed but never acted upon. The end of Peronism Mark I came in 1955 with a military coup backed by a range of civilian forces, and with the working class demobilised by Perón's constant admonition – 'De casa al trabajo y del trabajo a la casa' (From home to work and from work to home). Having said that, our analysis shows that Perón's relation with the labour movement was not simply a one-way process, and that the gains of this period were not just a hand-out from the state. The working class was an active agent in the making of Peronism.

17 October 1945

We saw in the previous chapter how Perón built up support within the trade union movement in 1943 and 1944. Perón's political ambitions coincided with a reformist labour project put forward by the union leaders. This must be said to avoid seeing Perón's success as simple manipulation. Even in 1945 the alliance between Perón and the unions was a two-way process.

The first major political test for this alliance came mid-way through 1945 when all the major employers' associations launched a manifesto condemning the reformist social policies of the military regime. The trade union response was not slow to come: first the commercial employees' union, then the state employees' union, and eventually all the major trade unions mobilised against the employers. The campaign culminated in a mass meeting where the main slogan was 'in defence of the improvements obtained by the workers through the Labour and Social Security Secretariat'. Even at this stage the unions were careful to avoid a direct identification with Perón himself. But this did not stop some of the trade union leaders growing apprehensive about the increasing links with the military politician.

Towards the end of 1945 the train drivers' unions *La Fraternidad*, along with textile and shoe-makers' unions, withdrew from the CGT. Perón responded with a new Law of Professional Associations which increased the power of the CGT but also gave the government the right to grant legal status (*personería jurídica*) to unions, as a precondition for collective bargaining on behalf of their members.

While Perón was consolidating his trade union base, the traditional ruling class of Argentina had been working on the other military rulers in a bid to displace Perón. They were not convinced by Perón's soothing response to employers' worries and believed he was embarking on a dangerous revolutionary adventure. Perón was duly relieved from his post as Minister for Labour and his other positions of Vice-President and Minister for War, and sent into internal exile.

This now placed the trade union leaders in the position of having to face the consequences of their alliance with Perón. Though they saw the reforms of the previous two years as the fruit of their own struggles, they now began to see to what extent they depended on Perón personally. A movement began pledged to the return of Perón. Attention has been focused traditionally on the role within the labour movement of Mercante, Perón's labour adviser; Eva Duarte, who was shortly to become his wife; and acolytes such as Cipriano Reyes, who were already unconditional supporters. Recent research has tended to stress the role of the organised labour movement as a whole which threw its still considerable weight behind the pro-Perón campaign.[1]

The fateful meeting of the CGT Central Committee to decide its response to Perón's enforced departure took place on 16 October. The minutes of that meeting show that only the *Unión Ferroviaria* was prepared to compromise with the military government over Perón's fate so as to protect the advances of the labour movement.[2] The remaining delegates, representing the old service sector unions as much as the new industrial unions, saw the need for a decisive counter-attack. They perceived that the attack on Perón was an attack on the new-found rights of labour. One thing which hastened this unanimity was a wave of strikes throughout the country protesting Perón's displacement but which also represented a potential threat to the established union leadership. Lombardi of the tram-workers union said openly that 'the situation is extremely grave because we run the risk of losing control of the labour movement which has taken so much work to organise. The working masses, why deny it, are steamrolling'.[3] This was effectively true: the general strike called by the CGT for 18 October was already unfolding on the 17th.

A whole network of labour organisers was at work throughout the popular quarters of Buenos Aires. The Berisso *frigorífico* workers led by Cipriano Reyes played a key role in this, linking up with the Tucumán sugar workers' union FOTIA, for example, which helped the movement spread to the provinces. But Reyes exaggerates when he says 'I made 17 October'.[4] Perelman's account shows the role played by the new rank-and-file activists among the metallurgical and other workers: 'the masses had swallowed the (official) trade union organisation and the thousands of factory delegates were at the head of the crowds, which came together from hundreds of streets and districts at the historical Plaza de Mayo'.[5] Those who stress the spontaneous nature of the 17th must perforce play down the level of organisation required for such a massive mobilisation. The street mobilisations of the 17th were headed fundamentally by the 'new' trade unions organised since 1943. The myth of the *descamisados*, Argentina's *sans-culottes*, is not simple invention because the 17th did see the mobilisation of tens and thousands of recently-organised workers. It would be wrong, however, to write off the crucial role of the official trade union leadership in preparing the conditions for this event. Nor can we detect any significant 'liberal' labour sector which did not throw its weight behind the pro-Perón campaign.[6] This was for the very good reason that Perón had created a certain democratic space since 1943 which the labour movement could not afford to lose. The victorious conclusion of 17 October was a mixed blessing because it marked the definitive linking of labour's fate with the 'worker colonel'. Perón himself, when he was called upon to defuse the mass protest after its demands were conceded, spoke of 'the creation of an indestructible bond of brotherhood between the people and the army'.[7] At the very moment in which the masses were mobilised politically (not, we hasten to add, for the *first* time, as some Peronist accounts would have it) they were being co-opted into a corporatist project led by a nationalist sector of the armed forces.

The Communist Party seriously misinterpreted the significance of the 17th. The party journal *Orientación* had this to say on 24 October about the events of the 17th:

> Peronism managed to fool some small sectors of the working class, especially youths and women recently incorporated into production and from the provinces, to whom the democratic message had not reached because of the repression of the labour movement. These misled sectors of the working class were in fact directed by the Peronist bandits (*malevaje*) who, repeating scenes of the Rosas period and reliving what occurred during the origins of fascism in Italy and Germany, showed their true colours by hurling themselves against the defenceless population, against homes, against shops, against modesty and honesty, against decency, against culture, and, imposing the official strike, weapons in hand and with the active collaboration of the police, who on that day

and the next, handed over the streets of the city to the barbaric and unrestrained Peronists.[8]

At this point the communists parted company with the real mass movement of the workers in Argentina and paved the way for the unrestricted dominance of Peronism in the labour movement. In spite of all its contradictions, the movement which burst on to the historical scene on 17 October was undoubtedly progressive and represented the face of the future. The liberal or anti-nationalist side of the official left-wing parties was to favour indirectly the more reactionary aspects of Peronism, whose nationalism took a decidedly authoritarian direction.

In the wake of 17 October the *Partido Laborista* (Labour Party) was formed by trade union leaders who had operated as a fraction within the labour movement since 1943.[9] Its leading figures were Luis Gay, of the telephone workers' union and head of the syndicalist USA, Cipriano Reyes and Luis Monzalvo. Its programme called for nationalisation of the major industries, an end to the *latifundio*, profit-sharing for workers and a comprehensive social security system. It threw its weight behind the Perón candidature for the forthcoming elections. In this way the trade union movement had achieved an autonomous political voice on a national scale and workers were to have a direct impact on state politics. The union leaders who formed the *Partido Laborista* were well aware of the recently victorious British Labour Party and its links with the trade unions. Their project was a broadly similar one of institutionalising the political power of the working class, with the added element of a strong nationalist orientation as befitted Argentina's dependent position in the world economy.

In the circumstances the choice of Perón as the labourist presidential candidate was inevitable, but it would seriously limit the degree of independence of this new political current. This was shown in the choice of candidates for the 1946 elections. The *Partido Laborista* was able to impose Mercante for Buenos Aires provincial governership against Perón's chosen candidate, but only after Perón had rejected their arguments in favour of Mercante as vice-presidential candidate against the dissident Radical, Hortensio Quijano, chosen by Perón.

Labour advances (1946–1950)

Perón was duly elected president in 1946 with over 50% of the vote. One of his early acts was to dissolve the *Partido Laborista* and form his own Peronist party. Monzalvo accepted this decision meekly, justifying it in terms of a statement by Cipriano Reyes that the movement had already surpassed its leader Colonel Perón, and arguing that a new party 'with cohesion and unity in its thought and action' was now called for.[10] Reyes maintained an intransigent attitude as a result of which he passed most of the Peronist period in gaol. Perón, logically enough, was now aiming at total *personal* control over the labour movement, and all intermediaries would be swept aside. Figures such as Gay had provided a mantle of legitimacy among working-class voters at a crucial period. The dilemma faced by the labourist current was, as Baily writes, that 'they thought they could support Perón and the social and economic revolution without supporting his undemocratic methods or losing their independence'.[11]

Nevertheless, this process was not inevitable and a major responsibility must rest with traditional labour leaders, such as socialist Pérez Leirós and communist Rubens Iscaro, who in 1945 were already arguing at a meeting of the International Labour Organization that Perón's regime was fascist and that the CGT was not an independent labour organisation. This accusation echoed the crude propaganda of the US's 'Blue Book' on Perón's alleged fascism, and revived the stark alternative of 'Braden (ex-US ambassador in Argentina responsible for the "Blue Book") or Perón'. This type of argument could only strengthen Perón's grip over the labour movement and prevent the emergence of an independent class-struggle tendency *within* the nationalist movement.

Even as the Peronist government was being consolidated there was a considerable degree of trade union independence, perhaps best expressed in the figure of Luis Gay. Having dissolved the incipient Labour Party, Perón decided to carry out a similar operation on the CGT when elections to its leading bodies took place towards the end of 1946. However, his proposed candidate, Angel Borlenghi, was roundly defeated by Gay, which to some extent represented continued support in the trade union ranks for the labourist project. Perón could not allow the trade unions – the backbone of his movement, as he never ceased repeating – to retain an independent political presence. In 1947 he was able to engineer Gay's resignation after an obscure incident involving a visiting US union delegation with whom Gay was accused of colluding against the government. Gay later explained how

> either the independence of the trade unions was maintained, without ceasing to support a particular social policy, or the trade union confederation became a political instrument in the hands of the government. Those of us in favour of the first option had to go.[12]

The workers themselves had named Perón the 'No. 1 worker' in Argentina; now he was taking that delegated political responsibility to its logical consequences. As Torre argues, this whole incident represents 'the end of the convergence between the reformist and autonomous project of the trade union old guard and the populist movement which so profoundly marked the political history of contemporary Argentina'.[13]

After the fall of Luis Gay, Perón moved rapidly to consolidate the position of subservient figures in the labour movement; the CGT rapidly lost any independent political presence. Aureliano Hernández, a faithful Peronist, became CGT general secretary and transformed it effectively into a transmission belt for government policies within the labour movement.

Eventually Hernández was dismissed, after a quarrel with Eva Perón – who was now playing a major role in the trade unions on behalf of Perón – and was replaced by the even more subservient figure of José Espejo. Perón's overall labour strategy was now becoming clearer, as were his words in 1944 when trying to reassure Argentina's employers:

> It is a grave error to think that workers' unions are detrimental to the boss. In no way is this so. On the contrary, it is the best way to avoid the boss having to fight with his workers . . . It is the means to reach an agreement, not a struggle. Thus strikes and stoppages are suppressed, though, undoubtedly, the working masses obtain the right to discuss their own interests at the same level as the employers' organisations, which, on analysing it, is absolutely just. . . . That is why we are promoting trade unions, but a truly professional trade unionism. We do not want unions which are divided in political fractions, because the dangerous thing is, incidentally, a political trade unionism.[14]

Perón never deviated from this essentially corporativist vision of social affairs and his 'revolutionary' image in a later period (see forthcoming chapters) was never reflected in practice.

Trade union expansion

Having stressed Peronism's negative influence on the independence of the labour movement we must now devote some space to the positive effects of his period in office. Since 1943 Perón had been promoting the formation of trade unions and providing legal and technical aid. Trade union membership grew by nearly 20% between 1941 and 1945, but if we examine selected industries we find that this growth is very uneven.

What stands out in Table 11.1 (which covers only selected industries) is that trade union membership fell in the construction, textile and graphic

Table 11.1   Trade union members, 1941 (July) and 1945 (December)

Sector	1941	1945	Relative difference 1945/1941 (in percentages)
Foodstuffs	29,171	97,426	+234
Construction	74,283	14,346	–81
Graphic	5,045	3,713	–38
Chemicals	250	5,884	+2,254
Textiles	12,504	2,613	–79
General	23,566	142,986	+507
Total	441,412	528,523	+20

Source: L. Doyon, (1975) El crecimiento sindical bajo el peronismo, *Desarrollo Económico* 15.57, p. 154.

industries, which were precisely those in which communist-dominated unions had been displaced. Union membership rose in foodstuffs and particularly in the chemical industry, where Perón virtually created the union. As to the spectacular rise in the general trades, Doyon suggests that this represents a 'dustbin' category, where opponents of the regime were placed so that pro-Peronist unions should have a clear majority in CGT voting.[15]

Trade union membership grew spectacularly after Perón came to power in 1946, from 877,000 in that year to 1.5 million in 1948, and to nearly two million in 1950. By the end of the Peronist regime the overall unionisation rate was 42% (which compares favourably with the advanced industrial societies) with the crucial manufacturing sector having 55% of the total number of workers unionised, though the agrarian sector showed only a meagre 6% unionisation rate.[16] The government openly encouraged unionisation throughout this period but it would be wrong to see this expansion purely as something imposed from above. The early period in particular saw a massive wave of rank-and-file activity throughout the country which the pre-Peronist union leadership encouraged. By the 1950s certainly, union membership in the state sector was a statutory obligation and did not represent increased activism. The first phase was crucial when we consider that in the first three Peronist years (1946–49) union membership rose by 190%, whereas in the next six years (1950–55) it rose by only 44%. One union leader recalls vividly the difference Peronism made to union organisers:

> There is no longer any fear about joining. There is no need to pay union duties in the toilets and changing rooms, but in the light of day ... The worker no longer has to bow when the boss of foreman passes by as in the old days and respectfully raise his cap. He can now argue freely with the boss and legitimately defend his rights ... The worker has achieved that most precious right of a human being–dignity.[17]

Peronism not only achieved the dignity of labour in Argentina, but much more besides. First, wages rose steadily after 1946 particularly for the unskilled, as we see in Table 11.2.

Table 11.2   Real wages, 1943–1950 (1943=100)

	1943	1944	1945	1946	1947	1948	1949	1950
Skilled	100	105	87	91	104	124	118	113
Unskilled	100	108	99	95	109	137	134	127
Payments per hour (includes fringe benefits)	100	111	106	112	140	173	181	174

Source: B. Silverman, (1968–9) "Labor Ideology and Economic Development in the Peronist Epoch." *Studies in Comparative International Development* IV.11, p. 245.

The last category of payments per hour in Table 11.2 includes family allowances, seniority payments and the famous *aguinaldo* (payment for a thirteenth month at the end of the year) introduced by Perón. Another way of expressing labour's advance is that the share of wages and salaries in the national income rose from 44% in 1943 to 60% in 1950.[18] Perón also introduced paid annual holidays, paid sick-leave, the extension of the pension system to all employees, redundancy and dismissal compensation, regulations on health hazards at work, compensation for workplace accidents, etc. In this context, we can understand the rhetorical question posed by one union leader:

> The unions built workers' homes, clinics, holiday camps, sports fields . . . What could the labour movement aspire to that Perón could not grant? He even gave us rights and benefits which even the trade union leaders themselves had never dared to ask for.[19]

The unions became a key intermediary in Argentina's equivalent of a welfare state.

The situation in the workplaces themselves also changed dramatically under Perón. As Perelman explains:

> The internal relations between management and employees in the factories had completely changed in nature. The internal democratisation which we impressed on the metallurgical union meant that the factory delegate became the axis of the whole organisation and the direct expression of the will of the workers in each establishment.[20]

Since 1944 a sophisticated system of direct democracy had developed in the large factories. Each shop or department elected a delegate in open assemblies. The delegates constituted the *cuerpo de delegados* (shop-stewards' plenary) which in turn elected a *comisión interna* (factory committee) which negotiated with management. A strong shop-stewards' organisation was thus created which gave the Argentine labour movement an unrivalled level of participation and activism in its best periods. The *comisión interna*, unlike the formal trade union structure outside the plants, could play a major role in pushing back the 'frontiers of control', as workers took away more and more of management's prerogatives.[21] For the first time in Argentina, workers could meet legally during working hours and elect shop stewards – often after a vigorous political debate – and these could go on to defend the workers' rights while being paid by the firm. The *comisiones internas* became important organs of self-defence which helped enforce the social gains made by the working class at the national level.

The 'dignity of labour' took concrete shape in this democratic shop-steward structure, the scourge of the employers. Without a clear-cut anti-capitalist consciousness, workers were nevertheless taking up issues – an unfair dismissal, an authoritarian foreman or a speed-up of the assembly line – which directly threatened management's 'right to manage'. These bodies were also political schools in which workers debated the major issues of the day, learned to organise and to strike. Workers would henceforth associate the social gains of the Peronist period with the growth of the *comisiones internas*. These would sometimes become bureaucratised, but at their best they functioned as genuine organs of workers' democracy or 'workers' parliaments'.

This qualitative growth of workplace organisation was in direct contradiction with Perón's overall bid to control the trade union movement. At that level the trade unions were being centralised and coming increasingly under state control. This contradiction will be a constant in the history of the labour movement from then on, but in that early period there was an uneasy coexistence between factory democracy and union oligarchy.

Another, broader, contradiction was posed between the working class social base of the Peronist movement and its bourgeois nationalist ideology. This was to be a major problem for the left and one not easily resolved, even after the death of Perón in 1974.

Strikes

It would be wrong to think that the social and economic gains of the Perón period were achieved without struggle. In fact, the first years of Perón's government saw a real upsurge of strike activity. This can be gauged partly by comparing the strike statistics for the first and second half of the 1940s in Table 11.3.

Table 11.3   Strikes, strikers and days lost, 1940–1949

Period	No of strikes	No of strikers	Working days lost
1940–1944	332	75,067	1,235,149
1945–1949	392	1,226,835	9,693,117

Source: Computed from year-by-year data in the Appendix.

Though the actual number of strikes does not increase dramatically, the number of workers involved is sixteen times greater and the number of working days 'lost' (i.e. gained by workers) is almost eight times greater. Most of the strikes in the first Peronist phase were short in duration, averaging four or five days, although, as we shall see, there were a number of longer strikes. On the whole the government intervened to favour the workers in these strikes, though this was not always the case. Luise Doyon distinguishes an early phase from 1943 to 1945 in which the strikes imposed fairly limited contracts with the employers dealing with wage increases, and another from 1947 to 1948 in which the labour process and working conditions were a major issue, and in which the *comisión interna* became the backbone of workplace organisation.[22] We now turn to some of the major strikes in this period which helped win the social and economic reforms usually associated with state paternalism.

The anti-Peronist labour histories lay great stress on Perón's 'taming' of the unions. This does take place later as we shall see, but the main characteristic of the first phase is that those unions which were directly promoted from the Secretariat of Labour and Social Security between 1943 and 1944 were in the forefront of strike activity after 1946.

A major strike by the *frigorífico* workers in March 1946 had as one of its major demands the reinstatement of those remaining out of work from the 12,000 sacked after a strike the previous year.[23] In November, another strike spread throughout the industry over a number of wage and working conditions demands. This strike continued even after Perón had denounced it. Various union leaders were imprisoned and union premises closed down. In 1947 over 100,000 textile workers in Buenos Aires went on strike over wages and conditions. The dispute was declared illegal by the government and the CGT 'intervened' in the textile workers' union, after having dissolved the *comisiones internas* in the plants affected.

Towards the end of 1947, the metal-workers' union launched a strike in Buenos Aires to impose a wage demand and to force the firms in the industry to implement the Peronist labour reforms. In spite of threats of government intervention the metal-workers were able to defeat the employers, who were forced to accept one of the most advanced contracts of the period. The more well-established dockers' union also launched a strike in 1947 which lasted several weeks. They achieved higher wages, shorter hours and canteen facilities, though their union was to remain under government control until 1950.

The year 1948 represents a turning point in terms of the nature of strikes. Compared with the previous year there were one and a half times more strikes, but only half the number of strikers. The average duration of strikes had risen from 6 to 11 days (rising to 20 by 1950).[24] This would seem to mean that strikes were being more severely repressed by the state and more fiercely resisted by employers. Doyon also argues that the decline in strikes after 1948 is due to the achievement of the major economic demands of the workers, and the loss of a great number of the more combative leaders.[25] This process can be seen with the sugar workers' union FOTIA, which launched a successful strike in 1948, but which in 1949 was defeated in a bitter month-and-a-half long struggle with the government which led to its effective demise as an independent union organisation. The *frigorífico* workers carried out a strike in defence of a limited worker-participation scheme in 1949 (and again in 1950) which only ended after the government intervened and established a new collaborationist union leadership. Towards the end of the year the bank workers launched a strike which achieved its wage demand but resulted in 1,200 sackings and 200 bank workers being imprisoned. In this last case, socialist and communist elements had 'politicised' the strike, but in most of the others the workers were not acting against Peronism but simply in defence of their living standards. This point is important because the anti-Peronist interpretation would see every strike in this period as a 'revolutionary' protest against Peronism.

Turn against labour (1951–1955)

The early expansive phase of Peronism was coming to an end in 1950, particularly after Perón's re-election in 1951 (with 60% of the vote) and the death of the more militant 'Evita' in 1952. In 1946 Perón had embarked on an ambitious industrialisation programme based in large part on the state monopoly of agricultural trade. Income from agricultural exports was redirected through the state-controlled banking system to promote industrialisation. Perón also laid the basis for heavy industrialisation in Argentina through the creation of a steel industry as part of an overall strategy of state-led industrialisation. International space for this strategy was provided by the fact that one imperial power (Britain) was in decline whereas the rising power (USA) had not yet turned its full economic and military power to the south. The considerable level of income redistribution achieved by Perón during this period had been achieved thanks to the substantial reserves accumulated during the Second World War. By 1950 this 'easy' phase of industrialisation/redistribution had entered into crisis.

Dissension within the armed forces increased; the Catholic Church threw its weight against Perón; and above all, the industrialists began to question their support for Perón's economic policies. They wanted to break out of state tutelage and prosper under a less restrained capitalism. It was simply no longer possible for profits and wages to keep on rising at the same time – the black and white struggle between capital and labour was imposing itself above the Bonapartist ambitions of Perón. Perón's anti-imperialism also had to adapt to the new situation. The buying of the British-owned railways by the state in 1947 was already of questionable benefit.[26] Then in 1953 a new law on foreign investment granted preferential treatment to international capital, which turned the nascent car industry over to US interests and allowed another US firm, Standard Oil, a free hand in Argentina's oil fields. Perón's much vaunted 'third position' in the international political field also went by the board as he consistently took a position alongside the US in the Cold War.

At home, those who bore the brunt of the new economic turn were, as usual, the workers. Real wages began to decline slowly in 1950 (see appendix) as economic growth rates fell and the rate of inflation rose to over 30%. Wages still represented 49% of the gross national product during the 1952–55 period, higher than the 41% of the 1946–48 period and the 48% for the 1949–51 period. As one writer suggests: 'What was shrinking was the cake and not the share of workers in its distribution'.[27] Perón did, in fact, strive to defend the interests of the working class, even in the more unfavourable climate of his second mandate. The start of the Korean War provided a certain amount of economic breathing space, as demand for Argentina's agrarian produce picked up. What happened in this period was a streamlining of state expenditure – which was truly profligate until 1950 – and the selling-off of some of the firms bought by the state between 1943 and 1948. Perón attempted to keep prices down and vowed that from then on wages would only increase in relation to rises in productivity. This strategy was consolidated, as we shall see later, in the *Congreso de la Productividad* (Productivity Congress) of 1955 in which workers were urged by their trade union leaders to tighten their belts. Perón was trying too late to forge a 'developmentalist' alliance between the national bourgeoisie and a working class delivered by a corporativist state. However, the dynamic unleashed by Perón – in particular the organisation and politicisation of the workers – made this impossible.

Strikes

As we noted above, strikes became longer and more difficult after 1948. By 1951, as government repression became more severe, the level of strike activity was becoming lower, as we see in Table 11.4.

Table 11.4   Strikes, strikers and days lost (1945–1954)

Period	No of Strikes	No of Strikers	Working days lost
1945–1949	392	1,226,835	9,693,117
1950–1954	125	254,426	4,006,204

Source: Computed from the year by year data in the Appendix.

Table 11.5   Trade union meetings, (1946–1954)

Year	Number of Meetings	Attendance
1946	3,858	759,497
1947	2,969	650,098
1948	1,530	505,467
1949	1,182	338,415
1950	914	257,306
1951	698	167,676
1952	740	226,604
1953	1,009	316,837
1954	1,109	321,703

Source: R. Sidicaro, (1981) "Consideraciones sociológicas sobre las relaciones entre el peronismo y la clase obrera en la Argentina: 1943–1955", *Boletín de Estudios Latinoamericanos y del Caribe*, no. 31, p. 54.

We see an accentuation of the trend noted for 1948: the number of strikes between 1950 and 1954 are about a third of what they were for the 1945–49 period, working days lost fall by half, and the number of strikers is only one-quarter of what it was previously. Alongside the fall in militancy, the internal life of the trade unions also declined in this period as we can see in Table 11.5.

From the strong trade union participation of the first two years (1946–47) we see a steady decline in the late 1940s with only a slight recovery beginning in 1952. We shall now examine some of the major strikes of this period to assess the implications of these trends.

Perhaps the major strike in the second Peronist phase was the action taken by the railworkers in 1950. Rank-and-file assemblies began pressing for a wage increase to meet the rising cost of living and a levelling up of the lower-paid categories. The *Unión Ferroviaria* leadership (by now in Peronist hands) refused to take the matter further because it did not want to break 'the existing equilibrium between prices and wages'. A second assembly led to the formation of a strike committee which turned the partial stoppages into an all-out strike and called for the resignation of the union leadership. As Iscaro describes, 'What had begun as a protest by the *peones* was transformed into a struggle by the whole union for social and economic rights and the democratisation and independence of the *Unión Ferroviaria*'.[28] When the strike action spread into 1951 the government declared it illegal and placed the railworkers under military rule. Some 3,000 workers were sacked and 300 gaoled, though the firmness of the workers after the strike led to these being released and reinstated.

The roots of the strike lay in the inability of the government to maintain the relatively high wages of this sector after having nationalised the ailing rail system. The open movement of the opposition, the *Movimiento pro Democratización e Independência de los Sindicatos* (Movement for the Democratisation and Independence of the Unions), rapidly politicised this strike. In this context it is significant that the main objectives of the strike were attained even though the Peronist state threw its full political weight against the strikers. Another major strike of 1950 was that by the port and maritime workers–another vital transportation sector–in which the workers were forced to retreat after six bitter weeks.

In the metal-workers union there was a fierce internal dispute in 1952 between the Peronist leadership and the Communist-dominated Rosario branch which supported the claims of a rival leader. The latter actually led an armed assault on the union headquarters. In mid-1954 discontent with the leadership sharpened when it tried to call off a strike before its full demands were met. Mass assemblies of workers elected a strike committee which had to confront fierce repression, unleashed by the government and also by the official union leadership (who, according to some reports, tortured workers in union offices). The wage demands were eventually satisfied and the union leadership forced to resign, but many workers remained in gaol.

Other strikes in this period which took a broadly similar course (though less intense) were those of the tobacco workers, of some major textile firm workers, and of the power workers' union *Luz y Fuerza* (Light and Power). There was also the major graphic arts workers' strike of 1953. The main motive was invariably the decline in real wages but the strikes were also directed at a subservient union leadership. The government displayed none of the benevolence of the earlier period and strikes were rapidly declared illegal. The capacity of self-organisation of the workers had strengthened, however, and their combativity was undiminished. The majority of these strikes ended with government or employer concessions granted, if for no other reason, to defuse a possible general spread of working-class discontent.

Bureaucratisation

As we have seen, the trade unions became more bureaucratic and less responsive to their members' needs after 1950. The CGT congress of that year dropped its previous commitment to socialism and declared its total subordination to Perón. May Day became a celebration of the Peronist 'revolution'. In 1954 the CGT General Secretary, Espejo, was replaced by Eduardo Vuletich, who was himself replaced by Di Pietro in 1955. Belloni describes how 'the CGT loses all autonomy, becoming just another branch of the state apparatus. The CGT leadership is not the authentic, natural and democratic expression raised from the most capable of the rank and file'.[29] The CGT threw its weight behind Perón's productivity drive in the 1950s. Its publications urged workers to produce more, and in 1954 one CGT editorial even explained that the trade unions had to ensure that workers 'who had received the logical and necessary social justice, do not extend their demands beyond that which is reasonably just'.[30]

Already, 1949 had been dubbed the Year of Productivity, but it was the 1955 National Congress of Productivity which best expressed the trend towards corporativism. The CGT joined forces with the employers' organisation, the *Confederación General Económica* (General Economic Confederation), formed in 1951 to call on workers and bosses to co-operate for the good of the nation. Vuletich declared that 'the social gains of Peronism would have to be defended', but praised the 'understanding and commitment' of the employers and pledged the loyalty and sacrifice of the workers in 'the new stage' being entered into with the signing of national productivity agreements.[31]

José Gelbard, head of the CGE, spoke at this same congress of what the bosses considered to be the main problem:

When one looks at the role of the *comisiones internas* in many firms, which alters the notion that it is a workers' duty to do a fair day's work for a fair wage, it is not exaggerated . . . to ask that they should contribute to consolidate the normal development of the firm and the drive for productivity. Nor is it acceptable that, for no reason at all, a shop-steward should blow a whistle and a factory be paralysed . . .[32]

That this statement could be made in 1955 would seem to indicate that the bureaucratisation of the CGT was not as total as is sometimes thought. In 1952 the CGT authorised the formation of opposition slates in many union elections.[33] This democratic opening was designed to prevent the growing labour discontent from being channelled by the CP. It led to the emergence of a new leadership, slightly less bureaucratic, which had to base itself on the activists to displace the old unconditionals. The collective wage negotiations of 1954 brought rank-and-file unrest to the fore, and dissident sectors of the metallurgical, textile and other unions organised unofficial stoppages. Mainwaring argues persuasively that during this period 'the higher levels of the labour movement were reduced virtually to being an agent of the government, but at the rank and file level there was still an important level of autonomy'.[34]

This more nuanced picture leads us to question the version of events hitherto accepted by both supporters and opponents of Perón. A left-wing Peronist, Roberto Carri, speaks for example, of how 'the new proletariat, without trade union experience . . . considered it natural that its gains *were granted* by the government,' and of 'the impossibility of acting without receiving instructions from above'.[35] We have seen that unionisation and the struggle for the betterment of labour conditions were as much a fruit of labour activity as of Perón's social policy. Nor were workers that reluctant to take on their own leaders when these failed to defend their interests. There were even independent figures who, like Luis Gay in the early period, called for the independence of the labour movement and the revival of the original Peronist revolution.[36] One of these was Hilario Salvo, head of the metal-workers union until 1951, who supported the social and economic gains of 1943–46 but opposed Perón's subsequent attacks on the autonomy of the labour movement. In many unions, 'independent Peronism' was a serious trend, and support for Perón was justified in terms of the material benefits for the working class. Walter Little, after examining several cases, concludes that 'the political relations between the unions and the Peronist state were by no means monolithic'.[37] Little also argues that in spite of the massive support Perón received from the unions after 1951, and the strict control over their activities, he 'never lost a deeply rooted fear of the spontaneous acts of the working class'.[38]

The labour movement of 1954 was quite different from what it had been a decade earlier. The old political tendencies – syndicalism, socialism and communism – were minority forces. On the other hand the unions had been immensely strengthened, though at the cost of a largely bureaucratic leadership. This fitted in with Perón's vision which he communicated to the industrialists:

Do not be afraid of my trade unionism . . . I want to organise workers through the state . . . to neutralise ideological and revolutionary currents in its midst which might place our capitalist society in danger.[39]

He went on to say, 'We have to give the workers some improvements and they will be an easily managed force.' This is precisely what did not happen. The corporativist project put forward by Perón was never completed successfully. Strikes continued, and Perón's vision of 'class harmony', replacing the outmoded class struggle, was never realised.

The working class had gained in numbers, organisation, confidence and combativity. The real labour movement of the factories, workshops and workers' districts became a dense network of social and political ties which could not be broken by repression. Even the trade union bureaucracy which Perón created was a double-edged weapon. It certainly muzzled the working class but it also became a powerful social force with its own independent interests. Its future was tied up with the survival of the trade unions and its fortune could prosper only on the basis of a strong labour movement.

By 1955 the position of the Peronist government had become very unstable indeed. One attempted coup in 1951 had threatened the regime, but this was not as serious as the one in June 1955 when planes massacred hundreds in the central Plaza de Mayo. The workers obtained arms and barricaded the access streets, blocking the entry of the rebel soldiers to the city centre. In August Perón told a trade union congregation at the same Plaza de Mayo that 'for each of ours five of theirs will fall'. This was an empty threat and the 'loyal' armed forces began organising the definitive blow.

It took place in September with a military revolt in the provincial city of Córdoba which spread through the armed forces as Perón faltered and refused to take defensive action. The military coup was sanctified by the Catholic Church which, in spite of the many concessions granted it by Perón, threw its weight behind the traditional ruling class. The military operation was not without its mass support, organised by the political parties of the *Unión Democrática*. Perón's failure to win over the significant sectors of the middle class – and the abstract anti-fascism of the traditional left – made these two groups easy prey for the 'anti-totalitarian' message. In Argentina in 1955, however, 'democracy' was the last thing that the ruling class could deliver. The real class content of the 1955 coup was a deep-rooted anxiety about the new role of the working class and a need to accommodate the new international relations now clearly dominated by the US.

In the last months of the Peronist regime there was some speculation that trade union militias either had been or would be formed to defend the government. According to recent research by Julio Godio, the oft-repeated myth of the trade union militias is just that – 'because there was no attempt to form them. What happened was something quite different, which was to appear to be forming such militias to placate the pressures from below and to blackmail the *golpistas* (military coup-makers)'.[40] In fact, in September

1955 the CGT leadership put the workers volunteer reserves at the disposition of the army to help defend Perón. That this manoeuvre was considered necessary to calm Perón's supporters testifies to the widespread discussions in factories and workshops on how to fight the coming coup effectively. It reflected the dramatic changes in Argentine society, and the armed forces took the prospect of an armed proletariat very seriously indeed. In maintaining this façade the trade union bureaucracy rendered one last service to Perón. The lack of widespread (or organised) resistance to the coup was not due to the lack of weapons. It was simply the logical result of the sudden end to the Peronist dream of *justicialismo*, when its great helmsman decided to leave the stage before things got out of hand. Perón was to say quite truthfully in later years that he left without calling for resistance in 1955 so as not to cause a civil war. Meanwhile the bourgeoisie was declaring a civil war on the working class.

The ten years from 1945 to 1955 were absolutely vital in the formation of the contemporary labour movement, which still looks back on this era as its golden period. It is not that the workers' movement began with Perón, as his more fervent admirers in the labour camp profess to believe, simply that this period marks a fundamental re-making of the working class and the setting of political and ideological co-ordinates which would determine its evolution over the next 30 years. These years saw the definitive consolidation of the trade unions which from then on represented the mass of the workers rather than a political vanguard. They marked the beginning of a remarkably resilient form of workplace organisation, the *comisiones internas*, which were to be the backbone of future labour resurgences. At the same time the Peronist period saw the beginning of a new type of labour bureaucracy, which at best prevented rank-and-file activity, and at worst indulged in open gangsterism in trade union affairs.

We can say overall that whereas 1930–44 saw the nationalisation of the working class (i.e. the predominance of native over immigrant workers) the period 1945–55 saw the Peronisation of the working class, whereby a bourgeois nationalist ideology was imposed on the mass movement. There was also a shake-up of the left-wing parties in this period, with many socialists joining the syndicalists in the Peronist movement, and the communists going into the political wilderness when they joined forces with the traditional enemies of the working class.

An almost forgotten episode of the Peronist period was the attempt to create an international Peronist trade union movement. In 1952 union delegates from various countries came together to form an international confederation taking up the Peronist 'third position': neither capitalism nor communism. But the *Agrupación de Trabajadores Latino Americanos Sindicalizados* (Association of Latin American Unionized Workers), or ATLAS, as it became known, affiliated only two national organizations: the Argentine CGT and the Colombian CNT (*Confederación Nacional del Trabajo*: National Labour Confederation). Until it collapsed in 1955, ATLAS was essentially reduced to the propagation of Peronist doctrine through the labour attachés of Argentine embassies in the other Latin American countries. If the Mexican CTM (*Confederación de Trabajadores Mexicanos*: Mexican Workers' Confederation) had joined the new international body it could have become viable, but they were keen to have the CGT join ORIT (Latin American regional organ of the ICFTU), as it eventually did.[41] The international communist organization, the World Federation of Trade Unions, for its part, tried to approach ATLAS, drawn partly by the Argentine CP's turn in 1949 towards the Peronist trade unions. They were repulsed by the fiercely anti-communist CGT leadership which also effectively controlled ATLAS. As Deiner concludes in his history of ATLAS: 'It offered, for the first time, an organizational structure which might truly represent Latin American trade union hopes and opportunities; ATLAS betrayed these hopes'.[42]

Appendix 2

Table 11.6 Strike volume and real wages in Buenos Aires – 1945–55

Year	No of Strikes	Strikers	Days Lost	Real Wages (1943: 100)
1945	47	44,186	509,024	105.8
1946	142	333,929	2,047,601	111.7
1947	64	541,377	3,467,193	140.0
1948	103	278,179	3,158,947	172.9
1949	36	29,164	510,352	181.4
1950	30	97,048	2,031,827	173.6
1951	23	16,358	152,243	161.3
1952	14	15,815	313,343	143.1
1953	40	5,506	59,294	249.3
1954	18	119,701	1,449,497	164.7
1955	21	11,990	144,120	163.0

Source: Strike volume: R. Rotondaro, (1971) *Realidad y Cambio en el Sindicalismo*, Buenos Aires, Pleamar, p. 241.
Wages: B. Silverman, (1968–9) "Labor Ideology and Economic Development in the Peronist Epoch", *Studies in Comparative International Development*. vol. IV. no. 11, p. 245.
Note These figures do not include general strikes or factory occupations.

Notes

1. In particular J.C. Torre, (1976) "La CGT y el 17 Octubre de 1945". *Todo es Historia*. 105. A major factual account is F. Luna, (1973) *El 45: Crónica de un año decisivo*. Buenos Aires, Editorial Sudamericana.
2. "La CGT y el 17 de Octubre de 1945". In *Pasado y Presente* (1973), IV. 2/3.
3. Ibid., p. 414.

4. See C. Reyes, (1973) *Yo Hice el 17 de Octubre*. Buenos Aires, G.S. Editorial. Less self agrandizing is the account by S. Pontieri, (1972) *La Confederación General del Trabajo y la revolución del 17 de octubre de 1945*. Buenos Aires, Ed. Pirámide.

5. A. Perelman, (1961) *Como Hicimos el 17 de Octubre*. Buenos Aires, Coyoacán, p. 74.

6. The very categories of "liberal" and "anti-liberal" are of course questionable in this context and this is the major fault of Baily's labour history (*Labor, Nationalism and Politics in Argentina*) which divides up workers according to these labels.

7. Cited in F. Luna, (1973) *El 45*, p. 295.

8. Cited in J.J. Real, (1976) *Treinta Años de Historia Argentina*. Buenos Aires, Ediciones Crisol, p. 94.

9. See C. Reyes, (1946) *Que es el Laborismo?*. Buenos Aires, Ediciones R.A. and L. Monzalvo, (1974) *Testigo de la Primera Hora del Peronismo*. Buenos Aires, Pleamar.

10. L. Monzalvo, (1974) *Testigo de la Primera Hora del Peronismo*. pp. 238-9.

11. S. Baily, (1967) *Labor, Nationalism and Politics in Argentina*. New Brunswick, Rutgers University Press, p. 92.

12. Cited in J.C. Torre, (1974) "La caída de Luis Gay". *Todos es Historia*. 89, p. 8.

13. Ibid., p. 82.

14. Cited in C. Fayt (ed.), (1967) *La Naturaleza del Peronismo*. Buenos Aires, Viracocha, p. 99.

15. L. Doyon, (1975) "Crecimiento sindical bajo el peronismo". *Desarrollo Económico*, 15, 57, p. 155.

16. Ibid., p. 160.

17. Luis Angeleri (Luz y Fuerza) cited in C. Fayt (ed.), (1967) *La Naturaleza del Peronismo*, p. 217.

18. B. Silverman, (1968-9) "Labor Ideology and Economic Development in the Peronist Epoch". *Studies in Comparative International Development*, IV, 11, p. 243.

19. M. Gazzera, (1970) "Nosotros los Dirigentes" in M. Gazzera and N. Ceresole, *Peronismo: Autocrítica y Perspectivos*. Buenos Aires, Editorial Descartes, p. 42.

20. A. Perelman, (1961) *Como Hicimos el 17 de Octubre*, p. 42.

21. On the role of the *comisiones* see the comparative analysis of A. Gilly, (1978) Los consejos de fábrica: Argentina, Bolivia, Italia. *Coyoacán* II, 5.

22. L. Doyon, (1975) "Conflictos Operários Durante o Regime Personista (1946-1955)", *Estudos CEBRAP* 13, p. 100.

23. For a description of strikes in this period see L. Doyon, (1975) "Conflitos Operários Durante o Regime Peronista (1946-1955)" and R. Iscaro, (1958) *Origen y Desarrollo del Movimiento Sindical Argentino*. Buenos Aires, Anteo, Ch XIII.

24. Data from R. Carri, (1967) *Sindicatos y Poder en la Argentina*. Buenos Aires, Editorial Sudestada, p. 47.

25. L. Doyon, (1975) "Conflitos Operários Durante o Regime Peronista (1946-1955)", p. 103.

26. On this episode and the general decline of British hegemony in Argentina see P. Skupch, (1973) "El deterioro y fin de la hegemonía británica sobre la economía argentina 1914-1947". In *Estudio Sobre los Origenes del Peronismo/2*. Buenos Aires, Siglo XXI.

27. S. Mainwaring, (1982) "El movimiento obrero y el peronismo",

1952–1955". *Desarrollo Económico* 21.48. p. 519.

28. R. Iscaro, (1958) *Origen y Desarrollo del Movimiento Sindical Argentino.* p. 249.

29. A. Belloni, (1960) *Del Anarquismo al Peronismo.* Buenos Aires, Peña Lillo, p. 63.

30. Cited in S. Baily, (1967) *Labor, Nationalism and Politics in Argentina.* p. 140.

31. Cited in R. Carri, (1967) *Sindicato y Poder en la Argentina.* pp. 53–9.

32. Ibid., p. 53.

33. See E. Gonzalez, (1974) *Que fué y que es el peronismo.* Buenos Aires, Editorial Pluma, p. 55.

34. S. Mainwaring, (1982) "El movimiento obrero y el peronismo", p. 515.

35. R. Carri, (1967) *Sindicatos y Poder en la Argentina*, p. 217.

36. For further reference see: J.C. Torre, (1974) 'La Caida de Luis Gay' in *Todo es Historia* No. 89.

37. W. Little, (1979) "La Organización Obrero y el Estado Peronista', 1943–1955". *Desarrollo Económico* 19, p. 373.

38. Ibid., p. 376.

39. Cited in C. Fayt, ed. (1967) *La Naturaleza del Peronismo*, p. 22.7

40. J. Godio, (1973) *La caída de Peron.* Buenos Aires, Granica Editor, p. 183.

41. For an overview of Argentine trade unionism's international contacts subsequently see NACLA (1975) *Argentina in the Hour of the Furnaces.* New York, NACLA.

42. Deiner, J.T. (1970) *ATLAS: A Labor instrument of Argentine expansionism under Perón.* Rutgers, The State University, PhD thesis, p. 405.

12. Labour Resistance and Trade Union Bureaucracy (1956–1967)

After the fall of Perón, a period of chronic political instability opened up with a succession of military regimes (1955–1958 and 1966–1973) civilian interludes (1958–1962 and 1963–1966) or a combination of both (1962–1963).[1] The major political question of this period was how to handle the Peronist labour movement. Both proscription and controlled legalisation were tried. This period saw the trade unions emerging as a solid organisational power and also becoming steadily bureaucratised. It was a period of militant strikes and factory occupations, though on the factory floor workers were coerced by the productivity drives of the employers' modernising strategy.

In this chapter we shall examine different aspects of labour resistance and union bureaucratisation through the various political phases. These are the two military governments of Lonardi and Aramburu from 1955 to 1958; the civilian Frondizi regime of 1958 to 1962 and his succession by Senate President Guido under military tutelage from 1962 to 1963; and finally the Radical government of Illia which came to power in 1963 and was followed by the Onganía dictatorship in 1966. Throughout this period the trade unions assumed the dual role of representing the workers' economic interests and being effectively the political party of the working class due to the collapse of political Peronism. The working class became linked to Peronism but the latter also became more firmly based in the working class once its grip on state power was broken.

Peronist resistance (1955–1958)

When Perón was overthrown in September 1955 by the so-called *Revolución Libertadora* (Liberating Revolution) power was assumed by the provisional government of General Lonardi. He represented a nationalist sector which was prepared to accept many of the advances made by labour under Perón and he put forward the slogan "Ni Vencedores Ni Vencidos" (Neither Victors nor Vanquished). This helped disarm the labour movement and accounts in part for the change in the CGT line. On 19 September CGT general secretary Di Pietro declared, 'Every worker will fight with arms and whatever means are at his disposal to annihilate the traitors to the people's cause . . . ', but only three days later the CGT advised workers to 'maintain the most absolute calmness and remain at your work . . . '[2]

Many workers failed to take this advice and this period is rightly known as the Peronist Resistance. Military sectors who remained faithful to Perón began organising and this resulted in the Valle revolt of June 1956 which failed miserably. There was also a semi-insurrectional situation in the provincial city of Rosario which was only suppressed by military intervention. In the meat-workers' quarters of Ensenada and Berisso, demonstrations and armed attacks were also suppressed by a virtual military occupation of the area. These spontaneous moves towards a general strike were thwarted by the collaborationist attitude of the CGT leadership.

The second phase of the resistance was much more organised and saw a combination of trade union and military methods. Thousands of *caños* (primitive explosive devices) were used during these years in sabotage actions. Union activists were a key element in this campaign and, among other things, this firmly established a tradition of using physical force during strikes. As military pressure this was clearly insufficient, however, and gradually the main emphasis was placed on trade union work. The old trade union leadership had clearly outlived its usefulness. Strikes without official support were too much for these cadres who were largely 'upstarts, smart-Alecs and charlatans without convictions, knowledge or principles' as one critic put it.[3] Their last act was to call a general strike in mid-November 1955 to halt the government's growing repressive measures. In the industrial belt around Buenos Aires the stoppage was almost complete, but, as Juan Vigo describes 'there were no protest marches, nor assault groups . . . it was a calm, peaceful strike as though the workers had still not got over the shock caused by the fall of the Leader . . .'[4] Lack of preparation by the leadership was matched by fierce repression from the state forces. The strike was defeated. The CGT and many trade unions were taken over by the government, and the two-month-long Lonardi interregnum ended. State power was now assumed by General Aramburu, who represented a more consistent 'liberal' orientation pledged to eradicate Peronism from political life in Argentina.

Whereas Lonardi had tolerated the Peronist old guard in the unions, Aramburu moved rapidly to sweep them aside. His essential aim is described by Cavarozzi as that of:

> promoting the atomisation and weakening of the trade unions and any other wage-earners' organisation, and, as a result of that, to achieve a lowering of wage earners' participation in the national income, and liquidate any more or less autonomous form of political action by the working class.[5]

A prerequisite for this was the 'de-Peronisation' of the trade unions, a task in which the socialist and communist trade unionists proved willing accomplices. State-managed elections were held in many unions in 1957, and these two parties gained control of several service and transport sector trade unions. Whereas socialists chided workers for heeding the demagogy of Perón, figures such as Pérez Leiros, who returned to power in the municipal workers' union, were seen by workers as government agents. The communists were slightly less paternalistic in their approach to Peronist workers and their support for the *Libertadora* in 1955 was not reciprocated by the new military government. They began working with the clandestine Peronist bodies in support of the *comisiones internas*. Their credibility suffered, however, when their trade union policy was moderated in return for the government's permission for CP participation in the 1957 Constituent Assembly elections.

The 'democratic' trade unionists were completely incapable of replacing the trade unionists' Peronist leadership. They had lost all credibility among the rank and file, and where they did gain some kind of a base, it was through militant action, hardly what the government wanted. The key industrial unions such as *Unión Obrera Metalúrgica* and the *Asociación Obrera Textil* were solid Peronist bases. Only the Buenos Aires print-workers, where the syndicalists were popular, and the traditionally Socialist *La Fraternidad*, represented any real anti-Peronist force.

The government gradually began to recognise the need for 'normalisation' of trade union affairs. Several laws were passed to ban the participation of any leaders who had held union posts during the Peronist government. These older cadre were organised in the *CGT-Negra* (Black CGT) but its mass base was negligible. The effect of this was the election of a new generation of union leaders, less tainted by collaborationism and in much closer contact with the rank and file. There were certain limits to this process and an attempt by CGT military overseer, Patrón Laplacette, to 'normalise' this body in 1957 ended in failure.

Shortly afterwards, the trade unions divided into political factions – the '62 Organisations' represented the Peronist unions, the '32 Democratic Organisations' organised the Socialist and syndicalist forces, and the Communist Party organised through the *Movimiento de Unidad y Coordinación Sindical* (Movement of Trade Union Unity and Coordination). These last two gradually declined and the '62 Organisations' became the undisputed political voice of the organised working class.

Labour resistance during this period was not contained by the government's repressive measures. Indeed, the strike statistics for 1956–1958 (see appendix) show an impressive level of working-class mobilisation. The first major strike was precipitated in 1955 by the government's decision to privatise rail transport in Buenos Aires. There were assemblies in all the stations and workshops, and when the police intervened a general strike across the capital was the result. This was followed in 1956 by the big metal-workers' strike which began over a wage demand and then continued to prevent victimisation. According to one report, 'the inexperience of the new [union] leadership and a provocation by a sector of the bureaucracy launched the strike prematurely. A direct confrontation with the united bosses and government was foolhardy'.[6] Certainly repression was severe: major plants were occupied by the army, tanks patrolled the workers' quarters, hundreds were arrested and thousands dismissed from work. The six-week long strike was hardly a victory, but the workers now knew that the state benevolence of the Peronist period was truly over. James concludes that:

> 'the strike was perhaps the worst example of the period of government-management intransigence but it was not a-typical. In the latter part of 1956 strikes in Construction, Shipbuilding and Transport were all declared illegal and the strikers subjected to similar treatment'.[7]

In the course of these confrontations a new working-class leadership was forged, relatively untainted by the state tutelage of Perón's last period in office.

In 1957 there were general strikes in July, September and October, largely organised by the '62 Organisations' to protest against the anti-union policies of the government. The ensuing repression of the Peronist-led unions could not alter the fact that the '62 Organisations' was becoming the stable and unified representative of the Peronist working class. A major aim of these strikes was to recover trade unions and the regional CGT bodies from the regime's overseers (*interventores*). The major centre of these strikes was Buenos Aires, but towards the end of the year there was a general strike in Mendoza and another in Tucumán which lasted a whole week.

It was in this general climate of resistance and combativity that the Córdoba branch of the CGT held a joint regional congress with the '62 Organisations' in La Falda. The anti-imperialist and anti-capitalist programme which it issued posed clearly the question of workers' power and was implicitly a threat to traditional Peronism. The 1957 La Falda Programme put forward a comprehensive economic plan based on state-supported industrialisation, a social policy which involved workers' control of production and a sliding scale of wages, and a political platform which called for Latin American unity and the hegemonic role of the labour movement in implementing the programme.[8] The official labour movement probably never intended to apply this radical programme, but it is indicative of the mood of the period, and had a certain educative role over the years. It is part of the heritage which would be taken up by the 'combative' unions after 1969.

In the wave of working-class mobilisations after 1955 the rank and file played a crucial role. The Aramburu regime directed much of its fire towards the *comisiones internas* which were either dissolved or simply appointed by the Ministry of Labour. Employers were given the go-ahead to sack Peronist union delegates (the *delegados de empresa*) and reassert 'the right of managers to manage'. This offensive was only partially successful. The 1956 metal-workers strike, for example, had brought to the fore a new generation of activists, a process which had been extended to many other sectors by 1958. Persecution of the trade union leaders could only lead to an increase in their prestige, especially when they participated in the Peronist Resistance, which was actively supported by even the more traditional sectors. Repression also heightened the ties between union leaders and the rank and file, as their official manoeuvring space was cut down.

The unofficial trade union federation known as the *Intersindical*, which was formed in 1955, and later the '62 Organisations', were forced by circumstances into a fairly democratic form of organising. There were plenary sessions held almost every week at which lively political debates took place. The members of the middle ranks of the trade unions who came to the fore during this agitated phase (such as Augusto Vandor in the metallurgical union and Eleuterio Cardozo in the meat-packers' union) were later to become part of a hardened bureaucratic caste. For the time being they rode the crest of working-class militancy.

One of the primary objectives of the post-1955 de facto governments was to drive down wages and restore 'healthy' rates of profit. The 10% wage increase granted in 1956 went a little way towards matching the rising rate of inflation (which reached 25% in 1957). The union wage-negotiating committees (*comisiones paritarias*) found the employers intransigent, though when disputes went to arbitration, some gains were made. Overall, the share of wages in the gross national income fell from 49.5% in 1955 to 47.3% in 1957. As James argues, 'the decline in living standards was rather the result of a political defeat than an economic one'.[9] The unions' capacity to take defensive action on wages was not impaired and the decline in real wages was not spectacular (see appendix). What the unions were losing was the capacity to hold back the 'frontier of control' in the workplaces. Increasingly employers were linking wage concessions to productivity deals and union cooperation with 'rationalisation'. The workers' 'restrictive practices' were condemned and piece-work was widely introduced along with various individual incentive schemes. The metallurgical industry employers' federation made its position clear in 1956 when it declared that it was 'urgently necessary to re-establish healthy discipline in the factories, which at the moment are something like an army in which the troops give the orders, not the generals'.[10] The semi-clandestine *comisiones internas* had lost the legal right to negotiate over these issues, but for most of this period maintained a vigorous defensive campaign against the new trends in capital-labour relations.

For Torre, the long-term effects of the strikes of 1956 to 1958 were more important than their immediate objectives because they 'reinforced a threatened mass movement [i.e. Peronism] and achieved its recognition as the trade union and political representative [*interlocutor*] of the organised working class'.[11] Perón remained the undisputed leader of the movement but he was in exile; the Peronist Party for its part had totally collapsed. Some of the political figures of Peronism such as the radical leader John William

Cooke had an important influence on the labour movement.[12] On the whole, the trade unions created their own leadership which, given the absence of any other credible power base in the country, became the political leadership of the Peronist movement as well. Thus began the famous 'dual role' (*juego doble*) of the unions: as organisers and mobilisers of the Peronist mass movement and as centralised negotiators of labour's social and economic gains with the state.[13] The identities of the labour and Peronist movements seemed to merge. This was expressed by one union leader, Augusto Vandor, when he said, 'If I take off the Peronist vest [*camiseta*] I'd lose the union in a week'.[14] While the Peronist/anti-Peronist division corresponded closely to the division between workers and capitalists, this could be a positive factor. The ambiguity of the Peronist project – its essentially capitalist economic strategy and its heavy-handed corporatist-style bureaucracy – would emerge more clearly later. For this to happen the working class would first have to suffer a severe defeat in the factories to match its earlier political defeat in 1955.

The rise of Vandorismo (1959–1963)

The year 1959 saw almost 1.5 million workers out on strike and 10 million working days 'lost' through strikes. It also marked a turning-point in the relations between labour and capital, because from that time the *comisiones internas* lost much of their previous power. On the basis of a partially demobilised working class, a trade union current known as *Vandorismo* – after Augusto Vandor – became the leading force in the labour movement.

The Frondizi government which came to power in 1958 with the tactical support of Perón, began to implement a coherent economic policy based on increased foreign investment and a rationalisation drive. The inevitable confrontation with the labour movement came over the plans to privatise the Lisandro de la Torre *frigorífico* near Buenos Aires. In January 1959 the workers organised a mass lobby of parliament to try to block the measure. This failed, and 9,000 workers occupied the plant with the support of tens of thousands from the surrounding district of Mataderos. The government sent tanks to break down the doors and a wave of indiscriminate repression began. The eviction of the *frigorífico* workers only increased the district's militancy. Barricades went up and Frondizi's local Radical Party office was burnt down. The 62 Organisations called a general strike – reluctantly supported by the 'democratic' 32 Organisations and the CP's trade union front (MUCS) – which rapidly developed into an insurrectional situation. The official union leadership called off the general strike after three days and although some areas continued unofficially, the *frigorífico* strike was effectively broken (though 6,000 workers never returned to work).

Later in April there was a month-long national strike by bank workers, which embraced both the state and private sectors and, according to the employers, brought the country to the edge of financial paralysis. In

August the metal-workers' union (*Unión Obrera Metalúrgica*) launched a national strike which lasted a month and a half in pursuance of a wage claim. In September the *Asociación Obrera Textil* called out its members for the same reason, and they remained on strike for nearly as long. These two unions, metallurgical and textile, were led by key Peronist figures, Augusto Vandor and Andrés Framini respectively. Though their collective contracts ran out at roughly the same time they refused to co-ordinate their action, and they both went down to bitter defeat, as the bank workers had done earlier. At the time these strikes were presented to the rank and file as a victory.

This view is reflected by Roberto Carri, who refers to 1959 as 'a year of great victories for the working class'.[15] Certainly 1959 was a high point of militancy and a culmination of the Peronist Resistance. Nor is the enthusiasm and participation of the rank and file in question. However, Daniel James is much closer to the truth when he says that 'the objective result of the conflicts was defeat rather than victory. These defeats marked the turning of the tide as far as working-class mobilisation and confidence was concerned'.[16] For most of the 1960s – except in part during the 1964 factory occupations – there was a downturn of labour militancy. In fact, the tide only really turned a decade later – with the *Cordobazo* of 1969.

In September 1959 there was a 48-hour general strike organised by the *Movimiento Obrero Unificado* (Unified Workers' Movement) which brought together the 62 Organisations, MUCS and some independent unions which broke away from the 'democratic' 32. This was the culmination of a year which saw four general strikes in which some twelve million workers participated. The combativity and resoluteness of the working class were unable to defeat Frondizi's economic plan however, and wages fell by one-quarter in 1959. A process had already begun to 'normalise' fully the government's relations with the trade unions, and in 1961 the CGT was returned to the labour movement. The union leadership was becoming increasingly collaborationist and was deeply worried by the militant strikes of early 1959 which had effectively outflanked it. The general strikes or stoppages (*paros*) were at least in part a means to defuse energy. It was noticeable that these stoppages were passive in general, and there was no mass picketing. Echagüe calls this a beginning of *huelgas domingueras* (Sunday strikes) meaning that they were formal measures with a sort of holiday atmosphere, and somewhat removed from the heat of the class struggle.[17] The unions had lost the initiative, which they clearly had had from 1955 to 1958, and from now on their role was primarily defensive. They could not even maintain the basic gains of the Peronist period – the socio-economic advances and the high level of workplace organisation.

A key factor in driving back the labour movement was the concerted productivity drive of the employers from 1959 onwards. The 1955 Productivity Congress had already set out the major aims of the employers: to reduce the power of the *comisiones internas* and clear away the obstacles to the 'rationalisation' of the labour process. This could not be achieved under the climate of Peronism, and the military governments after 1955 had only been partially successful. It was in the early 1960s that measures designed to achieve these aims were taken across industry as a whole. A prerequisite was a rank-and-file movement which had exhausted its reserves of combativity, as had happened in the 1959 strikes, and a labour bureaucracy which was willing to trade-off power in the plants for a respectable political role.

In contract after contract employers succeeded in gaining sole control over working arrangements and removing any remaining obstacles to labour mobility and *speed-ups* of the assembly lines. The *Unión Obrera Metalúrgica* signed a contract in 1960 which contained the following provision:

> The system of bonuses and other forms of incentive schemes do not form a proper matter for this contract . . . the UOM and/or its delegates in the different establishments cannot oppose the revision of existing schemes when it has become clear that failure to adopt wage systems, methods of work and to renew machinery will detract from the higher goal of giving incentives to optimise production.[18]

A fierce rear-guard action to reject the right of employers to determine unilaterally the 'rate for the job' and do away with mutuality clauses was met by lock-outs and widespread sackings. The *comisiones internas* were systematically deprived of the right to negotiate with employers at plant level and a centralised system of wage bargaining was consolidated. Severe restrictions were placed on the election of union delegates in terms of age and experience requirements and in terms of the numbers allowed. They were faced with complex procedures through which to take up grievances, and production arrangements were explicitly removed from their control. James concludes correctly that 'the prime result of the rationalisation drive which culminated in the early 1960s was radically to shift the balance of forces on the shop floor in favour of employers and to make the objective possibilities of rank and file activity centred on the internal commissions very poor'.[19]

This process was systematically implemented in the key metallurgical, textile, food-processing and meat-packing industries. At the same time it was applied with less resistance in the new high technology and capital-intensive industries based on an inflow of foreign capital. US investment alone increased from US$350 million in 1950 to US$472 million in 1960 and then jumped to US$992 million by 1965. Foreign investment was concentrated in the durable consumer and intermediate goods category such as the motor industry and allied trades. The local branches of the multinational corporations initiated a vigorous process of capital concentration in 1958 – the top 100 private industrial firms accounted for 20% of total sales in 1958, and this rose to 30% by 1968. Foreign participation in local manufacturing also increased dramatically: whereas in 1958 foreign companies controlled 14 of the top 100 manufacturing enterprises (and accounted for 30% of sales), by 1968 60 of the top 100 firms were in foreign hands (accounting for 60% of sales).

The importance of these tendencies for our purposes is that they led to a fundamental change in the composition of the working class. The dominant form of industrialisation until the mid-1950s was based on a relatively stable organic composition of capital and hence a steady recruitment of labour. From the mid-1950s, and particularly after 1958, the pattern of industrialisation had become much more capital-intensive and consequently less labour was absorbed. One indication of this is that the cumulative increase in capital stock of the manufacturing industry was 1.8% between 1946 and 1955, rising to 9.8% between 1956 and 1965. This marked a qualitative shift from manufacturing to big industry, to use Marx's terms, and consequently a change in the social organisation of work.[20] The absolute extraction of surplus value from workers (lengthening of the working day, etc.) was gradually superseded by the extraction of relative surplus value (increased labour productivity through more advanced machinery, etc.). The working class was passing from the stage of *formal* subsumption of labour (where capital dominates a labour process, characteristic of an earlier phase) to the *real* subsumption of labour (the specifically capitalist form of production based on a constant revolution of techniques and methods). We shall examine in the next chapter the effects of these changes, once they had matured, on the labour movement.

We return now to our account of the labour movement under the Frondizi government, starting with the return of the CGT to its legitimate leaders in 1961. The first conflict the CGT faced, once it had achieved independence from its military overseer, was the 1961 strike on the railways against the government's rationalisation and privatisation measures. The CGT was forced to call a three-day general strike in solidarity. After a month and a half the workers achieved a victory in spite of wide-scale repression. Shortly after this, state employees went on strike over the plans for administrative rationalisation, as did the *frigorífico* workers and the Tucumán sugar workers who also occupied 27 *ingenios* (sugar mills). The social and economic crisis of this period with its sequel of hunger and unemployment was driving workers to radical actions. In spite of the measures taken against them the *cuerpo de delegados* (shop-stewards' plenary) were in the forefront of these struggles, and exerted a powerful radicalising pressure on the leadership.

The spreading of factory occupations after 1960 provided a new element of concern to employers, who saw the sacred rights of private property being threatened. When Frondizi called legislative elections in March 1962 Peronists and their allies obtained 40 per cent of the vote, and militant trade union leader Framini was elected governor of Buenos Aires province. The military then overthrew Frondizi and installed the senate president as government caretaker under their tutelage. All the measures taken to co-opt Peronism, to 'normalise' Argentine politics, had been in vain. Governments could not govern (for long) with a thwarted, proscribed

Peronist movement, but when it was legalised they would also fall.

In 1962 there was a succession of factory occupations which involved considerable rank-and-file participation and were often successful. One example was the strike in the Acindar metallurgical plant in Villa Constitución where pay had been withheld and redundancies were planned. Echagüe describes how a movement 'based on strike committees [*comisiones de lucha*] carried out successful 4-hour strikes each shift, devoting the remaining four hours to mass meetings in the factory, demonstrations and picketing to guarantee the strike and mass participation in the assemblies'.[21] In many cases workers were practising rudimentary forms of armed self-defence using iron bars and 'molotov cocktails' to hold the occupied plants. A reflection of all this ferment at a national level was the adoption by the Peronist 62 Organisations of the Huerte Grande Programme which put forward ten points:

1) Nationalise the banks and establish a centralised state banking system.
2) Impose state control over foreign trade.
3) Nationalise the key sectors of the economy: steel, electricity, oil, *frigoríficos*.
4) Prohibit the direct or indirect export of capital.
5) Refuse to recognise the country's debts, signed behind the backs of the people.
6) Prohibit all imports which compete with our own production.
7) Expropriate the landed oligarchy without any type of compensation.
8) Impose workers' control over production.
9) Abolish commercial secrecy and rigorously control commercial associations.
10) Plan production efforts in terms of the interests of the nation and the Argentine people, fixing priorities and establishing minimum and maximum limits of production.

Here was a coherent workers' plan with an anti-capitalist as well as anti-imperialist content, but the union leadership offered no concrete means to achieve its implementation.

In January 1963 the CGT held its 'normalisation' congress and later adopted a comprehensive *plan de lucha* (struggle plan). Augusto Vandor emerged as undisputed leader of the organised workers' movement. For that reason we must now examine the basic elements of the *vandorista* strategy.[22] It can best be summed up in the phrase 'hit and negotiate' (*golpear y negociar*) which meant that Vandor was quite prepared to use militant action, but only as a bargaining tool with employers or the state. Mobilisation had to be carefully controlled, and this was nowhere more apparent than in the *plan de lucha* with its carefully orchestrated campaign of factory occupations. The plan was drawn up from above and the workers' only function was to obey instructions from head office. Workers were used as part of the union leadership's pressure politics. The main demands of the *plan de lucha* were economic ones, but a central objective was to block the government's bid to weaken the CGT through legal measures. This explains the relative benevolence of employers during the factory occupations.

This does not mean that the *vandorista* strategy was simply legalistic. It is worth recalling that in the 1959 metal-workers' strike there were a number of attacks with explosives against plants and offices of the industry. In fact the national treasurer of the *Unión Obrera Metalúrgica* was arrested for leaving a bomb in a bar; it had begun to detonate prematurely, before arriving at its objective at the Siam di Tella offices.[23]

Vandorismo was not simply a heavy-handed bureaucracy, as the level of grass roots organisation in the metal-workers' union (UOM) testifies. Cavarozzi describes how under Vandor's leadership the UOM 'had developed . . . a vast and representative network of delegates, factory committees and union branches effectively centralised by the Executive Committee . . . '[24] The usual emphasis on Vandor's use of union thugs (*matones*) to control meetings and discipline wayward elements, tends to neglect the extent of rank-and-file participation. Vandor, and others like him, had a long history of militancy and persecution behind them which afforded them considerable prestige. After the defeats of 1959–60 the rank and file was also quite prepared to support Vandor's pragmatic approach, or at least not fight against it. Lack of participation in internal union elections was an important indication of the rank and file's response: whereas in 1957 there was an 85% turn-out in the textile union internal elections, in the 1961 UOM elections in Buenos Aires there was a 59% abstention rate.[25] James concludes that this represented 'a system of institutionalised rank and file passivity which was independent of the specific antidemocratic machinations or actions of the Peronista union leadership . . .'[26] Whereas one can accept that the union bureaucracy can only occupy a space ceded by a demobilised working class, as another writer puts it,[27] this process cannot be seen as something *independent* of the union leaders' negotiations. Under Frondizi they had gained legal recognition with a new Law of Professional Associations, which had consolidated their position in return for their control over the rank and file.

The deleterious effects of *vandorismo* can best be seen in Vandor's own metallurgical union stronghold. After the militant strike of 1959 Vandor presided over a declining membership, as we see in Table 12.1.

Table 12.1   Workers employed in the metallurgical industry

Year	1959	1960	1961	1962	1963	1966
Number	309,000	296,000	284,000	252,000	219,000	121,000

Source: R. Walsh, (1969) *Quien Mató a Rosendo?* Buenos Aires, Editorial Tiempo Contemporaneo, pp. 152–3.

In examining these figures it is worth bearing in mind that the UOM had 100,000 members in 1946. The 'modernisation' of the metallurgical industry, which the union leadership collaborated in, also resulted in a dramatic increase in labour productivity (i.e. exploitation) as we see in Table 12.2.

Table 12.2   Productivity in the metallurgical industry (1950: 100)

Year	1950 (index)	1956 (first strike)	1958 (Frondizi government	1959 (second strike)	1961 (union/ employers alliance)
Productivity	100	108	136	114	150

Source: R. Walsh, (1969) *Quien Mató a Rosendo?* Buenos Aires, Editorial Tiempo Contemporaneo, p. 153.

The union went along with the concentration of the industry, which resulted in the closure of many smaller firms and workshops. In the larger firms dismissals were more selective, as Rodolfo Walsh describes: 'the most militant are thrown out, those previously called 'communists' or revolutionary Peronists. *Comisiones internas* are dissolved, or if necessary they are bought: a good redundancy payment ensures a peaceful future for the shop-steward who accepts it'.[28] In short, the considerable resources of the unions were used to discipline the work-force rather than the bosses.

Struggles and defeats (1964–1967)

In 1964 the *plan de lucha* entered its decisive second phase: in seven carefully planned operations 11,000 factories were occupied by nearly four million workers.[29] The centre of these mobilisations was Buenos Aires and its industrial suburbs, though the provincial capitals of Córdoba, Rosario, Tucumán and Mendoza were all affected. More than a quarter of the operations were centred around the metallurgical industry which was the real vanguard, followed closely by the textile, food-processing, construction and *frigorífico* sectors. The combativity of the artisan sectors was far less, as was that of shop and bank employees. According to one account, 'the objective of the mobilisations was to cancel out rank-and-file action, to continue wearing them down, and at the same time to create the appropriate climate for a coup d'état . . . '[30] We shall return to the trade union campaign against the Illia government which came to power at the end of 1963 (with only 25% of the vote after the banning of Peronism) but the first part of the statement must be qualified. In spite of the intentions behind the *plan de lucha* the actual mobilisations were a tremendously important experience for the working class. The power, organisation and combativity demonstrated in the factory occupations by the labour movement were undeniable. To a certain extent the bureaucracy was in practice outflanked by rank-and-file activists who impressed a more radical stamp on what was originally conceived of as carefully controlled 'revolutionary gymnastics' (*gimnasia revolucionaria*), as Perón was fond of saying.[31]

If the 1964 stage of the *plan de lucha* was the high point of *vandorista* strategy, the 1965 phase involving public meetings and demonstrations was a much more subdued affair. The independent trade unions withdrew from the mobilisation as they considered that most of its aims had been achieved. Vandor and the 62 Organisations continued the action with the clear aim of weakening Illia's Radical government. Ostensibly, the aim was to achieve the return of Perón from exile (*Operación Retorno*) but when this was prevented towards the end of the year, the *vandoristas* began actively to encourage a military coup. The general strike called in December 1965 to protest against Perón's non-arrival received only patchy support. It seemed that the *vandoristas* were now overstretching themselves, having an exaggerated view of their own power but failing to attend to the most pressing demands of the working class.

The rank and file, for its part, maintained a capacity to carry out militant action. One example was the violent occupation of the ASTARSA plant near Buenos Aires at the beginning of 1965 when 700 workers held the managers hostage. This thwarted the possibility of violent repression and the managers were forced to settle with the workers' representatives. Workplace occupations again became a favoured method of struggle and clearly posed 'political' issues when the state intervened. A favourable economic situation allowed the workers to recoup some of the purchasing power they had lost since 1959. The year closed with a month-long strike by the municipal workers of Buenos Aires, involving daily mass meetings and rank-and-file mobilisation, which led to the overthrow of the Pérez Leiros socialist leadership of the union after he refused to back their members.

In 1965, when the promised return of the leader did not materialise the political contradictions of the Peronist movement sharpened and the CGT entered an internal crisis.[32] Vandor then took the logical step of extending the power of the trade unions into the political arena, in short to establish a 'Peronism without Perón'. The political independence of Vandor came to a head in the April 1966 elections for the governorship of Mendoza, where he put forward a rival to the official Peronist candidate. Perón even sent his wife Isabel Martínez as a personal envoy to try to quell the *vandoristas'* pretensions of autonomy. José Alonso set up his own version of the 62 Organisations (the Peronist political trade union body) called 'standing alongside Perón' (*de pie junto a Perón*) to signify his unconditional allegiance. The left tended to support Alonso (as did a series of Vandor's rivals for more personal reasons) because he was confronting the bureaucratic monolith of *vandorismo*. In January 1966 this rivalry in the Peronist camp led to a split in the CGT. It is necessary to stress that this did not represent a split between fractions of the working class but simply a quarrel between rival bureaucratic cliques. The Alonso fraction took with it 21 unions, representing 417,000 workers, among whom were the mechanical, sugar and state workers. Vandor had a following of 20 unions, which represented 408,350 workers, including metallurgical, construction, port and oil workers. There were also seven independent unions representing 397,600 workers.

It was thus a divided labour movement which confronted the growing crisis of the Radical government. Illia had legalised the political presence of the Peronists in a bid to defuse their appeal, but as Frondizi had found out earlier, this did not win him any friends. In March 1965, congressional elections were held and the Peronists polled 38% of the national vote against 30% for Illia's party. As presidential elections were scheduled for 1967 the prospects of a Peronist government were becoming real. The armed forces reacted much as they had in 1962, and overthrew Illia's government in a well-organised military manoeuvre. This time they did not merely install a care-taker president, but assumed power directly.

Political ferment in the armed forces had been brewing since 1962, pitting the *Azul* faction, which was essentially in favour of a 'professional' military and some accommodation with the 'Peronist problem', against the *Colorado* group, which called for a permanent political role for the military and complete intransigence towards Peronism. General Onganía (of the *Azules*) emerged from these struggles as the new commander-in-chief, and it was he who led the military to power in June 1966.

Onganía's coup represented more than just another military take-over or 'preventive coup', and was to result in a basic restructuring of Argentine society. It was the most coherent attempt by Argentina's dominant classes to 'rationalise' the social and economic structures of the country. Its main beneficiaries were the dynamic industries which had emerged between 1958 and 1962 under Frondizi and which had become the leading economic sector. They were now assuming political power to match their economic role and therefore displaced the ineffective Illia regime which represented only the traditional middle class.

The majority of the trade union leaders supported Onganía's coup and even attended his inauguration. Juan Taccone, of the electricity workers' union, *Luz y Fuerza*, says that 'the support for Onganía was not opportunism of the leadership: it was a position which recognised national realities . . . Onganía represented hope for the majority of the Argentine people, over and above ideological differences . . . '[33] Onganía was deeply influenced by Catholic corporativist social thinking which sees a strong state mediating directly between the major power groups. The union leaders thought they could become the undisputed representatives of labour (as a pressure or interest group) cutting out the party political system. Taccone argues that 'the political parties were no longer representative of the totality and needed the complementary action of the dynamic groups in society.'[34] This was a logical outcome of the trade union bureaucracy's acceptance of 'integration' (*integracionismo*) under Frondizi which was now becoming 'participation' (*participacionismo*) under Onganía. There were in fact differences in the trade union position, with a minority sector maintaining an oppositionist role, Taccone and others openly collaborating with the government, and Vandor, as always, hedging his bets by working with the government but not too openly.[35] The acquiescence of the Peronists as a whole towards the 1966 coup – thinking that another process such as that of 1943–1946 was being ushered in – is best exemplified by the response of Perón himself, who told his followers to 'dismount until the storm blows over' (*desensillar hasta que aclare*).

In a sense it was not surprising that the trade union leaders would support a corporativist project such as Onganía's. They had effectively renounced the weapon of working-class mobilisations to carry out their aims, and were now clearly 'managers of discontent' to use an expression of C. Wright Mills. Their orientation was to achieve a larger share of the national income for workers by promoting industrialisation. They did not wish to challenge capital in the factories but rather to encourage further investment. The politics of *vandorismo* were pragmatic – including its allegiance to Perón – and there was nothing preventing its support for someone like Onganía.

In fact, support for the state and the military as an institution was inscribed in the logic of Peronist ideology from the start. Taccone, for example, says openly: 'I believe in a statist society [*sociedad estatal*], that is, in the possibility that social development will occur within the state . . . '[36] The trade union leaders also had material interests to defend, which no doubt reinforced their commitment to corporativism. Union membership dues were all funnelled to the Buenos Aires headquarters, a percentage of every wage increase they negotiated was retained by the union leaders, and they could also ask the government for one-off discounts from members' wages for the union coffers.[37] The considerable sums of money at their disposal – which gave them widespread powers of patronage – were matched by extensive material resources such as clinics, holiday resorts, etc. Though one can lay too much stress on the element of corruption in explaining the conduct of a trade union bureaucracy, this was undoubtedly a factor in leading them to maintain a cooperative attitude with the powers that were.

Trade union support for Onganía began to wane as the true complexion of the de facto government became clearer. When Krieger Vasena took charge of the economy in 1967 he began implementing measures clearly designed to favour monopoly capital.[38] Non-competitive enterprises were to be pruned – this meant rail cuts, closures of sugar *ingenios* in Tucumán and the sacking of public employees. Anti-inflationary policies were used as a pretext for freezing wages (see Appendix) while an open-door policy was practised with regard to foreign capital. The CGT was faced with a freezing of all collective contracts and the state take-over of its holiday resorts. The government control of union elections and over the management of funds which had begun under Illia was now stepped up.

The unions were simply taken aback by this frontal attack. The Buenos Aires port workers were one of the first to mount a lively rearguard attack on 'rationalisation' towards the end of 1966. After a month-long strike they were forced to retreat after having received little or no support from the organised labour movement. Ironically, the government's intervention in the union led to the imprisonment of its leader, Eustaquio Tolosa, who had expressed his complete confidence in Onganía until a few days previously. The next sector to feel the weight of the military-monopolist government was the railway workers. The railway network was to be completely restructured, as were the organisation and conditions of work. The unions resisted the implicit job losses and increased exploitation with a strike in January 1967. In spite of massive mobilisation the workers were defeated and the *Unión Ferroviaria* suffered government intervention.

In the threatened sugar region workers were not able to repeat the *ingenio* occupations of December 1965, and demonstrations were severely repressed by the police. The once proud sugar-workers' union FOTIA was unable to prevent the closure of twelve of the 27 *ingenios* in the Tucumán province.[39] The CGT called a general strike for 1 March 1967 as part of an action plan to protest against the government's economic policies and particularly the situation in Tucumán. Many unions simply refused to support the stoppage, and on the actual day only the railworkers came out solidly, though there was some support from the industrial unions in the Buenos Aires area. The overall downturn of the class struggle in 1967 is manifested in the strike statistics for that year: there were six strikes, 547 strikers and only 2,702 days 'lost' in Buenos Aires.

The failure of the general strike in March 1967 also represented the end of the road for *vandorismo* as a viable strategy for the labour movement.[40] Under all the governments prior to 1966 the trade unions had been able to gain concessions through their tight control over the labour force. Onganía's government was not weak, as most of the previous ones had been, and the ruling class was united as never before. For the time being at least there were few contradictions to exploit among the dominant classes. The working class had also been driven too many times up to the top of the hill and down again to no avail–it was now simply too tired and demoralised to respond.

Taking the whole period from 1956 to 1967 we can say that the fierce resistance of the first years and the big strikes and factory occupations which came later were not matched by a principled labour leadership. Peronism had promoted a trade unionism turned towards the state and not the working class. The trade union current know as *vandorismo* epitomised Argentina's version of business unionism. As solid organisations with enormous financial resources, these unions traded off their influence in the workplace for short-term economic gains. The defeat of the 1959 strikes led to a demobilised working class, paving the way for the *vandorista* strategy. This culminated in the *plan de lucha* by which carefully orchestrated mobilisations replaced the spontaneous energy of the working class.

The trade unions' advanced political programmes–exemplified by the one adopted in Huerta Grande in 1962–could not hide the essential pragmatism of the union leadership. This was displayed in full when the union leaders enthusiastically supported Onganía's military coup in 1966 in the vain hope that in his corporatist dreams there would be a place for them. Instead, 1966 led to the collapse of *vandorismo* as a credible option for the unions. A new period was beginning based on the objective transformation of the working class during the early 1960s. Out of the defeats of 1966 and 1967 a powerful wave of mobilisation and political ferment would emerge.

Appendix 3

Table 12.3   Strike volume and real wages in Buenos Aires, 1956–1967

Year	No. of Strikes	Strikers	Days Lost	Real Wages (1960: 100)
1956	52	853,994	5,167,294	117.1
1957	56	304,209	3,390,509	113.7
1958	84	277,381	6,245,286	128.5
1959	45	1,411,062	10,078,138	98.3
1960	26	130,044	1,661,519	100.0
1961	43	236,462	1,755,170	110.8
1962	15	42,386	268,748	—
1963	20	207,216	812,395	108.0
1964	27	144,230	636,302	119.0
1965	32	203,596	590,511	127.1
1966	27	235,913	1,003,710	125.3
1967	6	547	2,702	121.6

Source: Strike statistics: R. Rotondaro, (1971) *Realidad y Cambio en el Sindicalismo,* Buenos Aires, Pleamar, p. 241.
Wages: G. Ducatenzeiler, (1980) *Syndicats et politique en Argentine 1955–1973,* Montreal, Les Presses de L'Université de Montréal, p. 259.
Note: These figures do not include general strikes or factory occupations.

Notes

1. For an overview of this period see C. Fayt (1971) *El politico armado: Dinámica del proceso político argentino 1960–1971*, Buenos Aires, Penedille.
2. Cited in M. Cavarozzi (1979) Sindicatos y Política en Argentina 1955–1958, *Estudios CEDES,* vol. 2, no. 1, p. 17.
3. J. Vigo (1973) *Crónicas de la Resistencia*, Buenos Aires, Peña Lillo Editor, p. 72.
4. Ibid., pp. 73–4.
5. M. Cavarozzi, (1979) *Sindicatos y Política en Argentina*, p. 25.
6. E. González, (1974) *Qué fue y qué es el peronismo*, Buenos Aires, Ediciones Pluma, p. 74.
7. D. James, (1979) *Unions and Politics: The Development of Peronist Trade Unions, 1955–66*, PhD thesis, London School of Economics, p. 76.

8. The La Falda programme is reproduced in F. Cerro, (1974) *De Perón al Cordobazo*, Buenos Aires, Centro Editor de América Latina, pp. 210–11.

9. D. James, (1979) *Unions and Politics*, p. 74.

10. Ibid., p. 53.

11. J.C. Torre (1979) *El movimiento sindical en la Argentina*, mimeo, p. 19.

12. Of Cooke's work see in particular J.W. Cooke, (1973) *Peronismo y Revolución*, Buenos Aires, Granica Editor.

13. See R. Carri, (1971) Sindicalismo de Participación, "Sindicalismo de Liberación", in N. Ceresole (ed.) *Argentina: Estado y Liberación Nacional*, Buenos Aires, Organización Editorial, p. 148.

14. R. Walsh, (1969) *¿ Quien Mató a Rosendo?* Buenos Aires, Editorial Tiempo Contemporaneo, p. 171.

15. R. Carri, (1967) *Sindicatos y Poder en la Argentina*.

16. D. James, (1979) *Unions and Politics*, p. 183.

17. C. Echagüe, (1971) *Las Grandes Huelgas*, Buenos Aires, Centro Editor de América Latina, p. 97.

18. Cited in D. James (1981) "Rationalisation and Working Class Response: the Context and Limits of Factor Floor Activity in Argentina", *Journal of Latin American Studies*, vol. 13, no. 2, p. 394.

19. Ibid., p. 402.

20. This is explored in more detail in M. Peralta Ramos, (1972) *Etapas de acmulación y alianzas de clases en la Argentina (1930–1970)*, Buenos Aires, Siglo XXI.

21. C. Echagüe, (1971) *Las Grandes Huelgas*, p. 99.

22. For an insider's account of *Vandorismo* see M. Gazzera, (1970) Nosotros los Dirigentes, in M. Gazzera and N. Ceresole, *Peronismo: Autocrítica y Perspectivas*, Buenos Aires, Editorial Descartes.

23. M. Cavarozzi, (1979) "Consolidación del Sindicalismo Peronista y Emergencia de la Fórmula Politica Argentina Durante el Gobierno Fronalizista", *Estudios CEDES*, vol. 2, no. 7/8, p. 77.

24. Ibid., p. 74.

25. D. James, (1978) "Power and Politics in Peronist Trade Unions", *Journal of Interamerican Studies and World Affairs*, vol. 20, no. 1, p. 26 and p. 24. On trade union democracy more generally see J.C. Torre, (1974) "La Democracia Sindical en la Argentina", *Desarrollo Económico*, vol. 14, no. 55.

26. Ibid., pp. 27–8.

27. J.C. Torre, (1974). "The Meaning of Current Workers' Struggles", *Latin American Perspectives*, vol. 1, no. 3, p. 78.

28. R. Walsh, (1969) *¿Quien Mató a Rosendo?*, p. 154.

29. G. Bourde, (1978) 'La CGT argentine et les occupations d'usines de mai–juin 1964'. *Le Mouvement Social*, no. 103, p. 73.

30. C. Echagüe, (1971) *Las Grandes Huelgas,* p. 102.

31. See Perón's radical rhetoric in his correspondence with J.W. Cooke who was his representative in Argentina after 1965: *Correspondencia Perón–Cooke,* 2 vols, Buenos Aires, Granica Editor, 1973.

32. The internal union disputes are traced meticulously in G. Ducatenzeiler, (1980) *Syndicats el politique en Argentine (1955–1973)*, Montréal, Les Presses de L'Université de Montreal.

33. N. Dominguez, (1977) *Conversaciones con Juan José Taccone*, Buenos Aires, Hachette, p. 122.

34. Ibid., p. 127.

35. The documents produced by the various tendencies are reproduced in S. Senén Gonzalez, (1971) *El Sindicalismo Despues de Perón*, Buenos Aires, Editorial Galerna, Ch VI.

36. N. Dominguez, (1977) *Conversaciones con Juan José Taccone*, p. 42.

37. D. James, (1978) "Power and Politics in Peronist Trade Unions", p. 7. On the trade union bureaucracy generally see J. Correa, (1972) *Los Jerarcas Sindicales*, Buenos Aires, Editorial Polémica.

38. On Onganía's economic policies see C.R. Cepeda (1972) *Crisis de Una Burguesía Dependiente–Balance Económico de la "Revolución Argentina" 1966–1971*, Buenos Aires, Ediciones la Rosa Blindada.

39. For a study of the Tucumán sugar workers around this period see F. Delich, (1970) *Tierra y conciencia campesina en Tucumán*, Buenos Aires, Editorial Signos.

40. This interpretation is pursued in J.C. Torre (1979) "El Movimiento Laboral en Argentina: 1955–76" in J. Carrière (ed.)

13. The *Cordobazo* and a 'New' Working Class (1968–1972)

When President Onganía came to power through force of arms in 1966 he envisaged a lengthy period of office – some twenty years – to complete his ambitious plans for restructuring Argentina. This illusion lasted barely three years, because in May 1969 the workers and students of Córdoba launched the famous *Cordobazo*. Onganía's succcessor, General Levingston was similarly shocked by a mass revolt in 1971 – the second *Cordobazo*. With a declining range of options the third military president, General Lanusse, embarked on a policy of 'decompression' which was to lead to the return of Perón in 1973.[1] This chapter studies the upsurge of labour activity during this period, from the *Cordobazo* to the various class struggle tendencies which emerged subsequently in some trade unions.

The events of this whole period, and particularly those of 1969, mark a watershed in Argentina's labour history. New forms of struggle emerged, and the dichotomy between Peronism and anti-Peronism was broken as various forms of socialism took root. New layers of workers came to the forefront, symbolised by Córdoba's militant car workers. They were relatively well-paid and their claims went beyond economic issues to take up labour conditions and democracy within the unions. To set the framework for our narrative of events from 1968 to 1972 we begin with an analysis of this 'new' working class which emerged from the industrialisation process of the early 1960s.

A labour aristocracy?

If the 'typical' worker of the 1950s was from the textile plant or *frigorífico*, a more typical figure of the late 1960s was the worker from the car or chemical plant. The large foreign corporations established during the early 1960s needed a skilled work force and were prepared to pay above-average wages to obtain it. The unions agreed to supplementary wage bargaining at plant level over and above national negotiations for the industries. Considerable wage differentials developed and there was some speculation that a 'labour aristocracy' was developing in the new dynamic industries.

In his 1964 analysis of the Córdoba car industry, Aricó said:

The industrial proletariat of the big enterprises, which resulted from recent foreign investment, constitutes in a certain sense a relatively privileged group, a labour aristocracy which obtains privileges through the maintenance of the present structure, who enjoy high wages because their class brothers – unskilled workers, *peones*, rural proletarians, etc. – earn miserable wages.[2]

We must note that in this hypothesis, car workers, for example, obtain high wages *because* the rural *peón* does not. Other writers point to the supposed political effects of this 'new' working class. In particular the tendency for these dynamic industries to establish plant unions is attacked. Carri refers to a process whereby:

arguing that the specific conditions [of each plant] cannot be covered by entities which embrace the most varied situations, the plant level unions become the principal means of imperialist penetration in the working class, with its sequel of apoliticism and submission in exchange for a few more *pesos* in the wage packet.[3]

To assess the 'labour aristocracy' thesis we must begin by separating the economic and political aspects which the above analysis equates far too rapidly. There *was* a growing heterogeneity of the working class between 1955 and 1965 expressed in wage differentials between workers in the 'dynamic' industries (e.g. petroleum, chemicals, machinery, vehicles and in the 'traditional' sectors (e.g. food and beverages, clothing, textiles). This was simply 'accompanying the growing internal diversification of the industrial sector and increasing dispersion in the rates of growth of labour productivity', according to one analysis.[4] We can see the results of this process in Table 13.1.

Table 13.1   Rates of increase of wages and labour productivity in traditional and dynamic industries, 1950–1970 (annual average rate of increase in manufacturing as a whole: 100)

	Wages	*Productivity*
Traditional industry	81	36
Dynamic industry	128	164

Source: A. Marshall, (1980) "Labour market and wage growth: the case of Argentina", *Cambridge Journal of Economics*, no. 4, p. 56.

There were countervailing factors which prevented this tendency towards differentiation from increasing. Firstly, when the new stage of industrialisation was completed around 1965, employers no longer felt the need to grant bigger wage increases. Secondly, there was a growing rate of unemployment in the 1960s (around 6 per cent) comparable to an earlier period of labour shortage, which drove down wages as a whole. Thirdly, as Marshall notes, 'labour organisations were able to *spread* a large fraction of the wage increases obtained in leading industries to the rest of the manufacturing sector ...'[5]

Does heterogeneity of working conditions lead to a lack of cohesion and to centrifugal tendencies in the labour movement, as several authors argue? Peralta Ramos says that:

> the growing heterogeneity of the objective situation of the working class, which generates an internal fractioning with the appearance of a 'labour aristocracy' . . . generates the main upholders of reformist ideology in the new period.[6]

However, the few empirical studies of trade union attitudes in Argentina have found no clear-cut link between industrial sector and political attitudes. If anything, 'participationism' predominated in those unions formed under Perón which were the bastions of the traditional proletariat.[7] A strong sectionalist orientation, striving for higher wages in one's own particular sector, has never been incompatible with a broader class consciousness. The most important missing link is the political dimension which tends to unite workers across industry. Here we find little difference between workers in different sectors in their attitude towards unions or socialism. One major study of working-class attitudes in Argentina carried out by Silvia Sigal concludes that:

> the greater professional and economic integration which is produced in the modern enterprises is not accompanied by an important re-definition of class identity, nor does it place in doubt worker solidarity, nor does it lead to a significant decline in the conflicts linked to the work situation.[8]

In fact, the greater level of education of these sectors and their position in the most dynamic heartlands of capital, made them into a political vanguard in the 1970s.

The dynamic industrial sectors were able to achieve limited economic integration of their work-force, but this did not result in the formation of a labour aristocracy. As Jelin and Torre point out, 'relative economic privileges do not necessarily lead to greater social integration, [and] heterogeneity does not result in an automatic weakening of class solidarity'.[9] Plant level bargaining never completely replaced centralised or national collective bargaining to the extent that these plants became cut off from the labour movement. A union like the metal-workers' UOM negotiated wages and conditions for its members across industry, from the small workshop to the large factory. This in itself was a unifying factor, but one that was even more powerful was the high level of political identification with a mass movement, i.e. Peronism. Workers do not live in the closed world of the factory floor, and consciousness is not formed at that level alone, or even principally (see Chapter 16). The military government was also confused over this issue of the labour aristocracy when it saw the relatively well-paid workers in the forefront of the *Cordobazo* uprising in 1969. Economy Minister Krieger Vasena reputedly asked afterwards, 'How can we blame the government's economic policies for the May events if their protagonists are the best paid workers in the country?' Allowing for exaggeration his surprise was understandable. The Córdoba car workers were part of a 'new' working class only in the sense that they brought new issues – related to the labour process and labour bureaucracy – to the fore. We must not make the mistake, in relation to the rise of Peronism, of detecting and separating a 'new' working class from the overall evolution of the labour movement.

Towards the *Cordobazo* (1968–1969)

We can recall that in 1967 there was an unprecedented slump in strike activity. This picked up slightly in 1968 when 1,600 workers went on strike and 15,500 days were 'lost' by strikes in Buenos Aires. Between June and August there were several stoppages and marches by the IKA-Renault car workers in Córdoba and a national strike organised by the car mechanics' union SMATA (*Sindicato de Mecánicos y Afines del Transporte Automotor*). In Córdoba there were two issues which most concerned workers: a proposed end to the traditional *Sábado Inglés* (a 44-hour week paid as 48) and the *quitas zonales*, which were deductions on national wages claimed by the employers because of the provincial economy's poor state. In Buenos Aires the state petroleum workers of Ensenada and Berisso went on strike in September over working hours, though the underlying cause was the proposed privatisation of the industry. During the two-month-long strike the trade union bureaucracy did its best to contain the struggle and government repression was severe. A new, more militant style of unionism was evident, however, with long strikes replacing the token stoppages typical of the *vandorismo* era. This upsurge was consolidated in early 1969 with a long and bitter strike by the building workers at the Chocón damn project, where workers confronted their own union leadership and defended the site with barricades and dynamite. The Fabril Financiera graphic workers in Buenos Aires also went on strike (for 100 days) as did a number of the major car plant workers. In Tucumán the sugar workers began to mobilise once again to defend the *ingenios*, confronting the police with the support of a militant student movement.

In retrospect, the most significant event of 1968 was the split in the CGT which resulted in the formation of the militant 'CGT of the Argentines' (*de los Argentinos*) and the traditional 'CGT-Azopardo' (the street on which the CGT headquarters was situated).[10] A militant trade union tendency had already been organised by Amado Olmos before his death in 1968, and when a CGT congress was held in March that year it elected as its general secretary the militant leader of the Buenos Aires print-workers, Raimundo Ongaro.

At that stage the CGT-A (*de los Argentinos*) had some 600,000 affiliated members, but a year later this had declined to 280,000. It organised those sectors of the working class which had been most badly hit by Onganía's policies – rail-workers, sugar workers and generally the workers of the provinces. Its ideology was intensely radical and it promoted a campaign of mass mobilisation against the government's policies. Perón opportunistically supported the militant CGT-A against the more traditional CGT-Azopardo, but he later changed his mind and called for reunification. The CGT-A acted as a political pole of attraction for dissident workers, the increasingly confident student movement and the left generally. It continued to function sporadically until it called the general strike after the *Cordobazo*. It then declined as a mass force. The CGT-A tended to organise marginal or declining fractions of the working class and its outlook was more radical Christian than revolutionary Marxist, but it reflected the growing political ferment within the organised labour movement.

During 1969 there was a growing number of strikes, with the Córdoba workers playing a key role. In March, the Córdoba branch of the metalworkers' union UOM called a strike against the *quitas zonales* wage deductions. Early in May they repeated this action and were later joined by the car-mechanics' union, SMATA (7,500 members) which called a two-day general strike supported by the national leadership. Shortly before, the bus drivers' union, *Union Tranviarios Automotor* (UTA), led by veteran Peronist fighter Atilio López, had been out on strike over recognition of seniority. The involvement of the large and well-organised car workers' union led to a rapid politicisation of the dispute. The government responded with police repression, a sharp increase in food and transport prices and a law finally abolishing the *Sábado Inglés*.

The Córdoba unions were able to overcome the national political differences and UOM, SMATA and UTA called a joint general strike for 15 and 16 May. The Rosario metal-workers called a strike over factory closures, redundancies, the wage freeze and other issues. Both strikes were highly successful and the one in Rosario resulted in the reunification of the trade union federation and more general mobilisation. The metal-workers of Rosario showed eloquently why they went on strike:

> Every day the army of unemployed and the exploitation of workers increases, as does the delay in the payment of the miserable wages frozen by decree and by the increase in the cost of living. . . . We want to participate as actors. We are no longer spectators. The water has reached our noses and this is no time for puppets. All this is leading us to 'participate' actively and maturely in the only way that those who do not bear arms can – with the weapon of the general strike. . . .[11]

The immediate build-up to the *Cordobazo* began with the killing of a student in May 1969 after a demonstration by the university students of Chaco and Corrientes in the north-east of the country, protesting a rise in canteen prices. The provincial CGT called a general strike in protest, and organised a mass demonstration. The unrest then spread to Rosario after a student there was killed by the police. The local CGT supported a protest march, and as Laclau describes:

> On that day events exploded beyond all expectation: a mass of workers, students

and employees physically seized the centre of the city and threw up barricades, which they defended with Molotov cocktails, stones and anything that came to hand to beat off tear-gas bombardments by the police.[12]

The police were completely overwhelmed and the army intervened, declaring Rosario an 'emergency zone', in preparation for a decisive confrontation, as marches and clashes with the repressive forces spread throughout the country. The key element was the recovery of working-class combativity in Córdoba and elsewhere, which opened up a political space for a revitalised student movement to emerge. The students were the detonator for a more explosive phase and also the link between the working class and wider layers of the population, which now began to confront the dictatorship. The labour movement was acting as the vanguard of a broad social movement, both organisationally and politically. For the time being the 'participationist' current in the unions was forced into the background as the leadership was forced once again (as in 1956–58) to ride the crest of a militant wave.

May 1969

The growing unrest within the working class culminated in the national general strike called for 30 May 1969 by both CGT branches. The militant unions in Córdoba supplemented this measure with an 'active strike' (*paro activo*) on 29 May.[13] Preparations began in the car plants as SMATA members made up Molotov cocktails, distributed slings and the famous *miguelitos* (bent nails placed on the road to puncture tyres). The power workers' union, *Luz y Fuerza*, was also involved in this preparatory work, in fact there was a saying that 'SMATA provided the men and Luz y Fuerza the ideas'. The power workers' leader in Córdoba, Agustín Tosco, explains how the strike was far from spontaneous:

> We had said: on such a day everybody strikes, and this column heads to town along this route and so on. In our opinion the spontaneity consisted in the degree of popular support, but not in the organisation itself. The date and time of the strike were fixed at a mass meeting [*plenario*]. It was a concrete struggle, headed by the working class, for concrete demands.[14]

The workers' participation was planned by their unions. They marched in organised columns – the 4,000 IKA-Renault workers, 10,000 metallurgical workers, 1,000 power workers, and so on – towards the city centre. As they advanced, and confrontations with the police began, they were joined by students, white-collar employees and other workers. The city centre represented 'the powers that be': there were the police headquarters, the churches, the hotels, the banks and above all, the salesrooms of the big firms.

During the street fighting of 29 May the demonstrators confronted 4,000 police and, in the subsequent days, some 5,000 fully-armed soldiers. The police succeeded in splitting up the large groups but were then overwhelmed by hundreds of smaller groups who constructed barricades as they advanced. By early afternoon the police had been forced to retreat from the city centre where there was widespread destruction. Cars were dragged out of showrooms and set on fire, bank windows were smashed, the restaurants of the upper class were set on fire and at the Xerox offices someone said, 'This is an imperialist firm. Here the enemies of the people exploit us and that is why we must burn it.'[15] When the people had taken over the whole of the city centre the army declared the area subject to martial law and prepared to move in. The demonstrators withdrew to the workers' quarters and the student district, Barrio Clínicas, which were heavily fortified with barricades and makeshift weapons. In the early evening the army moved in and began moving from one barricade to the next. There was an attempt to win over the soldiers, but this was not at all successful. There was no mass organised resistance, which would have been suicidal, but throughout the night there was sniping and persistent isolated incidents. Local police headquarters were attacked as were electricity generators and railway installations. The military moved through the town, ruthlessly imposing the curfew order, though at certain points they came under severe pressure, especially when the electricity supply to the city was cut for several hours.

On 30 May the city woke to army patrols and constant demonstrations and attacks, centred around the Barrio Clínicas. In the afternoon the action shifted to the workers' quarters which were mobilised throughout, and here firearms were used persistently. Repression became more fierce – 16 people were killed – as the army moved to take control of the insurgent districts. Tosco and the SMATA leader, Elpidio Torres, were arrested along with other union leaders and countless rank-and-file militants. In the evening the last resistance in Barrio Clínicas was dealt with, and by the next day the army had the situation under control and proceeded with 'mopping-up operations' for a couple of days.

The government blamed communists, Castroists and even Cubans for the violence. The two CGTs issued a joint communiqué blaming the 'criminal and repressive behaviour of the so-called forces of order', pointing out that 'the measures taken by the government characterise it as an anti-popular, reactionary and pro-imperialist (*entreguista*) dictatorship'.[16] A general strike in the province was called for 1 July, and 2 July was declared a day of mourning for the victims of the repression. In Córdoba and elsewhere these events brought home the vulnerability of the dictatorship and the power of mass mobilisations. There was something missing, though, because even at the height of the *Cordobazo* (as it now became known) there was no clear immediate tactical objective. The CGT-A had proved its mobilising capacity but had not provided a clear political strategy to deal with the new situation. In the months to follow there was intense political debate, and new organisations were forged in preparation for 'the next time'.

The question now arises as to why Córdoba was the epicentre of the 1969 upsurge in labour activity. The city had gone through a process of intensive industrialisation after 1958, based on the automobile industry. The industry then stagnated, and whereas in 1960 the province accounted for 50% of national car production, this declined to 30% in 1966 and to 20% in 1970. This reflected Córdoba's position in the national economy, which has been compared to that of an 'internal colony'.[17] Though this may be exaggerated we must include the provincial dimension in any analysis of the crisis. Apart from that we can say that in Córdoba the factory had much greater weight in the community than it did in Buenos Aires. Torre describes how:

> the transparency of social antagonisms which results from this, as did the density of the links within and outside the workplace, which reinforce the internal cohesion of the working class community, create favourable conditions for the rapid articulation of discontent.[18]

The car industry – the IKA-Renault complex in particular with its 6,000 workers – played a dominant role in the society. There were also 6,000 metal-workers in medium-sized workshops organised by the UOM, 4,000 workers in Fiat's Concord and Materfer plants, and 2,500 workers in the state power company EPEC. This relatively young (i.e. largely post-Peronist) working class formed a strong homogeneous block which had broad alliances with employees and students. Córdoba was in many ways the Petrograd of Argentina and when the car industry caught a cold the whole province sneezed.

As to why the *Cordobazo* was so explosive, this was due primarily to the authoritarian military regime. By suppressing the political parties and generally freezing the political arena, the military had blocked any other outlet for social discontent. In more normal circumstances the unrest which had built up in Córdoba may well have been channelled through institutional paths; in 1969 there was no viable reformist alternative. Two separate, though related, revolts came to a head in 1969 – the demands of the most 'advanced' sectors of the working class and the more basic economic and democratic demands of the broad masses. The bourgeoisie had basically no strategy – except for repression – to deal with the crisis. In fact, sniping during the *Cordobazo* was most common in the middle-class areas, which meant that some sectors at least were losing confidence in their traditional political leaders. The *Cordobazo* showed that the labour movement was able to articulate the interests of society as a whole. It also broke the long-lasting Peronist hegemony over the masses, however partially and sporadically – the traditional *Marcha Peronista* was hardly heard on the marches. The direct action and street violence of these days created new methods of struggle which threatened to outflank the traditional labour leadership. In its aftermath there were to be concerted measures, as we shall see, to re-establish control over the mass movement, and prevent the development of a socialist tendency among the working class.

The *Cordobazo* had a long-term impact on Argentine politics and was recognised by conservatives and revolutionaries alike as a key turning-point. For the Córdoba Industrialists Association, 'Activities never before seen nor imagined followed each other with the exteriorisation of apparently inexplicable disorders. . . . What happened taught us the existence of real dangers. . . . our institutions and way of life find themselves in danger'.[19]

The *Cordobazo* completely disrupted the hegemonic project of the big bourgeoisie and shattered the internal unity of both the bourgeoisie and the military. It drove a wedge between the middle-class sectors which had been impoverished by the post-1966 economic policies and the military regime. After the *Cordobazo*, a series of unstable power coalitions could not hide the growing contradictions within the bourgeoisie which were constantly exacerbated by working-class struggles.

For the labour movement it represented a culmination of a long history of popular insurrections in Argentina, from the *Semana Trágica* of 1919, to 17 October 1945, to the Rosario Rising following the overthrow of Perón in 1955. The police were forced to retreat in the face of mass violence, and had the arming of the masses been ensured, a revolutionary situation could have resulted. Within the popular camp the *Cordobazo* acted as a catalyst for radical transformations and the emergence of solid politico-military organisations. New forms of struggle were popularised and a democratic anti-bureaucratic consciousness became widespread. In short, it led to the formation of a new mass vanguard. The *Cordobazo* constituted a decisive break in the rhythm of the class struggle in Argentina.

General strikes (1969–1971)

After the *Cordobazo* there were general strikes and insurrectional situations, and the emergence of a new class struggle tendency (*clasismo*) in the trade unions. There was a lull in the class struggle immediately following the *Cordobazo*, as its full implications sank in. It soon picked up again following a general strike in Córdoba on 17 and 18 June over wage demands, which also called for the release of the *Cordobazo* prisoners and an end to the repressive legislation. In August the town of Cañada de Gómez was seized by its inhabitants because the parish priest had been removed by the archbishop, and there was a regional strike in San Nicolás over redundancies in the textile industry. On 27 August the CGT called a national general strike, which through its massive impact on industry and the service sector, marked the beginning of a gradual regeneration of the organised labour movement.

In the rest of 1969 and throughout 1970 there were strikes, stoppages and factory occupations throughout the country, involving nearly every sector of the working class (see Appendix). The trade union bureaucracy had no option but to go along with the mass mobilisations. There was even an apparent radicalisation of this sector as seen in CGT Secretary General José Rucci's declaration early in 1971 that 'The working class is prepared for the struggle. We are not in politics to seek a *peso* more for workers or some other advance. We are struggling for a change of system. Socialism is irreversible. For the working class it is an imperative necessity'.[20]

One of the high points of this period was the so-called *Rosariazo* of September 1969. It began with a rail strike in Rosario organised by *Unión Ferroviaria* and *La Fraternidad* with the backing of the Rosario branch of the CGT. By 15 September the railworkers had been placed under military discipline and the local CGT responded with a 48-hour strike and a march on the CGT headquarters. Unlike the 1969 situation in Córdoba, here the strike call was posed clearly in terms of the Peronist movement's traditional demands. On 16 September columns of workers began to march towards the city centre where the CGT building was surrounded by heavily-armed police. Apart from the railway workers, the demonstrators came from electricity plants, textile and metallurgical factories, from the *frigoríficos* and the port.

The inevitable conflict with the forces of 'law and order' came with a liberal use of tear-gas and firearms, to which the marchers responded with barricades. With the city centre closed off, attention shifted in the afternoon to railway installations, banks and warehouses in the suburbs. The following day action escalated throughout the city with firearms and bombs complementing the demonstrators' arsenal of sticks and stones. A column of railworkers marched on a rail-coach factory and set it on fire. That evening army reinforcements arrived to help the local forces and to defend vital installations. Even so, there were mass confrontations the following day until finally things quietened down. As Jacobs points out, the *Rosariazo* saw the participation of all sectors of the working class:

> from the better paid to those who live and work in terrible conditions, the workers of the big factories and temporary workers, those from the most modern, expanding branches of industry and those that are obsolete and in permanent crisis, those who are recently incorporated into production and city life and those who have been there a long time, wage earners linked to production and those linked to commerce and credit.[21]

In Córdoba meanwhile a general strike was building up into a second *Cordobazo*. In March 1971 Governor Uriburu declared that the poisonous snake (*víbora*) of revolution was stalking Córdoba and he would cut its head off. Subsequent events were therefore dubbed the *Viborazo*.[22] They began with factory occupations and street mobilisations against Governor Uriburu and the national CGT's collaborationist policies. The power workers moved to seize the neighbouring Villa Revol district, and after a mass meeting in the city centre the revolt became generalised. At first the police did not intervene in this re-enactment of the *Cordobazo*, but two days later they moved in fiercely with the army, which by now had had intensive anti-guerrilla training.

The industrial working class was not as central to the 1971 mobilisation as it was in 1969 (see Appendix). This was partly because the car mechanics' union SMATA had suffered a severe defeat in mid-1970 after a month-long occupation of the IKA-Renault plant. This time there were new organisations present, namely the armed units of the ERP (People's Revolutionary Army) who were seen behind many of the barricades. For the first time armed revolutionary organisations were participating openly in mass mobilisations. Other key participants were the new militant unions of the Concord and Materfer Fiat plants (examined below) which advocated militant methods and provided a pole of attraction for students and other social forces. In the aftermath of the *Viborazo* Agustín Tosco was again imprisoned by the military government, but this time with the support of the national CGT, who were already seeking an end to militant mass unionism and a return to the *Vandorista* strategy.

The sugar workers of Tucumán had been a constant irritation to the military rulers since 1966. In September 1969, shortly after the *Rosariazo*, the sugar workers' union FOTIA called a two-day strike to obtain assurances from the government that no more *ingenios* would be closed. Exactly five years later, in spite of the decline of the sugar industry FOTIA called a strike which paralysed the industry and most of the province. It was this determination and militancy which helped promote a much wider process of rural organisation in the northern provinces of Chaco, Misiones, Formosa and Corrientes.

The *Ligas Agrarias* (Agrarian Leagues), which brought together small-holders and sharecroppers, began in earnest in 1970 and were soon organising 50,000 families.[23] Their militant actions in 1971 and 1972 were a definite contribution to the collapse of the dictatorship. The impoverished *campesinos* were learning the habits of solidarity in a period of working-class resurgence, and durable links were forged between rural and urban workers. For the great mass of *campesinos* the *Ligas* led 'on the basis of the struggles they protagonised . . . to visualising phenomena such as the monopolies, the relation between exploitation and repression, the nature of the political power of the dominant classes and the importance of independent organisations'.[24] The shock waves of the *Cordobazo* had reached the most remote corners of the working population.

Rosario, Córdoba and Tucumán all pointed to the weakening of central control over the trade union movement. After the *Cordobazo* there was great pressure for the CGT to be 'normalised', which was achieved at a congress in July 1970. The CGT-A had been virtually immobilised by government repression following the assassination of Vandor a month earlier by a group which was later to join the *Montoneros*. This left the field open for the 62 Organisations to ally with the 'participationists' and the non-aligned unions in the reconstituted federation. José Rucci, of the metal-workers' union UOM, was elected secretary general. He proceeded to seek an alliance with the 'nationalist' employers' association, the CGE, and isolate the trade union opposition. In the interests of 'national reconciliation' the CGT strove to demobilise the working class. President Levingston's economic policies (admittedly somewhat more pro-industrialist than Onganía's) were given a cautious welcome, and in return normal collective bargaining was restored. The CGT did call national stoppages in October and November 1970, but its main efforts were now set on negotiating with the government and building up its presence within the Peronist movement.

When Lanusse became president in 1971 the CGT declared that 'The people still hope to meet with the armed forces to work for the realisation of the Argentine project'.[25] Against the wishes of the combative *Comisión Intersindical* (Inter-union committee) of Córdoba and the provinces, the CGT became even more closely involved with the government. But as Miguel Gazzera, ex-collaborator of Vandor, was to write, 'Though the labour leader may agree to quieten down, the labour movement, the working class, as a legitimate revolutionary force, cannot give up the struggle...'.[26] Even a CGT 'patronised and regimented by the government' as Gazzera called it, could not stop the forward march of labour.

Clasismo

In the period after the *Cordobazo* there emerged a new class struggle or *clasista* leadership in some factories. This happened in Fiat's Concord (tractors) and Materfer (railroad material) plants in Córdoba where there were plant level unions: SITRAC and SITRAM respectively.[27] Fiat's policy was aimed at integrating workers through paternalistic programmes, and rebellious elements were simply dismissed. The unions were weak and quite inactive until March 1970 when a tumultuous factory assembly at the Concord plant elected a new leadership. Some 2,500 workers occupied the plant to obtain management recognition of the new leaders. The Materfer workers quickly followed suit and a joint plan of action was agreed upon and negotiations with management opened up.

The new SITRAC-SITRAM leadership–composed largely of Maoist militants and some independent Peronists–rapidly imposed a new style of trade unionism. The government's wage guidelines were simply ignored when negotiating with FIAT, productivity bargaining and wage differentials were rejected and the national trade union leaders were criticised for their collaborationism. They constantly tried to involve the rank and file in a process which became known as permanent mobilisation. The *clasista* current, which as well as SITRAC-SITRAM, took in the local water-workers and the private oil companies, became for a brief period the most powerful sector within the Córdoba labour movement. Its emphasis on rank-and-file participation and mobilisation spread further afield and

177

continued even after SITRAC-SITRAM was defeated.

In October 1971, barely a year after *clasismo* began, the military government, with the support of the CGT, moved in a massive force which included tanks to overthrow the *clasista* leadership. The membership did not mobilise to defend their imprisoned leaders, which led many to the conclusion that they had moved ahead too far and too fast. Certainly there was an element of revolutionary romanticism in their slogan 'Neither coup nor elections, but revolution' (*ni golpe ni elección, revolución*). A serious error was the sectarian attitude they maintained towards the combative Peronist unions which they basically treated in the same way as the 'participationist' current. To a certain extent they confused the role of trade union and revolutionary party. The experience was a positive one, however, because it focused on the role of the labour bureaucracy and it raised issues related to the labour process and working conditions which radically threatened the basis of existing union practice. This last element is precisely the terrain ceded by the union leadership in the 1960s when it left the workplace to the bosses. Above all, SITRAC-SITRAM gives the lie to those who justify the role of the union bureaucracy by saying that it was 'representative' of the membership. Thus Portantiero can say that the union bureaucracy 'expressed an intermediate, though numerically powerful layer of industrial development and the working class "common sense" which accompanied it. In this layer its representativity was unquestionable . . . .'[28] If the FIAT workers could question it, there seems to be no reason why the textile and metallurgical workers Portantiero presumably refers to could not do the same.

Another variant of radical trade unionism was that known as the combative (*combativo*) tendency, where again Córdoba led the way. The local power workers' union, *Luz y Fuerza,* was a prime example of this orientation with its emphasis on grass-roots democracy and militant action. Agustín Tosco first came to prominence in 1953 and he explains his outlook as follows:

> Though we were all Peronists our group was inclined towards socialism, the example of Algeria, the Cooke line on the national scene. We lived through the end of Peronism with the big metal-workers' strikes, the sugar *ingenio* strikes, and the oil contracts which represented a change in the old Peronist model . . . The generation of '53 was opposed to bureaucratism in the union . . . it proposed a form of revolutionary nationalism, the union had to do more . . . [29]

Under Tosco's leadership·*Luz y Fuerza* in Córdoba certainly did 'do more'. In union elections and assemblies there was open political debate and an absence of gangsterism (*matonismo*). Unlike any other union leadership the Tosco group regularly returned to the workplace and there was a genuine collective leadership. The union practised a militant solidarity policy and there was hardly a strike, stoppage or workplace occupation in Córdoba and even further afield that Tosco did not visit. Tosco and his union were among the major protagonists of the *Cordobazo* and the *Viborazo*. After these events especially, the union was regarded as a tool in the struggle for national and social liberation, and a formative school for workers. The aim was to establish a model for a revolutionary trade unionism (*sindicalismo de liberación*).

Luz y Fuerza placed great emphasis on the need for unity within the labour movement, while allowing the freedom to act politically. Tosco was against parallel unionism and urged the left to work as a class struggle tendency within existing unions. Unity was not an abstract slogan: it referred to 'unity in struggle, in mobilisation, [which] is fundamental for the workers' movement to achieve its objectives of liberation....[30] Political unity did not mean political quiescence or accepting the 'lowest common denominator', but rather 'fighting politically on the general question related to the rights of the workers and the people (*pueblo*)'.[31] *Luz y Fuerza's* high point was during the struggle against the military dictatorship when Peronists could easily work together with Communists and even Trotskyists.

As the return of Perón became a real prospect, divisions appeared and the social struggle became divorced from the political struggle—the dictatorship was no longer a unifying factor. The limitations of combative unions became apparent when sectors of *Luz y Fuerza* began to pose demands leading to workers' control. Tosco decided it would not be expedient to encourage an autonomous workers' movement which would escape the control of the union and go beyond traditional demands. The overall impact of the *Luz y Fuerza* experience in Córdoba was extremely positive, and it is no coincidence that it was one of the first unions to be 'intervened' in by the new Peronist government, for whom 'critical support' was not good enough.

The radical trade union tendencies with their emphasis on rank-and-file participation were to have a lasting impact. The class-struggle unionism of this period established a minority tendency committed to working-class autonomy. There were several attempts to bring together the dispersed *clasista* unions. In 1972 the 'combative' unions held a national meeting and in 1974 formed the *Movimiento Sindical Combativo* (Combative Union Movement) led by Tosco and René Salamanca, the new SMATA *clasista* leader. This brought in several independent Peronist unions, belonging to the historical *Peronismo combativo* current, who were opposed to the collaborationism of the leadership. The 1972 Plenary Session of Combative Unions reaffirmed its commitment to the 1962 Huerta Grande programme and set its aim as 'national socialism'.[32]

The results of military rule and monetarist economics were the *Cordobazo* and the subsequent labour struggles. Factory level conflicts and anti-bureaucratic revolts were among the major features of this period, and towards the end of 1972 they spread to the industrial belt around Buenos Aires. The atmosphere of this period can probably best be captured in the SITRAC-SITRAM programme of 1971:

The trade union organisations will remain *clasista* while the exploitation of man by man continues, because their function is to defend the rights of the workers within a social order based on the existence of dominant and oppressed classes. There can be nothing more repugnant than the treacherous cliques of bureaucrats ensconced in the leadership of trade unions who aim to obstruct the social struggles for liberation. It is one of the primary demands of the working class to call for the democratisation of the unions and the full subordination of the leaderships to the mandate and control of the rank and file.[33]

Decompression (1972)

The last phase of the military government did not see a complete end to mass struggles, though their nature did change. In April 1972 there were large demonstrations in Córdoba, Rosario and in the Mendoza region protesting an increase in electricity tariffs. The protest movement culminated in a massive mobilisation in Mendoza lasting four days, during which practically the whole city was on the streets. Repression was severe but the government gave way and cancelled the electricity price increase. The movement was supported by the industrial working class but the leaders were largely white-collar workers, particularly teachers. In the small town of General Roca there was a similar movement in April known as the *Rocazo* which caused the whole locality to come up against the central authorities. After a week of clashes with the army–during which the demonstrators tried to win over the soldiers–and massive arrests, the provisional government was forced to resign although it achieved the release of all the prisoners.

This type of social protest had occurred in the Cipoletti (1969) and Casilda (1971) town seizures or *puebladas*, as they became known.[34] In each case workers were involved, but the leadership was largely middle-class. This provincial revolt was a direct result of the military regime's rationalisation policies, but there was also a growing anti-dictatorial consciousness. The *Cordobazo* had broken the spell of fear cast by military dictatorship. The example of the working class was now being taken up by broader social groups who wanted to see an end to the economic and political policies of the military/monopoly regime.

Struggles also continued in the workplace but they were more dispersed than in the earlier period. Since mid-1971 the CGT had maintained an undeclared truce with the government to encourage the holding of elections. There were national general strikes called by the CGT in September 1971 and in February 1972 but these did not essentially affect the 'social peace' policy. They were designed to quell the unrest among the rank and file and the growing criticism of the combative unions. The CGT was playing an increasingly political role, which in July 1972 culminated in a declaration warning the government not to use fraudulent methods in the forthcoming elections. The government responded by freezing union funds and withdrawing legal recognition (*personería gremial*) from the CGT. This reduced the CGT's political role but the 62 Organisations did nothing to make up for this. In fact, Perón himself was backing the Rucci leadership's quiescent approach in the CGT. The Trelew massacre in August 1972 (when 16 political prisoners were killed in cold blood) produced protest declarations from the CGT and the closure of its Córdoba headquarters.[35] The underlying trend, however, was one of economic and political inaction to facilitate the return of Perón. This was only broken on his return in November 1972 with the calling of a 24-hour general strike, but the government pre-empted this by declaring a national holiday. The CGT, in spite of the growing role of class struggle tendencies in the unions, was thus able to restrain working-class struggles after the second *Cordobazo* and prevent their becoming generalised.

New social forces had emerged between 1969 and 1972 in a number of fields as *Pasado y Presente* outlines:

- in the factories, where workers struggled against the new forms of exploitation and to reconstruct their class organisations, confronting the trade union bureaucracy, the employers and the state;
- in the towns and villages, struggling against an increasingly irrational system to resolve housing, health, transport and pollution problems;
- in the marginalised regions impoverished by capitalist expansion, struggling against the economic, social and cultural break-up of whole provinces.[36]

These struggles against capital and the state were taking on a revolutionary dynamic and their activists could not be co-opted by superficial changes. Only a radical transformation of the social and economic system could meet the demands of these new social forces.

After a rapid succession of military presidents the armed forces began to reconsider their traditional antagonism towards Perón. Perhaps re-calling the legendary popular leader could defuse the potentially revolutionary situation building up in Argentina. President Lanusse had already posed the need for a Grand National Agreement (*Gran Acuerdo Nacional*) in 1971. Its objective was clearly to defuse the growing mass struggles and channel them into constitutional politics. By unfreezing party politics, Lanusse succeeded to a certain extent in shifting the energy of the new social opposition into the political arena.

Lanusse himself provides a clear analysis in his memoirs of why and how the 'decompression' of the dictatorship was carried out.[37] The *Cordobazo* was seen as the symbolic expression of the crisis of the government and the armed forces. He shows how 'the real discussion was not over *whether* to institutionalise the Republic, but simply how and when to institutionalise' (i.e. return to constitutional rule).[38] Perón was the only political figure who could possibly turn the working class towards a populist-nationalist solution compatible with the continued dominance of capital in the conditions of Argentina in 1972. Even a US State Department official was forced to admit, 'I think this is the moment for Perón. He alone can bring cohesion to Argentina. There is no-one else left. He has come to represent opportunity. . . . '[39]

It was the wave of working-class insurgency since 1969 which had forced this conclusion on Argentina's ruling class and armed forces. They certainly hoped to control the decompression process and possibly limit the independence of the ageing *caudillo*. In the end they had no choice and Lanusse answers those critics who say he opened up the political game prematurely: 'If all that anger manifested itself with the safety-valve of the elections opened, what might not have happened without elections?'[40] The question is hypothetical because negotiations with Perón began and the way was cleared for his return to Argentina.

In late 1972 Perón returned to Argentina after 18 years in exile. This objective victory – which *was* a victory, whatever the intentions of the military – was imposed by an unprecedented five years of struggle. In 1968 the recovery of working-class combativity had been patchy but the signs were there. In 1969 there had been a steady build-up of strikes, demonstrations and street battles culminating in the *Cordobazo* of late May and its sequel in other cities. The upsurge had continued unabated into 1971 – the second *Cordobazo* occurred in March – though in 1972 the trade union bureaucracy had begun collaborating with the military government to negotiate Perón's return. In this latter period there had been a number of popular insurrections – the *Mendozazo* and *Rocazo* – and a generalised tendency towards anti-bureaucratic struggles in many unions. A new tendency – *clasismo* – had become established as a minority view in the labour movement and attention had been focused on the labour process. The new working class which emerged during the intensive industrialisation of the 1960s had not become a labour aristocracy. Rather, it was a central element in the new mass vanguard which emerged during and after the *Cordobazo*, representing the most advanced organisational and political experience of the Argentine working class hitherto. Just as the traditional dichotomy between Peronism and anti-Peronism seemed to be breaking down, Perón returned to Argentina.

The labour movement of the 1970s was much more organised than that of the pre-Peronist period. Whereas in the early 1940s barely one-third of industrial workers were unionised (and only one-tenth of all workers) by the early 1970s it is estimated that fully half of the total workforce belonged to trade unions, and 60% of industrial workers.[41] The 3½ million workers who belonged to trade unions (out of a population of 25 million) were distributed in the organisations outlined in Table 13.2 Some of the largest unions are in the service sector, but the overall unionisation rates for that sector was only 30%. The metallurgical and textile trades remain key bastions in the industrial sector. Finally rural workers remain under-organised with only 25,000 members in their main union (although there are other co-operatives and agrarian leagues in this sector). The overall level of organisation in Argentina compares favourably with other Third

World countries: in India and Indonesia unionisation is below 10%, in Brazil and Nigeria it is below 20%, in Egypt and Mexico it is below 30% and only in a few countries such as Sri Lanka and Chile does it approximate to the 40% mark.[42]

Table 13.2   The top thirty trade unions (over 10,000 members), 1972

Trade Union	*Membership*
Commercial employees	171,000
Railway workers	168,000
Metallurgical workers	125,000
Municipal employees	121,800
State workers	111,200
Textile workers	105,000
Construction workers	75,000
Restaurant employees	56,500
Electricity workers	50,500
State employees	50,100
Meat packers	45,000
Clothing workers	43,000
Health workers	38,200
Mechanics	35,000
Wood workers	33,000
Telephonists	30,000
Oil workers	30,000
Postal & telecommunication workers	29,000
Alimentation workers	25,100
Rural workers	25,000
Sugar workers	19,000
Paper workers	14,200
Drivers	14,100
Miners	11,500
Water workers	11,000
Wine workers	11,000
Glass workers	10,800
Rubber workers	10,600
Telegraph workers	10,400
Milk workers	10,100

Source: *Documentación e Información Laboral*

Appendix 4

Figure 13.1   Chronology of labour upsurge, 1968–1972

1968
June; August: Sporadic action by SMATA mechanics' union in Córdoba.
September: Two-month strike by Buenos Aires petroleum workers.

1969
January: Chocón building workers and Fabril Financiero graphic workers' strikes.
February: Citroën, Chrysler and General Motors stoppages.

March: Strikes by metal-workers (UOM) and mechanics (SMATA) in Córdoba.
May: Insurrectional general strikes in Córdoba, Rosario and Tucumán.
July: CGT-A calls general strike – its last major action.
August: National general strike and reunification of CGT tendencies.
September: Insurrectional general strike in Rosario; general strike in Tucumán, Cipolletti town seizure.
October: General strike in Córdoba.

1970
February: General strike in Córdoba.
March: General strike in Córdoba.
May: General strike in Córdoba.
October: Two national general strikes.
November: National general strike.

1971
January: General strike in Córdoba; Fiat-Concord plant occupied.
March: General strike in Córdoba (19th since May 1969), followed by second *Cordobazo (Viborazo)*.
April: Casilda town seizure.
June: SMATA factory occupations in Córdoba.
July: Chocón building workers' strike.
September: National general strike.

1972
January: National meeting of 'combative' unions.
February: National general strike.
April: *Mendozazo*, city occupied for four days.
July: *Rocazo*, local uprising takes over town.
November: Perón returns to Argentina.

Appendix 5

Table 13.3   Strikes by region and sector, 1968–1972

Year	Total strikes	Percentage outside Buenos Aires	Percentage involving state employees
1968	50	63.3	25.0
1969	93	71.8	41.2
1970	116	76.4	32.6
1971	237	67.5	53.6
1972	187	55.1	60.9

Source: G. O'Donnell, (1982) *1966–1973 – El Estado Burocrático Autoritario*. Buenos Aires, Editorial de Belgrano, p. 439.

Notes

1. For an overall analysis of this period see G. O'Donnell, (1986) *The Bureaucratic–Authoritarian State. Argentina 1966–1973*, Berkeley, University of California Press.

2. J. Aricó, (1964) "Examen de conciencia", *Pasado y Presente,* 1, 4, cited in E. Jelin and J.C. Torre, (1982) "Los Nuevos Trabajadores en América Latina: Una Reflexión Sobre La Tésis de la Aristocracia Obrera", *Desarrollo Económico,* 22, 85, 4.

3. R. Carri, (1967) *Sindicatos y Poder en la Argentina,* Buenos Aires, Editorial Sudestada, p. 106.

4. A. Marshall, (1980) "Labour market and wage growth: the case of Argentina", *Cambridge Journal of Economics*, 4, p. 55.

5. Ibid., p. 56.

6. M. Peralta Ramos, (1972) *Etapas de Acumulación y Alianzas de Clases en la Argentina (1930–1970)*, Buenos Aires, Siglo XXI, p. 170.

7. R. Zorrilla, (1974) *Estructura y Dinámica del Sindicalismo Argentino*, Buenos Aires, La Pleyade, p. 183.

8. S. Sigal, (1974) *Attitudes ouvrières en Argentina. Rapport d'enquète*, Paris, Centre d'etudes de Mouvements Sociaux, cited in E. Jelin, and J.C. Torre, (1982) "Los Nuevos Trabajadores en América Latina", p. 10.

9. Ibid., p. 20.

10. For a critical appraisal of the CGT-A see G. Ducatenzeiler, (1980) *Syndicats et politique en Argentine 1955–1973*, Montréal, Presses de l'Université de Montréal, Ch 5.

11. Cited in R. Jacoby, (1978) "Conciencia de Clase y Enfrentamientos Sociales: Argentina 1969", *CICSO Serie Estudios* no. 32, p. 14.

12. E. Laclau, (1970) "Argentina – Imperialist Strategy and the May Crisis", *New Left Review*, no. 62, p. 16.

13. For a detailed description of the *Cordobazo* see B. Balvé, J. Marin, and M. Murmis (1973) *Lucha de Calles Lucha de Clases. Elementos para su análisis: Córdoba 1971–1969*, Buenos Aires, La Rosa Blindada.

14. Cited in M. Roldán, (1979) *Sindicatos y Protesta Social en la Argentina (1969–1974)*, Amsterdam, CEDLA, p. 14.

15. Cited in B. Balvé, et al. (1973) *Lucha de Calles Lucha de Clases*, p. 119.

16. Cited in E. Delich, (1974) *Crisis y Protesta Social Córdoba, 1969–1973*. Buenos Aires, Siglo XXI, p. 184. This book along with Balve, et al. (1973) and Jacoby, (1978) cited above is an essential source on the *Cordobazo*.

17. See R. Massari (1975) "Le 'cordobazo' ". *Les Temps Modernes*, 4–75.

18. J.C. Torre (1979) "El Movimiento Laboral en Argentina: 1955–76 – de la Exclusión a la Participación en el Poder", in Carriere J.C. (ed.), *Industrialisation and the State in Latin America*, Amsterdam, CEDLA, p. 362.

19. Cited in R. Jacoby, (1978) "Conciencia de Clase y Enfrentamientos Sociales", p. 75.

20. Cited in B. Balvé, et al. (1973) *Lucha de Calles Lucha de Clases*, p. 180.

21. Cited in R. Jacoby, (1978) "Conciencia de Clase y Enfrentamientos Sociales", pp. 95–6 on which the account above draws.

22. For a description of the *Viborazo* see B. Balvé, et al. (1973) *Lucha de Calles Lucha de Clases*, Part 1.

23. For a discussion of the Agrarian Leagues see F. Ferreira, (1973) *Qué son los ligas agrarias*, Buenos Aires, Siglo XXI.

24. Ibid., p. 485.

25. Cited in G. Ducatenzeiler, (1980) *Syndicats et politique en Argentine*, p. 226.

26. M. Gazzera, (1970) "Nosotros los dirigentes", in Gazzera M. and Ceresole, N. *Peronismo: Autocrítica y Perspectivas*, Buenos Aires, Editorial Descartes, p. 186.

27. On the SITRAC-SITRAM experience see E. Jelin, (1975) "Espontaneidad y organización en el movimiento obrero", *Revista Latinoamericana de Sociología*, 2, and F. Delich, (1974) *Crisis y Protesta Social*, Part 3.

28. J.C. Portantiero, (1977) "Economía y política en la crisis argentina: 1958–1973", *Revista Mexicana de Sociología*, XXXIX, 2 p. 555.

29. Cited in M. Roldán, (1979) *Sindicatos y Protesta Social en la Argentina*, p. 120. This book is an excellent case study of *Luz y Fuerza*, Córdoba.

30. Ibid., p. 227.

31. Ibid., p. 199.

32. The 1972 declaration is reproduced in NACLA (1975) Argentina: *In The Hour of the Furnaces*. New York, NACLA, pp. 81–83.

33. Cited in F. Delich, (1974) *Crisis y Protesta Social*, p. 132.

34. These are examined in Aufgang, L. (1980) "Las Puebladas", *Cuadernos de CICSO*.

35. The rise of the guerrilla movements is outside the remit of this work but see R. Gillespie, (1982) *Soldiers of Perón – Argentina's Montoneros*, Oxford, Clarendon Press, for a useful summary.

36. Pasado y Presente (1973) "La crisis de julio y sus consecuencias políticas", *Pasado y Presente* IV 2/3, p. 194.

37. A. Lanusse, (1977) *Mi Testimonio,* Buenos Aires, Lasserre. See G. O'Donnell, (1986) *The Bureaucratic-Authoritarian State* to set this partisan account in context.

38. Ibid., p. 264.

39. Cited in NACLA (1975) *Argentina in the Hour of the Furnaces*, p. 27.

40. A. Lanusse, (1977) *Mi Testimonio*, p. 274.

41. A. Abós, (1983) *La Columna Vertebral. Sindicatos y Peronismo*, Buenos Aires, Editorial Leyasa, p. 35.

42. International Labour Organization (1985) *World Labour Report 2*, Geneva, ILO, p. 11.

14. The Return of Peronism and Labour Divided (1973–1976)

The period between 1973 and 1976 saw Perón's return to power, his death, the succession of Isabel Perón to the presidency and her overthrow by the armed forces.[1] The working class saw these Peronist governments as *their* governments and their reward for 18 years of loyalty and struggle. The Peronist promised land did not materialise, however, and instead an undeclared civil war began within the Peronist movement. The guerrilla campaign divided the political left from the organised trade union movement, and the trade union bureaucracy's offensive against dissidents alienated the combative sectors. There was even an unprecedented general strike *against* a Peronist government in July 1975. First, the contradictions inherent in the anti-dictatorship movement had begun to come into play and then, following the death of Perón in July 1974, the contradictions within his movement burst into the open. In spite of all the illusions and the confusion which followed, workers fought vigorously for their rights throughout this period (see Appendix). But we must describe these years as 'labour divided', because when the military seized power again in March 1976 the labour movement was divided and demoralised. The 1973–76 period was extremely important because the parameters set by Perón 30 years earlier began to break down, even before his death. In that sense they will probably be seen retrospectively as a watershed in the history of the labour movement.

'Cámpora to government, Perón to power' (May–September 1973)

This was the slogan coined by the radical Montonero movement to express its aims during the election campaign in the first months of 1973. When Perón returned to Argentina in late 1972 he forged an electoral alliance with a broad range of forces and then went back to Spain because he was not allowed to stand in the elections himself. His chosen candidate was Héctor Cámpora, a loyal figure from the political wing of the Peronist movement. The main force behind the election campaign was the radicalised Peronist Youth movement, led by the Montoneros. The trade union leadership was effectively marginalised with Perón declaring angrily:

187

'In the trade union field there is a lot of bureaucracy. Nobody has a more painful experience of this than I, because I have seen many union leaders defect at the most decisive moment in our whole political history'.[2] Perón complained that the union leaders had got mixed up in politics (his prerogative) instead of restricting themselves to their professional (i.e. trade union) duties. For the time being the union leadership had to stand aside and allow the political and youth wings of the Peronist movement to take the initiative. Perón still had to concede a certain amount of power to the radicalised social forces which had caused the collapse of the military government. But his essential policy was in line with the aspirations of the armed forces and the bourgeoisie: to create a climate of national unity through conciliation and collaboration between social classes and political forces.

The linch-pin of Perón's new 'national reconstruction' strategy was the Social Pact (*Pacto Social*) between the CGT and the nationalist employers' association (the CGE) which was implemented from July 1973 after Cámpora had been elected president with nearly 50 per cent of the vote.[3] Its basic stipulations were a price freeze for all goods and services on the one hand and an agreement by the unions to suspend the wage negotiating councils for two years on the other. Wages were to be increased once a year by the *Gran Paritaria Nacional* (National Negotiating Council) in accordance with average productivity rates. The Social Pact was preceded by an across-the-board wage and family allowance increase which had the effect of lowering differentials. The initial wage increase of 200 pesos added nearly 20% to the basic wage of an industrial *peón* (unskilled worker) but only 10% to that of workers in the intermediate wage category. For this reason the metal-workers' union (UOM) soon came to oppose the social pact whereas the lower-paid textile workers continued to support it. The levelling of wages continued, and between December 1973 and March 1975 the basic wage (*salario básico de convenio*) rose by 6.9% whereas wages in the intermediate category fell by 8.0%, and those of workers at the top of the scale fell by 13.3%.[4] Taking the real basic wage of the industrial *peón*, we see in Table 14.1 that Peronism Mark II did lead to an increase but not as pronounced as during its first period in office.

We see that inflation was controlled quite effectively in 1973, but it began rising in 1974, partly as a result of the international economic crisis, but also due to the gradual breakdown of the Social Pact as businesses allowed their prices to rise. The substantial wage increases of mid-1975 are to a certain extent illusory, because by then inflation was rampant. Towards the end of the period the deterioration of real wages was severe. We can say that the Social Pact was an overall failure in terms of its objectives, but its main impact was the legitimate aura it gave to the Peronist project. It was the symbol of national unity, and helped to demobilise the combative trade union sectors, as negotiations were removed to the remote *Gran Paritaria Nacional*.

Cámpora's government was not as smooth as the Social Pact architects

Table 14.1   Real wages and cost of living, 1973–1976 (Wages: 1968=100; cost of living: % increase over previous month)

| | 1973 | | 1974 | | 1975 | | 1976 | |
	Wages	Cost of living	Wages	Cost of living	Wages	Cost of living	Wages	Cost of living
Jan	113.4	10.3	111.0	−0.6	104.0	8.5	106.4	14.6
Feb	105.4	7.9	108.4	1.9	99.4	4.9	90.8	11.3
Mar	97.0	8.9	107.1	1.5	114.5	8.4	80.5	38.0
Apr	92.9	5.0	123.8	3.4	104.4	10.2		
May	90.9	4.4	120.3	4.3	100.5	4.8		
Jun	111.8	−0.8	117.4	3.9	183.5	21.3		
Jul	115.3	0.1	114.8	2.4	136.2	34.9		
Aug	114.3	1.9	112.8	3.0	111.2	23.8		
Sept	113.8	0.6	109.1	3.4	100.4	10.9		
Oct	113.1	0.6	105.1	2.7	88.2	12.6		
Nov	112.2	−0.1	120.5	3.3	108.5	8.0		
Dec	103.8	0.9	107.0	5.2	90.8	11.5		

Source: E. Jelin, (1977) 'Conflictos laborales en la Argentina, 1973–1976', *Estudios Sociales*, Buenos Aires, CEDES, p. 49.

had hoped for. There was a general feeling among the working class that victory at the polls should now be consolidated in the factories. As in the months building up to the elections the emphasis was on mass mobilisations. In fact, the whole tone of the Cámpora period was set during his inauguration on 25 May 1973 when people attacked Villa Devoto prison, and in what became known as the *Devotazo*, freed most of the political prisoners, thus forcing Cámpora to grant an amnesty. Cámpora's political programme was no more advanced than Perón's, but the manner in which it was implemented was profoundly worrying to the bourgeoisie. Soon after he became president there was a wave of office and public building occupations by radical political factions within the Peronist movement keen to set their stamp on the new administration. An admonishment from Perón was enough to send them home, however. The growing mobilisation in the factories was not to be stopped so easily. Though the context was different, there was something reminiscent of 1946 in the workers' offensive during what they saw as a favourable political situation. Within 20 days of Cámpora taking office there were 176 factories occupied by their workers, and though the Social Pact had suspended collective bargaining, the class struggle in the plants continued unabated.

As workers were unable to negotiate wage increases directly, they sought to do this indirectly by reinterpreting labour contracts, having jobs reclassified as well as generally improving working conditions. We find that between July and September 1973 a quarter of labour disputes (see Appendix) included demands concerning legal, statutory or contractual matters. A third of all disputes contained demands over the withholding of back-pay by management, and a similar percentage called for the re-hiring of unemployed or suspended workers. White-collar workers also joined these struggles in great numbers, striving to extend the principles of collective bargaining and achieve parity with other sectors. As Jelin notes 'the expansive economic climate, of both export-linked activities and those linked to the internal market . . . was without doubt favourable for initiating worker actions of this type'.[5] To this we must add the favourable political situation which meant that many of these demands were met.

The trade union leadership was often in the forefront of struggles, but working conditions were increasingly tackled by an in-plant leadership. On the factory floor the weakness of the *comisiones internas* after long years of inactivity or reduced functions, meant that a new rank-and-file leadership had to assert itself. New groupings emerged and challenged the rule of the existing leadership in a climate of continuous grass-roots mobilisation. *Pasado y Presente* describes how 'when they rise up against the foreman or the boss in the factory, the workers can no longer be manipulated, they begin to organise for themselves, and a process breaks out in which *the workplace demands and the anti-bureaucratic challenge fuse in a single struggle for the recovery and reaffirmation of workers' power*'.[6] In this context Perón's renewed advice to workers: 'From home to work and from work to home' (*de casa al trabajo, del trabajo a casa*) was unable to demobilise the working class.

In these struggles there was a growing presence of 'workers' control'-type demands. In May 1973 a fatal accident at the huge Astarsa ship-yard in Buenos Aires led to a demand by a spontaneous assembly of workers for the sacking of the safety officers.[7] This escalated into an occupation of the yard, with the managers being held hostage against the demand for full workers' control over health and safety at work. In some cases, as in the Molinos Rio de la Plata food-plant occupation in June, workers called for safety improvements, recognition of health hazard areas and a plant doctor, and forced the resignation of an inert *comisión interna*.

The pressures of the new 'rationalised' labour process also led to demands in that area. The big General Motors specialist vehicle plant in Barracas in Buenos Aires decided in June 1973 to raise the quota from 71 to 80 vehicles per shift. The assembly workers refused to accept the new quota and the company responded by sacking 32 workers, among them all the shop-stewards. The car workers' union SMATA called out the 8,000 workers on an indefinite strike and the dispute went to arbitration. The Ministry of Labour decreed the reinstatement of the dismissed workers and its technical experts eventually rejected the increased quotas as impossible. Once again, as during the first Peronist period, workers were beginning to make their presence felt within the factory. The class struggle was shifting to the factory floor now that the government was in the hands of the popular movement.

Though the industrial belt of Buenos Aires had now become the epicentre of labour struggles the provinces were also active. In Salta the local CGT was going through an inter-bureaucratic dispute and called a meeting in July 1973 to resolve it.[8] Hundreds of rural and urban workers from the combative unions overwhelmed the *matones* (union thugs) and invaded the CGT headquarters, turning the meeting into a popular assembly. The old leadership was voted out and a provisional committee established to supervise new elections. National CGT leader José Rucci called on the police to restore bureaucratic privilege, which they did, but a new parallel CGT was set up in Salta under the militant leadership of Armando Jaime. In other areas unions were 'recovered' by their membership from corrupt bureaucratic leaderships. Paradoxically, Ricardo Otero, the Minister of Labour, who was a member of the powerful metal-workers' union, often ruled in favour of the new rank-and-file groupings when the established leadership took the inter-union disputes to arbitration. In other situations the existing leadership was forced to adopt militant positions. In July 1973 the workers in a pasta factory in the town of San Francisco in Córdoba province occupied the plant to claim back-pay and the CGT was forced to call a general strike. Thousands of workers marched through the town, burned down the owner's house and sacked an armoury. These wildcats were deeply worrying to the national union leadership and it began to seek ways to restore its power. A necessary element in this was a frontal assault on the forces of the left and in particular on the Peronist Youth.

The confrontation between the right and the left in the Peronist movement had begun in earnest when Perón returned to the country on 20 June 1973. Hundreds of thousands of his supporters had gathered at Ezeiza airport to welcome him back, but the right-wing old guard and union bodyguards had control over the podium. Though the exact cause is unclear, these elements began firing at the crowd which was largely composed of young people and where the banners of the left predominated. At the end of the day there were nearly one hundred dead with many more being brutally tortured in the airport hotel. Perón responded with a strong attack on the radical wing of his movement, which was a sign of things to come. At the time the Peronist Youth blamed his reactionary entourage and not the old man himself.

The trade union leadership saw the time was ripe to move against Cámpora, who had begun to incur the displeasure of Perón by his apparent inability or unwillingness to control mass mobilisations. The palace revolution came in mid-July when CGT leader José Rucci came out of Cámpora's office and told the press that 'there will be no more messing around' (*se acabó la joda*). Raúl Lastiri, president of the Chamber of Deputies and, more importantly, son-in-law of López Rega, the *éminence grise* of the new Peronist right, became provisional president of the nation. In the new electoral campaign the trade union movement threw its considerable financial and organisational resources behind Perón's candidature.

Perón governs and dies (October 1973–June 1974)

General Perón was duly elected president on 23 September 1973 with 62% of the vote. The recent military coup in Chile allowed him to claim that precedent to legitimise a right-ward turn. One of his first moves was to seek a reconciliation with the trade union leadership. Contrary to his views earlier he now declared that 'the CGT is a guarantee for all workers because I have known its leaders for 30 years. . . . The CGT can be secure and contented with the leaders it has, even though some fools say they are bureaucrats'.[9] The main instrument he used to strengthen the position of the trade union leadership was a new Law of Professional Associations approved in November 1973.[10]

The essence of this new law was to increase the level of centralisation in the unions, granting head office the right to intervene in local branches and overturn decisions taken by the shop-stewards' committees. The position of the leadership was further strengthened by extending the period of office for elected posts from two to four years, and the role of national conferences was severely curtailed. To call an emergency conference one-fifth of the entire membership had to petition the leadership – a practically impossible requirement to meet. A secondary element was a built-in preference for the bigger, more powerful unions, which was reflected in a demarcation dispute between the powerful metal-workers' union UOM, and the car mechanics' union SMATA. A complementary Redundancy Law (*Ley de Prescindibilidad*) authorised the state to sack any employee with compensation. The left supported it on the basis that it would be used to weed out supporters of the military dictatorship in the administrative apparatus. In fact it was used to sack 200 workers at the State Mechanical Industries (*Industrias Mecánicas del Estado*) in Córdoba and 58 employees of the Banco de la Nación, among others.

The radical Montoneros organisation provided little political leadership against the new rise of the trade union bureaucracy. In fact, left-wing Peronism had always maintained a somewhat moralistic view of the labour bureaucracy.[11] Emphasis was placed on the leaders' individual corruption and their treacherous role, to the detriment of an understanding of their structural and political role in the labour movement. According to the militaristic logic of the Montoneros the answer to these traitors was 'execution'. Vandor had been killed in 1969, his rival José Alonso in 1970, now in 1973 it was the turn of CGT leader José Rucci, and a year later building workers' union leader Rogelio Coria. Perón himself had approved of the first two operations, but Rucci was a key element in his political strategy for 1973. Anyway, this was not a progressive labour policy as union leaders were simply replaced by others. The Montoneros labour front, the *Juventud Trabajadora Peronista* – JTP (Peronist Working Youth) never became a major tendency in the labour movement, nor did it articulate a coherent class-struggle orientation. As Gillespie writes, 'though it won control of the State Workers Association (ATE) regional councils in Córdoba, Rosario, Misiones, and though it won strong positions among the bus drivers (UTA), State Gas workers, and bank employees of Buenos Aires, the JTP never acquired industrial muscle'.[12] Nor could it hope to win influence in the bastions of the industrial working class by shooting its leaders with one hand and supporting the Social Pact with the other.

Perón took the purging of Cámpora's government furthest in the provinces where leftist governors had been elected. As part of the electoral pact between the leftist and traditional wings of Peronism, the left gained the provincial governorships of Buenos Aires, Córdoba, Mendoza and elsewhere. A new law, the Act of Obligation to National Security, gave the national government the right to intervene in the internal affairs of the provinces in the interests of 'national security'. A wave of federal interventions in the provincial governments became an integral element of the orthodox Peronist campaign against leftist 'infiltrators'. In January 1974 Perón forced Oscar Bidegain, governor of Buenos Aires, to resign because he was 'soft on terrorism', using as a pretext an ERP (People's Revolutionary Army) attack on the Azul barracks. This was followed in February by a move against the Córdoba government of Obregón Cano and Atilio López (a leader of the *Cordobazo*). Perón simply sanctioned a rebellion by Córdoba's police chief Navarro (the event became known as the *Navarrazo*) which displaced the elected government.[13] During the Córdoba events officials from the textile, metal-workers' and construction workers' union supported the rebels, whereas SMATA, *Luz y Fuerza* and the bus drivers (UTA) opposed them. It represented essentially a settling of accounts between the signatories of the Social Pact, and the car workers simply worked normally throughout the dispute. Here we can see already the deep fracture within the labour movement. After the *Navarrazo*, federal interventions followed in Mendoza, Santa Cruz, Salta and Catamarca until by the end of 1974 the process was complete.

During all these events the mobilisation of the working class in defence of living standards continued. During Perón's government (see Appendix) the average monthly strike rate reached a peak of nearly 40, and nearly a third of all disputes led to factory occupations. The deteriorating economic situation meant that whereas wage demands were present in only 5% of disputes during the Cámpora/Lastiri period, they now occurred in nearly one-third of all disputes. In May 1974 Perón forced the *Gran Paritaria Nacional* to grant a larger wage increase than the employers wanted, which helped reinforce the position of the trade union leadership. Demands over working conditions and for reinstatement were still the most frequent cause of disputes. As Jelin notes, 'the reinstatement of dismissed or suspended workers was often linked to the mobilisation over working conditions and the attempts to create an active trade union structure in the factories'.[14] Management would simply sack activists and shop-stewards when faced with a long list of demands, and if there was rank-and-file support, a protracted dispute would ensue, until the Ministry of Labour imposed its arbitration. There was also an increasing number of disputes in the public sector, specifically concerned with abuses of the new Redundancy Law. Taken overall, the continued mobilisation of labour during this period fundamentally undermined the Social Pact and seriously questioned the position of the labour bureaucracy.

Among the notable strikes of this period we should mention the 22-day stoppage in March 1974 at the INSUD lead plant, which won compensation for lead poisoning and a reduction of the working day to six hours.[15] Apart from trade union and local community support, the strikers were backed by the ERP which kidnapped one of the managers. In November the INSUD-owned mine El Aguilar (in the north-east) saw a bitter strike and occupation, over a reduction of over-time, which led to the death of a worker in confrontations with the police. Another strike in November was that at the big Terrabusi biscuit factory in Buenos Aires, for a 30% wage increase, job stability, medical facilities and so on, to which the management responded by sacking 30 workers. This led to an immediate occupation of the factory's two plants, which only ended after the Ministry of Labour decreed compulsory arbitration of the dispute.

One of the most interesting of all the disputes of this period was led by the 700 workers of the petrochemical plant PASA in July 1974, where protests began over the quality of canteen food. So as not to lay themselves open to intervention by the Ministry of Labour and the CGT, the workers decided to run the plant themselves, setting up committees in charge of production, information and medical services. Against the management, the Ministry of Labour and the CGT, the workers achieved their original demands by setting an example of workers' control. They also demanded that the US-owned firm be nationalised. A characteristic of many of these disputes was that they occurred in relatively recently organised sectors where the *Juventud Trabajadora Peronista* (JTP) and other left-wing organisations had a considerable role.

The combative sectors of the post-*Cordobazo* phase were also active under the Peronist government. The Córdoba car workers at the Renault, Ford and Fiat plants again elected a militant class-struggle leadership for their union SMATA in May 1974. In June, mass meetings of these workers showed they did not consider themselves bound by the Social Pact. They demanded a 60% wage increase but management responded with massive suspensions and a lock-out. The national SMATA leadership stepped in to expel René Salamanca and the rest of the Córdoba branch committee with the help of the police. From then on the Córdoba leadership had to act clandestinely. The national overseer of SMATA, Brigadier General Raul Lacabanne said that 'this was not a struggle between leaders or bureaucrats, but a struggle by a Peronist union to expel from its midst mercenary elements, enemies of the workers and allies of foreign imperialism . . .'[16]

The Córdoba branch of the power workers' union (*Luz y Fuerza*) under Agustín Tosco, also came under attack after the *Navarrazo* in February

1974, suffering a similar fate to SMATA–national headquarters intervention and a leadership on the run. As Tosco himself explains, '*Luz y Fuerza* maintained its total solidarity with the SMATA workers and was in turn attacked. The motivation was clear: *Luz y Fuerza* was the last of the militant unions which hadn't been taken over, and was able to organise the fight against the rightist deviation'.[17] In April 1974 there was a conference held in Villa Constitución organised by Tosco, Salamanca and Jaime (Salta CGT) but apart from issuing an anti-bureaucratic manifesto, it was unable to co-ordinate the fight-back in a general climate of repression and demoralisation.

Throughout this period the distance between Perón and the radical youth wing of his movement became greater. This came to a head with the May Day rally of 1974 at the Plaza de Mayo, which the Montoneros saw as a chance to renew the mystical 'dialogue' between the leader and his followers. Soon after Perón appeared at the rostrum surrounded by the trade union leaders, the crowds began to chant, '*Se vá acabar, se vá acabar la burocracia sindical*' (the union bureaucracy is going to end).[18] A furious Perón replied that for 20 years the trade unions had remained intransigent and that the 'callow youth' shouting slogans were no match for them. As he uttered threats against the 'pernicious elements' and 'mercenaries' in the movement, the Montonero columns filed out of the Plaza de Mayo leaving it practically deserted. In his last speech to the masses in June 1974 Perón tried to repair some of the damage caused to his credibility at the May Day rally by attacking the oligarchy and the pressures exerted by imperialism upon his government.[19]

Perón died on 1 July 1974, and although he had recently stated that his only heir was the people (*mi único heredero es el pueblo*) his widow Isabel stepped into his position from her vice-president's role. Isabel Perón inherited the tarnished mantle of Peronism and a severe political crisis, aggravated by the effects of the international recession on Argentina's economy. On top of this, she did not have the prestige, charisma and historical dimension which Perón had used to control a contradictory nationalist-labour movement.

Repression and resistance (July 1974–September 1975)

In the wake of Perón's death the right-wing *déclassé* elements around López Rega consolidated themselves under the protection of President Isabel Perón. A prime target was the combative wing of the trade union movement which had emerged in the period following the *Cordobazo*. Here Isabel Perón pursued the same policies already begun under General Perón's presidency. In Buenos Aires the militant leader of the telephone workers, Julio Guillán, was removed in October 1974 when the Ministry of Labour declared the conference that elected him invalid. Another highly symbolic act was the gaoling of Raimundo Ongaro, head of the *Federación*

Gráfica Bonaërense and ex-leader of the CGT-A.

Towards the end of 1974 the Ministry of Labour, after withdrawing recognition (*personería gremial*) from Ongaro's union, set up a new *Sindicato Gráfico* (Argentine Graphic Workers' Union). When the parallel union was set up, Minister for Labour Ricardo Otero declared that it

> would return to graphic workers . . . the respect that they are owed as Peronist workers who have always been at the service of the ideals of General Perón, as workers who never dared question the undisputed leader of the movement – General Perón – and who, at this moment, as is proper, follow loyally the absolute authority [*verticalidad*] of our dear President, señora María Estela Martínez de Perón . . .[20]

In Tucumán, the sugar workers' union (FOTIA) launched a campaign for a wage increase in September 1974, when the price of sugar was allowed to rise. After a hard struggle, in the course of which its legal recognition was withdrawn, the demands were met and recognition restored. During this period a clandestine meeting was held in Tucumán organised by FOTIA, the Córdoba branches of SMATA and *Luz y Fuerza*, and the Buenos Aires graphic workers' union, to try to organise a coordinated fight-back. This body was shortlived, as Isabel Perón's government launched a full-scale repressive wave. The murderous AAA (Argentine Anti-Communist Alliance) stepped up its assassination of worker militants, journalists and labour lawyers.[21] The battle launched in 1973 between the orthodox slogan of *Patria Peronista* (Peronist Fatherland) and the radical's alternative *Patria Socialista*[22] (Socialist Fatherland) was now clearly being won by the first. In fact it looked as if a narrow *Patria Metalúrgica* (Metal-workers' Fatherland) based on corporatist thinking was beginning to take shape.

The CGT began a process of reorganisation and reorientation following the death of Perón. Reluctantly brought into the Social Pact by Perón, the union leaders were aware of their contradictory position. Once they were subjected to the political dictates of Perón they could no longer defend their corporative interests adequately. As Torre explains:

> the end of the mandate of the CGT general council [in July 1974] provided the opportunity to resolve the conflict between those trade unionists who believed that the unions were one branch more of the governing political movement and that they must subordinate themselves to it, and the others who, on the contrary, understood that they should behave as an independent pressure group.[23]

They argued persuasively that whereas governments come and go, the trade unions were always there. After the death of Perón the trade union leaders around Lorenzo Miguel of UOM carved out a position freer of commitments and burdensome loyalties. Supporters of Lorenzo Miguel – who remained as the power behind the scenes, as Vandor had done, by controlling the 62 Organisations – now took control of the CGT. Adelino Romero remained the titular head of the CGT for a short while, but when he died he was replaced by Casildo Herreras, leader of the Textile Workers' Union (AOT) who was close to Miguel.[24]

There was now considerable distance between the CGT and the government of Isabel Perón. The union movement was a major power centre nevertheless – it controlled the Ministry of Labour and later it even gained a leading role at the Ministry of Economy. But all this power was dissipated in a series of internal disputes and ritual confrontations. The logic of *Vandorismo* was again having its effect – the CGT simply wanted a bigger slice of the cake and played no role in its possible redesign. The organised labour movement did not use its great weight and influence to launch a hegemonic project which could lead a broad class alliance to socialism, or even social democracy. The long years of negotiation and compromise were matched now by an arrogant assumption that power was theirs. The union leaders neither sought social allies for a transformation strategy nor took responsibility for the disastrous policies of what was after all 'their' government. They pursued the politics of a clique and not the politics of a class movement.

The right-wing offensive under Isabel Perón led to a dramatic decline in labour struggles (see Appendix) with only eleven strikes per month on average between November 1974 and March 1975. Just as significantly, the percentage of disputes which led to factory occupations dropped to barely 10% under Isabel Perón. As Jelin describes, the Ministry of Labour used a new Security Law (*Ley de Seguridad*) to 'ban factory occupations and strikes or stoppages in pursuit of wage claims. It also began to intimidate and threaten unions and suspend their legal recognition [*personería gremial*] more frequently than previously'.[25] In this situation disputes involving union issues increased considerably and shifted from the previous anti-bureaucratic issues to direct conflicts between the unions and the Ministry of Labour over the new legislation. Absenteeism increased to around 20% in many sectors, in large part as a protest measure and one which was relatively safe, given a new labour contract law which guaranteed job security.

The working class did not respond immediately to this situation, and for a long time it was the revolutionary organisations which suffered the brunt of the repression, in isolation from the mass movement. Then a number of important strikes in Córdoba marked a gradual recovery of the workers' movement and there was a growing realisation that it was necessary to confront the Peronist government. The strike in Villa Constitución in early 1975 was the first large-scale response to the government's offensive.[26] In March 1974, the 6,000 workers at the Acindar, Marathon and Methcon steel factories has occupied all three plants demanding that their union, the UOM, should hold local elections, which had not taken place since 1970. After dockers, bank employees, textile workers, teachers, railway workers, shop assistants – in short all 30,000 workers of Villa Constitución – stopped work for a week in sympathy, the union headquarters gave in. In December 1974 elections were held which resulted in an overwhelming victory for the class-struggle slate which displaced the old Peronist bureaucracy. The new leadership demanded a 70% wage increase and, quite significantly, workers' control over industrial health and over the pace of work. This led to an occupation of the big steel plants in the region and a month-long struggle in which four successive strike committees were arrested. In spite of severe repression, the strike received widespread support throughout the country, and clearly demonstrated a militant determination to resist the economic policies and the repression of late Peronism. Though the Villa Constitución strike did not achieve its objectives, it was not a defeat for the working class as a whole, as it marked an end of fragmented, defensive struggles and a turn towards a working-class offensive. As a contemporary observer noted:

> The government put its prestige on the line in this confrontation, and the test of strength, which was a prolonged one, damaged it. . . . Day after day the conflict was on the first page of the newspapers, and soon the automobile industry will be paralysed if the Villa factories do not start working again quickly. . . . Whatever negotiations the government may undertake, the masses of the country will see them as a triumph and will adopt the road and methods of Villa Constitución in order to push their struggles forward.[27]

In the wake of the Villa Constitución strike the government named a new economy minister, Celestino Rodrigo, whose aim was to implement drastic austerity measures. This involved a new devaluation of the peso, so as to stimulate exports, a big increase in the price of public services, and a severe limitation on wage increases under the guise of holding down inflation – the government spoke of holding wage increases at 38–45% while the cost of living was going up by 150% per annum. The aim of the Rodrigo plan was clearly an attempt to reduce mass consumption drastically, even at the risk of provoking a deflationary turn so sharp that a serious economic recession would result.[28]

At this time the periodic collective contracts of key sections of the working class (metal-workers, construction workers, bank employees, public sector employees, etc.) were coming up for renewal. After wage increases of up to 100% had been negotiated the government stepped in and set a 50% limit, with an extra 15% in October 1975 and another 15% in January 1976. Isabel Perón also sharply attacked the workers for going back on the promise they made to her late husband 'to work harder and produce more'. She was at least conscious of the gravity of the situation: 'The Argentine nation is now facing what I would call the zero hour of our decision to obtain definitive freedom on all fronts. . . . Production is going down. Speculation seems to be spreading beyond all limits. . . . ' Her solution was predictably to maintain 'a just and healthy austerity'.[29] What this meant was that as real wages were dropping, the rate of unemployment was rising.

The working class did not accept this affront passively, and launched a series of strikes which culminated in a 48-hour general strike in July, forced on the CGT by a massive wave of wildcat strikes which had spread through the country. The situation was chaotic as Jelin describes:

> Spontaneous protest, uncontrolled by the unions, dominated the scene. The workers from one plant would start a street demonstration and soon the workers from neighbouring plants would join in. Within minutes, thousands of workers would be marching through the streets of Córdoba, Mendoza, Rosario or Buenos Aires.[30]

The country was paralysed as far as production was concerned and there was a deepening crisis which could only be resolved through concessions across the board. In Córdoba and Santa Fé provinces particularly, a new type of rank-and-file organisation was formed by co-ordinating bodies of factory activists and workers' commissions on a district level. These were known as *coordinadoras*. The participants of these bodies were, as Thompson describes, 'the local branches of the unions (as in Córdoba) shop-steward committees, plant representatives and activists (as in Greater Buenos Aires). In other cases, as in San Lorenzo, the *coordinadora* included the participation of factory unions (PASA Petroquímica)'.[31] In general they resulted from initiatives by the combative Peronists and other left-wing groupings to meet the leadership crisis caused by the inaction of the CGT during the June–July days of 1975.

The emergence of the *co-ordinadoras* as a potential alternative leadership highlighted the crisis of Peronism, in which the tension between the rank and file and the leadership had never been as sharp. Workers had downed tools and marched to CGT headquarters to demand action, without a word from their shop-stewards, and without the transport usually laid on by the unions. Important sections of the working class broke with the bourgeois leadership of Peronism as embodied in the Isabel-López Rega *camarilla*. As well as ratifying the wage agreements, the government was forced to dismiss López Rega, thus satisfying one of the demands of the strike.

However, this social break, and the success of the first ever general strike against a Peronist government, was not consummated in a *political* break with Peronism, nor did an independent working-class political leadership emerge. After the July 1975 general strike, which was referred to as a *Cordobazo amortiguado* (Cordobazo with shock absorbers) there was a crisis in the government's economic and political strategy. The strike had effectively blocked the attempts to rationalise the economy on the basis of renewed integration with international monopoly capital, and showed the limits of trade union collaborationism.

After the July 1975 upsurge the energy of workers focused on the basic demand for free collective bargaining without government intervention. The advance of some categories of workers had produced a lop-sided wage structure so that there were a series of struggles through to October designed to catch up with the front-runners. From mid-1975 to the end of the year disputes over wages predominated (see Appendix) and there were also many strikes over job classification (*escalafón*) issues which also affected wages. An ominous sign was the increase in strikes protesting against violence – this was the period in which workers were kidnapped, imprisoned or simply murdered as the factory floor became part of the growing war between the right and left of the Peronist movement.[32] In this context the post-July political compromises reached within the government – such as the appointment of a pro-trade union economy minister – could not mask the fundamental contradictions which had emerged within the Peronist movement. This growing discord had its effect on mass mobilisations and when the 30th anniversary of 17 October – the key date in the Peronist calendar – was held in 1975, only 30,000 people turned up. The massive organisation of the CGT, a huge propaganda campaign and free transport could only turn out a small crowd composed mainly of trade union employees and lumpen elements, with a marked absence of shop-steward committee banners. The dream of the Peronist *retorno* was turning sour for hundreds of thousands of Peronist workers.

Crisis and collapse (October 1975–March 1976)

Two events took place in October 1975 which indicated clearly the growing crisis of the Peronist movement and government. Victorio Calabró, governor of Buenos Aires and No. 2 in the metal-workers'union UOM declared himself openly against *verticalismo* (unquestioning obedience to Isabel Perón). He stated categorically that if things continued as they were there would be no elections in 1977 (*así no llegamos al 77*) and called for Isabel's resignation.[33] Calabró was eventually expelled from the UOM, the CGT and 62 Organisations for 'insubordination', but there was considerable support for his *anti-verticalista* position. This current was also known as the *acuerdistas* or compromisers because they wanted to reconstruct the social alliance expressed earlier through the Grand National Agreement.

The other main event was an attempt towards the end of the month to set up a new social pact which would ban strikes and sackings for 180 days. Economy Minister Cafiero, sympathetic to the unions, was able to establish an agreement between the CGT, the CGE and the government, but this compromise was no longer possible given the growing economic crisis.[34] The economic policy of populism – which had to maintain profits *and* wages – was simply no longer viable. The Central Bank was in the red, the IMF refused further credits, inflation had reached 335% in 1975 and was completely out of control in early 1976, and real wages were declining. Strikes were to continue (although they dropped off in early 1976) with wage demands coming to represent over half the causes of all disputes (see Appendix).

The armed forces were already deeply involved in the war against 'terrorism' but they were as yet reluctant to seize political power.[35] They knew that with the split in the trade unions – the backbone of the Peronist movement – there would be no effective opposition but it was best to leave the 'popular government' to discredit itself further. There were two currents of opinion in the armed forces – one wanted to see a generalised, long-term repression of the mass movement and another preferred a more selective and temporary repression of trade-union and political activists. The second current gained the upper hand after an abortive coup attempt in December 1975 by a section of the air-force. Though ex-president Onganía supported the plot, and the armed forces were in general sympathetic, army-chief General Videla opted to hold back. His timetable for military intervention was laid out early in 1976 when he made it clear that the armed forces would seize power in order to counter the anticipated wave of strikes against the new austerity measures then being prepared. The Chilean variant was explicitly rejected and the aim of the coup was expressed in terms of putting an end to 'mis-government, corruption and subversion'. In the circumstances of the very real chaos, terror and corruption of late Peronism, there was widespread support for a coup to restore 'order and decency'. The fact that the CGT had called a general strike towards the end of the coup dress-rehearsal, and that it failed miserably, was a good omen for the military conspirators.

In January 1976 Isabel Perón had reshuffled her government, getting rid of those figures such as Cafiero who were linked to the Peronist trade union or political wing. Instead, elements from the López Rega clique were brought back into prominence, thus reducing the chances of consensus. The trade union leaders were furious, but decided on a passive course, arguing that to do otherwise would lead to the fall of the government. The new economy minister, Mondelli, was meanwhile called upon to restore the austerity measures which had been defeated by the labour movement in the *Rodrigazo* of mid-1975. This time not only were rigorous wage limits set, but there were a proposal to sack around 500,000 public sector employees.

The employers, for their part, had regrouped their forces with the *Asamblea Permanente de Asociaciones Gremiales* (Permanent Assembly of Employers' Associations), condemned the government's economic policies and in March 1976 called an 'employers' strike' (unprecedented in Argentina) successfully paralysing urban and rural activities. The workers were not prepared to wait for the industry-wide collective negotiations (*paritarias*) coming up in April 1976, and began to mobilise. The CGT in Córdoba declared its 'rejection and repudiation of the Mondelli plan, which does not follow the national *Justicialista* doctrine; because it unloads the weight of the crisis on the working class'.[36] The *verticalista* element was now clearly becoming a minority within the organised labour movement.

It was not only the combative union branches of the provinces which launched the struggle, but whole unions and even regional bodies of the CGT. In the first weeks of March 1976 workers in Córdoba, Mendoza and Rosario stopped work in their thousands. In Buenos Aires, Calabró called out his supporters in the metallurgical industry and even threatened a series of 24- and 48-hour strikes. There was a similar dynamic to the events of

June–July 1975 with the *coordinadoras* (inter-factory coordinating committees) this time pursuing a more radical project.[37] The CGT could no longer support the Mondelli plan, but nor could it place itself at the head of the powerful and spontaneous wave of strikes and factory occupations without endangering the government. Calabró vacillated, began negotiating with the armed forces over the impending coup, then retreated. The *coordinadoras* were not sufficiently established to offer an alternative national leadership. Most of the left-wing organisations – including the Montoneros, the ERP and the Communist Party – did not throw their full weight behind the strikes, concentrating their activity on preparations for the supposedly inevitable coup.[38] Thus the only process which could defeat the coup – a development of the mass mobilisation which had begun against the economic plan – was allowed to collapse. As one contemporary observer put it:

> The road was finally open to the putschists. There was no leadership or force sufficient to detonate a generalised mobilisation of the entire working class. Thus Peronism, while preparing its own defeat, rendered the capitalist system one last great service: the division, disillusionment, and lack of confidence it provoked among the masses in turn deprived the masses of the only leadership they had known.[39]

The military coup finally came on 24 March 1976 and a new phase in Argentina's history as well as a new government began. If we were to seek one essential cause for the coup it would have to be the failure of the Peronist government to contain the combativeness of the working class within a framework of national unity and class collaboration, under a charismatic 'Bonaparte', and supported by a powerful trade-union bureaucracy able to maintain its hegemony among the workers. The key element, with Perón himself dead, was the trade union bureaucracy: it had begun to lose control over sections of the rural proletariat in the north such as the sugar workers, the core sections of the Córdoba proletariat, and increasingly sectors of the dynamic industries in the crucial Buenos Aires region, such as the metallurgical workers. The labour bureaucracy had also failed to give any sort of lead as the crisis deepened. Interviewed by journalists across the River Plate in Uruguay where he had fled on 22 March, Casildo Herreras, head of the textile workers' union and CGT general secretary, could only say that he was 'getting off-side' (*me borré*). This memorable phrase was a good epitaph for the labour bureaucracy. In spite of important labour struggles around the time of the coup, including a general strike in Córdoba the day before, the isolated and demoralised working class did not respond to defend a government it no longer saw as its own. By March 1976 the pre-revolutionary situation had been exhausted, and the working class was on the defensive, not through a direct confrontation with the ruling class, but rather from the effects of a Peronist government.[40] When the final collapse came the working class had already withdrawn from the political scene, leaving the way clear for an offensive by the armed forces.

Looking back to the heady days of May 1973 when Cámpora assumed power we can see how far things had changed. Between June and September 1973 workers had launched a wave of anti-bureaucratic struggles and posed the need for workers' control. These were the days of the Peronist Youth and their mass mobilisations. Under Perón, between October 1973 and June 1974, the trade union bureaucracy had regained the initiative and had begun to attack the militant class-struggle bastions. By shooting trade union leaders, the Montoneros could not change this fact. When Isabel Perón assumed the presidency in July 1974 the Peronist right wing took the offensive more openly to complete this process, but workers responded in Villa Constitución and shortly afterwards with the July 1975 general strike. This strike represented a social, if not political, break with Peronism, and the internal struggles within the movement became fiercer. It did not lead to an alternative leadership for the labour movement, and the political crisis only deepened from then on.

By the end of 1975 it was clear that the military were just biding their time until the appropriate moment to step in. The crisis of late Peronism was such, that when the armed forces made their move in March 1976, not one section of the working class rose up in protest. A general strike called by the CGT leadership was largely ignored. The legacy of Peronism's return between 1973 and 1976 was a demoralised working class and a weakened trade union movement. The new military government was going to try to make this weakness permanent and finally break the mould of Argentine politics set between 1943 and 1945.

Appendix 6

Table 14.2   Strikes in Argentina 1973–1976 by causes of dispute

	June–Sep 1973	Oct 1973–Feb 1974	Mar–Jun 1974	July–Oct 1974	Nov 1974.–Mar 1975	April–Jun 1975	July–Aug 1975	Sep–Jan 1976	Feb–Mar 1976
					Period				
Monthly Average	30.5	30.8	39.0	22.5	11.6	24.7	33.0	31.2	17.0
Percentage with factory seizures	43	31	19	11	10	4	9	7	–
Causes (%)									
National negotiations	–	–	–	–	–	31	29	–	–
Against violence	–	6	3	6	10	–	3	12	15
Opposition to management	12	5	6	7	5	4	–	3	6
Trade union affairs	15	16	18	11	28	26	8	21	9
Legal or contractual affairs	25	20	17	24	24	18	14	28	12
Overdue wages & back-pay	32	23	16	27	24	14	21	22	15
Fear of redundancy or closure	11	9	8	8	5	1	3	4	–
Working conditions	17	31	17	19	16	20	9	12	9
For rehiring of unemployed or suspended workers	30	36	25	24	17	9	17	19	12
Wage demands	5	21	32	27	16	26	45	39	65

Source: E. Jelin, (1977) "Conflictos laborales en la Argentina, 1973–1976", *Estudios Sociales* no. 9, Buenos Aires, CEDES pp. 46 and 47.
Note: The data for July 1975 does not include the general strike; the data for March 1976 ends on the 24th with the military coup. Due to multiple causes for disputes the total adds up to more than 100%.

Notes

1. For an overview of this period see L. De Riz, (1981). *Retorno y Derrumbe – el ultimo gobierno peronista*, Mexico, Folios Ediciones.
2. Cited in L. De Riz, (1981) *Retorno y Derrumbe*, p. 48.
3. For a detailed analysis of the Social Pact see R. Ayres, (1976) "The Social Pact as anti-inflationary policy: The Argentine experience since 1976", *World Politics*, vol. XXVIII, no. 4.
4. All wages data from R. Ayres, (1976) "The Social Pact as anti-inflationary policy", p. 483.
5. E. Jelin, (1977) "Conflictos laborales en la Argentina, 1973–1976", *Estudios Sociales* 9, Buenos Aires, CEDES, p. 11. (There is a briefer English version of this article: E. Jelin, (1979) "Labour Conflicts under the Second Peronist Regime, Argentina 1973–1976", *Development and Change*, 10, 2). For a complementary analysis of labour disputes during this period see J. Pegoraro (1979) "Los conflictos laborales, 1973–1976", *Cuadernos de Marcha*, II, 2.
6. *Pasado y Presente* (1973) "El significado de las luchas obreras actuales", *Pasado y Presente* IV, 2/3, p. 279. (there is an English version of this article: J.C. Torre, (1974) "Workers Struggle and Consciousness", *Latin American Perspectives*, 1, 3).
7. This and following disputes described in *Pasado y Presente* (1973) "El significado de la luchas obreras actuales".
8. Episode described in F. Gèze and A. Labrousse, (1975) *Argentine: Révolution et Contre-Révolutions*, Paris, Editions Du Seuil, p. 225.
9. Cited in L. De Riz, (1981) *Retorno y Derrumbe*, p. 94.
10. For a detailed analysis of the Law of Professional Associations see P. Aguirre. (1973) "La reforma de la Ley de Asociaciones Profesionales", *Pasado y Presente*, IV, 2/3.
11. See D. James, (1976) "The Peronist Left: 1955–1975", *Journal of Latin American Studies*, 8, 2.
12. R. Gillespie, (1982). *Soldiers of Perón – Argentina's Montoneros*, Oxford, Clarendon Press, p. 139.
13. For an account of the *Navarrazo* see B. Balvé, (1978) "Crisis Institucional, Experiencia y Conciencia de Poder", *Estudios Sociales Centroamericanos* 20.
14. E. Jelin, (1977) "Conflictos laborales en la Argentina", p. 19.
15. Dispute mentioned in CEDETIM (1974) "Argentine: Mobilisation Populaire Contre L'Imperialisme", *Bulletin du CEDETIM*, 32/33, p. 35.
16. Cited in S. Senén Gonzalez, (1978) *El Poder Sindical*, Buenos Aires, Plus Ultra, p. 28.
17. C. Knowles, (1975) "Revolutionary Trade Unionism in Argentina: Interview with Agustín Tosco", *Radical America*. 9, 3, p. 29. For more details of Luz y Fuerza in this period see I.M. Roldán (1979) *Sindicatos y Protesta Social en la Argentina (1969–1974)*, Amsterdam, CEDLA.
18. Episode described in R. Gillespie (1982) *Soldiers of Perón*, pp. 148–150. See also J. Godio (1977) *Perón y los Montoneros*, Maracaibo, Universidad de Zulia.
19. On Perón's last year in power and its underlying significance see J. Godio, (1981) *El ultimo año de Perón*. Colombia, Colección Universidad y Pueblo.
20. Cited in S. Senén Gonzalez (1978). *El Poder Sindical*, p. 37.
21. For a perceptive analysis of repression during this period see J.C. Marín (1980) *Argentina 1973–1976: Armed Events and Democracy*, Canada, LARU Working Paper no. 8.

22. On their underlying social projects see R. García, (1980) *Patria sindical os Patria Socialista*. Buenos Aires, Colección Humanismo y Terror.

23. J.C. Torre (1979) "El Movimiento Laboral en Argentina: 1955–1976", J. Carrière (ed.) *Industrialisation and the State in Latin America*. Amsterdam, CEDLA, p. 384.

24. On the intricacies of CGT politics during this period see S. Senén Gonzalez, (1980) *El Poder Sindical* and also the useful journalistic account P. Kandel and M. Monteverde, (1976) *Entorno y Caída*, Buenos Aires, Editorial Planeta.

25. E. Jelin, (1977) "Conflicto laborales en la Argentina", p. 25.

26. For a detailed description and assessment of the Villa Constitución strike see B. Galitelli, (1980) "La Huelga de Villa Constitución", *Apuntes* II, 2.

27. E. Raisin (1975) "Villa Constitución", *Inprecor*, 29, p. 15.

28. On the economic crisis of 1975 and on Peronist economic policies generally see T. Di Tella (1983) *Argentina under Perón, 1973–76. The Nation's Experience with a Labour-Based Government*, London, Macmillan. Also A. Ferrer (1977) *Crisis y Alternativas de la Política Económica Argentina*, Buenos Aires, Fondo de Cultura Económica.

29. Cited in P. Kandel and P. Monteverde, (1976) *Entorno y Caída*, p. 175.

30. E. Jelin (1977) "Conflicto laborales en la Argentina", p. 31.

31. A. Thompson (1982) *Labour Struggles and Political Conflict. Argentina: The general strike of 1975 and the crisis of Peronism through an historical perspective*, MA thesis, Institute of Social Studies, The Hague, p. 112.

32. See J.C. Marín (1980) *Argentina 1973–1976*.

33. On the Calabró split see S. Senén Gonzalez (1978) *El Poder Sindical*.

34. On the growing inviability of the Peronist economic project see A. Canitrot, (1977) "La viabilidad económica de la democracia: un análisis de la experiencia peronista 1973–1976", *Estudios Sociales*, 11, Buenos Aires, CEDES.

35. On the "private war" between the armed forces and the guerrilla organisations, see M. Días (1978) *A Guerra da Argentina*, Lisbon, Al Regra do Jogo.

36. P. Kandel and M. Monteverde (1976) *Entorno y Caída*, p. 200.

37. A. Thompson (1982) *Labour Struggles and Political Conflict*, p. 123.

38. For a critical balance sheet of the Montoneros' strategy see R. Gillespie (1982) *Soldiers of Perón* and for a self-criticism on the ERP see L. Flores (1980) "La cuestión de 'Las vias' en Argentina", *Rearme*, 11, 6.

39. I. Rodriguez (1977) "Argentina: one year after the coup". *Inprecor*, 68, p. 6.

40. Interpretation developed by O. Landi (1979) Argentina 1973–1976: "La génesis de una nueva crisis política", *Revista Mexicana de Sociología*, XLI, 1, p. 127.

15. Labour Recomposition and Trade Union Resistance (1976–1985)

A new period of military rule began in 1976 with the objective of decisively defeating the mass movement and thus breaking the 'pendulum' pattern of politics in Argentina which began in 1930.[1] The guerrilla movement was ostensibly the main enemy, but by defining shop-stewards and activists as 'industrial guerrillas', the war was extended to the factory floor. Repression by itself was not sufficient – a fundamental restructuring of the working class was to be a prime element in weakening the labour movement.

We turn our attention first to the systematic recomposition of labour through various economic, social and legal means. This sets the scene for a reconstruction of the various stages of trade union resistance from 1976 to 1983.[2] We examine the early spontaneous and inorganic expressions of labour resistance through to the period of recovery beginning with the 1979 general strike. An important element to consider is the role of the trade union bureaucracy which, under attack from the government, found itself (as from 1955 to 1958) forced to play a more militant role. By 1982 the trade union movement had become strengthened to such an extent that the Malvinas adventure was launched to defuse labour protest. With the elections in 1983 labour returned to the centre of the political scene and showed conclusively that this military offensive, far more thorough than either 1955 or 1966, had failed. Successive military presidents – Generals Videla (1976–1981), Viola (1981), Galtieri (1982) and Bignone (1982–83) – found that the labour movement was their main problem.

Repression

The repression of the working class and the trade union movement after 1976 took many forms.[3] In the weeks following the coup armed police detachments stood at the doors of offices and factories to arrest shop-stewards and union activists. Army detachments would simply march into factories to 'settle' disputes at the point of a bayonet. The 'disappearance' of militants was stepped up, and the less dramatic sacking of 'trouble-makers' became routine practice. All this must be mentioned first, but terror in itself would not have been sufficient to inflict a historic defeat on

207

the labour movement. To do that Argentina's capitalists and new military rulers needed to restructure the economy completely so as to reduce the social weight of the working class. Essentially the military junta's monetarist policies were aimed at returning Argentina to the pre-1930 'golden era' based on a thriving agro-export economy with only a subsidiary industrial sector.[4] The public sector was to be reduced, and uncompetitive industrial sectors would simply be allowed to sink. The main beneficiaries were the agrarian oligarchy and a new financial oligarchy dedicated to profiteering over the de-industrialising economic system. The strong national industrialist class traditionally organised through the CGE–which had provided an important element in the Peronist alliance–was destined to disappear, or at best become a minor partner in the new arrangements. To a large extent these economic policies did not come to fruition, but they were effective in reducing the homogeneity of the working class and caused considerable disorganisation in labour ranks.

The drastic restructuring of the labour market after the coup is best expressed in the decline in the number of workers in manufacturing, from 1,030,000 in 1976 to 790,000 in 1980.[5] The effects on the labour movement are obvious–the car workers' union SMATA lost 36,000 members, the textile workers' union AOT calculated that only 40,000 of its 120,000 members in 1976 still had work in 1980. We see in Table 15.1 what monetarist economic policies led to in some key industrial plants.

Table 15.1 Employment in selected firms, 1976–1981

| Firm | Personnel | | Reduction |
	1976	1981	
Sevel (Fiat and Peugeot merger)	6,000	2,400	60%
Mercedes Benz	4,000	3,200	20%
Dodge-Volkswagen	4,000	2,200	45%
Deutz	2,000	240	88%
Renault	8,000	5,800	27%

Source: Various SMATA press statements.

In the state sector, half a million employees lost their jobs over this period. The remodelling of the labour market severely weakened the traditional solidarity of the working class, which had been based on a homogeneous labour market and strong links between the factory and the community.[6] Now thousands of workers were thrown off the labour market to become self-employed or to move to another area. This process of atomisation was sharpened by a conscious policy of increasing wage differentials. As we saw earlier, the wage structure in Argentina had been traditionally homogeneous, which increased solidarity and union power. Now wages for skilled workers and those in bigger firms were allowed to rise disproportionately, creating an internal hierarchy within the labour force based on wage differentials between industrial sectors of up to 75% in 1978.

The restructuring of the labour market did not lead immediately to an increase in unemployment.[7] In fact the military government was keenly aware of the effects a drastic rise in unemployment could have on labour militancy. Several factors served to mask the decline in the labour force from eight million to 7,200,000 between 1974 and 1978. Those withdrawn from the labour market were made up of some 300,000 who became 'self-employed' in the service sector, 150,000 women and young people who left waged employment, and some 300,000 immigrant workers from neighbouring countries who were expelled. Thus the official unemployment rate was kept around 3–4% until 1980.

By 1981 the government was admitting that unemployment had doubled, and one report suggested that fully 40% of the economically active population was under-employed.[8] The service sector could no longer act as a refuge for those thrown out of the industrial sector, and the economic recession was deepening. By 1981 there were possibly 1,500,000 people unemployed and some studies put the figure as high as 4,000,000. Though full employment had always been a myth this was the first time that the Argentine labour movement had had to cope with such a level of unemployment. The divisive effects of such a large reserve army of labour were bound to test the traditional solidarity of the workers' movement.

To increase the rate of profit in industry a key condition was the reduction of wages. The stark result of the political defeat and military repression of March 1976 was a 50% wage reduction within a year. The workers' share of national income fell from nearly 50% in 1975 to around 30% in 1980. The economic recession meant that there was less over-time, social benefits were cut and so on. The decline in real wages cannot even be fully expressed in these figures. The continued resistance of the working class, however, was able to halt this decline in living standards by 1979, as we see in Table 15.2.

Table 15.2   Real industrial wage, 1976–1980 (1977: 100)

Year	1975	1976	1977	1978	1979	1980
Wage	175	114	100	95	114	125

Source: *Boletín Semanal de Economía* no. 408 (1981), p. 2169.

While wages were generally falling (and the 1980 rates were still well below 1975) labour productivity was increasing dramatically as restrictive practices were eroded. Though manufacturing output per capita fell by 11% between 1975 and 1980, productivity rose by an incredible 37%. There was an increased work effort due to repression and unemployment, and an introduction of new technology in key areas designed to accelerate the process of de-skilling (and hence the interchangeability of workers). The effects of this super-exploitation of labour can be seen in one report which states that the biggest industrial plant in Córdoba required 172 man-hours to produce one vehicle in 1975 and in 1979 it only required 90 hours; in another plant 1,300 workers had been required to produce 2,000 engines per month, and in 1979 half the number of workers produced twice as many engines.[9]

Having examined the social and economic effects on the working class of the military government's policies we must now turn to the junta's offensive against the trade union movement. As had happened after previous military take-overs the government intervened in the CGT and in some 45 unions representing 75% of the unionised working class. Among these were all the unions which were important in terms of influence or numbers: the metal-workers' (UOM), the construction workers' (UOCRA), the bank workers' (*Asociación Bancaria*), the textile workers' (AOT) and the car workers' (SMATA) unions. These organisations had been the base of the organised labour movement since the 1940s. The military government took the following legislative measures to reduce the power of the unions:

Law 21356: suspended all trade union activity, banned assemblies, conferences, meetings and elections; the Ministry of Labour was empowered to replace shop-stewards and *comisiones internas*;

Law 21400: (of Industrial Security) banned any concerted measure of direct action, go-slow (*trabajo a desgano*) etc: striking workers came under military jurisdiction.

Law 21297: annulled most of the measures favourable to workers in the previous labour contract law: the onus of proof is on the workers in any dispute, workers can be dismissed before guilt is proved by a tribunal, etc.;

Law 21576: changed the collective bargaining conventions so that special pay structures, holidays, union participation in tribunals and other advances were cancelled; all previous declarations regarding unhealthy working conditions were subject to revision, etc.;

Law 22269: withdrew all social services including clinics, rest homes, etc. from trade union jurisdiction.

This battery of repressive legislation was unprecedented in Argentina's labour history and its effects were considerable.[10] It deprived the unions of all their basic functions; the social services law (22269) broke the link between unions and basic welfare rights and greatly weakened the economic power of unions; many of the historic conquests of the working class were annulled at a stroke. For the conservative newspaper *La Nación* these measures were designed to put an end to 'the economic and political power with which the trade unions overpowered the state and the political parties for more than two decades'. The government's aim was ostensibly to democratise and de-politicise the unions. In reality it was to fragment the basic organisations of the working class and to consolidate the dispersion of the labour movement.

Not only were the trade unions as institutions severely attacked – the grass-roots of the labour movement in the factories were also. Where the trade union structures were concerned, the military government was careful not to jeopardise completely the role of the leadership. Its role was merely suspended and taken over by military overseers, who would presumably in due course hand back the unions to a chastened bureaucracy. When tackling the 'real' or grass-roots labour movement in the workplace the military rulers were far less ambiguous in their mission. The new Law of Professional Associations, finally approved in 1979 after some hesitation, decreed a number of measures in this respect:

- the number of shop-stewards was reduced to 1 per 100 workers instead of 1 per 50 as previously;
- to be eligible for a shop-stewardship candidates had to have worked four years in the plant and have no police record;
- the Ministry of Labour was empowered to intervene in union recognition, negotiations, and union finances at a local level;
- branch meetings could only discuss items on a pre-approved agenda, there would be no speeches or debates or involvement in politics;
- the closed shop system was abolished.

All these measures were aimed at destroying workers' power at factory level as established during the first Peronist period and revived between 1973 and 1976. The main target was the *comisión interna* and the democratically elected union representatives. Many of these were killed in the 'dirty war' waged against the people by the armed forces. Others were sacked by the factories' internal security services; some simply resigned in the very real climate of terror. The result was that a major factory such as the General Motors plant in Buenos Aires only had one union representative (*delegado de empresa*) for every 2,000 workers in 1979. A visiting trade union delegation found that 'at Ford in Córdoba the number of shop-stewards was lowered from 300 to six, depriving workers in the plant of any effective means of communication'.[11] In other plants, such as Mercedes Benz and the Deutz tractor works, a shop-steward structure was the exception rather than the rule, and this lack of a generalised organic union structure at factory level greatly impeded working-class resistance in the years following the coup. It is well to remember, when the military justifies its repression in terms of a guerrilla campaign, that out of 15,000 prisoners in Argentina's gaols in 1978, fully 5,000 were workers and trade union activists. Of those killed during the dirty war between 1976 and 1978 one-fifth were workers and union activists.[12]

Labour resistance (1976–1978)

Though the labour movement did not mobilise to defend the government of Isabel Perón, there was a widely-felt need to confront the military dictatorship's offensive. At the Renault plant in Córdoba there was a strike on 24 March, the very day of the coup, and the Buenos Aires metal-workers launched strikes in various plants around the city. These first actions against the regime were of great importance because they laid the basis for the accumulation of forces and concerted fight-back campaign in the months that followed. Despite the repression unleashed by the government the working class was able to organise strikes, go-slows, lightning stoppages and various ingenious forms of sabotage. At the IKA-Renault plant in Córdoba production dropped from 40 to 14 units a day in June 1976 and the government administrator declared that 'obviously this was caused by industrial sabotage'. One of the most persistent and effective forms of labour protest was the so-called 'sad working' (*trabajo a tristeza*).

The Montoneros somewhat rashly called for a 'CGT in the Resistance' to replace the body suspended by the government and to help co-ordinate these struggles. This proposal, as they themselves later admitted 'was incorrect, because it proposed a totally clandestine structure, forcing legal structures to go underground, thus ceding, gratuitously, spaces of legality'.[13] Nor could this type of vanguardist movement mobilise the millions of Argentine workers, and it rapidly became a propaganda front which did not really impinge on the life of the masses. After this attempt, energy was focused on recovering the trade unions from their military overseers, as in the 1956–58 period.

The early strike movements were largely defensive, designed to ward off government attacks on strategic sectors which had in the previous period been in the forefront of labour struggles. One of these was the car industry. In 1976 there were partial stoppages in the Fiat, Renault and Ford plants, which by September had spread across the industry. Repression against the car workers was severe. Early in 1977 six workers were kidnapped from the Mercedes Benz works and only one reappeared in spite of the workers' protest. A strike at the Córdoba Renault plant in October 1977 led to intervention by the armed forces to 'restore order', resulting in 75 arrests and 175 dismissals. In June 1978 a paramilitary group entered the Deutz factory and took away busts of Perón and Evita in order to intimidate the workers who were in dispute with management over wages. The *comisión interna* called a general meeting and a half-hour protest strike was called.

Another form of repression was the dramatic increase in the level of exploitation in the plants. A report on Ford notes how the already rapid pace of production on the line was accelerated, the working day was extended from 8 to 9 hours (10 for the late shift) and those who did not accept the new working practices were summarily dismissed.[14] The true significance of the coup was becoming brutally clear – it had little to do with fighting corruption and a lot to do with implementing conditions which would favour a super-exploitation of workers and the virtual destruction of the organised labour movement.

With the most combative unions under military overseers, some previously less militant unions came to the fore. One of these was the electricity company workers of the *Luz y Fuerza* union who faced a general revision of working arrangements, including an increase in the shift from six to eight hours. In October 1976 they launched a go-slow and a series of partial stoppages which were to continue for six months, in defence of their rights. The workers engaged in widespread sabotage actions, and when their general secretary, Oscar Smith, was 'disappeared' they mounted an unprecedented march on the Ministry of Labour. Though the power workers' struggle was defeated it served as the axis for a general process of reactivation within the union movement. This culminated in a rail strike in Buenos Aires in October 1977 which spread to the underground and power workers. At the time of the first power strikes the Buenos Aires port workers began a work-to-rule over wages and conditions which seriously hindered the grain export drive. In June 1978 another port workers' strike began in Buenos Aires and rapidly spread to other ports throughout the country, calling for extra pay for over-time. Unlike the port workers' defeat in 1966 which led to widespread demoralisation, this dispute transmitted a spirit of resistance to the whole labour movement. In the rest of 1978 there was a downturn in labour struggles – after the successful rearguard battles of 1976 and 1977 – apart from some high-points such as the national railworkers' strike in November which not only achieved its economic demands, but succeeded in freeing the union leaders detained by the junta.

We must now attempt an analysis of the causes of the strikes, the sectors involved and the forms of struggle taken during this period. From the data in the Appendix (which understates by about one-third the number of disputes, owing to its reliance on the press, but which is useful for trends) we can draw several conclusions. In 1976, 1977 and 1978 wage demands constituted 60%, 87% and 65% respectively of all disputes. Clearly there were no anti-bureaucratic struggles as between 1969 and 1976, and where working conditions were an issue (10% of disputes in 1978) these generally concerned the defence of previous gains rather than a demand for new concessions. In short the labour struggles in this period were purely defensive. In 1976 80% of all disputes occurred in the manufacturing sector and this declined sharply to 44% and 48% in the two following years, whereas the service sector *increased* its share in disputes from 15% in 1976 to 49% in 1977 and to 53% in 1978. In terms of the number of workers involved we find that the transport sector alone accounted for three-quarters of all disputes in 1978. This reflects the serious state offensive against the transport sector after the industrial working class had been forced to retreat after the confrontations of 1976. Nearly half of all disputes took the form of stoppages, and a quarter were work-to-rules (*quite de colaboración*). There was only one factory seizure in the whole three years and just nine public demonstrations. This again shows that the whole tenor of labour activity in this period was defensive.

Data on the results of the strikes is very difficult to obtain. However, in a survey of 174 major disputes between March 1976 and March 1981 we found that in 61 of them workers' demands were fully met, in 54 workers' demands were partially met and in 59 they were completely rejected.[15] This means that over the whole five years there were practically the same amount of disputes won and lost by workers and a similar proportion where negotiations led to some advance. In the context this was a considerable achievement. When we consider that the vast majority of disputes during this period were called at plant level, with very few regional, national or solidarity strikes, the dominant picture is one of dispersed, isolated struggles. The labour movement had lost its cohesion and its mass mobilising power based on its centralised structure.

It had not lost it totally, however, and the junta was unsuccessful in its bid to use widening wage differentials as a source of disunity. The extent of strikes in the metallurgical and mechanical sectors, and the lead given by the highly skilled workers in many disputes, shows that no labour aristocracy was created by the new policies. A confirmation of this tendency is the fact (see Appendix) that between one-third and a half of all disputes occurred in the largest industrial establishments (where pay was usually higher than average). Our conclusion can only be that the drive by the junta to fragment the labour movement was only partly successful. The trade unions maintained a residual element of mobilising power, and developed a vigorous – though defensive and dispersed – resistance to the government's austerity policies and repression.[16]

One of the most remarkable features of this period was the emergence of a new rank-and-file leadership in the factories. It is estimated that of the 100,000 shop-stewards present in Argentine industry in 1976 10,000 were killed or imprisoned by the regime. After the coup it was not surprising that most struggles were not led by an organic plant leadership. Previously unknown people were elected unofficially as provisional union delegates who would take turns in leading negotiations with management. Given the weakness of the *comisiones internas* this new semi-spontaneous leadership came to play an important role in more than half of all disputes after 1976. Sometimes this leadership was recognised by the firm, and in some cases the unions concerned would declare a dispute official. In most cases they remained a fluid, somewhat inorganic presence in the plants.

One newspaper report in 1977 expressed a general concern over this phenomenon when it noted that though the 'industrial guerrilla' had been rooted out in most plants since March 1976, 'in many firms it has been discovered that the true thinking and organising agents of trade union activity did not appear on the list of union delegates'.[17] This concern even took the ludicrous form of military detachments entering factories in dispute and demanding that management allow union representatives to negotiate freely. Once again the reserves of combativeness and the dense supportive social networks of the labour movement had allowed at least a partial recovery from what was, after all, the worst defeat in its history.[18]

As for the trade union bureaucracy, there was a split after 1976, reflecting previous divisions in the mid-1960s, between openly collaborationist and supposedly 'hard' sectors. The so-called 'Group of 25' followed the *verticalista* line of the last Peronist government which was based on a strict hierarchy within the Peronist movement; its main strength lay in the smaller unions in which the government had not intervened. A second federation, the *Comisión Nacional de Trabajo* (National Labour Commission) based on many of the large unions, such as the textile workers', metal-workers', construction workers' and power workers' unions, concentrated on putting forward a more professional image, along US business unionism lines.

The Minister of Labour distinguished between one sector which defended the interests of workers through 'a dialogue with the different productive sectors' and which 'believe that dialogue and participation are the most appropriate means' and others, less to his liking, who, he said, 'believe that it is appropriate to carry out the defence [of workers' interests] through "days of protest" and direct action'.[19] It was this latter body, more attuned to the international labour federations, which usually represented Argentina at the tripartite (state, business, labour) meetings of the International Labour Organization (ILO). With much of the national field of action closed to them, the trade union leaders took an unprecedented interest in the annual ILO delegation, which provided an international platform. At home they were constantly competing for the favours of the government, only going about it in different ways. This division within the organised labour movement was undoubtedly a source of weakness, and some unions, such as the metal-workers' UOM, split over the claims of the rival federations. The railworkers' union, *La Fraternidad*, took a more principled line, emphasising 'its efforts to unify the labour movement without participating in any sector'.[20] It would take several more years before pressure from the rank and file would lead to a process of reunification of the CGT.

Labour recovery (1979–1980)

After the downturn of labour struggles in 1978 there was a new phase of recovery in 1979 which culminated in the first general strike against the military dictatorship on 27 April. In March 1979 a series of disputes in Córdoba brought that city to the brink of the struggles it had known ten years previously. Workers at the State Mechanical Industries (IME) run by the Ministry of Defence began a series of stoppages in support of wage demands. The authorities decided to apply the redundancy law and dismissed 50 workers, and the Labour Ministry applied the new Security Law. This dispute spread to the car-part manufacturer, Thompson Ramco, and to 6,000 workers in four Renault plants. At the Renault works the demand was for a 50% wage increase timed to coincide with a visit from the managing director of the French parent company. After 100 workers were sacked, negotiations began with the military overseers of SMATA, the motor mechanics' union, and the dispute was settled favourably for the workers.

This example led to a series of strikes in Buenos Aires metal-working plants such as Santa Rosa, Centenera, Decker, etc. A business review made the following worried comment after the events:

> The chieftains of the labour movement . . . are out of touch with popular demands and the prospects for continued labour peace are going to be complicated by a series of shop-floor strikes. For all its defects, union bureaucracy acted in the past as a shock-absorber, and this is not possible at the moment.[21]

Indeed, there was a real prospect that union leaders would be brushed aside by shop-floor members because of their failure to secure wage increases, and militant action was seen to be the only way forward.

It was partly as a result of these pressures that the union leaders called for a National Day of Protest on 27 April 1979. The stoppage was called for by one of the union fronts, the Group of 25, in protest at the government's economic policies and for the release of imprisoned trade unionists. Given the fact that only one of the federations called the strike, the turn-out of approximately 30% was quite respectable, and in the circumstances the other federation, the CNT, lost ground because many of its member unions supported the strike. The unions had effectively re-established their role in national politics, and at gross-roots level the stoppage increased self-confidence. In the months which followed, some disputes (such as that of the Peugeot plant) were successful, others were hard and long (over a month at the Santa Rosa metallurgical plant) and there was even a workplace occupation (ITT).

The crucial links between unions and the community were being re-established and the union structures themselves were being rebuilt. This movement of recovery culminated in the events of October 1979. The Ministry of Labour even began issuing a daily bulletin on the strike movement and was at pains to stress that it was due to misinterpretation of the new wage guidelines and not 'subversion'. Many disputes were solved by ministerial intervention, as a snowball effect could have led to a general strike. As it was, the last week of October saw 17 concurrent disputes involving nearly 10,000 workers. In these circumstances the Secretary of Finance, Juan Alemann, declared openly that union power in Argentina was too strong and that the government's economic policy was designed explicitly to weaken it.[22] Considering that strikes were still illegal, this upsurge of labour activity was most significant.

In several ways October 1979 represents a turning-point in the pattern of strikes. From then on struggles against the effects of the economic recession, such as factory closures and lay-offs were to achieve more prominence. In the twelve months prior to October 1979 nearly 80% of all conflicts were due to wage demands and only 9% were related to the recession.[23] By contrast, in the twelve months after October 1979 the disputes over wages had fallen to 40%, and those concerned with the effects of the recession had risen to 44%. Another way of observing this trend is that whereas in the earlier period the large, leading firms had accounted for nearly 45% of all disputes, this proportion had fallen to 30% in the second period. This may indicate that those firms squeezed by the capital concentration process implicit in the recession were becoming more strike-prone. This change in the rhythm of strike activity was also reflected in the type of unions in the forefront of labour struggles. In the first years after the coup those unions which were previously in a strong economic position, such as the metal-workers' UOM and the power workers' *Luz y Fuerza*, were in the forefront of the struggle. Later it was unions such as the car mechanics' SMATA, operating in a sector which was hit hard by the recession, which came to the fore, playing a key role in the 27 April general strike and the massive mobilisations of labour in the following months. New sectors also came to the fore in 1980, such as the bank workers, who carried out several combative stoppages at regional levels, obtaining important economic concessions.

In the course of 1980 there were several important disputes. In June there was a national seamen's strike to protest new laws allowing foreigners not resident in the country to serve on Argentine ships. The strike was organised by unoffical 'struggle committees' (*comisiones de lucha*) bringing together the various trades involved. The admiral in charge of the Secretariat of Maritime Interests pointed out that 'the legitimate union leaders had neither declared nor led the strike, and they had shown themselves to be impotent to control the activities they were supposed to be in charge of'.[24] The union leaders meekly responded that the strike was 'a spontaneous reaction by the workers'. The strike marked a new level of autonomous working-class organisation.

In July, a major rail strike was led by a coordinating committee of the various unions involved, train drivers, signallers, guards, and the intervened-in union of unskilled railworkers. Demands centred around the closure of railway workshops as well as wage increases. The government remained intransigent, but as one contemporary account noted, 'this is the fourth railway strike in four years of military government and the railway workers' union is supervised which makes the spontaneous activity the more surprising'.[25] It is also significant that the disputes of the seamen and railway workers (also the taxi-drivers and cinema operators) were not led officially by the union but by local rank-and-file committees. In a way, the militant tactics of *clasismo* were being adopted, more due to official union inactivity than choice.

Another area of dispute in 1980 was the fight against lay-offs and sackings in many car, machinery and textile factories. Though the redundancies produced worker protests there was little response from the union hierarchy, and each group tended to act alone. The closure of General Motors and Citroën affected other related industries, and it appeared that the crisis would spread to Villa Constitución, centre of the 1975 struggles. In Córdoba there were uninterrupted dismissals in Fiat-controlled companies and one business magazine speculated on a repeat of the *Cordobazo* 'which will shatter ideas about general tranquillity that have been gaining ground lately'.[26] These disputes came to a head in November when the Deutz tractor company announced that it was to cease production. The 800 workers at the plant held a meeting and decided to occupy the factory in reaction to the first 100 sackings. The car workers' union SMATA declared a 'state of alert' in defence of its members' jobs and in solidarity with the Deutz workers. The company rapidly reinstated the 100 workers and pledged to negotiate over the proposed closure. At around the same time the workers at the Inort chemical laboratories started a go-slow to force management to discuss poor working conditions. Four years of frozen collective bargaining had left a vast area of accumulated grievances over safety, hygiene, lighting and hours worked.

From the data in the Appendix we can now draw some general conclusions about the strikes of 1979 and 1980. We find that stoppages in the manufacturing sector increase in importance once again, representing 71% and 66% of all disputes in 1979 and 1980 respectively, whereas the service sector share declines from over half, to 27% in 1979 and 29% in 1980. Wages still represent the main cause in three-quarters of all disputes in 1979, but as we have already mentioned, this proportion declines to one-third in 1980, whereas recession-related disputes rise from 11% to 50% over the same period. The stoppage is still the main form of struggle in over half of all disputes, but we see a dramatic increase in the number of assemblies and petitions and there is even a handful of workplace occupations. Sabotage practically disappears. It would seem that strikes were becoming more structured and more organic as a certain level of organisation and confidence was recovered. This is confirmed by the level at which disputes originated: whereas previously there were few regional stoppages and virtually no sympathy strikes, between 1979 and 1980 there were at least 44 strikes called by regional union bodies and 56 major sympathy strikes. Though the facts are hard to come by, it seems that many strikes were being won in this period. This masks the fact that many, if not most, struggles over the effects of the recession were unsuccessful. This should lead us to a complex picture of a certain recovery by labour with a growing number of struggles occurring on the unfavourable terrain set by economic recession and growing unemployment. The closure of the State Mechanical Industries (IME) in Córdoba in April 1980 without a major union response was a clear example of this.

In analysing this period the question of the trade union bureaucracy became an important issue again. Time and again the employers lamented the lack of a 'representative interlocutor' (*interlocutor válido*) for labour.

We have mentioned several strikes above in which observers lamented the lack of a regular union structure. By mid-1980 this pressure had become severe and one economic journal said that 'the government, by depriving union leaders of room for manoeuvre, are leaving a vacuum that may be filled by moderates today, but by someone quite different tomorrow'.[27] A visiting delegation of the AFL-CIO had earlier concluded that the 'junta's subversive paranoia is misplaced in the strongly anti-Communist CGT'.[28] As the trade union federations began regrouping in 1979, one of their statements pointed out that if the government did not normalise union affairs rapidly, 'alien structures' would grow within the movement which would be much more difficult to control.[29]

Another source of pressure towards normalisation came from the rank and file. There were numerous incidents in these years where workers called on, and obtained, the solidarity of local union leaders, even in cases where there had been bitter anti-bureaucratic struggles under the previous Peronist administration. There were pressures from all directions – if for different reasons – for a restoration of normal trade union structures. The government, however, had not yet decided to accept defeat in its bid to virtually decapitate the union structures and prohibit the operation of a central union confederation.

The unification of the trade union hierarchy did advance slightly in this period. In September 1980 the CNT and Group of 25 came together to form the *Conducción Unica de Trabajadores Argentinos* (United Leadership of Argentine Workers) which, though illegal, began to take on the role of the old CGT. An independent sector, the Group of 20, composed of a heterogeneous group of unions such as *La Fraternidad* and the collaborationist *participacionista* current, remained on the side-lines. This unity was shortlived. By the end of 1980 the 'big battalions' such as the metal-workers' UOM were playing a more prominent role in labour struggles, displacing the smaller marginal unions which had played a disproportionate role until 1979 owing to the anomalous legal situation. After several permutations a rump CGT was formed.

Labour offensive (1981–1983)

By 1981 the recovery of the labour movement had become consolidated to such an extent that we can realistically speak of a labour offensive from then on. Now it was the military regime which was on the defensive and not the labour movement, as in the difficult period between 1976 and 1978. In early 1981, as one firm after another laid-off workers or simply closed down, strikes and go-slows spread with unheard-of frequency in spite of the junta's anti-strike laws. In March the workers at the Borgward clutch factory in Buenos Aires occupied the plant for twelve days until a court order forced them to leave; the strike then continued until the police dispersed the picket lines. The bank and insurance company workers also launched a battle plan, involving go-slows and lightning strikes protesting the new regulations eliminating job security. The union also accused the economy minister, Martínez de Hoz, of corrupt banking deals and fraudulent bank closures.[30] The workers' economic struggle was now being extended to a general offensive against the dictatorship and in particular its economic policies. In April the new labour minister, General Porcile, promised to seek 'social peace' and an agreement between capital and labour.

This all reflected a new climate in which indiscriminate repression was no longer viable and workers frequently resorted to wildcat strikes and factory seizures. Around this time internal union elections were allowed for the first time, in the first instance in five small unions, but over the next two years 'normalisation' of union affairs accelerated. By mid–1983 the government was forced to repeal law 21400 thus restoring the right to strike. It ended military control over the key car workers' union SMATA, and eventually reformed the Law of Professional Associations to allow the formation of 'third level' union organisations, i.e. confederations such as the CGT.

In July 1981 the car workers' union SMATA called a 12-hour national strike to protest the growing run-down of the industry and in support of the Mercedes Benz workers' fight against redundancies. In the course of the strike the union leaders and more than 1,000 workers who were meeting at the union headquarters were arrested. A strong police contingent blocked the march of car workers coming from the industrial suburb of Avellaneda towards the capital. This street mobilisation of a key sector of the working class had a strong impact on the whole labour movement. The pressure from this action and from more strikes at Borgward, and at the Celulosa Argentina plant and others, led to a general strike on 22 July 1981. One union federation denounced the strike call and demanded a social truce instead. Many reports suggested the action was a failure considering that important sectors such as the railworkers did not heed the strike call. Participation in the strike was solid in the industrial belt around Buenos Aires, nevertheless, with absenteeism in some sectors such as engineering and the paper industry exceeding 50%. In the provinces the response was more patchy, but there was more support in Córdoba, Mendoza, Santa Fé and Tucumán than during the previous national stoppage on 27 April 1979.[31] The level of organisation was stronger, with labour activists mounting strike pickets, distributing leaflets and in parts using *miguelitos* (bent nails) to stop traffic. In spite of the division in the trade union leadership, over two million workers demonstrated their rejection of an economic policy which was leading to daily factory closures and lay-offs.

The whole picture changed in 1982, the year of the Malvinas war, which represents a watershed in Argentina's recent political history.[32] Even as the military adventure was starting, the labour movement was challenging the dictatorship with a major demonstration on 30 March 1982. It seemed at first that the protest would be called off due to the looming confrontation, but labour leader Saúl Ubaldini declared that 'the role of the people cannot be subordinated on the sole grounds of defending national sovereignty'.[33] In the circumstances the union demonstrators were met with police repression, and 400 arrests were made. In Córdoba four people were seriously wounded when the police opened fire.

During the war the unions supported the recovery of the Malvinas islands and repudiated the attack by British imperialism. They did not go as far as the political parties and actually support the junta. In tours abroad the union leaders were at pains to draw their distance from the dictatorship and its military adventure designed to draw attention from the growing labour unrest in the country. In fact after the war there was a concerted drive to obtain higher wages to meet the rising cost of living. In August when the railway, transport and seamen's unions all threatened industrial action the new labour minister, Héctor Villaveiran, took the side of the unions, arguing their case in cabinet meetings. The defeat of Argentina's armed forces in the south Atlantic had given a boost to the labour movement and seriously weakened the cohesion of the regime.

In 1982 'normalising committees' were established for the unions' transition back to democratic procedures. This was a concession to the labour bureaucracy, and was again necessary as a stabilising element, as during the 'decompression' of 1972. But, as General Nicolaides declared, the military government 'could reconsider recognising the CGT and study the question of the [CGT's] social services, but there can be no movement on the rule of one union delegate per 100 workers'.[34] Even so, there was a series of shop-floor elections during this period which helped re-establish the *comisiones internas*. Union delegates were elected for the railways, for Buenos Aires municipal workers, in the banks and in the metallurgical plants.

In many cases normalisation went beyond official channels and regulations, as the rank and file made a leap forward in factory floor organisation. This pressure from below led towards a new general strike which the union leadership called for 6 December 1982, partly to defuse the ground swell of protest. The one-day strike was highly successful, being joined this time by the independent unions such as the railworkers, bus drivers and railway workers who had remained outside the July 1981 general strike. On 16 December 1982 the opposition parties organised another protest march in which the workers' movement was clearly the main force. As Alberto Piccinini, a leader of the 1975 Villa Constitución strike, described soon after his release from gaol, 'The climate has changed drastically. There is a real resurgence of a determination to join in activity, to act'.[35]

This resurgence went wider than the ranks of organised labour. There were mobilisations of small farmers and agricultural workers in many areas; there were popular movements against the increase in municipal rates; the Mothers of the Plaza de Mayo received increased popular support for their denunciations of disappearances; even the police force kept to barracks in Buenos Aires in a protest over wages. An important strike early in 1983 which showed a new pattern was the three-week stoppage at the Volkswagen plant near Buenos Aires. Led by young left-wing activists, the strikers obtained massive support from the neighbourhood and showed total determination. The upsurge of activity came to a head with a new general strike on 28 March 1983, which was successful in spite of being declared illegal by the government – even the Ministry of the Interior spoke later of an 85% effectiveness.

Two days later a mass rally was called and several newspaper reports commented on the presence of a far-left contingent which came close to matching the organised columns of the official trade union movement.[36] This turn to the left was also reflected in the trade unions. The MAS (*Movimiento al Socialismo*) had become active in the car workers' union SMATA, and among building and transport workers. The Trotskyist-oriented *Partido Obrero* re-established a presence in the metal-workers union UOM and among journalists and teachers, and also played a prominent role in the Volkswagen dispute. The Communist Party was by far the most successful in breaking out of the intellectual world, establishing a significant role in the UOM and in the port, railway, bank and state employees' unions. It also controlled over one-fifth of the union delegates in the staunchly Peronist power-workers' union *Luz y Fuerza*.[37] The time appeared to be ripe, as some labour activists suggested, for the left to strive not only for union democratisation, but to build class-struggle tendencies which could actually assume the leadership of unions, and change their policies and form of operating.[38] There had also been a serious split between the top- and middle-level union leadership (especially in the provinces) since 1976 which was to the advantage of a new combative union movement.

The trade union leadership went through further splits and re-alignments during this period. By the beginning of 1983, one sector known as CGT-RA (*República Argentina*) had brought together the ostensibly hardline Peronist CGT-Brasil, led by Saúl Ubaldini, and most of the non-aligned unions. A smaller sector, the CGT-Azopardo, followed a more conciliatory line, though it, too, was forced to take militant action in this phase to protect its credibility. The military government had favoured the Azopardo group, but towards the end of 1982 turned more towards the CGT-RA, and particularly to Lorenzo Miguel, leader of the 62 Organisations and effectively the 'kingmaker' in the Peronist movement. There was even considerable speculation in 1983 that sectors of the armed forces were proposing a new military-labour alliance to Miguel.

The terms of the military withdrawal to barracks were, however, increasingly set by the mass movement after the defeat of the regime in the Malvinas adventure. The union leaders, though they emerged as a credible political force once again during this period, also had their terms of reference set by the mobilisation of the masses. The freezing of most anti-bureaucratic struggles for seven years did not mean that the issue of union democracy was resolved. In the new democratic political period opening up the rank-and-file organisations naturally will seek a democratic renewal of their trade unions. The recent establishment of 'coordinating commissions' outside official union structures points to a resurgence of the type of bodies which emerged after the 1975 general strike. The union bureaucracy has not yet realised to what extent a new generation of trade unionists, which has had to defend wages and conditions with no help from a national organisation, has emerged. As one report states, 'the real trade union power at present is in the hands of factory delegates and local coordinating committees. No one speaks for them, or can claim to represent them, at a national level. Yet they may well determine the future shape of Argentine trade unionism, and of the Peronist movement itself'.[19]

Labour and democracy (1983–1985)

The general elections of October 1983 saw the unexpected victory of the middle-class Radical Party. The Peronists had suffered from the rumours of their pact with the military, their undemocratic image and lack of a coherent and viable political alternative. The popular support for the Radicals was a vote for a clean break with the military state and the fullest restoration of economic and political rights. The labour movement remained on the offensive until the very eve of the elections – on 4 October the fifth general strike since the military seized power in 1976 gained the advance of the traditional Christmas bonus (*aguinaldo*). As the 'military party' of the bourgeoisie gave way to its 'civilian party' there were increased demands over housing conditions, educational provisions, health facilities and so on, which capital could ill afford to meet, but which is required for the continued stability of capitalist rule in Argentina.

With the advent of democratisation a new era began for the labour movement. The Radical government of Alfonsín, which came to office in the wake of the military débâcle, had a contradictory labour policy. One of their election promises was to democratise the trade unions and clip the wings of the 'trade union barons'. The president also argued that 'the worker has a right to his political beliefs: what he does not have a right to is to put his union at the service of a political party' (i.e. Peronism).[40] Thus the quite legitimate aim of introducing an element of internal democracy in the unions was allied with a prospect of trade union pluralism which would break the organic tie between the unions and Peronism. The CGT, reunified in January 1984 after a period of division under the military regime, mounted a strong campaign against the proposed trade union law, and it was eventually defeated by the Peronist deputies. There had indeed been a growth of Radical influence within the trade unions, with the party's dynamic trade union tendency, *Franja Morada*, gaining many recruits in some industries as well as the leadership of the university students. At a national level, out of 250 trade union organisations, only the leadership of two supported the Radical Party. The question of trade union democracy was one which could only be settled within the working class organisations where there was a long tradition of anti-bureaucracy struggles, and could not be settled from above by the government.

After seven years in which the internal life of the trade unions was virtually frozen, the democratic opening of 1984 led to a process of intense debate and renewal. Internal elections were gradually held across all levels of the trade union movement, and the results are an indicator of how the movement will act in the future. Some of the bastions of the trade union bureaucracy remained secure; such was the case with Lorenzo Miguel's group and the metal-workers' union (UOM). In other cases, such as the car workers' union, SMATA, the old leaders loyal to Miguel's 62 Organisations (the political leadership of the Peronist trade unions) were replaced by supporters of the Group of 25 which had led many of the struggles against the military regime. Sectors even more radicalised came to the fore in the Buenos Aires print-workers' union, where Raimundo Ongaro (who once headed the *CGT de los Argentinos*) regained control of the union, and the telephonists' union, where Julio Guillán stood for revolutionary Peronism. What was most significant was the union members' high turn-out in the internal elections: in many cases this reached 75% and in the power workers' union *Luz y Fuerza* it was 90 per cent. A major process of renewal had begun within the trade union movement, with a significant increase in rank-and-file participation and a marked turn towards a more combative and democratic union leadership.

Though the latter years of the military dictatorship had seen a considerable recovery of working-class living standards, there was inevitably an outburst of pent-up demands in 1984. In the first place there was a series of strikes aimed at regaining list purchasing power, with claims of 50% and even 100% wage rises. There were also strikes which reflected concern over working conditions in the context of the military regime's rationalisation bid and flouting of health and safety regulations. Finally, there were many disputes over job losses, against further redundancies and for the reinstatement of those dismissed under the old regime. These partial struggles culminated in the general strike of September 1984, called to protest the effects of the government's economic policies. It won a massive response from the industrial unions, and a partial one from the service sector.

In the course of 1984 there were 717 recorded strikes affecting 4.5 million workers: of these 62 occurred in the sugar industry (496 hours lost to capital), 29 took place in the car industry (149 hours lost), 608 hours were lost in the metallurgical sector and 584 in the construction industry.[41] In November 1984 the CGT warned the government of a possible 'social explosion' if the economic situation was not rectified. By then the trade union leadership was firmly committed to the *concertación* process which gave rise to the accusation of a Radical–trade union pact, ironic given the Radicals' previous accusation of a military–trade union pact during the 1983 election campaign. The union leadership is now seriously concerned that it will be outflanked by its social base. An indication of this was the strikes and rioting in Córdoba in January 1985 which served notice on the union leadership that its members would not accept the austerity plan implicit in the *concertación social* (social contract) treaties, which were being signed at that time. In May 1985 a general strike against the government's economic policies was preceded by a series of unprecedented CGT-organised provincial mobilisations. By mid-1985 any hopes of a Radical–CGT pact were dashed with a wave of stoppages caused by an ever-worsening economic situation. July's 20-day-long factory occupation by Ford workers in protest against redundancies, was the high-point of this agitation.

In the new democratic era, political scientists stressed the role of political parties in the democratisation process, against the previously dominant role of 'corporations' such as the armed forces and the trade unions. De Riz argues in this respect that the political parties' mediation can become 'the principal instrument for the regulation of social conflicts', and urges the trade unions 'to subordinate the logic of their sectoral interests to that of party politics, which must reconcile the exigencies of the trade unions with the demands of other social sectors'.[42] Other authors have argued even more explicitly that the closed shop which the Argentine trade unions won under Perón 'annuls liberty' and leads inevitably to 'despotic regimes'.[43] This perspective lay behind the new government's aborted trade union reform law and had its practical counterpart in the government's policy of *concertación social* (social contract) designed to bring the trade unions, employers and the state into a united front. After various ups and downs, caused by some reluctance on the part of the trade unions to be absorbed by this corporatist project, an agreement was reached in February 1985.

The anti-inflationary package agreed included a commitment to a wage-freeze for 1985, which caused unrest among trade union members. The government promised a tax reform to 'avoid the worsening of social in-equalities', but the employers, significantly, only reluctantly agreed to a price-freeze. One cannot prejudge the prospect of the government's 1985–1989 plan, but 'social pacts' have been tried before in Argentina (and else-where) and have failed. They seek basically to achieve an agreement or compromise between capital and labour which the class conflict of dependent capitalism will inevitably disrupt. Grossi and Dos Santos write that '*concertación social* can be seen as one of those modes of mediation between society and the political systems'.[44] They recognise that this may be just another way to legitimise domination, but argue that the involvement of the social movements may turn this type of pact into a means for the 'progressive transformation of the social order'.[45] All we can say at this stage is that neither national nor international experience in this respect suggests that a 'social pact' between labour, capital and state can be a means of achieving radical social transformation.

Increased political participation after the fall of the military regime was not matched by increased economic participation. Nor can the Radicals' inroads into the Peronist vote be expected to continue unless this situation is remedied. As one journal put it somewhat crudely, *'Sin puchero no hay movimiento'* (without stew there is no movement).[46] The 1983 elections have clearly not dissipated social inequality nor condemned to oblivion the traditional nationalist–popular project of Peronism. However the new politics have at least partly broken the sterile antinomy between Peronism and anti-Peronism in Argentina. For the first time since 1955 the Peronista–*gorila* (reactionary) mould of politics has been broken. A long cycle which began with the 'remaking' of Peronism between 1943 and 1946, has now been closed. In many ways Peronism died with Perón in 1974, but in the confused and repressive decade which followed it survived. The defeat of old-style Peronism in 1983 signalled the end of the road for a certain authoritarian populist labourism. Peronism remains, in a diffuse way, a source of class identity for workers, but its hitherto unchallenged claim to democracy and nationalism within the working class was shattered by Alfonsín. One can safely predict another political remaking of the working class in Argentina in the period now opening up.

Notes

1. For an overview of this period see A. Rouquié, (ed.) (1982) *Argentina, Hoy* Mexico, Siglo XXI, and the special issue on Argentina of *Amérique Latine*, no. 11 (July–September 1982).

2. This chapter draws on previous work by the authors: R. Falcón, (1982) "Conflicto Social y Regimen Militar, La Resistencia Obrera en Argentina (marzo 1976–marzo 1981)" and R. Munck, (1982) "Restructuración del Capital y Recomposición de la Clase Obrera en Argentina desde 1976" in B. Galitelli and A. Thompson (eds.) *Sindicalismo y Regimenes Militares en Argentina y Chile*, Amsterdam, CEDLA.

3. For a general survey of repression see CADHU (1977) *Argentina, Proceso al Genocidio*, Madrid, Elías Quejereta Ediciones.

4. On the economic policy of the military government see A. Ferrer, (1981) *Nacionalismo y Orden Constitucional*, Mexico, Fondo de Cultura Económica and G. Hillcoat, (1981) *Notas sobre la evolución reciente del capitalismo. El programa económico del regimen militar. 1976–1980*, Paris, CIAL, Université de Paris VIII.

5. On changes in the labour market after 1976 see L. Beccaría, (1980) "El mercado de trabajo urbano en Argentina 1975–1978", *Desarrollo Económico*, vol. 20, no. 78.

6. This interpretation is developed in G. Almeyra, (1980) "La clase obrera en la Argentina actual", *Coyoacán*, no. 9.

7. On unemployment see C. Sanchez, F. Ferrero, and W. Schultness (1979) 'Empleo, desempleo y tamaño de la fuerza laboral en el mercado de trabajo urbano de la Argentina", *Desarrollo Económico*, vol. 19, no. 73.

8. Report cited in *Buenos Aires Herald* (2 July 1981).

9. Report cited in *Somos* (9 May 1979).

10. For a discussion on the effects of the new labour legislation see B. Galitelli

and A. Thompson (1982) "La Situación Laboral en la Argentina del 'Proceso', 1976–1981". in B. Galitelli and A. Thompson (eds.) *Sindicalismo y Regimenes Militares*, p. 182. F. Delich, (1982) "Después del Diluvio, la Clase Obrera" in A. Rouquié (ed.) *Argentina, Hoy;* and J.C. Torre, (1980) "La cuestión del poder sindical y el orden político en la Argentina", *Criterio*, LII, no. 1843.

11. M. Boggs and A. McLellan (1978) Argentine Trade Unions, *AFL-CIO Free Trade Union News*, no. 33, p. 16.

12. Vance Report, cited in B. Galitelli and A. Thompson (1982) "La Situación Laboral en la Argentina", p. 153.

13. G. Chavez, (1981) "Movimiento obrero-consecuencias del plan económico", *Vencer*, no. 6, p. 9.

14. *Política Obrera* leaflet, cited in Latin American Bureau (1980) *Unity is Strength. Trade Unions in Latin America. The case for Solidarity*. London, Latin American Bureau, p. 44.

15. R. Falcón, (1982) "Conflicto Social y Regimen Militar", p. 132.

16. For a closer analysis of this period apart from the work cited above, D. Fernandez, (1980) *Política laboral de Estado y características de la respuesta obrera en la Argentina (1976–1979)*, Mexico, CEHSMO conference and N. Liffschitz, (1981) "Luttes Ouvrieres et Repression", *Tricontinental*, New Series, no. 2.

17. *Somos* (27 May 1977).

18. For a development of this theme see J. Petras, (1981) "Terror and the Hydra: The Resurgence of the Argentine Working Class", J. Petras, *Class, State and Power in the Third World,* London, Zed Press.

19. *La Prensa* (7 July 1981), p. 4.

20. *The Review of the River Plate* (11 April 1979), p. 492.

21. *The Review of the River Plate* (11 April 1979), p. 492.

22. *La Prensa* (23 October 1979), p. 3.

23. From data in *Vencer*, no. 6, (1981), p. 7.

24. *The Review of the River Plate* (18 June 1980), p. 887.

25. *The Review of the River Plate* (18 July 1980), p. 96.

26. *The Review of the River Plate* (8 August 1980), p. 206.

27. *The Review of the River Plate* (11 June 1980), p. 835.

28. M. Boggs, and A. McLellan, (1978) *Argentine Trade Unions, p. 5.*

29. *Latin America Economic Report* (11 October 1979), p. 329.

30. *Latin America Weekly Report* (20 March 1981), p. 11.

31. See report in *Vencer*, no. 9 (1981).

32. For a socialist view on the war from Argentina see A. Dabat and L. Lorenzano (1984) *The Malvinas and the Crisis of Military Rule*, London, New Left Books.

33. *Latin America Weekly Report* (2 April 1982), p. 6.

34. *Política Obrera* (12 October 1982), p. 5.

35. *International Viewpoint* (18 May 1983), p. 9.

36. *Solidaridad Socialista* (7 April 1983), pp. 4–5.

37. *Latin America Weekly Report* (6 May 1983), p. 10.

38. See J. Gaibur and E. Gutierrez, (1980) "Documento presentado para la discusión del IV Encuento del TYSAE", *En Lucha*, no. 2.

39. *Latin America Weekly Report* (21 November 1980), p. 6.

40. *Redacción*, January 1984.

41. *El Bimestre*, no. 19 (1985), p. 15.

42. L. De Riz, (1984) "La hora de los partidos", *Debates*, no. 1, p. 15.

43. E. Corbiere, "Organizaciones Corporativas y proceso democrático", in O. Oszlak (ed.) *Proceso, crisis y transición democrática/1,* Buenos Aires, Centro Editor de América Latina, 1984, p. 136.

44. M. Grossi and M. Dos Santos "La concertación social: una perspectiva sobre la instrumentos de democratización" in O. Oszlak (ed.), op. cit., p. 138.

45. Ibid., p. 159.

46. *El Perodista* (17 January 1985), p. 4.

	Strikes					Workers involved				
Year	1976	1977	1978	1979	1980	1976	1977	1978	1979	1980
Total	89	100	40	188	261	191,660	514,710	212,140	318,020	362,447
Sector										
Extractive industry	2	6	0	2	10	500	38,732	0	5,020	2,280
Manufacturing (large or leading firms)	71	44	19	133	171	118,610	69,600	49,080	164,757	136,844
Total Service sector	13	49	21	51	75	70,650	406,286	163,060	148,060	222,893
(Transport)	8	29	16	30	26	4,650	288,246	162,160	134,040	154,727
Cause										
Wage demand	53	82	26	141	88	79,520	386,948	194,400	278,332	165,039
Recession	6	3	7	21	130	7,540	6,300	6,280	15,430	88,869
Working conditions	6	3	4	2	18	34,000	62,000	6,660	2,100	34,900
Union organisation	8	2	0	1	6	26,800	20,100	0	100	13,747
State sector restructuring	1	0	0	2	3	20,000	0	0	5,100	5,100
Others	1	0	2	2	13	100	0	1,100	0	52,170
Measures taken										
Stoppage	43	54	19	113	132	180,120	356,022	145,480	244,744	194,218
Withdrawal of cooperation	24	23	11	28	21	64,020	113,150	52,200	30,410	21,841
Public demonstration	6	0	3	10	26	25,950	0	1,300	15,800	22,620
Factory seizure	0	0	1	5	5	0	0	2,000	8,200	2,660
Factory assembly	2	0	0	13	58	250	0	0	24,500	85,287
Petition	0	0	3	11	38	0	0	660	23,970	74,164
Sabotage	7	19	4	0	0	13,250	37,646	11,380	0	0
Strike call										
Factory	51	46	19	69	155	101,790	96,470	46,600	138,140	133,271
Regional	3	7	9	15	29	6,100	118,232	47,200	16,300	81,190
National	3	8	2	7	3	60,000	182,200	115,200	105,100	114,100
Sympathy	0	0	1	17	38	0	0	115,200	45,330	155,092

Source: *Vencer*, no. 8 (May–June 1981), pp. 6–7.
Notes: The data for 1976 begins with April. The data for 1979 does not include the general strike of 27 April.

16. The Social History of Labour

We have stressed that the working class should not be reduced to its formal political and trade union organisations in analysis, and we have referred to the community aspects of Argentine labour history. In this chapter we make explicit this community dimension, develop some ideas about working-class culture in Argentina, and point to the complexity of working-class consciousness. Donzelot has recently defined 'the social' cryptically as 'a general solidarity and the production of a life-style'.[1] The social is a set of means by which the members of society are cushioned from the effects of economic fluctuations and political uncertainties. It establishes a set of relations that may avert the dislocations attendant on social and economic transformations. And in doing so it builds up a form of consciousness, the 'common sense' of a class or social group. This consciousness is often embodied in a particular culture. By culture we mean, as Richard Johnson writes, 'the common sense or way of life of a particular class, group or social category, the complex of ideologies that are actually *adopted* as moral preferences or principles of life'.[2] Working-class culture is formed through an interaction of capital's demands and that form of 'the social' known conventionally as community. This chapter launches a preliminary analysis of these questions in relation to the Argentine working class.

Community

Workers are shaped not only by the factory, shop or dockyard, but by a whole range of experiences, particularly the community they live in. In early 20th Century Argentina the immigrant worker was largely socialised by two parallel processes: free, obligatory and non-clerical primary education and obligatory military service for all males. Education promoted the values of the New Republic, encapsulated in the 'Order and Progress' motto, and military service reinforced this. This dual process was largely successful in forging a national identity out of a diverse mass of foreign workers. Yet working-class culture was not a simple mirror image of the élite's public ideology. In its communities the working class elaborated its own values: an alternative social world which over time the élite was forced to borrow from to maintain its hegemony.

We have already mentioned the importance of the *conventillo*, the predominant form of working-class housing until the first decades of the 20th Century. Social networks were established between those of the same national origin and of similar occupations. There were also recreational and cultural associations, such as clubs, popular libraries, theatre groups, and the libertarian schools of the anarchists. The trade unions themselves were social organisations with deep roots in the community, above and beyond their economic functions in the workplace. Eduardo Gilimón, an anarchist activist from this period, describes how in 1907 the first general strike on the railways was followed by a rent strike in the *conventillos:*

> Socialists, anarchists and others had for some time agitated against the constant increase in rents, inciting the people to direct action or electoral action according to whether the speaker was an anarchist or had political tendencies. It seemed that the Buenos Aires population had become used to bad living [*mal vivir*] and that the preaching had fallen on stony ground, but just as the railwaymen could not escape the strike fervour, demonstrating with their strike [of 1907] that the idea of solidarity had rooted in their minds, so the tenants [*inquilinos*] of Buenos Aires proved by their deeds that the propaganda against rent rises and in favour of rent strike was not in vain. One bright day the inhabitants of one *conventillo* resolved not to pay their rent until it was reduced. This resolution was treated as a joke by half the population but the joking soon stopped. From *conventillo* to *conventillo* the idea of not paying rent spread, and in a few days the whole proletarian population adhered to the strike. The *conventillos* became clubs. There were street demonstrations in all areas, which the police could not prevent, and with an admirable spirit of organisation, committees were set up in all areas of the city.[3]

In this one event we see how solidarity and organisation had become an integral element of the proletarian consciousness.

As the *conventillos* gave way to small houses on the outskirts of the city, so the neighbourhood (*barrio*) became the new focus of working class sociability. As the PEHESA research group on popular culture describes, new networks of solidarity were created in the *barrio*, which included the café, the club dance and the community development society (*sociedad de fomento*).[4] The relatively homogeneous environment of the workshop and the *conventillo* was giving way to a more diffuse and heterogeneous working-class community. Civil society became a rich tapestry of social, political, educational and cultural institutions. The diversity of social groups in the new *barrios* tended to dilute the harsh proletarian experience of the pre-1930 period. As PEHESA explains, 'In its place, a new conception slowly emerges, less confrontationist, more conformist perhaps, of a society that could be reformed and improved gradually, a society which could become more just'.[5] Perón's doctrine of *Justicialismo* therefore operated on fertile terrain and his nationalist appeal also conformed to a new pattern of working-class consciousness as the sons and daughters of the first immigrants became fervent devotees of their new country.

The social arena of the *conventillo patio* was now replaced by the café, local store (*almacén*) and football field of the new *barrios*. After 1945 the sense of community was strengthened with the rise of Peronism which provided essential political cohesion. The earlier moulding of a working class from diverse nationalities was followed by a synthesis between these and the new internal immigrants. As Gutiérrez writes in a popular working-class history: 'Attracted by industry and expelled from the land, the human contingents from the provinces brought fragments of their own culture, clashed with the jacket and tie of the bank workers and filled the city with *mestizo* [mixed-race] faces'.[6] A vast process of social, cultural and ethnic transformation was now under way. It was Peronism, as politics but also as cultural milieu, which provided the catalyst with its nationalist populism.

The trade unions were not submerged in the populist sea and continued to play a vital role in forming a working-class community. One essential way in which this occurred was through the trade unions taking on the role of the welfare state. Trade unions began to run their own clinics, pharmacies, shops, housing schemes, holiday hotels and training centres. The 'social wage' in Argentina was a trade union conquest and not a concession by the state.[7] The importance of this link between the unions and welfare was recognised by the military dictatorship which withdrew all the 'social workers' from union control in 1980. The importance of the vast network of cooperative, welfare, recreational and sporting associations connected with the unions cannot be over-estimated. As Abós argues,

> Through the offer of concrete services, which often helped them overcome difficult situations which could not be resolved by any other means, many workers took the first step towards discovering the trade union dimension, the existence of a union which was 'for' them and which could be 'theirs'.[8]

That some trade union leaders used the funds derived from this alternative welfare state for their own purposes does not alter its fundamental role in forging a working-class community. Juan Carlos D'Abate of the commercial employees' union tells of how their social service organisation embraced 2.5 million people and had a monthly income of $2 million in 1976.[9] The extent of social benefits provided by the unions in Argentina becomes evident in Table 16.1, which shows the unions providing for 17.5 million people out of a total population of 27 million.

The working-class community was also an important element in the overall class struggle as we have seen at several points in our historical account. From 1930 the working-class family had increased in importance compared to the political interpellations of the anarchist resistance society of an earlier era. The move from the *conventillo* to the *barrio* had not dissolved politics into the family. The extended family acted as a nucleus

Table 16.1   Sources of social service funding in Argentina, 1976

	No. of funds	Persons affected (in millions)	Percentage of population affected
Trade unions	362	17.5	70
Provincial and municipal government	22	2.0	8
Armed forces	5	1.0	4
Totals	389	20.5	82

Source: J.C. D'Abate, (1983) "Trade unions and Peronism" in F. Turner and J.E. Miguens (eds.) *Juan Perón and the Reshaping of Argentina,* Pittsburg, Pittsburg University Press, p. 69.

for a new set of self-help relations. As Silvina Ramos writes: 'The frequency and durability of these exchanges took shape in a dense matrix of interactions'.[10] It is this social network which plays a constant defensive role against the onslaughts of capital and the state. It also serves as a platform for new advances by the working class when conditions are ripe. Military regimes have never been able to destroy this dynamic element in civil society, that set of organisms usually called private, as against the public domain we call political society, where the state reigns supreme. O'Donnell notes perceptively in this respect that: '*Barrio* Committees, self-help organisations, trade union or *barrio* grass-roots movements, popular institutions of the Catholic and other churches, are part of a long list through which–above all–the popular sector distils the lessons derived from the previous difficult period'.[11]

The working-class community in Argentina has been formed precisely through such difficult 'learning experiences' as dictatorships and, at best, semi-democratic regimes. The trade union aspect of the workers' struggle merges imperceptibly with the community dimension. Hector Lucero refers to:

Organisations and leaderships without recognised headquarters which emerge and disappear to the rhythm of the struggle and repression, united by an ever more dense and closed network of the very collective life of the proletariat, its families, the factory and the *barrio.*[12]

It is this lived experience of millions of women and men which has created a genuine labour *movement* and allowed the working class to 'soak up' repression and live to fight another day. Even a visitor to Argentina such as James Petras cannot fail to appreciate this particular community aspect of working-class life: he refers to the 'powerful informal bonds, expressed through family, neighbourhood, and work place, which reinforced class bonds and links among the working class and against the ruling class'.[13] It is this shared experience which provides the anchor of class solidarity, and the social base for many of the most spectacular episodes in the class struggle.

During the 1959 strike against privatisation of the Lisandro de la Torre *frigorífico* (see Chapter 12) the workers were forced out of their workplace by the army and fell back to the nearby *barrio* of Mataderos. There the struggle continued with barricades, the burning of government party offices and stoning of the troops, extending the strike into a semi-insurrectional situation. In a similar way, during the 1969 *Cordobazo* (see Chapter 13), marching columns of workers coming into the city from the surrounding industrial areas were joined by citizens opening up with sniper fire from their windows against the state forces. In many smaller strikes, up and down the country, it is common for the community to rally round providing food, clothing and, above all, solidarity. Indeed the community soup kitchens (*ollas populares*) are a regular feature of strike actions, and are just the visible sign of a genuine working-class community behind the struggle of apparently isolated groups of workers.

Under the second Peronist government in the 1970s there was a prolonged strike in Villa Constitución, near Rosario, which severely shook the administration (see Chapter 15). The strikers were spread out in towns and villages over a 50-mile stretch from Rosario to San Nicolás and thus could not easily be concentrated in one place.[14] That, and the factor of police repression against union headquarters, led the district committees (*comités barriales*), to take on a particular significance. They organised food collections for the strikers' families, helped spread the factory stoppages to regional strikes, and were the prime organisers of flying pickets and self-defence activities. Relatives of strikers, but also students and neighbours, were the activists of the *barrio* organisations. The strike itself was spread through this means to the student sector, to small shopkeepers and to the sharecroppers (*chacareros*) of the *Federación Agraria Argentina* (Argentine Agrarian Federation).

During the struggle against the military dictatorship which came to power in 1976 (see Chapter 15) community mobilisations also played a vital role. One particularly important mobilisation occurred during the urban protests of 1982.[15] A series of neighbourhood protests (*vecinazos*) set the seal of defeat on a military regime beaten in the South Atlantic and weakened by a series of strikes. Their motives were not always political – they were more often typical municipal or ecological complaints – but the *vecinos* (neighbours) helped shake off the mantle of fear caused by military repression, and mobilised wider popular layers in the final struggle to end the dictatorship.

Culture

As Raymond Williams writes, 'The primary distinction between bourgeois and working-class culture is to be sought in the whole way of life', and working-class culture is not merely a sum of incidental differences but 'the basic collective idea and the institutions, manners, habits of thought and intentions which proceed from this'.[16] The individualism of the middle class is matched by the collective or community orientation we have outlined above. In this section, without falling into a conception of culture as 'the arts', we examine some of the specifically cultural manifestations of this community.

Universal education, though designed to incorporate the immigrant into the ideological domain set by Argentina's rulers, also allowed workers to read political tracts. Eduardo Gilimón, anarchist activist of the early 20th Century, recalls that new books were relatively cheap and 'reading had more devotees in Argentina than in Europe, and thus the diffusion of anarchist ideas was more rapid and extensive. People read more and attend public conferences in greater numbers than in Europe . . .'.[17] Gilimón puts this cultural urge down to the lack of alternative entertainment and the pressures of *conventillo* life, but even if this is true its political significance is considerable. Argentina achieved high (almost universal) rates of literacy at an early stage which sets it apart from most other Third World countries in this respect.

Working-class culture took a diversity of forms, in accordance with the mixed origins of the class. From 1880 to the 1920s two distinct socio-cultural currents developed in Argentina: that of the *criollo* and that of the immigrants. The immigrants simply reproduced the culture of their country of origin and the *criollos* developed their particular blend of Hispanic and indigenous customs. The experience of a shared exploitation, and increasingly a common struggle against it, gradually helped overcome the mutual suspicions and antagonisms. The popular literature of the 1920s and 1930s reflects the growing process of social integration between these two groups. This 'social digestion', as Arturo Jauretche calls it, took place in the *conventillo* and assumed musical, literary and theatrical forms, for example, the *sainete* (short farce).[18] The image of the *gaucho* was often the archetypal figure in this synthesis. As Sosa Pujato writes, 'By the 1930s what had once seemed two irreconcilable modes of expression were becoming one'.[19] The nascent mass media would take up themes, in particular the *gaucho* and the *arrabal* (urban slum), which reflected the melancholy frustrations and resentment of the urban masses. Peronism captured this discontent and launched a movement which was as much social and cultural as it was political.

The *tango*, of obscure, possibly African, origins, was one of the prime expressions of the transnational culture mode of the 1930s. As Horacio Ferrer writes, the *tango* was 'a constant and important cultural phenomenon, an indispensable element in the life of our people'.[20] It reflected the tensions, frustrations and aspirations of urban working-class life, it spoke of the economic and social uncertainties of the period and looked back to a simpler and more secure past. Celedonio Flores writes in the popular *tango* 'La Cumparsita':

Y yo me hice en tangos;	I was made by the tango,
Me fui modelando en odio, en tristeza	I was moulded by hate and sadness,
En las amarguras que da la pobreza . . .	In the bitterness of poverty . . .
En llantos de madres . . .	In the tears of mothers . . .
En las rebeldías del que es fuerte y tiene	In the rebelliousness of those who who are strong and must
Que cruzar los brazos cuando el hambre viene.[21]	Stand helpless when hunger comes

Displaced from the abstract thought of the élite, the people built up their own ideal of 'the new person'. An early ideal was the *gaucho* Martín Fierro, banished in his own land, as recounted in the epic verses of José Hernández.[22] Later, he was replaced by '*tango* man' who lived in the *arrabal* (urban slum), was constantly accosted by the élite, and lived off his *viveza criolla* (native cunning). He was of course a man, and women played a distinctly subordinate role in his discourse. The *tango* culture was immortalised in the figure of Carlos Gardel, a popular idol who died in the mid-1930s, and has since become deified in popular culture.[23] His cool grin, of the working-class boy made good, still hangs over the heads of *colectivo* (collective taxi) drivers and his songs are immensely popular.

Peronism did not create a culture of its own in the orthodox sense: indeed, Peronist-realism was not a memorable cultural revolution. Yet it did create a popular culture, where nationalism was never totally able to drown out the rebellious contestatory elements. A mediocre piece of theatre, '*Camino Bueno*' (Good Road) played in 1947 illustrates this quite well.[24] Set in Santa Fé province on the eve of the 1946 elections, a group of *peones* (labourers) discuss the prospects in the *almacén* (local store):

> Romero: Yo no sé nada de política, Lindoro
>   (I don't know anything about politics, Lindoro).
> Sergeant: ¿ Pero usté é' peronista?
>   (But you are a Peronist?)
> Romero: Todos somos
>   (We all are)

They then hear Colonel Perón speaking on the radio (a vital organ in the diffusion of popular culture, then and now) and Lindoro, another *peón*, expresses their views:

> Al fin y al cabo el hombre lo único que quiere e' que no haiga más unos muchos todos pobres y unos pocos todos ricos . . . Lo unico que quiere e' que haiga una nivelada.
> (At the end of the day, all the man wants is that there should not be many who are all poor and a few who are all rich. . . . He only wants to have a levelling.)

They swear that if Perón is cheated of victory they will burn the factories, destroy the *estancias* (estates) and string up the bosses.

Peronism, as we saw in Chapter 11, burst on to the national political scene on 17 October 1945. That popular demonstration was also a cultural event, at least in a negative sense, for the dominant class. Jorge Abelardo Ramos, a pro-Peronist Marxist describes those fateful events:

> Buenos Aires was occupied by hundreds of thousands of furious workers. Their slogans are primitive but unequivocal: 'Death to the oligarchs!' or 'No top hats and walking sticks!' (*Sin galera y sin bastón!*) 'We want Perón!' The columns of workers flowed into the Plaza de Mayo and turned the full weight of their frustration on the deserted Government House. Tired by the march, many demonstrators washed in the Congress fountains; their modest dress, their provocative attitude, their distempered shouts, caused horror for the spectators from the 'democratic' parties who witnessed in stupefaction the conquest of Buenos Aires.[25]

The marchers walked along in their shirt-sleeves, or rode on horseback, or on the backs of lorries or in hijacked buses. The well-dressed city gents of Buenos Aires – who could compare with the best of Rome, Paris or London – stared in horror. Beyond its political significance this was a cultural event, with the culture of the élite being swamped by the masses. The left-wing parties and especially the Communists, joined the chorus of 'civilised' protest at this invasion of their city by the unwashed hordes. Many recalled President Sarmiento (1868–1874) warning that Argentina faced a choice between 'civilisation or barbarism'.[24]

From 1945 springs the myth of the *descamisados*, which literally means shirtless, but in fact refers to the workers' sensible habit of not wearing coats in hot weather and rolling up their shirt-sleeves. General Perón, as a good populist, adopted this habit and praised the humble virtue of 'his' *descamisados*, and his campaign train during the 1946 elections was called 'El Descamisado'. Eva Perón defined the *descamisados* as those 'who feel themselves part of the people' (*es el que se siente pueblo*).[27] This whole discourse harks back to Sarmiento's fear of 'barbarism' represented in his era by the *gaucho*. Now a new figure, the *descamisado*, was taking on this role, and attacking the symbols of 'civilisation' which in Sarmiento's days were the educated immigrants who would civilise the rude inhabitants of the *pampas*. Peronism made a virtue out of the popular and elevated the *descamisado* to the status of a cult figure. Lined up against them were the oligarchy, the traditional left, and 'people of culture' like Jorge Luis Borges. At various stages of the Peronist saga slogans were adopted which reflected this divide, such as: '*Alpargatas* (rope sandals worn by the poor) *sí, líbros* (books) *no!*' and '*Haga patria, mate un estudiante!*' (Build the nation, kill a student!). The haunts of the oligarchy, such as the Jockey Club, the traditional newspaper *La Prensa*, churches and the university were all subject to mob attacks.

Many of the marchers on 17 October came from the provinces and they were dubbed '*cabecitas negras*' (literally black heads) by the press. The *cabecitas negras* were not defined by the colour of their skin: they included blond-haired people from Entre Rios, those with indigenous features from Jujuy, and many Italians, Poles and others from the interior. *Cabecita negra* was simply the latest epithet used by the oligarchy to label a social sector it feared: the labouring masses. The *gaucho* had been a vagabond (*vagabundo*) and knife-man (*cuchillero*), the early artisans were simply urban scum (*chusma*), Yrigoyen's supporters were the plebs (*plebe*) and now Perón had his *cabecitas negras*. These themes were reflected in an immensely popular film of 1942 *La guerra gaucha* (The gaucho war).[28] The film depicts the epic liberation struggles of the *gauchos* of Salta who fought the royalist armies at the beginning of the century. The film tells the story, of a young Spanish officer who thinks he is fighting for civilisation against barbarism until he is captured by the *gauchos*. Love leads him to see the virtues of the other side and join the guerrilla army (*montonera*) of the insurgents. As Sosa Pujato explains, 'The true protagonist of the film is the anonymous *gaucho*, selfless and courageous, who spontaneously sacrifices his life in the struggle for national independence'.[29] In the 1940s the slogan was to be *La vida por Perón* (My life for Perón).

The Peronist myth which stands above all others is that of 'Evita': a secular saint or a sordid social climber according to one's viewpoint. No simple verdict on Eva Perón would be possible, or indeed appropriate, given her importance. Evita played a vital role in the making of Peronism, through her work with the trade union leaders, her social work and her general mediation between Perón and the masses. The *Fundación Eva Perón*, a social aid foundation over which she presided, is a good example of her contradictory image. For many this was simply charity designed to buy votes and encourage submissiveness. Marysa Navarro describes its work thus:

> Besides granting old-age pensions, building *hogares para ancianos* (old people's homes) and *hogares de transito* (halfway homes) for women and children, organising soccer championships for children and teenagers, and every Christmas distributing *sidra* (cider) and *pan dulce* (raised bread), dolls and soccer balls, she gradually expanded the Fundación's goals to include the construction of schools, union headquarters, a building for the CGT, luxurious hotels where workers could spend their vacations at low cost, four modern hospitals where they received free medical care, numerous clinics, and housing.[30]

Faced with this catalogue of achievements – and their undoubted symbolic significance for workers and their families – it somehow misses the point to say it is simply the beneficence of a *grande dame*.

Evita did undoubtedly capture the anxieties and fantasies of the poor, in particular those of women. For the humiliated she represented one of their own kind (she was from a poor provincial background) in power. The élite certainly saw her that way, and her image was even more shocking for the 'people of culture' than Perón's, because she was a woman and she spoke the language of the people. In her autobiography, Eva Perón wrote of the situation before Perón: 'A few rich and many poor. The wheat of our land, for example, fed those abroad but the *peón* who sowed and harvested that wheat had no bread for his children. Our wealth was an old lie for the sons of this land. For one hundred years they sowed poverty and misery in the fields and cities of Argentina.'[31] The innate radicalism of Evita is hardly in question, whatever her appeals to compromise over struggle. She legitimised women's participation in politics, and women played a major role in the Peronist resistance of the 1950s and in the guerrilla movements of the 1970s.[32] Not surprisingly, the major Peronist guerrilla movement, the Montoneros, had as one of its most popular slogans, '*Si Evita viviera, sería Montonera*' (If Evita were alive she would be a Montonero). Perhaps she would have become an Isabel Perón, but the myth of Evita the *guerrillera* struggling on behalf of the humble (*los humildes*) is an integral part of popular consciousness.

In this section we have traced elements of the common sense of Argentine workers, defined by Gramsci as the complex, lived culture of a social group.[33] It is fragmentary, even incoherent, but the solidity of these popular beliefs cannot be denied. Culture is a contested terrain, and the much vaunted homogeneity of culture in Argentina is essentially a myth. Working-class culture does not stand fully-formed confronting the culture of the dominant classes but interacts with it, in a complex manner. One aspect of this, as described by Angel Rama, is the way in which the dominant culture 'did not negate or ignore the products of the sub-cultures (as the culture of domination in the Andean region did) but integrated them within its ideological domination plan, neutralising them and removing their revindicative violence . . . '[34] Thus the *gaucho* and the *tango* were incorporated into a sanitised 'popular culture', carefully packaged in a de-politicised delivery. In spite of the acknowledged success of the dominant class in Argentina in creating a mass culture, a genuine popular alternative has persisted. That is because ideology is not just composed of ideas but materialises in social structures and practices. It is the working-class way of life in Argentina which has created and reproduced a common sense which is essentially incompatible with the barren prospects of dependent capitalist development.

Consciousness

Quantitative studies of class consciousness are notoriously unreliable: they freeze and individualise a dynamic and collective phenomenon. We have in the pages above already made an estimation, of what constitutes working-class consciousness in Argentina, in which community and culture are prime ingredients. Now, we examine some individual experiences and some general studies of class consciousness to complete our analysis.

The life history of an individual worker cannot be representative in a sociological sense but can be at a deeper level of social meaning. In reading a letter by José Wanza, an immigrant to Argentina in 1891, we are not only reading an individual experience:

> What one suffers here is indescribable. I came to the country impressed by the great promises made to us by the Argentine agent in Vienna. These sellers of human souls lacking in conscience related such brilliant descriptions of the wealth of the country, and the welfare workers could expect there, that together with some friends, I came. It had all been lies and trickery.
>
> In Buenos Aires I could not find a job, and at the Immigrants' Hotel, a filthy dump, we were treated as though we were slaves. They threatened to throw us out on the streets if we did not go as day workers (*jornaleros*) to the plantations of Tucumán . . . I realized I had no choice but to obey.
>
> The journey to Tucumán took two nights, a day and a half. We travelled like sardines in a can. It was very cold and an icy wind blew through the railway carriage. Pounded mercilessly, dying of hunger, and many of us ill, we arrived in Tucumán. We were met by an immigration official who shouted at us like a Turkish pasha. After another journey we arrived . . .
>
> Next day work, and it's been like this for three months. We live on maize and soup (*puchero*) which does not kill the hunger of a working man. Our sleeping quarters have the stars for a roof. How miserable! And we just have to put up with it. There are so many people looking for work they would offer to work just for the *puchero*. We are always a month behind in wages so we cannot leave. At the store (*pulpería*) they let us have goods on tick at inflated prices and then knock it off our wages on pay day. The poor devils with wives and children never receive a cent in cash and are always in debt.
>
> I beg you comrades, publish this letter so that the proletarian press in Europe can warn the poor not to come to this country. If only I could return.[35]

José Wanza arrived in Argentina during the slump of the 1890s and by no means all immigrants had such a raw deal. Yet essentially, the 'golden era' of 1880–1930 was more prosperous for capital than it was for workers. Though recently some workers such as Cortés Conde have argued against an earlier orthodoxy which saw steadily declining wages throughout this period, the opposite case is far from proven.[36] As Leandro Gutiérrez points out, 'Even assuming a rise in real wages . . . the conditions of housing, health, food, the uncertainty of the labour market and the hopelessness of attaining the promises made by the promoter of immigration, would appear to have detracted from the assumed advantages'.[37]

Consciousness is moulded by experience, and here the record of the 'golden era' was a mixed one. Some authors, such as Gino Germani, stress the immigrants' rosy prospects of upward mobility.[38] Others, such as Robert Shipley, suggest that inter-class mobility was certainly not the norm and only applied to a few workers.[39] Working conditions were in some ways better in Buenos Aires than in comparable European cities because of a lower level of mechanisation. Yet workers were affected by poor ventilation and lighting, long hours and inadequate safety precautions, especially on construction sites and in the docks. Unemployment rates in

Buenos Aires averaged 17% between 1914 and 1930, reaching 30% in 1917. In terms of the consciousness generated by this set of experiences the verdict is mixed. For conservative observers, the Argentine worker would not be subject to the class appeal because 'class hatred' was not present. Most academic writers agree that the level of class solidarity and political sophistication among workers was not high. Yet workers did join unions led by radicals, even if for non-political reasons, and most importantly, they did perceive that improvements in their position were gained through struggle. Class solidarity may have been uneven, but it certainly affected wide layers of the working population during Argentina's mythical 'golden era'.

From the overseas immigrant worker at the turn of the century, we move on to the immigrant from the impoverished interior provinces during the 1930s. One of these immigrants, by no means typical in terms of his later career as a communist militant, was a typical figure in his trajectory towards the city. José Peter, later leader of the *frigorífico* workers, describes his experience:

> Many of us have arrived from our provinces, chased away by poverty and unemployment, obliged to spread out across other territory, other *estancias* and what industry was available, in search of a dignified life. We arrived, covered in the scars of our rural labours, from the *chacras* (farms) of Entre Ríos, from the *quebrachales* (*quebracho* woods) and *algodonales* (cotton fields) of the Chaco, the jungles of Misiones the *estancias* of Corrientes, the dry lands of Santiago del Estero, and from every corner of our vast national territory. We brought in our veins the blood of the *charrua*, the *araucano* and the *guaraní* (indigenous peoples), the blood of *gringo* peasants and workers, to become mixed in the *frigoríficos* and thus forge proletarian unity to fight for a better life.'[40]

As Peter came down by train to the big city he was hypnotised by the sight of his first *frigorífico*, which appeared as a monster devouring thousands of workers, and which attracted him with an irresistible force. For a rural *peón* like himself, the industrial proletariat was a pole of attraction: 'We perceived the multi-faceted and varied message of the big industrial enterprise, which spoke a very different language from the *chacras* and *estancias* of Entre Ríos'.[41] Moving in to the domain of the *frigorífico* Peter continues:

> In the cold chambers I met many foreign workers: Poles, Russians, Germans and others who had fled the coming war. Some had rich trade union experience. . . . The *criollo* workers like myself suffered a regime of brutal exploitation without a class understanding, with a mentality moulded by the surroundings of our upbringing. . . . The company tried to divide the workers whom it exploited equally and without any national distinctions.'[42]

Eventually José Peter became a communist activist and the *frigorífico* became a bastion of trade union power, uniting skilled and unskilled, foreign and *criollo* workers. This process of assimilation and developing class consciousness took place under the hegemony of Peronism, an essentially nationalist labourist ideology. A wide-ranging survey of attitudes in Argentina during the early 1960s, known as the Harvard Project, allows us to probe the complexity of the popular consciousness which resulted from this process.[43] Industrial workers were found to be significantly more class-conscious, radical, solidaristic, and hostile towards the traditional élites, than their rural counterparts. There is, however, no appreciable difference in the class consciousness of industrial and non-industrial workers in urban areas. Tiano, in analysing these results, concludes that 'this finding corresponds rather closely to Marx's theoretical expectations. Marx predicted that conditions of industrial production would steadily increase the cohesiveness of the industrial working class'.[44] As workers became concentrated in large establishments, communication increased accordingly, and provided the basis for cohesive worker networks. According to this study, duration of industrial work experience significantly increased Argentine workers' class consciousness.

On the vexed question of Peronism, opinions diverge regarding its association with class consciousness: whether it reduces or increases it. Tiano argues that the data gathered by the Harvard Project supports the view that Peronism was 'a major consciousness-increasing force among Argentine workers'.[45] Peronism leads to higher solidarity levels, but a certain lack of radicalism, measured in orthodox left-right terms. This is not surprising given the nature of the Peronist ideology and its hostility towards leftists (*zurdos*). Against the orthodox socialist viewpoint however, Peronism can be seen as an overall consciousness-raising factor, and the ideological cement for the cohesive and solidaristic social structures of the Argentine working class.

From the overseas and internal immigrant, we turn to the settled Argentine worker of the 1950s who had gone through the experience of Peronism and now faced the long resistance period. Vicente Armando Cabo, a metallurgical worker who became a union activist in 1939, was a leader of the Peronist resistance. He remembers the pre-Peronist era:

> In 1939 I was thrown out of the Istilart factory in Tres Arroyos, when I started to organise a union, though I was reinstated six months later through the efforts of my comrades. At that time we were treated as rubbish [*piltrafas*]: I have seen comrades thrown out of the factory gates. My three sisters were in domestic service and I only saw them two or three hours each week. . . . This whole undignified situation was transformed through a great popular movement.[46]

After the Peronist heyday came the days of illegality:

> Our struggle during that period was extremely hard, the majority of the leaders were without work and the employers would not take them on. The lack of funds made our situation even more difficult. Correspondence was sent by friendly bus- or train-drivers as we did not have the means to travel. We had few union buildings and pamphlets and leaflets were written from gaol. The struggle in

those days was truly heroic. To overcome all these difficulties there was a will of iron, and people – especially in the factories – responded very well.[47]

Yet by the 1960s Cabo seemed disillusioned and his faith in Peronism was by no means uncritical:

There is a big difference between the Peronism which we struggled for in those days and the Peronism in the minds of some of today's leaders, who have perverted the true meaning of the movement. Compared with the actions we developed during the resistance period, many of today's declarations seem ridiculous. This is not Peronism, this is not what we fought for.[48]

A new generation of worker activists would now take over from Cabo and lead the factory occupations of 1964, the *Cordobazo* of 1969 and eventually the first general strike *against* a Peronist government in 1975.

The new working class in the advanced capitalist sector would develop a consciousness distinct from the textile and metallurgical worker produced by the first wave of industrialisation. Sigal's survey of class consciousness in Argentina in the mid-1960s focuses particularly on this sector.[49] This study finds a certain level of economic integration in this sector, with expansive dynamic industries being seen as a ticket to personal social mobility. These attitudes shift as the working environment is left behind and broader social attitudes are tested. This corresponds with the findings of Patrick Peppe's study of Chilean workers and John Humphrey's study of Brazilian car workers.[50] Workers' consciousness is not formed only in the workplace and we must always incorporate the broader social, political and cultural aspects.

The attitudes of Roberto Nagera, who became a trade union activist in Ford's Córdoba plant in 1969, probably show more than most sociological surveys:

The working class of Argentina, looked at as a social class, is like every other working class: revolutionary. However, this strategic concept . . . was applied to the repressed and submerged working class. Over the years, through struggle and sacrifice, the working class won things from capital, and it is common to see the worker's son going to unversity. This makes the working class essentially Peronist, because all we have won was through General Perón. At the same time I think the working class here is reformist, and until something happens to break daily routine it will remain so . . . This is a bit what happened in Córdoba in 1969 . . .

The *Cordobazo* is linked to 17 October, with that man who granted the Statute of the Peón and made a series of concessions to the labour movement through the Labour and Social Security Secretariat. When these conquests were taken away from the labour movement it reacted spontaneously. It seems that the labour movement reacts in a revolutionary way and abandons its reformist condition when it is attacked . . .

Throughout its history this labour movement has reacted to aggression but has not taken the offensive. In the *Cordobazo* the workers outflanked their own leadership. It is then due to the lack of appropriate leadership, that the class struggle tendency (*clasismo*) appeared.[51]

No general analysis of class consciousness can capture the complexity of the proletarian experience. A general study of the conditions of the working class is subject to the same reservations as statistics on average wage rates. As Leandro Gutiérrez points out: Certainly, though we may compare them, the life situation of a docker, a self-employed dressmaking out worker, a factory seamstress, a shoe repairer working in a *conventillo* room, the butcher who slaughters a cow daily, and that of the factory proletariat as such are not the same.[52]

To this day there is considerable heterogeneity in the forms of production in Argentina, with sub-contracting and the putting-out system not necessarily representing a transitional form to modern capitalism.[53] The working class is differentiated by occupation but also by place of residence and, above all, by age and gender. The urban workers we have concentrated on were also in a quite different situation from that of the rural workers. In the mid-1930s approximately 95% of military recruits from the north-western provinces were found physically unfit for service.[54] Chronic malnutrition, disease, and rampant poverty were the essential reality of the provincial worker. Even the small-holders, the *colonos* in the relatively rich province of Entre Ríos, were forced to join the exodus to the city, as they were driven under by debts and mortgage foreclosures. Even Peronism, in spite of its fervent support in the impoverished provinces, failed to improve the lot of the rural workers.

Notes

1. J. Donzelot (1979) *The Policing of Families*, London, Hutchinson, p. xxvii.
2. R. Johnson, (1979) "Three problematics: elements of a theory of working-class culture" in J. Clarke, C. Critcher and R. Johnson (eds) *Working Class Culture*, London, Hutchinson) p. 234.
3. E. Gilimón, (1971) *Un Anarquista en Buenos Aires (1890–1910)*, Buenos Aires, Centro Editor de América Latina, p. 85.
4. PEHESA (1983) "La cultura de los sectores populares: manipulación, inmanencia o creación histórica", *Punto de Vista*, no. 18, p. 14.
5. Ibid., p. 14.
6. G. Gutierrez, (1975) *La Clase Trabajadora Nacional*, Buenos Aires, Crisis, p.67.
7. On the 'social wage' generally, see A. Marshall, (1984) "El 'salario social' en la Argentina", *Desarrollo Económico*, vol. 24, no. 93.
8. A. Abós, (1983) *La Columna Vertebral: Sindicatos y Peronismo,* Buenos Aires, Editorial Legasa, p. 93.
9. J.C. D'Abate, (1983) "Trade Unions and Peronism", in F. Turner and J.E. Miguens (eds.) *Juan Perón and the Reshaping of Argentina,* Pittsburgh, University of Pittsburgh Press, p. 68.

10. S. Ramos (1981) "Las relaciones de parentesco y de ayuda mutua en los sectores populares urbanos", *Estudios Cedes*, vol. 4, no. 1, p. 55.

11. G. O'Donnell, (1979) "Notas para el estudio de procesos de democratización política a partir del estado burocrático–autoritario", *Estudios Cedes*, vol. 2, no. 5, p. 24.

12. H. Lucero, (1977) "La larga marcha de la clase obrera argentina", *Coyoacán*, vol. 1, no. 1, p. 73.

13. J. Petras, (1981) "Terror and the Hydra: The Resurgence of the Argentine Working Class" in J. Petras, *Class, State and Power in the Third World,* London, Zed Press, p. 261.

14. For more details see B. Galitelli, (1980) "La huelga de Villa Constitución", *Apuntes*, vol. 11, no. 2.

15. See CEDES (1984) "La protesta urbana en 1982", *Debates*, vol. 1, no. 2.

16. R. Williams, (1961) *Culture and Society,* Harmondsworth, Penguin, p. 312.

17. E. Gilimón (1971) *Un Anarquista en Buenos Aires*, p. 36.

18. A. Jauretche, (1962) *FORJA y la Década Infame*, Buenos Aires, Editorial Coyoacán.

19. G. Sosa-Pujato (1975) "Popular Culture" in M. Falcoff and R. Dolkart (eds.) *Prologue to Perón. Argentina in Depression and War, 1930–1943*, Berkeley, University of California Press, p. 136.

20. H. Ferrer, (1960) *El tango, su historia y evolución*, Buenos Aires, cited in Sosa-Pujato (1975) "Popular Culture", p. 138.

21. Cited in Sosa-Pujato (1975) "Popular Culture", p. 140.

22. J. Hernandez, *Martin Fierro*, various editions.

23. See E. Zimmerman, (1984) "Gardel, un mito", *Debates*, vol. 1, no. 1.

24. Cited in E. Goldar, (1973) "La Literatura Peronista" in G. Cárdenas et al. *El Peronismo*, Buenos Aires, Ediciones Cepe, p. 176.

25. J. Ramos Abelardo (1981) *La era del peronismo 1943–1976*, Buenos Aires, Ediciones del Mar Dulce, p. 80.

26. See D. Sarmiento, *Facundo*, various editions. The theme of "civilisation of barbarism" was further explored by E. Martínez Estrada (1971) *X-Ray of the Pampa*, Austin, University of Texas Press.

27. E. Perón, (1952) *La Razon de Mi Vida,* Buenos Aires, Ediciones Peuser, p.117.

28. Sosa-Pujato (1975) "Popular Culture", p. 159.

29. Ibid.

30. M. Navarro, (1983) "Evita and Peronism" in F. Turner and J.E. Miguens (eds.) *Juan Perón and the Reshaping of Argentina*, p. 24.

31. E. Perón, (1952) *La Razon de Mi Vida*, p. 159.

32. See N.C. Hollander, (1974) "Si Evita Viviera", *Latin American Perspectives*, vol. 1, no. 3.

33. A. Gramsci, (1971) *Selections from the Prison Notebooks,* London, Lawrence and Wishart, pp. 419–424.

34. A. Rama, (1982) "La narrativa en el conflicto de las culturas" in A. Rouquiè (ed.) *Argentina Hoy*, Mexico, Siglo XXI, p. 255.

35. In H. Spalding, (1970) *La Clase Trabajadora Argentina (Documentos para su historia–1890/1912)*, Buenos Aires, Galerna, pp. 200–202.

36. R. Cortés Conde, (1979) *El Progreso Argentino 1884–1914*, Buenos Aires, Editorial Sudamericana.

37. L. Gutierrez, (1981) "Condiciones de la vida material de los sectores

populares en Buenos Aires: 1880–1914," *Revista de Indias*, vol. XLI, no. 163–164, p.171.

38. G. Germani (1968) *Política y Sociedad en una Epoca de Transición*, Buenos Aires, Paidos.

39. R. Shipley, (1977) *On the Outside Looking In: A Social History of the Porteño Worker During the "Golden Age" of Argentine Development 1914–1930*, New Brunswick, Rutgers University, PhD thesis which we draw on for the rest of this paragraph.

40. J. Peter, (1968) *Crónicas Proletarias*, Buenos Aires, Editorial Esfera, p. 10.

41. Ibid., p. 20.

42. Ibid., p. 27.

43. See S.B. Tiano, (1979) *Authoritarianism, Class Consciousness, and Modernity: Working Class Attitudes in Argentina and Chile*. Brown University, PhD thesis.

44. Ibid., p. 255.

45. Ibid., p. 545.

46. O. Calello, and D. Parcero, (1984) *De Vandor a Ubaldini/1*. Buenos Aires, Centro Editor de América Latina p. 29.

49. Ibid., p. 26.

48. Ibid., p. 28.

49. Cited in E. Jelin and J.C. Torre (1982) "Los nuevos trabajadores en América Latina: una reflexion sobre la tesis de la aristocracia obrera", *Desarrollo Económico* Vol. 22, no. 85.

50. See P. Peppe, (1971) *Working Class Politics in Chile*, PhD thesis, Columbia University, and J. Humphrey, (1982) *Capitalist Control and Workers' Struggle in the Brazilian Auto Industry*, New Jersey, Princeton University Press, respectively.

51. O. Calello, and D. Parcero, (1984) *De Vandor a Ubaldini/2*. Buenos Aires, Centro Editor de América Latina, pp. 127–132.

52. L. Gutierrez, (1982) "Condiciones Materiales de Vida de los sectores Populares en el Buenos Aires Finisecular" in *De Historia a historiadores. Homenaje a Jose Luis Romero*, Mexico Siglo XXI, p. 434.

53. See B. Schmukler (1977) "Relaciones actuales de producción en industrias tradicionales argentinas", *Estudios Sociales Cedes*, no. 6.

54. D. Tamarin, (1977) *The Argentine Labor Movement in an Age of Transition, 1930–1945*, University of Washington, PhD thesis, p. 57.

17. By Way of Conclusion

Our historical account began with the outward-oriented growth experienced by Argentina after 1850, which gave rise to a subsidiary industrial (artisanal-workshop) sector in the 1870s. A labour movement did not emerge immediately and for a whole period mutual-aid societies predominated. As Hobsbawm notes 'The habit of industrial solidarity must be learned. . . . There is a natural time-lag, before new workers become an "effective" labour movement'.[1] This learning period was completed in Argentina between 1880 and 1900 with the emergence and consolidation of trade unions along with the first strikes. The class struggle had become a permanent fact of life, with the interests of labour being expressed by the early anarchist and socialist groupings. The workers' press, which we examined in its various manifestations, played a crucial role in forging a social and political identity for the working class. Symbolically, the Argentine labour movement became part of the international labour movement in 1890, when 1 May was first celebrated as a symbol of workers' autonomy.

The first decade of the 20th Century saw a great upsurge in the capital accumulation process in Argentina. Predictably, immigration increased dramatically as the small farmers and artisans of Europe were attracted by tales of fabulous wealth. For a time the immigrants displayed a form of 'dual consciousness', part worker, part upwardly-mobile immigrant. Eventually, the proletarian condition imposed itself and national differences between the various immigrant groups were overcome. At this stage one person in every two in Buenos Aires would be foreign-born, and of every ten foreigners there would be five Italians, three Spaniards, one person from north-western Europe and one from the Balkans or Eastern Europe. These largely prosperous years for capital were also ones of labour's first 'explosion'.[2] As Hobsbawm writes, 'All social movements expand in jerks: the history of all contains periods of abnormality, often fantastically rapid and easy mobilisations of hitherto untouched masses'.[3] The high level of working-class self-activity continued at least until 1913, when a general downturn set in. The massive repression of the 1910 general strike had already signalled the beginning of the end for anarchist hegemony within the labour movement. It should be noted that until 1910 the working class had the advantage of a relatively disorganised capitalist class, which made rapid gains possible.

The First World War marked a transition phase for capital–labour relations in Argentina, as the agrarian economy reached the limits of its expansion and industrialisation accelerated. The war marked a global shift in class relations, as the transition from the handicraft or petty commodity production stage of capitalism to that of manufacturing and the systematic extension of the division of labour was completed (or at least its basis laid). This had serious implications for the labour movement because, as Roxborough points out:

> As the leading sector shifts over time from one industry to another, there will be a break in the institutional pattern of class relations. . . . The older pattern [of class conflict] will almost certainly be substantially modified in the process, and labour organizations will be restructured.[4]

As capital was restructured so the labour movement went through a process of recomposition: once the artisan type-setter was the vanguard of the movement, then the bakers and dockers, then the railway workers, and then the *frigorífico* (meat-packing plant) workers and those in the textile industry were poised to take over the leadership of the movement. In the 1940s it would be the turn of the metallurgical workers as the transition to large-scale industry was completed.

With the electoral reform of 1911 the urban middle class was incorporated into the political process, but it was still too early for labour to be incorporated. While in Europe the First World War marked the high point of the labour movement's political integration with the bourgeoisie, in Argentina the immigrant workers' level of social integration was still too low to allow this. The immigrants were integrated into society first of all as workers, and only later did they become citizens in the full sense of the word. The bloody events towards the end of the decade – the *Semana Trágica* of 1919 and the Patagonia massacre of 1921 – showed the clear limits of the ruling class reformist strategy. The events of 1919 also marked the limits of the anarchist strategy – since 1910 the syndicalist current had become the leading political trend within the labour movement and their more cautious position was now consolidated.

By 1919 the Argentine labour movement's achievements were considerable. Julio Godio notes that in spite of its failure to organise a revolutionary workers' party capable of leading a popular struggle against the conservative regime, 'the successes in the trade union and parliamentary terrains were so notable as to make the labour movement of Argentina, in spite of its limitations, the greatest in development and prestige throughout Latin America during the 1880–1919 period'.[5]

Indeed, in terms of organisation, numbers and combativeness the labour movement was ahead of all others on the continent. Its precocious development was due in no small measure to the leavening of the local working class by anarchists and socialist militants from abroad, who fused with a pre-existing radical tradition stretching back to the gaucho *montoneras*.

After a continued upsurge of strikes in the early 1920s, the labour movement went into a serious decline. The trade unions probably lost about half their members, though earlier figures were quite inflated so it is difficult to estimate precisely. The political expressions of the labour movement were radicalised, partly as an effect of the ripples produced by the Russian revolution in Latin America, and partly as the last expressions of a bygone radical era. What occurred in the 1920s was that the labour movement had lost its traditional identity, but had not yet found a new role in society. The process of social and political integration of the working class had cut the ground from under the feet of the anarchists and the revolutionary syndicalists. The reformist socialists, with their rigid separation of the economic and political aspects of the labour movement, had taken root but offered no overall strategy for labour. The trade union movement did achieve a certain degree of unification with the formation of the CGT (General Confederation of Labour) in 1930. The first labour confederation had been formed in 1901, but the trade unions had been plagued by divisions between the various political currents thereafter. The formation of the CGT, in spite of some later divisions, did provide organic political representation for the working class, and helped to forge a degree of cohesion and unity in the labour movement unparalleled in the rest of Latin America.

The great slump of 1929 led to profound changes in Argentina and a conservative restoration which put an end to the strategy of incorporating labour, but which also promoted limited industrialisation. The composition of the working class also began to change as internal migration began to predominate over international migration. The labour movement remained subject to the disorientation and demoralisation it had suffered in the 1920s. The CGT remained quiescent in the face of the 1930 military coup, on the basis of non-intervention in political affairs. The bourgeoisie took advantage of the situation with a concerted attack on the social and economic gains made by labour in the previous period.

Perhaps the greatest 'could have been' in this period relates to the role of the Communist Party which, since its emergence from the Socialist Party, had established a solid foot-hold in the labour movement. Its leading role in a number of notable strikes in the mid-1930s placed it in a good position to make a bid for the leadership of the labour movement. The Communists were by far the most dynamic force during this period, but as happened elsewhere, their subordination to an international movement proved their downfall. Following the dictates of Soviet foreign policy, in the lead-up to the Second World War, the Communist Party had already begun to lose ground when Colonel Perón became Secretary of Labour in 1943 and began the second or co-optive phase in Argentina's labour history.

The conventional explanations for the rise of Perón have been found to be unsatisfactory, particularly those based on the distinction between an 'old' working class–of immigrant origin, unionised and socialist or syndicalist–and a 'new' working class–of recent national immigration, non-unionised and nationalist-populist in outlook. Perón, according to this interpretation, simply wooed this second group with promises of higher wages, holidays and so on, and organised them in trade unions under his direct control. The truth was more complex, because it was some of the 'traditional' leaders of the labour movement who played a key role in securing labour support for Perón. Furthermore, it was the working class as a whole which supported Perón, and not because they were duped, but because they saw him as the best guarantee of the benefits they had won in struggle.

Perón overcame the reluctance of the ruling class to adopt a co-optive strategy towards labour, or rather he ignored their objections. The number of workers employed in manufacturing had doubled between 1935 and 1945, and the industrial proletariat had become the backbone of the labour movement. There was a long list of pent-up grievances within the factories which were waiting to burst into the open. The previously dominant political currents within the labour movement–anarchism, socialism, syndicalism–were either in decline or in such a state of disarray that they could not express the current needs of the working class. The Communists had isolated themselves, and repression could always be used as well as co-option. Perón seized his chance, and solved one problem for the ruling class while creating another.

The political crisis of the state and the inability of the ruling classes to forge a stable system of bourgeois rule created the conditions for Perón's rise to power. The massive demonstration in October 1945 which sealed his bid for mass support also marked the eruption of the working masses on to the political scene. Unionisation 'from above' and the forging of a pliant trade union leadership (or bureaucracy) was designed to turn workers into citizens and class demands, into 'popular' ones. From then on the working class became part of a mass non-class nationalist movement. On the other hand, under the Peronist governments between 1946 and 1955, the working class established a dense social network of proletarian organisation in the workplaces. Stable organs of workers' democracy were established in the factories, which served as a countervailing weight to the bureaucratic propensities of the leadership. It would be stretching reality to call this a system of workers' autonomy, but workers did maintain a permanent class presence within the broader nationalist movement. The very fact that strikes never stopped under the Peronist governments, contrary to popular belief, is proof in itself that Perón did not succeed in 'buying off' the working class. This period is looked back to with nostalgia by older workers because it helped establish a basic human dignity for the worker, who was previously looked on by the oligarchy and its government as rather less important than the cattle on their *estancias*.

Under Perón the labour movement had made another leap forward in terms of organisation, especially if we compare the situation with that of

1919. Milcíades Peña, a vigorous socialist critic of Peronism, writes:

> General integrated unionisation of the factory proletariat and wage workers as a whole; democratisation of the worker-boss relations in the workplace and in dealings with the state; 33% increase in the wage earners' share of the national income: this is what the 'Peronist revolution' boiled down to.[6]

Yet this is a considerable achievement: the trade unions were no longer the preserve of a minority of militants but mass organisations of the working class. Through the *comisiones internas* these bodies achieved a considerable degree of workers' democracy, and the workers' economic and political participation in the life of the country increased to an unprecedented extent. Peronism established a new 'industrial legality' (Gramsci's phrase) in Argentina in which the role of the working class and the trade unions was firmly established. There was of course a political price to pay for these organisational achievements.

The internationalism of the early syndicalists and anarchists had tended to ignore the question of economic dependence (as outlined in Lenin's *Imperialism*) for the case of Argentina. In 1928 the anarchist journal *La Protesta* had declared: 'For the anarchists and the working people the invasion of foreign capital does not matter a great deal, in that it is the same to be exploited by one capitalist as another'.[7] Following the 1930 Roca-Runciman treaty with Britain, which codified Argentina's condition of dependence, nationalism became increasingly important within the labour movement. The abstract internationalism of the anarchists had paved the way for the rise of nationalism within the ranks of labour in so far as dependence was an issue which affected the fate of the working class. Yet before the labour movement became integrated in the nationalist Peronist movement, there was one key episode of labour autonomy. The *Partido Laborista* (Labour Party) which flourished briefly at the rise of Peronism, was, as Pont writes, 'one of the clearest expressions of autonomy of the organised working class, and its dissolution signalled the first and most decisive step in the breaking of the political autonomy of the trade union movement in Argentina'.[8] The internal democracy of this trade-union-based labour party was henceforth present only within the trade unions, and there only during periods of labour activism. The lack of political autonomy, as Peronism commenced to set the parameters of the trade union movement, meant that the working class lacked a coherent and consistent political representation to match its undoubted vitality in the class struggle.

Taking a long view of the labour movement's history we can say that the making of the working class in Argentina took place between 1880 and 1900 but that it went through a fundamental remaking between 1935 and 1945. As Stedman Jones writes in a different context, 'This remaking process did not obliterate the legacy of that first formative phase of working-class history. . . . But it did transform its meaning'.[9] The historical experience of Peronism led the working class to reinterpret rather selectively its previous history, which was relegated to a simple pre-history, somewhat in the way in which Marx calls all modes of production prior to communism a 'pre-history' before the real history of humankind begins.

At this point it might be worth emphasising the particular way in which the making and remaking of the working class took place in Argentina. For the orthodox Marxist Kuczynski, there were simply various social groups and then 'the factory fused these various groups, these men [sic] who came from such different strata of society, into one unit.'[10] This economistic approach, whatever its merits in the British case, simply will not do for Latin America where the factory never acted as a unifying factor to this extent. To understand how the working class was formed we need to examine, as done partially above in Chapter 16, the much broader social context of working-class life.

One popular labour history argues that in Argentina the working-class tenements, the *conventillos*, were 'the bitter site of a new cultural synthesis', uniting *gringo* and *criollo* workers.[11] In this case, the unification of the working class operated largely outside the factory, and this explains the strong community element in the class solidarity forged by the workers' movement in Argentina. With the rise of Peronism we see how the political arena – the streets – was the site of labour mobilisation and political integration. As Sigal and Torre write, 'This early experience of political unification became in fact inseparable from its identity as a class'.[12] This is correct, but we would not stress quite so much as Sigal and Torre the role of the state in the political integration of economically fragmented workers. In the rise of Peronism the working class was not passive, it made its own history in this phase, as it had earlier.

After Perón was overthrown by the military in 1955 a long period of political instability opened up in Argentina. Successive military and civilian governments showed that a basic stalemate had been arrived at in Argentine society. The labour movement, in alliance with the middle sectors and the national industrialists, could make the rule of the old agrarian oligarchy impossible. Yet the nationalist movement could not impose its solution on society, partly because international conditions had changed and a nationalist economic strategy no longer seemed viable. Indeed, from the late 1950s onwards there was an influx of foreign capital into Argentina which radically altered the pattern of capital accumulation. The industrial structure built up under Perón was based largely on labour-intensive industry (accumulation of absolute surplus-value), but now the leading sectors were decidedly capital-intensive (and shifted towards the extraction of relative surplus-value). There had been a remaking of the working class under Peronism, and now further economic transformations were leading to another fundamental restructuring of the labour movement. Throughout this period the labour movement maintained a high level of militancy, for example the 1964 general strikes and factory occupations, but in the workplaces the new changes in the labour process led to capital extending the 'frontiers of control' over labour. Another military coup in 1966 represented an attempt by the new internationalised section of the bourgeoisie to seal its economic predominance with political power. New levels of repression called forth renewed labour resistance.

The anti-dictatorial resistance culminated in the semi-insurrectional general strike in the provincial capital of Córdoba in 1969. Among its protagonists were the car workers, a fact which greatly shocked the economy ministers who thought high wages would deal with this 'new' modern sector of the working class. In fact, this advanced sector of the proletariat found itself leading popular resistance to the regime and establishing new practices of workers' autonomy in the workplace. It confronted capitalist control of the labour process, raising demands for workers' control which went far beyond Peronist labour policy. It also attacked the linchpin of the Peronist labour movement, the labour bureaucracy. Clear-cut struggles for workers' democracy were henceforth to be an integral element of the class struggle in Argentina. When a series of general strikes led to a serious weakening of the military regime, Perón was called back from exile and was duly elected to office in 1973. His death in 1974 only set the seal on a process of realignment which had already begun within the Peronist movement. The two wings which had emerged – one socialist, the other right-wing nationalist – now clashed openly. In 1975 the growing strength of the rank-and-file class struggle tendencies was demonstrated in the first ever general strike against a Peronist government (that of his widow Isabel). As the threat of workers' autonomy grew, so too did the calls for a new intervention by the armed forces to defend capital.

What had the labour movement achieved by the eve of the military intervention in 1976? In 1971 Agustín Tosco, one of the leaders of the *Cordobazo*, wrote from his prison cell:

> The Argentine workers have achieved an important role on the national scene. Their standard of living has risen, their representatives have been admitted on to state bodies and their working conditions have generally been determined by collective contracts.[13]

This is a sober estimate of the solid achievements notched up by the labour movement in 100 years. By Third World standards these achievements are indeed considerable, even though they may sound banal to the workers of the advanced industrial societies. Tosco's experience at the head of the Córdoba power workers also allows us to clarify some of the most pressing problems in Third World labour studies.

The labour aristocracy theory is now fading in popularity though it is still quite common. For example, Hewlett and Weinert assert categorically (though without empirical foundation) that in Brazil and Mexico, 'The industrial work-force . . . emerged as a labour aristocracy with more to lose than to gain from sharing the benefits of economic growth with the mass of the people, and the trade union movement grew up as an instrument to control and co-opt this élite group'.[14] The experience of the power workers in Argentina – an established and well-paid work-force – belies this set of statements. Certainly at a national level the power workers were led by the conservative J.C. Taccone, admirer of US business unionism and promoter of 'participation' schemes, but in Córdoba the Tosco leadership group pioneered liberation trade unionism (*sindicalismo de liberación*). With this conception the trade unions acted as 'schools for revolution', mobilising and developing class consciousness. Even writers who accept the framework set by the labour aristocracy concept, such as Ducatenzeiler, find that reformism is not the sole prerogative of this sector, but permeates all labour sectors.[15]

As to the labour bureaucracy, the 'managers of discontent' within the workers' movement, Tosco makes the dividing line clear. His combative union leadership in Córdoba had as its immediate priority the same administrative tasks as the bureaucrat. But the combative leader is not merely an administrator and, in Tosco's words, 'must struggle for social and national liberation'.[16] In Argentina, national, popular and democratic rights have often been violated; it is the task of the organised labour movement to defend them, according to Tosco. The political struggle over general questions is what differentiates the labour bureaucrat from the class struggle leadership, more than any individual elements of corruption.

In 1976 a determined effort was made by the ruling class and the state to inflict a decisive and permanent defeat on the labour movement. The economy minister appointed by the military state, and therefore unconstrained by electoral considerations, was able to declare quite openly that the economic and political power of the trade unions needed to be smashed before a stable political solution (for the bourgeoisie) could be found. The new military strategy was certainly far-reaching, and it was designed to restructure the labour market fundamentally so as to reduce the social weight of the working class, and then to weaken the trade unions through legislation and repression so as to discipline them under the new regime. This strategy was only partly successful. It did succeed in remodelling the labour market and seriously weakening the core sections of the working class, and the structures of the trade unions received the hardest blows in their whole history. It did not succeed, however, in its central aim of inflicting a political defeat on the labour movement. As the struggles of the working class continued, culminating in a series of general strikes in the early 1980s, so the economic policies of the military state began falling into disarray. In a final desperate bid, the nationalist card was played again with the invasion of the Malvinas islands, whose repossession was always part of the Peronist programme. Defeat of the military in this adventure was sealed in an upsurge of working-class and democratic struggles from 1983 onwards, which continued under the newly-elected Radical Party government.

The Radical government of Raúl Alfonsín, which came into office in the wake of the military débâcle, had a contradictory labour policy. Many rank-and-file workers and socialists agreed with Alfonsín's pledge to 'democratise' the unions, but in reality he was simply seeking to reduce

Peronist political power based on the trade unions, and to encourage a Radical tendency within the trade union movement. Eventually a broad coalition of trade union leaders and political figures succeeded in defeating Alfonsín's trade union bill. The price paid seems to have been the bureaucracy's agreement not to mount an offensive campaign against the austerity plan imposed by the International Monetary Fund.

Rank-and-file enthusiasm was dampened when the Radical government banned several internal elections for shop-steward committees in key workplaces. The cause of democracy was now seen to mean different things to different people. Meanwhile, the pent-up demands accumulated under the military regimes since 1976 erupted in the new constitutional era. The working class in Argentina today is still largely Peronist, but this no longer signifies blind allegiance to a charismatic leader; rather it is an integral element of working-class consciousness, part of that historic memory which stretches back to the legendary mobilisation of 17 October 1945. Another current in the labour movement, born from the *Cordobazo* of 1969, looks back to an earlier era at the turn of the century, when a class struggle movement was first formed in Argentina.

To speak of myths and popular memory introduces a new dimension into our analysis, perhaps a disruptive one in what has been an essentially objective account of labour's history. Yet Jeff Crisp recognised recently that 'political action is informed not only by contemporary circumstances, but also by past experiences and the mythology of these experiences'.[17] Crisp finds evidence to support this statement in the continuity of the pattern of collective worker resistance among the Ghanaian gold miners he studied. The 'myth' of the general strike proposed by the revolutionary syndicalists also had a real factual content and purpose. In Argentina there are three main labour myths: the *Semana Trágica* of 1919, 17 October 1945 and the *Cordobazo* of 1969. Each of these has been analysed factually in the pages above, but they also have a meaning and significance beyond this. The bloody and heroic events of 1919 have particular significance in that they mark the high point of the insurrectional period dominated by the anarchists. As Bilsky writes,

> The *Semana Trágica* will remain in the history of the Argentine labour movement as a symbol which represents the tradition of struggle of the first years of this century. As with all traditions, it is an inheritance which deserves reconstruction and which the Argentine working class will recover.[18]

The recovery and reconstruction of the other two traditions is more problematic.

The mass mobilisations of 17 October 1945 and the *Cordobazo* represent the founding myths of the national-popular and the class struggle (*clasista*) discourses respectively. For the Peronist tradition the events of 1945 represent a victory of the national and popular over the liberal oligarchic regime. The myth of the *descamisado*, who walked the streets of Buenos Aires that day, was a victory over that oligarchy but also over the 'Marxism of select minorities', as Geltman calls it.[19] The iconography and mystique of Peronism derive from that day and at the same time sanctify it. For the socialist tradition the mobilisation of workers and students in Córdoba in 1969 operates in a similar way to legitimise a class struggle discourse. It is the tradition of Agustín Tosco and SITRAC-SITRAM constructed as an antidote to that of Perón and the bureaucratic leaders of the CGT. Today, both the nationalist and socialist traditions of 1945 and 1969 are challenged by a democratic myth ably mobilised by Alfonsín's government. This classless democratic tradition can be countered, and undoubtedly will be, by the tradition of workers' democracy present in the cataclysmic events of 1919, 1945 and 1969 and also in the day-to-day life of the factory and community grass-roots. This was manifested most recently in the ultimately successful struggle against the military dictatorship which came to power in 1976 with the aim of closing the history of the Argentine labour movement.

Notes

1. E. Hobsbawm, (1971) *Labouring Men*, London, Weidenfeld and Nicolson, p. 144.
2. For an analysis of the relationship between economic fluctuations and labour militancy see R. Munck, (1985). *Cycles of Class Struggle and the Making of the Working Class in Argentina (1890–1920)*, Centre for Developing-Area Studies, McGill University, Discussion Paper Series, no. 25.
3. E. Hobsbawm, (1979) *Primitive Rebels*, Manchester, Manchester University Press, p. 105.
4. I. Roxborough, (1981) "The Analysis of Labour Movements in Latin America: Typologies and Theories", *Bulletin of Latin American Research*, I 1, p. 91.
5. J. Godio, (1980) *Historia del movimiento obrero latinoamericano/1*. Mexico, Editorial Nueva Imágen, p. 219.
6. Peña, M. (1973) *Masas, Caudillos y Elites*, Buenos Aires, Ediciones Fichas, p. 130.
7. Cited in H. Matsushita, (1983) *Movimiento Obrero Argentino 1930–1945*, Buenos Aires, Siglo Veinte, p. 42.
8. E. Pont, (1984) *Partido Laborista: Estado y sindicatos*, Buenos Aires, Centro Editor de América Latina, p. 37.
9. G. Stedman Jones, (1983) *Languages of Class*, Cambridge, Cambridge University Press, p. 236.
10. J. Kuczynski, (1967) *The Rise of the Working Class*, London, Weidenfeld and Nicolson, p. 76.
11. G. Gutierrez, (1975) *La Clase Trabajadora Nacional*, Buenos Aires, Crisis, p. 37.
12. S. Sigal, and J.C. Torre, (1979) "Una reflexion en torno a los movimientos laborales en America Latina", in R. Katzman and S.L. Reyna (eds.) *Fuerza de Trabajo y Movimientos Laborales en América Latina*, Mexico, El Colegio de Mexico, p. 142.
13. J. Lannot, R. Amantea and E. Sguiglia (eds.), (1984) *Augustin Tosco,*

conducta de un dirigente obrero, Buenos Aires, Centro Editor de América Latina, p. 18.

14. S.A. Hewlett and R.S. Weinert, "Characteristics and consequences of late development" in Hewlett and Weinert, (eds.) *Brazil and Mexico: Patterns in late Development*, Philadelphia, Institute for the Study of Human Issues, p. 7.

15. G. Ducatenzeiler, (1980) *Syndicats et politique en Argentine 1955–1973*, Montreal, Les Presses de l'Université de Montréal.

16. Cited in M. Roldán, (1979) *Sindicatos y Protesta Social en la Argentina*, Amsterdam, CEDLA, p. 199.

17. J. Crisp, (1984) *The Story of An African Working Class. Ghanaian Miners' Struggles 1870–1980*, London, Zed Books, p. 183.

18. E. Bilsky, (1984) *La Semana Trágica*, Buenos Aires, Centro Editor de América Latina, p. 161.

19. P. Geltman, (1973) "Mitos, Simbolos y Heroes en el Peronismo", in G. Cárdenas et al. *El Peronismo*, Buenos Aires, Ediciones Cepe, p. 120.

Select Bibliography

Though most of the sources for the study of the labour movement in Argentina are obviously in Spanish, a basic bibliography of works in English should be useful.

Alexander, R. (1962) *Labor relations in Argentina, Brazil and Chile,* McGraw Hill, New York.

Baily, S. (1967) *Labor, Nationalism and Politics in Argentina,* Rutgers University Press, New Brunswick. For long the standard reference work; now slightly dated by recent research and vitiated by its "modernisation" framework, but still a useful source.

Doyon, L. (1978) *Organized Labour and Perón (1943–1955),* University of Toronto, Toronto, PhD thesis.

Di Tella, T. (1981) "Working-class organization and politics in Argentina", *Latin American Research Review*, vol. XVI, no. 2, 1981. A wide-ranging survey of labour and politics based partly on oral-history archives.

Epstein, E. (1975) "Politicization and income redistribution in Argentina: The case of the Peronist worker", *Economic Development and Cultural Change*, 23, (4).

—— (1979) "Control and co-optation of the Argentine labour movement", *Economic Development and Cultural Change,* 27, (3).

Evans, J.; Hoeffel, P.H.; James, D. (1983) 'Reflections on Argentine Auto Workers and Their Unions', in R. Kronish and K. Mericke (eds), *The Political Economy of the Latin American Motor Vehicle Industry*, MIT Press, Cambridge, Mass.

Germani, G. (1977) *Authoritarianism, National Populism and Fascism*, Transaction Books, New Brunswick. Contains classic statement of the position stressing the role of internal migrants in the rise of Perón.

Gordon, E., Hall, M. and Spalding, H. (1973) "A Survey of Brazilian and Argentine materials at the International Instituut Voor Sociale Geschiedenis in Amsterdam", *Latin American Research Review*, 8, 3.

Guy, D. (1981) "Women, peonage and industrialization: Argentina, 1810–1914", *Latin American Research Review* VXI, 3.

Hollander, N. (1977) "Women workers and the class struggle: the case of

Argentina", *Latin American Perspectives* 4 (1/2). A useful contribution on a sorely neglected subject.

Horowitz, J. (1979) *Adaptation and change in the Argentine labor movement (1930–1943)–A study of five unions*, PhD thesis, University of California, Berkeley.

—— (1983) "The impact of the pre-1943 labor union traditions on Peronism", *Journal of Latin American Studies*. 15, 1. Argues for continuity between pre- and post-Peronist periods.

Imaz, L. (1970) *Los que mandan (Those who rule)*. State University of New York Press, Albany, Chapter 11. "The Union Leaders" deals with the development of the trade union bureaucracy.

James, D. (1978) "Power and politics in Peronist trade unions", *Journal of Interamerican Studies and World Affairs*, 20, (1). Examines the role of the trade union bureaucracy during the 1950s and early 1960s.

—— (1981) "Rationalisation and working class response: the context and limits of factory floor activity in Argentina", *Journal of Latin American Studies*, 13, (2). A rare focus on the importance of the labour process in industrial relations.

Jelin, E. (1979) "Labour conflicts under the second Peronist regime, Argentina 1973–76", *Development and Change*, 10, (2). A definitive piece of work by one of Argentina's foremost labour analysts.

Johnson, L. (1981) "The impact of racial discrimination on black artisans in colonial Buenos Aires", *Social History*, 6, (3).

Kenworthy, E. (1970) *The Formation of the Peronist Coalition*, Yale University, PhD Thesis. Chapter 5 "Capturing Labor" deals with Perón's strategy for building a trade union base.

Knowles, C. (1975) "Revolutionary Trade Unionism in Argentina: Interview with Agustín Tosco", *Radical America*, 9 (3). An insight into the thinking of the legendary leader of the *Cordobazo*.

Laclau, E. (1973) Peronism and Revolution, *Latin American Review of Books*, 1.

Latin American Bureau (1980) *Unity is Strength–Trade Unions in Latin America*, Latin American Bureau, London. The chapter on Argentina provides a useful overview.

Lawrence Stockell, A. (1972) "Peronist Politics in Labor, 1943", in A. Ciria (ed.) *New Perspectives on Modern Argentina*, Latin American Studies Program, Indiana University, Bloomington.

Little, W. (1975) "The Popular Origins of Peronism", in D. Rock (ed.) *Argentina in the Twentieth Century*, Duckworth, London. Rejects the view of a split between the "new" and "old" working class in relation to Peronism.

Marshall, A. (1980) "Labour market and wage growth: the case of Argentina", *Cambridge Journal of Economics*, no. 4. Comprehensive discussion of labour market segmentation and heterogeneity of the labour market segmentation and heterogeneity of the working class.

Munck, R. (1984) "Formation and development of the working class in

Argentina (1857–1919)", in B. Munslow and H. Finch (eds.) *Proletarianization in the Third World*, Croom Helm, London.

—— (1986) "Labour in Argentina and Brazil: a comparative study", in R. Boyd, R. Cohen and P. Gutkind (eds.) *International Labour: Subordination, Structure and Conflict*, London, Gower.

NACLA (1975) *Argentina: in the hour of the furnaces,* North American Congress on Latin America, New York. Contains a survey of the labour movement in the late 1960s stressing the role of U.S. "labour imperialism".

Petras, J. (1981) "Terror and the Hydra: The Resurgence of the Argentine Working Class", in J. Petras, *Class, State, and Power in the Third World*, Zed Press, London. Stress on the informal solidarity networks within the working class since 1976.

Rock, D. (1975) *Politics in Argentina 1890–1930. The rise and fall of Radicalism*, Cambridge University Press, Cambridge. Extensive coverage of workers' struggle during this period, particularly Semana Trágica of 1919.

Roxborough, I. (1981) The analysis of labour movements in Latin America: typologies and theories. *Bulletin of Latin American Reseach*, I, (1). Develops a critique of Spalding's approach, also commenting on work by Torre on labour in Argentina. (See reference below).

Shipley, P. (1977) *On the Outside Looking in: A Social History of the Porteño Worker during the "Golden Age" of Argentine Development*. PhD thesis, Rutgers University, New Brunswick.

Silverman, B. (1968–9) "Labor ideology and economic development in the Peronist epoch", *Studies in Comparative International Development*. IV, (11).

Smith, P. (1972) "The social base of Peronism", *Hispanic American Historical Review* 52 (1).

Solberg, C. (1970) *Immigration and Nationalism in Argentina and Chile, 1890–1914*. University of Texas Press, Texas.

—— (1971) "Agrarian unrest and agrarian policy in Argentina, 1912–1930", *Journal of Interamerican Studies and World Affairs*, no. 13 January.

Spalding, H. (1977) *Organized Labor in Latin America*, Harper and Row, New York. Contains a general study of the formative period up to 1930 and a specific study of labor and populism in Argentina.

Tamarin, D. (1985) *The Argentine Labor Movement, 1930–1945: A Study in the Origins of Peronism,* University of New Mexico Press, Albuquerque.

Thompson, A. (1982) *Labour Struggles and Political Conflict. Argentina: The general strike of 1975 and the crisis of Peronsim through a historical perspective*. MA Thesis, Institute of Social Studies, The Hague.

Torre, J.C. (1974) "The meaning of current workers' struggles". *Latin American Perspectives*. 1 (3). A discussion of the relationship between rank and file and labour bureaucracy during early 1970s by Argentina's foremost labour historian.

Waisman, C. (1982) *Modernization and the Working Class,* University of

Texas Press, Austin. Contains two sociological studies of sugar workers and internal migrants in Argentina.

Walter, R. (1977) *The Socialist Party of Argentina, 1890–1930*, Institute of Latin American Studies, University of Texas, Austin.

Yoast, R. (1975) *The Development of Argentine Anarchism: A Socio-Ideological Analysis*, PhD thesis, University of Wisconsin.